Divining Margaret Laurence

Divining
Margaret Laurence

A Study of Her Complete Writings

NORA FOSTER STOVEL

McGILL-QUEEN'S UNIVERSITY PRESS | Montreal & Kingston • London • Ithaca

© McGill-Queen's University Press 2008

ISBN 978-0-7735-3376-9 (cloth)
ISBN 978-0-7735-3437-7 (paper)

Legal deposit third quarter 2008
Bibliothèque nationale du Québec

Printed in Canada on acid-free paper that is 100% ancient forest free
(100% post-consumer recycled), processed chlorine free.

McGill-Queen's University Press acknowledges the support of the Canada
Council for the Arts for our publishing program. We also acknowledge
the financial support of the Government of Canada through the Book
Publishing Industry Development Program (BPIDP) for our publishing activities.

Library and Archives Canada Cataloguing in Publication

Stovel, Nora Foster
Divining Margaret Laurence : a study of her complete writings /
Nora Foster Stovel.

Includes bibliographical references and index.
ISBN 978-0-7735-3376-9 (bnd)
ISBN 978-0-7735-3437-7 (pbk)

1. Laurence, Margaret, 1926–1987 – Criticism and interpretation.
I. Title.

PS8523.A86Z835 2008   C813'.54   C2008-900875-8

This book was designed and typeset by studio oneonone in Sabon 10.5/13.5

Contents

For Bruce

Preface

Margaret Laurence is one of Canada's most respected writers. She is, naturally, most popular in Canada and most famous for her Manawaka cycle – and justly so. But her genius extends beyond the limits of nation, culture, or genre. Her oeuvre includes African as well as Canadian works, life-writing texts as well as creative fiction, children's books as well as adult literature. *Divining Margaret Laurence: A Study of Her Complete Writings* examines her achievement in all these areas and explores the development of her artistic genius throughout her career. To this end, it addresses all her major works, establishes a framework of introduction and conclusion, and provides a bibliography and annotations. This inclusive structure reveals the development of Laurence's artistic vision and vehicle.

While Laurence wrote five books about Canada, her famous Manawaka cycle, she wrote an equal number of books about Africa. In fact, she published four books about Africa before she ever published fiction set in Canada. Therefore, the first major section of *Divining Margaret Laurence* deals with all her African writings, devoting chapters to two non-fiction texts – her translation of Somali folk literature, *A Tree for Poverty: Somali Poetry and Prose* (1954), and a critical study, *Long Drums and Cannons: Nigerian Dramatists and Novelists, 1952–1966*

(1968) – and one chapter to her travel-memoir *The Prophet's Camel Bell* and her fictions – her first novel, *This Side Jordan* (1960), and her first collection of stories, *The Tomorrow-Tamer and Other Stories* (1963) – in order to demonstrate how she developed her voice through translating Somali folk literature, her themes through a critique of Nigerian literature, and her skilful characterization and narrative method through her Ghanaian fictions.

The second section of *Divining Margaret Laurence* focuses on her Canadian fiction, with one chapter devoted to *The Stone Angel* (1964), one to *A Jest of God* (1966) and *The Fire-Dwellers* (1969), one to *A Bird in the House* (1970), and one to *The Diviners* (1974). In this Manawaka cycle Laurence creates what I call the Family of Woman, exploring women's conflicted, changing roles in the family and in society – as mother, daughter, sister, wife, lover, friend, and, most important, writer – as she portrays each heroine discovering her individual identity beneath the role-playing and gender constructions. Writing about Ghanaian independence at a political level influenced her portrayal of self-empowerment for her Canadian protagonists at a personal level in these increasingly explicit feminist texts. Her artistry also progresses from modernist use of myth and metaphor to include postmodernist use of narrative techniques in these semi-autobiographical fictions. "A Town of the Mind," a discussion of her microcosm of Manawaka, a mythologized version of her hometown of Neepawa, Manitoba, introduces the chapters on her Manawaka fiction. A chapter on her final, unfinished novel, "Dance on the Earth" – an ambitious plan spanning three generations of Ukrainian and Scots immigrants to Canada that was intended to complete the Manawaka cycle – concludes this complete study of Laurence's Canadian fiction.

The discussion of her African and Canadian texts is framed, first, by an introduction and conclusion, second by studies of her juvenilia and children's fictions, and third by her two autobiographical texts, *Heart of a Stranger* (1976) and *Dance on the Earth: A Memoir* (1989). A substantial introduction outlines the multi-layered argument, contextualizing it in the large body of critical work on Laurence, including the three recent biographies. A conclusion summarizes the argument, focusing first on her use of closure in her texts, as she strives for affirmative resolutions of difficult dilemmas, second on her approach to closure in her career, as she turns her attention to public issues including disarmament, ecology, and feminism, and third on closure in her life, as she chooses to end her struggle with cancer.

The second frame includes two largely ignored areas of her writing – her juvenilia and children's fiction. "Embryo Words," the chapter on her juvenilia, demonstrates how her early writings anticipate the themes of love of nature and hatred of war that she develops in her mature fiction. Many of her early works are poems, and this focus on poetry contributed to making her prose works highly poetic in terms of imagery, diction, and musical rhythm. Her tendency to recycle her early stories in her Manawaka *Künstlerromane*, *A Bird in the House* and *The Diviners*, is also of meta-autobiographical interest. It is, therefore, essential to consider her juvenilia, collected in *Embryo Words* and *Colors of Speech*, as an important element in exploring the development of her oeuvre. "Embryo Words" also explains how her early life – the loss of both her parents in her childhood and the outbreak of war in her adolescence – influenced her early writing, and it demonstrates how her early writing developed her artistry. "Snow Angels and Monarch Butterflies," the chapter on her four children's fictions – *Jason's Quest* (1970), *The Olden Days Coat* (1979), *Six Darn Cows* (1979), and *The Christmas Birthday Story* (1980) – shows how her children's books reflect her adult fiction in portraying the quest for identity and community through metaphor and myth. Laurence's children's fiction is an intriguing adjunct to her oeuvre that has been largely ignored by critics to date.

These sections on Laurence's African, Canadian, and children's fiction are further framed by chapters on her life-writing, texts that are not included in most previous studies of her work. The chapter on *Heart of a Stranger*, her collection of twenty travel essays describing her life-journey, introduces the chapters on her African texts. A chapter on her autobiographical *Dance on the Earth: A Memoir* concludes this discussion of her oeuvre, as it enables us to appreciate her artistic alchemy as she transforms facts into fiction.

This is a timely point for such a study of Laurence's writings. Three recent biographies of Laurence by James King, Lyall Powers, and Donez Xiques have publicized new facts of her life and renewed interest in her work. The Laurence Estate has made available unpublished material, including Laurence's unfinished novel and final journal, which contribute valuable new information. Numerous articles, published in journals and recent *festschriften* edited by Greta M. Coger, Kristjana Gunnars, Colin Nicholson, Christian Riegel, and Christl Verduyn since Laurence's death in 1987, suggest valuable new approaches to Laurence's work. Laurence's correspondence with other writers – Al Purdy, Gabrielle Roy, Adele Wiseman and others – has been published in recent collections by John Lennox and Ruth Panofsky, Paul Socken and J.A. Wainwright, providing invaluable material. New studies of the Manawaka cycle by Christian Riegel and Paul Comeau suggest novel approaches. Most existing studies of Laurence's work do not include her children's fiction; her final, unfinished novel, "Dance on the Earth"; her memoir, *Dance on the Earth*; or her collection of travel essays, *Heart of a Stranger*. For all these reasons, *Divining Margaret Laurence: A Study of Her Complete Writings* contributes significantly to an appreciation of Laurence's work in particular and also of Canadian, African, women's, children's, and fictional writing in general.

Acknowledgments

First and foremost, I want to thank the Margaret Laurence Estate, especially Jocelyn and David Laurence, for permission to research and publish Laurence materials. I am grateful to the Social Sciences and Humanities Research Council of Canada for awarding me a research grant that enabled me to examine Laurence's manuscripts at McMaster University and her correspondence and papers at York University. I am also grateful to the Faculty of Arts of the University of Alberta for awarding me a McCalla Research Professorship that enabled me to bring this study to completion. I wish to thank Charlotte Stewart-Murphy and Carl Spadoni and the staff of the William Ready Division of Archives and Research Collections at the Mills Memorial Library at McMaster and the late Kent Haworth and the staff of the Scott Library of York University for valuable assistance in researching their Laurence Archives, as well as the staff of the University of Manitoba for assisting me with Laurence's juvenilia. I wish to thank friends of Margaret Laurence, especially Jean Murray Cole, Joan Johnston, Walter Swayze, Alice Williams, and the Reverend Dr Lois Freeman Wilson, for their valuable information and encouragement. I want to thank

Mrs Florence Campbell Henderson and the friendly staff of the Margaret Laurence House in Neepawa for helping me to copy Laurence materials. I want to thank my colleagues who have given me helpful suggestions throughout the process of composing this study: Neil Besner, Greta McCormick Coger, Lorna Irvine, Fran Kaye, Jon Kertzer, James King, John Lennox, Barbara Pell, Michael Peterman, and Clara Thomas. I also want to thank the students with whom I discussed Laurence's works in Honours English tutorials, graduate seminars, and graduate supervisions: Jennifer Adrain, Micaela Brown, Anne Coté, Myrl Coulter, Laura Davis, Lisa Fiander, Robyn Fowler, Jill Garrett, Tracey Gillespie, Kathryn Holland, James Hutson, Krissy Lundberg, Jill Manderson, Nicole Marshall, Matthew Martin, Brent McKeown, Christian Riegel, Kim Solga, Tanya Stewart, Mario Trono, Anne Vimtrup, Tracy Wright, and Liu Yangyang. I especially want to thank Myrl Coulter, Laura Davis, Lisa Fiander, and Kathryn Holland, who read sections of this work and made valuable suggestions. I want to thank my research assistants Rebecca Babcock, Diana Davidson, Al Fleishman, Jay Smith, Jennifer Smith, Olivia Street, and Tracy Wright for bibliographical help. I want to thank the late Dr Malcolm Ross and Jack McClelland for their encouragement of this project and for permission to research and quote from their correspondence. I also wish to thank support staff, especially Marcie Whitecotton-Carroll, who assisted me with technical matters. I want to thank copy-editor Kate Merriman, designer David LeBlanc, Managing Editor Joan McGilvray, and Production Manager Susanne McAdam for expert work in the production process. And I want to thank Philip Cercone for believing in this book and for shepherding it through the publishing process. Last, but never least, I want to thank my family – my husband, Bruce Stovel, my daughter, Laura Stovel, and my son, Grant Foster Stovel – for their unfailing faith and support.

Chronology of Margaret Laurence's Life and Works

1926 Jean Margaret Wemyss born 18 July in Neepawa, Manitoba, to Robert Wemyss and Verna Simpson Wemyss.

1930 Verna Simpson Wemyss dies. Her sister, Margaret Campbell Simpson, returns to Neepawa to care for niece.

1931 Margaret Campbell Simpson marries Robert Wemyss.

1933 Robert Morrison Wemyss born.

1935 Robert Wemyss dies.

1938 Margaret Simpson Wemyss moves with children Margaret and Robert to home of her father, John Simpson.

1940–44 Attends the Viscount School, now Neepawa Collegiate, edits its newspaper, wins Governor General's Medal.

1944–47 BA in Honours English at United College, Winnipeg. Publishes poetry and stories in *Vox* and *Manitoban*.

1947–48 Works as a reporter on *The Westerner* and *Winnipeg Citizen* and as Assistant Registrar at Winnipeg YWCA.

1947 Marries Jack Laurence, born 1916 in Prince George, British Columbia, a war veteran and civil engineering student.

1949 Jack graduates from University of Manitoba. Laurences move to England.

1950 Laurences move to British Protectorate of Somaliland. Laurence collects material for *A Tree for Poverty*.

1952 Laurences move to the Gold Coast, now Ghana. Daughter Jocelyn born.

1954 *A Tree for Poverty: Somali Poetry and Prose* published in Nairobi.

1955 Son David born.

1957 Ghana achieves independence. Laurences move to Vancouver. Laurence's stepmother dies in Victoria.

1960 *This Side Jordan*, a novel set in Ghana, published.

1962 Margaret Laurence moves to Hampstead, London, with children. Jack Laurence takes up post in East Pakistan.

1963 Margaret Laurence moves to Elm Cottage in Penn, Buckinghamshire, and publishes *The Tomorrow-Tamer and Other Stories*, set in Ghana, and *The Prophet's Camel Bell*, based on her Somali journals.

1964 *The Stone Angel*, first Manawaka novel, published.

1966 *A Jest of God* published and awarded Governor General's Award for Fiction.

1968 *Long Drums and Cannons: Nigerian Dramatists and Novelists, 1952–1966* published.

1969 *The Fire-Dwellers* published. Laurences divorced. Margaret returns to Canada as Writer-in-Residence at Massey College, University of Toronto. Purchases cabin on Otonabee River near Peterborough, Ontario.

1970 *A Bird in the House*, a collection of Canadian short stories, and *Jason's Quest*, children's novel, published.

1971 Companion of the Order of Canada.

1972 Honorary degrees conferred by Trent, Dalhousie, and University of Toronto.

1973 Writer-in-Residence at University of Western Ontario. Sells Elm Cottage and buys house in Lakefield, Ontario.

1974 *The Diviners* published, winning Governor General's Award for Fiction. Writer-in-Residence, Trent University.

1975 Awarded Molson Prize and D Litt by the Universities of Brandon, Mount Allison, and Western Ontario.

1976 *Heart of a Stranger* published. Controversy over teaching *The Diviners* in Peterborough high schools begins.

1979 *Six Darn Cows* and *The Olden Days Coat*, children's fictions, published.

1980 *A Christmas Birthday Story*, a children's version of the Nativity, published.

1981–83 Chancellor, Trent University. Begins works with Probe, Project Ploughshares, Operation Dismantle. Censorship controversy regarding her books redevelops.

1987 Dies 5 January in Lakefield, Ontario.

1989 *Dance on the Earth: A Memoir* published posthumously, edited by daughter, Jocelyn.

BOOKS BY MARGARET LAURENCE

A Tree for Poverty. 1954. Translation.

This Side Jordan. 1960. Novel.

The Prophet's Camel Bell. 1963. Memoir.

The Tomorrow-Tamer and Other Stories. 1963. Stories.

The Stone Angel. 1964. Novel.

A Jest of God. 1966. Novel.

Long Drums and Cannons: Nigerian Dramatists and Novelists, 1952–1966. 1968. Criticism.

The Fire-Dwellers. 1969. Novel.

A Bird in the House. 1970. Stories.

Jason's Quest. 1970. Children's Book.

The Diviners. 1974. Novel.

Heart of a Stranger. 1976. Essays.

The Olden Days Coat. 1979. Children's Book.

Six Darn Cows. 1979. Children's Book.

The Christmas Birthday Story. 1980. Children's Book.

Dance on the Earth: A Memoir. 1989. Memoir.

Abbreviations

ESSAYS (IN ALPHABETICAL ORDER)

AC "Author's Commentary." Unpublished. York University. Typescript

  G "Geography–Outer or Inner?" Unpublished. York University. Essay

GG "Gadgetry or Growing: Form and Voice in the Novel." 1980. Essay

  IT "Ivory Tower or Grass Roots?: The Novelist as Socio-Political Being." 1978. Essay

TVN "Time and the Narrative Voice." 1977. Essay

TYS "Ten Years' Sentences." 1977. Essay

SECONDARY WORKS (IN ALPHABETICAL ORDER)

AH Powers, Lyall H. *Alien Heart: The Life and Work of Margaret Laurence.* 2003. Biography

CA Nicholson, Colin, ed. *Critical Approaches to the Fiction of Margaret Laurence.* 1990. Criticism

CR Gunnars, Kristjana, ed. *Crossing the River: Essays in Honour of Margaret Laurence.* 1988. Criticism

CS Stovel, Nora Foster. *"Colors of Speech": Margaret Laurence's Early Writings.* Edmonton: Juvenilia P, 2000. Poems and stories

CT Riegel, Christian. *Challenging Territory: The Writing of Margaret Laurence.* 1997. Criticism

EW Stovel, Nora Foster. *"Embryo Words": Margaret Laurence's Early Writings.* 1997. Edition

FL Lennox, John, ed. *Margaret Laurence-Al Purdy: A Friendship in Letters: Selected Correspondence.* 1993. Correspondence

LJ Morley, Patricia. *Margaret Laurence: The Long Journey Home.* 1981. Criticism

LJH Morley, Patricia. *Margaret Laurence: The Long Journey Home, Revised.* 1991. Criticism

LML King, James. *The Life of Margaret Laurence.* 1997. Biography

MLWC New, William, ed. *Margaret Laurence: The Writer and Her Critics*. 1977. Criticism

ML Thomas, Clara. *Margaret Laurence*. 1969. Criticism

MLA Verduyn, Christl, ed. *Margaret Laurence: An Appreciation*. 1978. Criticism

MW Thomas, Clara. *The Manawaka World of Margaret Laurence*. 1976. Criticism

NP Coger, Greta, ed. *New Perspectives on Margaret Laurence*. 1996. Criticism

OCCL Coldwell, Joan. "Margaret Laurence." *The Oxford Companion to Canadian Literature*. 1983. Criticism

PS Woodcock, George, ed. *A Place to Stand On: Essays by and about Margaret Laurence*. 1983. Criticism

RC Stovel, Nora Foster. *Rachel's Children: Margaret Laurence's A Jest of God*. 1992. Criticism

SC Stovel, Nora Foster. *Stacey's Choice: Margaret Laurence's The Fire-Dwellers*. 1993. Criticism

SL Lennox, John and Panofsky, Ruth, eds. *Selected Letters of Margaret Laurence and Adele Wiseman*. 1997. Correspondence

TV Hind-Smith, Joan. *Three Voices: The Lives of Margaret Laurence, Gabrielle Roy, Frederick Philip Grove*. 1975. Biography

VLS Wainwright, J.A. ed. *A Very Large Soul: Selected Letters from Margaret Laurence to Canadian Writers*. 1995. Correspondence

PART ONE

Beginnings
"A Place to Stand On"

CHAPTER 1

Introduction: "The Promised Land of One's Own Inner Freedom"

Laurence (1926–87) has been called "Canada's most successful novelist" by Joan Coldwell in *The Oxford Companion to Canadian Literature* (1983), "the most significant creative writer in Canadian literature" (vii) by J.A. Wainwright in *A Very Large Soul: Selected Letters from Margaret Laurence to Canadian Writers* (1995), "the best-known and most successful Canadian novelist of her generation" (4) by John Lennox in *Margaret Laurence: A Friendship in Letters* (1997), and "the most renowned writer in Canadian literary history" (xix) by James King in *The Life of Margaret Laurence* (1997). In fact, Laurence was not just respected, but revered: she was called "the most beloved woman in Canada" (*PCB* 268) by Clara Thomas, "the most loved writer in Canada" (*VLS* 111) by Dennis Lee, "one of the most famous and beloved of Canadians" (xviii) by James King in *The Life of Margaret Laurence*, and "one of the most respected and beloved writers of her day" (10) by Donez Xiques in *Margaret Laurence: The Making of a Writer* (2005).

Laurence has been iconized as the quintessential Canadian writer. There are two major reasons for Laurence's importance to Canadian literature: first is her stature as an artist in her own right, and second is the degree to which she, as "den mother," fostered the success of her "tribe" of Canadian writers, as she called them. Sam Solecki declares, in *The Oxford Companion to Canadian Literature* (1997), "Laurence had a central influence during the literary renaissance of the 1960s and 1970s. Showing the way by example, she became a creative godmother to an entire generation" (825).

Certainly, her importance to the development of Canadian literature cannot be overestimated. Kristjana Gunnars, in *Crossing the River: Essays in Honour of Margaret Laurence* (1988), calls her "a founding mother of Canadian literature" (viii), and Wainwright claims she had an "unparalleled influence on Canadian writers and readers" (vii). Paul Comeau concludes, in *Margaret Laurence's Epic Imagination* (2005), "Margaret Laurence helped to give us our place to stand on and continues to exert a compelling and guiding influence on Canadian literature" (144). Matt Cohen, in his memoir, *Typing: A Life in 26 Keys* (2000), says, "It is difficult today to recreate the extent to which, in the 1970s, Margaret Laurence was the massive and dominating presence on the Canadian literary scene ... Of all those writers who had been born in Canada or lived here, she was considered the best, the most Canadian, the most universal, the most gifted and the most accomplished" (179–80). Cohen echoes the maternal metaphor: "Margaret Laurence was the *primus inter pares*, the Queen Bee, the mother, grandmother, and all the aunts of the 'tribe' ... of Canadian writers" (179).

Laurence's stature is reflected in the impressive amount of material published on her work, including monographs by J.M. Kertzer, Patricia Morley, Christian Riegel, and Clara Thomas; reader's guides to her Manawaka texts by J.M. Kertzer, Nora Foster Stovel, Susan Warwick, and George Woodcock; collections of essays edited by Greta M. Coger, Kristjana Gunnars, William H. New, Colin Nicholson, Christian Riegel, Christl Verduyn, and George Woodcock; collections of her correspondence with Al Purdy, Gabrielle Roy, Adele Wiseman, and others edited by John Lennox, Ruth Panofsky, Paul Socken, and J.A. Wainwright; and biographies by Noelle Boughton, James King, Lyall Powers, and Donez Xiques.

Margaret Laurence is, of course, most famous for her Manawaka cycle of Canadian fictions – *The Stone Angel* (1964), *A Jest of God* (1966), *The Fire-Dwellers* (1969), *A Bird in the House* (1970) and *The Diviners* (1974). When Malcolm Ross, editor-in-chief of McClelland and Stewart's New Canadian Library, asked Canadian teachers and critics in 1982 to name the best Canadian novels, *The Stone Angel* topped "List A." Laurence book-ended "List B," framing the top ten, with *The Stone Angel* as number one and *The Diviners* as number ten (Steele, 150).[1] More recently, the University of Toronto's 1999 survey of the top one hundred Canadian novels placed both these novels in the top ten again, with *The Diviners* as number one and *The Stone Angel* as number six.[2]

The Stone Angel, as the first of her Manawaka texts, made a powerful impression on Canadian readers and critics. Cohen continues, "And of all her many books, which were considered to be indubitable classic masterpieces, the most masterful masterpiece of all was considered to be *The Stone Angel*" (280). W.H. New judges *The Stone Angel* "one of the most illuminating literary experiences in recent Canadian fiction" (*MLWC* 135). Clearly, *The Stone Angel*, followed by the other four Manawaka texts, established Laurence as a major Canadian novelist. John Lennox and Ruth Panofsky claim, "with the appearance of *The Stone Angel* (1964) and the subsequent works in the Manawaka cycle, Laurence steadily became the best-known and most successful Canadian novelist of her generation" (*SL* 4). George Woodcock asserts, in *Introducing Margaret Laurence's* The Stone Angel: "*The Stone Angel* established Margaret Laurence as a leading Canadian novelist … the publication of *The Stone Angel* was hailed as marking the appearance of a new and original literary talent on the Canadian literary horizon, and rapidly made Laurence the most important novelist in that vitally formative period of Canadian writing – the late 1960s and early 1970s" (15, 110).

Laurence's Manawaka cycle of Canadian novels resonated in the Canadian mind, establishing her as the quintessential Canadian writer. Christian Riegel claims in his introduction to *Challenging Territory: The Writing of Margaret Laurence*, "Margaret Laurence touched Canadians like no other writer during her celebrated life and career. A nerve was struck in the Canadian psyche" (xi). Ironically, however, this lionizing of Laurence as the quintessential Canadian writer by Canadian readers and reviewers – at a time when Canada was establishing its own sense of national identity, as witnessed by the Great Flag Debate, which coincided historically with Laurence's Manawaka books – has worked against her because it has led her greatest admirers to ignore or neglect other significant segments of her oeuvre. Laurence's genius extends beyond the limits of nation, culture, or genre. Her oeuvre includes

African as well as Canadian books, life-writing as well as creative fiction works, children's books as well as adult texts. Only by considering her corpus of work can one appreciate the full range of her achievement. *Divining Margaret Laurence: A Study of Her Complete Writings* explores her achievement in all these areas, and by examining her entire oeuvre, it traces the development of her artistic genius.

THE AFRICAN WRITING: "A SEVEN YEARS' LOVE AFFAIR WITH A CONTINENT"

First, her African work is highly significant. Canadians do not think of Laurence as an author of African texts, although she deserves that title, because the fame of her Canadian fiction has overshadowed her earlier African writing. While she did write five fictions set in Canada, she wrote an equal number of books about Africa. Her first book, *A Tree for Poverty* (1954), was the first translation or publication of Somali folk literature, appearing two decades before the Somali language developed any orthography. Her first novel, *This Side Jordan* (1960), her first collection of stories, *The Tomorrow-Tamer* (1963), her first memoir, *The Prophet's Camel Bell* (1963), and her first and only critical study, *Long Drums and Cannons: Nigerian Dramatists and Novelists, 1952–1966* (1968) were all written about Africa, where she lived from 1951 to 1957 – a year and a half in the British Protectorate of Somaliland, later Somalia, and five years in the Gold Coast, soon to become Ghana. Donez Xiques concludes, in *Margaret Laurence: The Making of a Writer*, her African texts form "a significant part of her legacy as a writer and need to be placed beside her Manawaka fiction" (311). Indeed, Laurence published her first four African texts before she published a book set in Canada. This experience, at a critical point of decolonization in Somalia and Ghana, influenced her Canadian writing greatly. Clara Thomas states in *The Manawaka World of Margaret Laurence*, "Her experience of Africa, between 1950 and 1957, acted as a kind of dynamic culture shock, a catalyst, on the talents of Margaret Laurence" (17). And Patricia Morley claims in *Margaret Laurence: The Long Journey Home*, "The way to Manawaka lay through Ghana, Nigeria, and the searching desert sun" (39).[3]

Laurence's African texts have been so overshadowed by her subsequent Canadian books that many readers and even scholars are still unfamiliar with her African writing. Only recently has it begun to attract the critical attention it deserves, and even then it is often considered in isolation from her Canadian writing. Indeed, it is dismissed as "apprentice work" by certain Canadian critics. As Clara Thomas declares in *The Manawaka World of Margaret Laurence*, "The writing of *The Prophet's Camel Bell* marked the end of the apprenticeship experiences that the years in Africa had given her; the book was her acknowledgement of that apprenticeship and her farewell to it" (33). Other critics value the African writing in its own right. In his afterword to *This Side Jordan*, George Woodcock judges, "*This Side Jordan* proved to be more than a mere apprentice's exercise by the audacity with which it handled the vital conjunction in the mid-twentieth century of the African tribal consciousness and the European rational and individualized consciousness" (*SJ* 284). He concludes that *This Side Jordan* "anticipated almost all that Laurence eventually achieved in her Manawaka novels" (*SJ* 88). There is no trace of the apprentice in her next fiction set in Africa: *The Tomorrow-Tamer and Other Stories* is manifestly the work of an accomplished artist.[4] G.D. Killam, in his 1976 introduction to *This Side Jordan*, judges Laurence "the best expatriate writing about Africa": "no other expatriate writer has attempted and achieved as much as Margaret Laurence" (x). If she had not published her Canadian fiction, she would still be regarded for her African writings.

Most significant is the influence of her African work on her Canadian writing. Because critics, especially Canadian critics, often regard her Manawaka cycle in isolation from her other writing, the important connections between the two bodies of work, and indeed the influence of her African writing on her subsequent Canadian fiction, have not been fully appreciated. I argue, however, that her African experience made her a great Canadian novelist. Her experience of living in Africa led her to perceive Canada as a post-colonial nation, and her observation of African women led her to perceive how women can be colonized under patriarchy. Writing of emerging independence in her African fiction inspired her to write about the self-empowerment of women in her Canadian fiction.

One key to the influence of Africa on Laurence's Canadian writing may lie in colonial theory. Laurence was greatly influenced by French psychologist Olivier Mannoni's "Prospero complex" theory (110) advanced in his study *Prospero and Caliban: The Psychology of Colonization* (1950). She read Mannoni in 1961 in Vancouver while she was editing her Somali journals in preparation for publishing her travel memoir, *The Prophet's Camel Bell*, in 1963. She affirms in *Dance on the Earth: A Memoir*, "That book was a revelation. Mannoni said things about colonialism and the people who had been colonized that struck me deeply" (155). In her 1981 essay, "Books That Mattered to Me," she calls it one of the epiphanic "moments of Recognition and Revelation" (242) that changed her forever: "To me, this book meant a real, literal revelation. It opened up to me an understanding of some of my own feelings and experiences in East and West Africa, and in the end, perhaps, taught me as much about my own land and the terrible injustices and outrages committed by imperialism against *our* native peoples, as it did about the peoples of Africa" (244). She affirms the connection between her African and Canadian writing thus. She adds, "I made use, I hope, of these insights in my African stories, especially in a story called 'The Voices of Adamo,' and in my book on Somaliland, *The Prophet's Camel Bell*" (244). In "The Voices of Adamo," she portrays the fatal dependence of drummer Adamo, sole survivor of his village, on Captain Fossey, in a story that reflects the powerful portrait of colonialist dependency in the 1939 novel *Mister Johnson* by Anglo-Irish author Joyce Cary, one of Laurence's literary heroes. Although Mannoni's theories have been challenged subsequently, notably in Frantz Fanon's 1952 study, *Black Skin, White Masks*, the fact remains that they influenced Laurence's thinking indelibly. Again, she reaffirms connections between her African and Canadian fiction in this colonial regard: "Much later, some of [Mannoni's] insights were to return, informed this time by more knowledge of my own land and peoples, in my novel *The Diviners*" (244–5). In *Heart of a Stranger*, she explains how her observation of African tribalism influenced her perception of the Scottish clan system, as well as the tribal system of Aboriginal Canadians, when she was writing *The Diviners* (HS 113).

Heart of a Stranger (1976), Laurence's collection of twenty travel essays, illuminates connections between her African and Canadian writing. Because travel inspired her creativity, it also constitutes a concealed autobiography that reveals how her travels, especially her sojourn in Africa, inspired her fiction, especially her Canadian fiction. Since it was out of print for several years between its first publication in 1976 and its republication in 2003, it has not been available to students of Laurence.

This is unfortunate, because it provides an ideal introduction to an examination of her African texts. Therefore, a chapter on *Heart of a Stranger* serves as a preface to the chapters on her African work.

Because of its significance in its own right and also because of its influence on her Canadian writing, I address all her African works here, devoting one chapter to two non-fiction texts – her translation of Somali folk literature, *A Tree for Poverty*, and her critical study, *Long Drums and Cannons: Nigerian Dramatists and Novelists, 1952–1966* – and one chapter to her Somali journal, *The Prophet's Camel Bell*, and her fictions – her first novel, *This Side Jordan*, and her first collection of stories, *The Tomorrow-Tamer and Other Stories* – in order to demonstrate how she developed her voice through translating Somali folk literature, her themes through composing a critique of Nigerian literature, and her characterization and narrative technique through writing her Ghanaian fictions. As Patricia Morley affirms, "Africa was catalyst and crucible for much of Laurence's work" (44).

Each of Laurence's African literary studies demonstrates influence on her Canadian work. *A Tree for Poverty: Somali Poetry and Prose* taught her significant lessons: her translation of Somali poetry, a difficult language with no orthography, honed her skills as a "Wordsmith" (*D* 33), making her a poet in prose; her translations of Somali and Arabic folk tales developed her skills as a storyteller; and the acting skills of her translator, Hersi Half-Tongue, led her to become a dramatic writer. No wonder she called her translations "a labour of love" (*PCB* 248).

Long Drums and Cannons: Nigerian Dramatists and Novelists, 1952–1966 also taught her many lessons, influencing her focus on the individual's dilemma, her regard for the ancestors and gods, her emphasis on myth and metaphor, her interest in vivid symbolic locales for moralized landscapes, and her grasp of individual idiom. It is not surprising that the qualities she celebrates in Nigerian writing are the qualities we admire in her Canadian fiction, for Nigerian literature taught her to view Canada as a post-colonial nation that had to heal the scars caused by colonialism. Fiona Sparrow, in her 1992 study, *Into Africa with Margaret Laurence*, declares, "the effects of her journey in Africa are evident not only in her African writing, but also in the Manawaka works that bring her writing career to its climax" (206). An exploration of both her African and Canadian texts can confirm this connection.

COMING HOME: "CANADA VIA AFRICA"

In the first essay in *Heart of a Stranger*, "A Place To Stand On" – originally titled "Sources," as it explains the origin of her creativity in her own cultural background – Laurence says, "I was fortunate in going to Africa when I did" (6), and she proceeds to parallel her own themes with African writers': "This sort of exploration can be clearly seen in the works of contemporary African writers, many of whom re-create their people's past in novels and plays in order to recover a sense of themselves, an identity and a feeling of value from which they were separated by two or three generations of colonialism and missionizing. They have found it necessary, in other words, to come to terms with their ancestors and their gods in order to be able to accept the past and be at peace with the dead, without being stifled or threatened by that past" (*HS* 6).⁵ In both her African and Canadian fiction, Laurence writes about her characters' struggle with the past because "the past and the future are both always present," as she asserts in her 1972 essay, "Time and the Narrative Voice" (157). She affirms, "My writing, then, has been my own attempt to come to terms with the past. I see this process as the gradual one of freeing oneself from the stultifying aspects of the past, while at the same time beginning to see its true value" (*HS* 8).

Laurence learned her distinctive themes of freedom and independence from the African writers she read and wrote about, and so her critique of Nigerian writing can illuminate her concerns. Clara Thomas writes, in her afterword to *The Prophet's Camel Bell*, "She had found her themes in Africa – exile, the journey towards wholeness, personhood, knowing the 'heart of a stranger,' the unique dignity of every individual, the drive to freedom, faith, and the recognition of grace" (266). In her preface to *Margaret Laurence: The Long Journey Home*, Morley claims, "The themes that shaped her Manawaka fiction – roots, ancestors, human complexity, acceptance of the Other, and the search for inner freedom and growth – these concerns first emerge in her African writing" (7–8). *Long Drums and Cannons* can reveal the origins of these influences, but, because it was out of print from its original publication in 1968 until its republication in 2001, readers have not been fully aware of the influence of Nigerian writing on her Canadian work. Therefore, an examination of this text and an exploration of its parallels with Laurence's Canadian fiction can be illuminating.

Laurence parallels Canada with certain African countries as post-colonial nations. In her 1978 essay "Ivory Tower or Grass Roots?: The Novelist as Socio-Political Being," she claims, "Canadian writers, like African writers, have had to find our own voices and write out of what is truly ours, in the face of an overwhelming cultural imperialism" (253). She compares herself to Chinua Achebe, labelling them both "Third World novelists" (253), as she discusses Nigerian writing: "In Nigeria, as in many parts of Africa, people lost their own self-value, their own distinctive voices, throughout three generations of colonialism. They were taught as children to despise their ancestors and the old gods, and the result was, of course, that they learned to despise themselves. Chinua Achebe's generation of writers (which includes very many writers of distinction such as Wole Soyinka, John Pepper Clark, Cyprian Ekwensi, T.M. Aluko, Elechi Amadi, Flora Nwapa, and Gabriel Okara)[6] has drawn on their relatively newfound sense of self-worth and on their people's past, and has tried consciously to impart these values to their own people, to combat the psychic damage done during the years of domination by British imperialism" (IT 253). She applies this post-colonial situation to her native land: "In Canada, our dilemma was perhaps more subtle. We ostensibly gained our independence in 1867, and yet we remained colonial in outlook for many years. In literary terms, our models remained those of Britain, and more recently of America" (IT 254). In *Heart of a Stranger*, she explains, "for many years we valued ourselves insufficiently, living as we did under the huge shadows of those two dominating figures, Uncle Sam and Britannia" (172). She credits literary pioneers, whom she terms "sodbusters," like Ethel Wilson and Sinclair Ross, with being "the first generation of non-colonial Canadian writers" (IT 254). She claims, "Sinclair Ross, Hugh MacLennan, Morley Callaghan, Gabrielle Roy, Ernest Buckler, Ethel Wilson ... were really the pioneering generation. They were the first generation of Canadian novelists to write out of their own people and their own culture, the sight of their own eyes, not taking as their models British or American writers, but developing the consciousness of their own people and culture" (Sullivan 78). In *Dance on the Earth*, she credits both Canadian and African writers of her generation with producing "a truly non-colonial literature" (185) – that is, a post-colonial literature, as we would now term it, a literature independent of colonial influences.

In "Ivory Tower or Grass Roots," Laurence defines her progression as "Canada via Africa" (257), as she learned from her African experience to view Canada as a post-colonial nation and to perceive how women can be colonized under patriarchy. She explains, "I had come back home to Canada via Africa, both physically and spiritually. In writing my first novel, *This Side Jordan*, set in Ghana, it had finally become clear to me why I had chosen the theme of an independence which was both political and inner. I was from a land that had been a colony, a land which in some ways was still colonial" (IT 257). She adds, "Our situation at the time, like that of all peoples with colonial mentalities, was not unlike that of women in our society" (IT 257). She parallels the political with the personal: her fictional portrayal of Ghana's emerging independence at the critical moment of decolonization reflects her emphasis on self-empowerment for her African protagonists and, later, her Canadian heroines. Laurence, whose position in Africa was complicated by race and gender, says her anti-colonialism, developed in Africa, extended to Canada and to women:

> My sense of social awareness, my feelings of anti-imperialism, anti-colonialism, anti-authoritarianism, had begun, probably, in embryo form in my own childhood: they had been nurtured during my college years and immediately afterwards, in the North Winnipeg of the old Left; they had developed considerably through my African experience. It was not very difficult to relate this experience to my own land, which had been under the colonial sway of Britain once and was now under the colonial sway of America. But these developing feelings also related very importantly to my growing awareness of the dilemma and powerlessness of women, the tendency of women to accept male definition of ourselves, to be self-deprecating and uncertain, and to rage inwardly. (IT 257)

In her original, unpublished introduction to *Long Drums and Cannons*, Laurence explains how she found her individual voice in travelling from Africa to Canada both in fact and in fiction: "My own first novel and a subsequent book of short stories were set in Ghana, where

I lived for a number of years. I began to realize, however, that if I wanted to go on as a novelist, I could really only write about people whom I knew from the inside, my own people who came out of the same background as myself – Scots Presbyterian, in a Canadian prairie town – people who were (as Muslims say about Allah) closer to me than my own neck-vein. It was probably fortunate that I came to this conclusion at the moment I did, for the time for outsiders to write about Africa was then nearly over."[7] In "Ten Years' Sentences," Laurence writes, "*This Side Jordan* and the two other books I wrote which were set in Africa, *The Prophet's Camel Bell* and *The Tomorrow-Tamer*, were written out of the milieu of a rapidly ending colonialism and an emerging independence of African countries" (18). She continues, "They were written by an outsider who experienced a seven years' love affair with a continent but who in the end had to remain in precisely that relationship, for it could never become the close involvement of family" (TYS 18). In *Heart of a Stranger*, Laurence affirms, "I always knew that one day I would have to stop writing about Africa and go back to my own people, my own place of belonging" (6). When she did return to Canada in her writing, however, it was with the knowledge gained from her experience of living in and writing about Africa.

Laurence was not then concerned with questions of cultural appropriation, a concept that was not current until decades later, but she was concerned about the issue of authenticity. In an unpublished essay entitled "Geography: Outer or Inner," she explains, "With the writing which was set in Africa, I felt I had gone as far as I personally could, in getting inside the mind of characters whose background was very different from my own. But I could never be certain how true the characters were, because one can never penetrate far enough into a different culture. I began to see that if I was going to go on as a novelist, and go deeper, I could only write about my own people."[8] She writes to Adele Wiseman on 20 January 1979, "After I finished writing the stories later collected as The Tomorrow-Tamer [*sic*], I had an entire novel planned, set in Africa. A beautiful plan it was, too. But I could not write it. I had really said everything about Africa that I had to say. Some guiding spirit has always prevented me, thank God, from writing a mock-up" (SL 353). In "Geography," she explains, "The real place of belonging is the culture within which one was born – that heritage of responses which one does not always like and indeed may have to battle desperately to break away from but in the end must come to terms with. Gradually I came to realize that the outer geography was less important to me than the inner, and that was why I felt I had to write out of my own Canadian-prairie-Scots-Presbyterian background. It took me a long time to dare to come home, but I finally did" (np).

THE RETURN OF THE NATIVE: *THE STONE ANGEL* AS THE TRANSITIONAL NOVEL

The Stone Angel was her homecoming novel. She completed a draft in 1961, while she edited her Somali diaries to prepare *The Prophet's Camel Bell* and *The Tomorrow-Tamer* for publication in 1963.[9] In her afterword to *The Prophet's Camel Bell*, Clara Thomas observes that this text was "the book in which she closed the door on her African years, her apprentice years and prepared the way for Manawaka" (266). There are therefore many parallels between *The Stone Angel* and her African texts, especially *The Prophet's Camel Bell*.

The Stone Angel was Laurence's first fiction set in Canada. After living in Africa for seven years and after composing her first four books about Africa, Laurence felt the need to come home. She felt that she had written as a stranger in a strange land, as an outsider about an alien culture, long enough; it was time to write about her own place, her own people: "For many years I had written not about Canada but about Africa where I had been living. And then in some way I had to come back to my roots, spiritually, I mean. Even though this return took place at about the same time I returned from Africa, actual geography was less important than this spiritual return out of which, in part, *The Stone Angel* grew" (Fabre 203). In "Books That Mattered to Me," Laurence describes another "Recognition and Revelation": "I saw, reading [*As For Me and My House*] that a writer *could* write out of a background similar to my own ... It was these writers [Sinclair Ross and W.O. Mitchell] who showed me what I would ultimately have to do, namely to write out of my own place, my own time, my own people" (243). *The Stone Angel* marked "the transition from writing about Africa to writing about my own people, the only ones I know from the inside" (quoted in King 183).

The Stone Angel was hailed as Laurence's first Canadian novel. But it could also be considered as her last African novel. As George Woodcock observes in *Introducing Margaret Laurence's* The Stone Angel, "just as *The Stone Angel* looked forward to the Manawaka novels, and in some ways set a pattern for them, it also looked back to Margaret Laurence's African experiences and bore their traces" (54). Thus, *The Stone Angel* is Laurence's transitional novel – transitional between Africa and Canada, male and female. Her heroine's name, "Hagar," is the first clue to this missing link: while the old lady owes much to her biblical namesake in Genesis, as various commentators have noted, *hhagar* is also the Somali word for "thornbush," virtually the only form of vegetation that flourishes in the desert landscape of Somalia. Laurence's attachment to the word is evidenced by the fact that, in translating Somali poems for *A Tree for Poverty*, she declines to translate the word "*hhagar*," choosing, instead, to let it stand but framing it in quotation marks to signal its Somali origin. For example, in her translation of the Somali *gabei*, "To a Friend Going on a Journey" by Mohamed Abdullah Hassan, she writes of "airless forests thick with 'hhagar' trees" (*TP* 53). And in translating Salaan Arrabey's *gabei*, "To a Faithless Friend," she writes, "'hagar' bushes tore my flesh" (*HS* 189). What name could be more appropriate for the cantankerous Hagar Currie? Like the word *sabra*, the Hebrew word for cactus, prickly on the outside but tender on the inside, which has come to stand for the tough-but-tender Israeli people, "Hagar" suggests this termagant's prickly personality. The fact that Laurence titled the embryo novel *Hagar* – until, on the eve of publication, her publishers objected (*HS* 145) – suggests the importance of the word and the name to the author. The Somali suggestions of the name *Hagar* are appropriate, for Hagar is proud, like the Somalis. In *The Prophet's Camel Bell* Laurence writes, "The Somalis are proud, not groveling, and in their own eyes, they are aristocrats and warriors" (*PCB* 206). Hagar says she is "proud as ... Lucifer" (*SA* 191).

Pride is not the only parallel between *The Stone Angel* and Laurence's African texts, however. Freedom is also central to both her African and Canadian writing, as the Somali people strive for political independence, and her Canadian protagonists aim for personal independence. "Freedom, in the profoundest sense even in colonial situations, must ultimately be an inner thing," she insists; "I think this theme has been an obsessive one, in my writing" (King 302). The quest for "the promised land of one's own inner freedom" (*TYS* 21) is crucial to all her Canadian heroines. She affirms, "I was very concerned,

[and] still am, with the whole question of freedom, both political and personal" (Sullivan 65). She cites the "quest for freedom" as central to all her fiction (IT 258). Hagar's tragedy is her failure to be free, as she tries "to recall something truly free that I've done in ninety years" (307). All Laurence's Canadian protagonists seek freedom from their shackles: from Hagar, who realizes on her deathbed that she was chained by her own pride – "Pride was my wilderness, and the demon that led me there was fear" (SA 292) – to Vanessa, who hopes, "if I sounded all my trumpets loudly enough, his walls would quake and crumble" (BH 184).

Freedom is closely linked to survival for Laurence. In "Ivory Tower or Grass Roots?" she asserts, "The quest for physical and spiritual freedom, the quest for relationships of equality and communication – these themes run through my fiction and are connected with the theme of survival, not mere physical survival, but a survival of the spirit, with human dignity and the ability to give and receive love" (258). She adds, "The themes of freedom and survival relate both to the social/external world and to the spiritual/inner one, and they are themes which I see as both political and religious" (259). She comments, "It will be obvious that these themes relate to Hagar, in The Stone Angel" (157).

"The theme of survival" (HS 8), which she identifies in "Sources" as the central theme of her fiction, especially The Stone Angel,[10] is clearly crucial to the desert life of the nomadic Somalis. In her introduction to A Tree for Poverty, she says, "the actual process of survival demands so much effort and tenacity from each tribesman" (47) that "Individualism and independence are a necessary step to survival" (40). By "survival," however, she intends more than mere physical survival. For Hagar, she explains in "Ten Years Sentences,'" it is spiritual rather than physical survival: the point is "to survive with some dignity, toting the load of excess mental baggage that everyone carries, until the moment of death" (21). She affirms, "The theme of survival – not just physical survival but the preservation of some human dignity and in the end some human warmth and ability to reach out and touch others – that is, I have come to think, an almost inevitable theme for a writer such as I, who came from a Scots-Irish background of stern values and hard work and puritanism and who grew up during the drought and depression of the thirties and then the war" (HS 8).

Survival is clearly crucial in the African desert, and Hagar's situation in the Canadian prairie is a parallel case. Laurence parallels these two locales explicitly in *The Prophet's Camel Bell*, affirming, "when we lived in Somaliland in the desert, this was a kind of country I took to right away because, as in the prairies, you can see from one side of the horizon to another" (*PCB* 33). Her description of the Canadian prairies, especially during the drought and depression of the Thirties, parallels them with her descriptions of the Somali desert, especially during the *jilal*, or dry season, when the land lies parched by the sun. Hagar's description of "the sun that grinds bone and flesh and earth to dust as though in a mortar of fire with a pestle of crushing light" (*SA* 54) is as applicable to the blazing sun of the African desert, "steeped in heat, stifling and dry" (*TP* 53) during the *jilal*, as it is to the Canadian prairie summer. The crucial importance of water in such arid landscapes is emphasized by Laurence's description in *The Prophet's Camel Bell* of the time she and Jack stopped their jeep to offer water to a young mother with a child crossing the desert of the Haud (77). This scene haunted Laurence, and the cup of water surfaces as a grail in the final scene of *The Stone Angel* (308).

In drawing on this African experience, Hagar paves the way for Laurence's Canadian heroines. In citing "Hagar's final journey toward self-knowledge and freedom," Clara Thomas states, in "Margaret Laurence and the Patterns of Pilgrimage," "Hagar sets the pattern for all the Manawaka heroines – she is a pilgrim, a seeker – and all the seekers (Rachel, Stacey, Vanessa and finally Morag), reflect the patterns of Margaret Laurence's own continuing quest" (97), for "Margaret Laurence's fiction presents patterns of pilgrimage that reflect her own life's quest" (96). Hagar does set the pattern of pilgrimage for Laurence's Manawaka heroines, for each of them must leave Manawaka in order to find herself, as Laurence herself did: and just as Hagar journeys to Shadow Point to find salvation, so Rachel and Stacey embark on a voyage of self-discovery both literally and figuratively. Vanessa leaves Manawaka to attend university in Winnipeg, just as Laurence did, near the end of *A Bird in the House*, and, like Laurence, Morag journeys far away before returning home in *The Diviners*. As Barbara Pell declares, in her essay "The African and Canadian Heroines: From Bondage to Grace," "The publication of *The Stone Angel* in 1964 liberated the

Canadian heroine from being primarily a prisoner of the male imagination and paved the way for the feminist creations" of women (33).

THE PROSPERO COMPLEX: "THE NOVELIST AS SOCIO-POLITICAL BEING"

The Stone Angel was Laurence's transitional novel in more ways than one: not only did it mark her movement from African to Canadian characters, but it also signaled her transition from male protagonists, as in *This Side Jordan*, to female protagonists in her Manawaka cycle. In her 1969 essay, "Gadgetry or Growing: Form and Voice in the Novel," Laurence acknowledges, referring to *This Side Jordan*, "I actually wonder how I ever had the nerve to attempt to go into the mind of an African man" (82). She determines, "I would never write with a male character as a protagonist" (Sullivan 74–5). In 1974, she remarks to Valerie Miner, "I think my main characters will continue to be women ... I'm a novelist and I'm a woman. I write about what I know" (20). She writes to Marian Engel, "More and more I want to speak about women" (King 368). Conrad Gross observes, "It does not come as a surprise that in contrast to *This side Jordan* her Canadian novels have women as main characters who, as mothers and wives, are painfully aware of their dependence and make constant efforts, therefore, to assert their individual identities" (78–9). Interestingly, the transition from African to Canadian subjects and from male to female protagonists coincided with Laurence's change of name from Peggy to Margaret (King 184). Transferring her faith in independence from the political to the personal corresponds with her movement from Africa to Canada. She employs the same themes for Canadian individuals that she used for African nations: "Understanding, respect, communication – these are possible among individuals as among nations" (IT 257).

As Laurence applies the political to the personal and the public to the private realm, Mannoni's theories of dependence are once again crucial to Laurence's perception of personal, as well as racial, or political, relations, for each of her Manawaka protagonists must discover independence in these narratives of self-empowerment. Each heroine is oppressed by an authority figure, whether it be a parent or a spouse. In *The Stone Angel*, Hagar lives her life under the shadow of her father, the self-made man Jason Currie: in attempting to be the strong son he never had, Hagar rejects her womanhood, becoming a patriarch in petticoats. In *A Jest of God*, Rachel Cameron is imprisoned in a prolonged adolescence by her hypochondriacal mother, May. In *The Fire-Dwellers*, Stacey feels oppressed by her uncommunicative husband, Mac, and his bizarre boss, Thor Thorlakson. In *A Bird in the House*, Vanessa MacLeod hates and fears her authoritarian grandfather, the arch-patriarch Timothy Connor, modelled on Laurence's own grandfather, John Simpson. In *The Diviners*, Morag Gunn is dominated by her condescending husband, Professor Brooke Skelton, who calls her "Child." Laurence makes the colonizer/colonized symbiosis, articulated by Mannoni as his Prospero Complex, quite clear in *The Diviners* by having Brooke born and raised in India under the British Raj. In case we miss the imperialist implications, Morag alludes to Shakespeare's *Tempest* (270).[11] Morag is an Ariel figure who must free herself from her dominating husband, a Prospero figure, by discovering her own voice as a writer. In fact, Laurence titled this section "(W)Rites of Passage" in her typescript.[12] In *Dance on the Earth: A Memoir*, she confesses, "I questioned my right to write" (159).

Morag's marriage may be inspired by the Laurence's own, as Jack was a decade older than Margaret and had spent four years during the Second World War with the Canadian Air Force in Burma, where he was known as "Driver" Laurence (*DE* 102). Although Margaret accompanied Jack to Somaliland, where he took up a post with the Department of Public Works to build reservoirs in the desert to conserve the rains for the *jilal* in 1951, and to the Gold Coast in 1952, where he helped to construct a port at Tema, she declined to accompany him when he took up a post in East Pakistan in 1962 because, as she explained to Ethel Wilson in a 23 January 1964 letter, she did not wish to be a Memsahib again.[13] *The Stone Angel*, as she explains in *Dance on the Earth*, was also instrumental in their separation because Jack, a civil engineer, did not like the novel and believed that it should be rewritten in the third person and in chronological order: "When I wrote the draft of *The Stone Angel*, Jack wanted to read it. I didn't want him to. I think I knew his response would be pivotal to our marriage ... I allowed him to read it in the end and he didn't like it much, but for me it was the most important book I had written, a book on which I had to stake the rest of my life" (*DE* 158). So Margaret moved to London with her children, Jocelyn and David, and the manuscript of her first Canadian novel, *The Stone Angel*. Thus, *The Stone Angel* was crucial to her career *and* to her life.

In her essay, "Ivory Tower or Grass Roots?: The Novelist as Socio-Political Being," Laurence identifies her writing as a political act: "Fiction has many facets ... It speaks first and foremost of individual characters, and through them it speaks of our dilemmas and our aspirations, which are always in some way or other those both of politics and of faith" (259). An artist is not generally conceived of as political, but Laurence believes she is. In fact, writing a novel about an old woman on the point of death is a courageous political act. So is writing a novel about a "spinster" school-teacher. So is writing a novel about a middle-aged housewife. So is writing a novel about a woman who has a child out of wedlock by a Métis man. Laurence was a courageous writer who brought the political to the personal and the public to the private in influential feminist fictions.

Laurence's experience of observing and writing about African women developed her nascent feminism. All her work is implicitly feminist, especially her Canadian fiction, but in her later years her feminism became explicit – notably in her last published work *Dance on the Earth: A Memoir*, where she labels herself a feminist and laments "the downgrading of women in every field" (*DE* 4). "Writing by women ... was generally considered by critics and reviewers in this country with at best amused tolerance, at worst a dismissive shrug. It still makes me angry how thoroughly I had been brainwashed by society" (*DE* 5), she complains. "In one of my early stories, ["*Tal des Walde*" (*EW* 36)] I actually used a first-person narrative, but the narrator was a man. How long, how regrettably long, it took me to find my true voice as a woman writer" (*DE* 5), she laments.

Laurence was lucky – despite growing up in a "world in which communications and the arts have been dominated by men and herstory either ignored, condescended to, or forgotten" (*DE* 4) – to have grown up "among determined women, intelligent and talented women" (*DE* 7): her pianist mother, Verna, her two distinguished nursing aunts, Velma and Ruby, and her Aunt Marg (who became her stepmother upon the death of her own young mother), who was an intellectual, but who was "denied university because she was female" (*DE* 27). She explains, "Their father, my grandfather Simpson, was a male chauvinist of the first order" (*DE* 8). This arch-patriarch bred rebellion in the bones of young Peggy Wemyss, as Laurence was known, who spent her adolescence in his brick house – fictionalized in her short story collection, *A Bird in the House*. Lyall Powers states in *Alien Heart*, "Except for her grim, ursine Grandpa Simpson, Peggy lived mainly in a world of females, a world of strong, independent-minded women" (25). Laurence explains, "because of these strong independent-minded women, I always had the vague but powerful feeling that I, too, could participate in exciting events" ("Books" 240–1).

Laurence explains the origins of her feminism in her foreword to *Dance on the Earth*: "I was not a person for the first three years of my life. It was only in 1929, because of the enormous and valiant efforts of such women as Nellie McClung and Emily Murphy, that Canadian women were finally legalized as 'persons'" (*DE* 8). In "Books That Mattered to Me," she writes, "Were there no women writers who spoke to my childhood? Not many" (240). She cites McClung and L.M. Montgomery as portraying intelligent, independent heroines: Montgomery's *Anne of Green Gables* and *Emily of New Moon* gave Laurence "the sense that a woman could be – and it was *all right* for her to be – an intelligent, independent-minded person who was determined to pursue her own vocation as well as to be a wife and mother" ("Books" 241). In describing the impact of the writing of Gabrielle Roy, she states, "When I read *The Tin Flute* for the first time, I began to understand what a woman writer can do, in portraying women characters" ("Books" 48).

THE FAMILY OF WOMAN: LAURENCE'S MANAKAWA FICTION

And Laurence did portray women powerfully in her Manawaka cycle. As Morley states, "This cycle of fiction constitutes a remarkable gallery of vital individuals, a composite portrait of women's experience in the late nineteenth and twentieth centuries, and the imaginative recreation of an entire society" (8). Many feminist critics have commended Laurence for giving women their own voice. As Diana Brydon states, in "Silence, Voice and the Mirror: Margaret Laurence and Women," "Her books give ordinary women their voices back. They reach out to their readers to establish a sense of community. And in claiming full humanity for all her female characters, her novels challenge the stereotypes that have limited women to preordained and constricting roles" (203).

Moreover, the five Manawaka texts form a cohesive unit, like Scott's Waverley novels. Laurence explains, "When I wrote *The Stone Angel* I had no idea there would be other books coming out of the Manawaka background, and indeed it turned out that there were five books … even though each of these books is, of course, quite independent of any of the others, they can be seen as a kind of whole" (Sullivan 77). Numerous critics, including Clara Thomas, George Woodcock, and David Blewett, to name just a few, have written persuasively about the coherence of the Manawaka cycle. In fact, the five heroines are related. Hagar is the grandmother of it all, since she is the generation of Laurence's own grandparents, for Hagar "incorporates many of the qualities of my grandparents' generation. Her speech is their speech, and her gods their gods" (*HS* 7), as Laurence affirms in *Heart of a Stranger*. Stacey is "Hagar's spiritual grand-daughter" (22), Laurence observes in "Ten Years' Sentences": "She's not particularly valiant (maybe she's an anti-heroine), but she's got some guts and some humour" (TYS 22). She remarks, "In *The Fire-Dwellers*, Stacey is Rachel's sister (don't ask me why; I don't know; she just is)" (TYS 21).

In the last two Manawaka books, *A Bird in the House* and *The Diviners*, Vanessa MacLeod and Morag Gunn play bit parts in each other's dramas. In *The Diviners*, for example, Vanessa sings the solo in the Christmas pageant, to Morag's disgust; but, when Vanessa's father, Dr Ewen MacLeod, dies, Morag is ashamed of having wished her ill. Both these heroines, as well as Rachel and Stacey, were also to have had bit parts in the novel "Dance on the Earth," which was to have concluded the Manawaka cycle. The Métis Tonnerre family connects all the Manawaka texts, threading through the cycle. The Currie plaid pin that John Shipley trades for the Tonnerre hunting knife in *The Stone Angel* is inherited by Morag Gunn, and the knife is returned to her on the death of Jules Tonnerre in *The Diviners*, where the two emblems, Aboriginal and settler artifacts, are reunited, to be inherited by Pique Gunn Tonnerre, Morag's daughter by Jules, knitting the entire Manawaka cycle together.

Just as modern American photographer Edward Steichen created a pictorial *Family of Man*,[14] so Margaret Laurence creates a fictional Family of Woman in her Manawaka cycle, as she portrays her female protagonists in every possible familial and social role – as mother, daughter, sister, and wife, and as lover, friend and, most important, writer. But within those roles, each heroine must discover her individual identity beneath the role-playing and gender construction – the selfhood that precedes and informs all those roles. For example, Hagar Shipley, the "holy terror" (304) who dominates *The Stone Angel*, is uncomfortable in her female roles as wife and mother because she is uneasy being a woman; before the nonagenarian can die, this petrified woman with the heart of stone must first come to life; before she can come to life, however, she must accept her identity as a woman.

Rachel Cameron, a neurotic, thirty-four-year-old elementary school teacher, is a case of arrested development, still living at home with her aging, widowed mother as an adolescent no more mature than her own students. She must outgrow the juvenile role of daughter and forge new adult roles and relationships for herself and, finally, give birth to her self as an adult woman in *A Jest of God*. Rachel's sister, Stacey MacAindra, has taken the other road in *The Fire-Dwellers* and married and borne four children: buried under the multiple roles of wife and mother, daughter and sister, she must learn to know and love herself before she can continue to love others. Vanessa is, literally, a child in *A Bird in the House*, and her adult retrospective chronicles her escape from the cage created by her Grandfather Connor and her emergence from the chrysalis suggested by her name, *Vanessa*, the Greek word for butterfly *and* for soul. Morag Gunn must outgrow the role of "Child" imposed on her by her authoritarian husband, Brooke Skelton, by finding her own voice as a writer in *The Diviners* – as Laurence did in writing her Manawaka cycle – her "(W)Rites of Passage."

In "Matriarch of Manawaka," Valerie Miner comments on the rejection of roles by Laurence's Manawaka heroines: "Morag's biggest step is her rejection of external roles. We see Hagar battling her father's expectations, Rachel fighting her mother's demands of propriety. Certainly Stacey is aware of role playing. Toward the end of *The Fire-Dwellers*, she is able to externalize at least some of her thoughts, to become a fuller person. Morag carries the whole process further. She rejects the traditional strictures of marriage, motherhood and housewifery" (20). While Morag does reject her confining marriage, however, she certainly does not reject motherhood. Indeed, Laurence does not portray her heroines as rejecting their responsibilities but, rather, as finding the confidence, through discovering their own identity, to reach out and help others. In fact, Laurence portrays her heroines as developing from solipsism to community. Hagar recognizes, too late, the devotion of her rejected husband, Bram Shipley, realizing, "*His banner over me was love*" (80). She also recognizes, finally, the value of community when she is confined in hospital, as she comes to appreciate women *and* her long-suffering son, Marvin, saying, "You've been good to me, always. A better son than John" (304). Rachel adopts, not rejects, her mother, now her "elderly child" (208), announcing, "I am the mother now" (203). Stacey reaffirms her commitment to her husband, Mac, and their children and even agrees to welcome her father-in-law, Matthew, into her home as she anticipates the arrival of her mother and sister from Manawaka. Morag comes to appreciate her foster-parents, Christie and Prin Logan: Morag tells Christie on his deathbed, "you've been my father to me" (420), prompting him to respond, "I'm blessed" (420). Laurence does not portray her heroines as rejecting their roles, but, rather, as accepting them with grace, with the knowledge that their sense of self-worth is now strong enough to support their responsibility to others. As Lyall Powers states, "The Manawaka fiction favours enlightened love and respect of self, the proper self-love that is the basis on which love of neighbour must rest" (37). Self-empowerment for Laurence spells charity, not selfishness.

Indeed, each of Laurence's Manawaka women feels sympathy, rather than animosity, toward her husband or lover. We saw how Hagar comes to appreciate Bram. Rachel says, of Nick Kazlik, "He had his own demons and webs" (*JG* 197). Stacey realizes that her husband, Mac, needs support as much as she does. And Morag consoles Jules Tonnerre as he lies dying. Vanessa acknowledges how much she inherits from Grandfather Connor. While Laurence identifies herself as a feminist who believes in equal rights for women, she is primarily a humanist who advocates empathy for others. She affirms, "I really think that with the main male characters in all my writing, I do feel great sympathy for them" (Sullivan 74). She writes to John Metcalf on 28 March 1972, "With women, although our culture has indeed tended to make them 2nd class citizens, men are not the enemy – that is, men are our brother, lovers, the fathers of our children. This makes it much more subtle and difficult, in some ways, because the efforts of women to re-spect and free themselves *must* be done without damaging men" (quoted in King 301). Laurence succeeds in her Manawaka novels.

"METHOD WRITER": LAURENCE'S AUTOBIOGRAPHICAL IMPULSE

Laurence frequently affirms the paramount importance of character to her fiction: "For me, fiction is primarily a matter of portraying indi-vidual characters as faithfully as I am able to do" (IT 251). In "A Place to Stand On," in *Heart of a Stranger*, she affirms, "I can feel a deep sense of connection with the main character" (6). In fact, she says, "I must be a kind of Method writer" (TNV 157): "I write ... what I would call a Method novel. Like a Method actor, you get right inside the role. I take on, for the time I'm writing, the *persona* of the character" (Cameron 102).

Laurence asserts, "my books deal basically with human dilemmas ... I always start with the main character or, as it may be, characters. Usually there are a number of people who have been inhabiting my head for a number of years before I begin on a novel, and their dilem-mas grow out of what they are, where they come from" (Gibson 193, 195). She claims that each protagonist is faced with a dilemma or con-flict that she must resolve so that she may continue to function. The nature of the character's dilemma varies, of course, depending on the culture. For her African characters, like Nathaniel Amegbe of *This Side Jordan*, the dilemma lies in the fact that they are caught between the old gods of their ancestors and the new gods of the Christian missions that educated them. For her Canadian heroines, the conflict is between the past generation, like Vanessa's Grandfather Connor in *A Bird in the House*, and the modern desire for independence, but it is also be-tween her heroines' need to discover their identities amidst the plethora of role constructions and their duty to fulfill the responsibilities in-volved in those roles, as we can see most clearly in the case of Stacey MacAindra of *The Fire-Dwellers*. Laurence recalls in *Dance on the Earth* the "impossible juggling act" (157) involved in being a writer and a wife and mother. She remarks to Rosemary Sullivan, "Role con-flict – I know exactly what that means" (73). Her heroine's dilemma consists of a conflict of roles or a conflict between her duty to others and responsibility to herself. Each novel portrays the character resolving that conflict through self-knowledge and relationships with others, so that she is able to find the strength, within and without, to carry on. Laurence believes, "Whatever strength one finds, ultimately, must come from inside oneself, and in a literal sense, no one can save anyone else, although you can reach out to touch others" (King 302). Thus, we can trace a development in the degree of self-empowerment of her Manawaka heroines.

Laurence's need to identify with her protagonists also helped to lead her home to her native land. In returning from Africa to Canada in her fiction, Laurence returned to the culture that informed her best work: "Writing, for me, has to be set firmly in ... some outer and inner territory which might be described in anthropological terms as 'cultural background'" (HS 9). She writes, "I began to see that if I was going to go on as a novelist, and go deeper, I could only write about my own people. Which in some ways means aspects of myself ... My characters had to be people whom I could know from the inside; people whose responses to life and to their own dilemmas I could be almost certain about; people whose idiom was mine" ("Geography"). Laurence explains in her interview with Robert Kroetsch that in her Manawaka works she is concerned with coming to terms with "my roots and my ancestors and, if you like, with my gods" (55).

Her Manawaka fiction is more autobiographical than mere "cultural background," however. She labels A Bird in the House "semi-autobiographical fiction" (HS 8) and The Diviners a "spiritual autobiography" (DE 6). While none of her Manawaka books are autobiographical in fact, they are autobiographical in impulse, for Laurence's life experience inspired and informed her fiction, as the biographies by King, Powers, and Xiques confirm. Laurence acknowledges in her essay "On 'The Loons'": "The character of Vanessa is based on myself as a child, and the MacLeod family is based on my own childhood family" (805).[15] A parallel may illustrate her claim: in "Sources," she explains how writing A Bird in the House led her to understand her grandfather's pioneering spirit: "I don't think I knew any of this, really knew it, until I had finished those stories. I don't think I ever knew, either, how much I owed to him. One sentence near the end of the final story may show what I mean. 'I had feared and fought the old man, yet he proclaimed himself in my veins'" (*HS* 8). Her discussion of her fiction in the essay "On 'The Loons'" demonstrates how she alters autobiographical facts: for example, the young Métis girl with tuberculosis of the bone who visited the Wemyss cottage at Clear Lake was several years younger than Peggy, while Peggy's father was, of course, a lawyer, not a doctor. She states, "The ways in which memories and 'created' events intertwine in this story probably illustrate a few things about the nature of fiction" (805). Examining the artistic alchemy by which Laurence transforms fact into fiction in the Manawaka cycle is extremely illuminating.

In her 1972 essay, "Time and the Narrative Voice," she insists none of her heroines is herself, but she acknowledges that they are all aspects of herself: "the character is one of the writer's voices and selves" (TNV 157). She writes to Gordon Elliott, "One's writing is not meant to be bound up with one's life, but only jerks believe this" (quoted by King xx). Clearly, she would not subscribe to the theory of the death of the author. Laurence explains to Adele Wiseman, "a character like Morag, just as with Stacey and even Rachel, is both me and not me" (*SL* 341). King agrees: "Indeed, she was very much like Hagar and Morag" (xxi): "The inner world of Margaret Laurence was intense and filled with drama, and her writings are intimately interconnected with her life. More than that, hers is the very human story of a woman's struggle to find – and define – herself in a male-centred world" (xx). He affirms, "The adversities she herself faced went into the making of all her heroines, each of whom is a mixture of great strengths and great weaknesses – a reflection of the powerful, vibrant and tormented woman who wrote the Manawaka novels" (xxi). Laurence's connection with her female protagonists is complex and problematic, but fascinating.

The character's dilemma often reflects Laurence's own personal conflicts, suggesting that fiction may provide a form of self-therapy for the author. Laurence acknowledges, "even though most of us don't write autobiographically, in any direct sense, our characters are partly formed by both our own experience and the experience of women that we have known" (Sullivan 74–5). She says, "in doing the writing I've discovered a lot about my own dilemmas" (King 302). Powers claims the pressure of her personal problems "made her feel the need, the genuine urgency, to resort to her fiction as a kind of therapy" (459). Consequently, he refers to Laurence's fiction to illustrate his theories about her life, as he attempts "to justify consideration of the 'autobiograph-ical' quality of the Manawaka books" (458) in *Alien Heart*: "I sug-gested strongly, in focusing on the autobiographical features of the first four Manawaka books, that in addition to their value as accomplished works of fiction they served Margaret as a necessary means of man-aging her own personal problems" (402). He explains, "There is a re-ciprocal illumination available as well to the informed biographer. I do not mean the facile reading into the fiction of a superficial 'confes-sional' or autobiographical feature" (xix). As Laurence acknowledges to Al Purdy on 7 September 1971, "The division between fiction and so-called reality in my life seems an awfully uncertain one" (*AH* 373).

Interestingly, each of her Manawaka heroines comes closer to Lau-rence's own experience and becomes more contemporaneous with her creator. She proceeds from Hagar, a nonagenarian, who represents her grandparents' generation, through Rachel, an unmarried schoolteacher based on her older cousin, to Stacey, a married mother of four living in Vancouver, as Laurence was at the time of composing the novel. She then creates Vanessa, acknowledged to be a version of her childhood self, a rebellious granddaughter who grows up to be a writer, like Lau-rence. Finally, she creates Morag, a middle-aged writer who is the same age as Laurence and resembles her physically – even to the long, straight black hair and the dark-rimmed, owlish glasses. Morag escapes the small town of Manawaka only to settle in a small Ontario town that resembles Manawaka and Neepawa, as well as Lakefield, Ontario, where Laurence lived the last years of her life. Lyall Powers concludes, "The difficulties and sacrifices in Morag's life as she creates her five books of fiction repeat those of Margaret's life as she created the five books of the Manawaka Saga" (402): Allie Pryce Chorniuk, protago-nist of Laurence's final, unfinished novel, "Dance on the Earth," may also be modelled on Laurence: not only is she the same age the author was, but she is also criticized by evangelicals, as Laurence was in the "Controversy" (*DE* 213), surrounding *The Diviners*, which fundamen-talists labelled blasphemous and pornographic. Allie also moves east from Manawaka to Jordan's Landing, a small Ontario town similar to Morag's McConnell's Landing and to Laurence's own Lakefield. All Laurence's Canadian heroines hail from Manawaka, a thinly disguised version of Laurence's own hometown of Neepawa, and all of them, eventually, escape – as Laurence herself did.

"A TOWN OF THE MIND:" THE MYTHICAL MICROCOSM OF MANAWAKA

Like Scott's *Waverley*, Hardy's *Wessex*, and Faulkner's Yoknapataw-pha County, to name but a few, Laurence creates a mythical microcosm in Manawaka. As Patricia Morley observes, "Laurence has turned the town of her youth into a metaphor of universal human experience" (18). Alan Bevan states, in his introduction to the 1973 NCL edition of *The Fire-Dwellers*, "Manawaka is more than a place: it represents its creator's point of reference. It is a world from which each of the three protagonists tries to escape, but which is always there" (viii). In "A Place to Stand On," the first essay in *Heart of a Stranger*, Laurence asserts, "Manawaka will probably always be there, simply because whatever I am was shaped and formed in that sort of place, and my way of seeing, however much it may have changed over the years, re-mains in some enduring way that of a small-town prairie person" (*HS* 9). And in "Where the World Began," the last essay in *Heart of a Stranger*, she affirms, "Because that settlement and that land were my first and for many years my only real knowledge of this planet, in some profound way they remain my world, my way of viewing. My eyes were formed there" (*HS* 169). My chapter on her microcosm of Man-awaka, which she labels "a town of the mind, my own private world" (*HS* 7), will therefore introduce the subsequent chapters on her five Manawaka fictions and her unfinished novel.

As Joan Coldwell remarks in *The Oxford Companion to Canadian Literature*, Second Edition, "Laurence's greatest achievement lies in the four Canadian novels dominated by the town of Manawaka" (634). Therefore, the second major section of *Divining Margaret Laurence*, following the first section on her African texts, focuses on the Man-awaka cycle, with chapters devoted to *The Stone Angel*, *A Jest of God* and *The Fire-Dwellers*, *A Bird in the House* and *The Diviners*. A chap-ter on her unfinished novel, titled "Dance on the Earth" – an ambi-tious plan spanning three generations of Ukrainian and Scottish immigrants to Canada intended to complete the Manawaka cycle – a work that has not been discussed by critics, concludes the study of her Canadian fiction.

"(W)RITES OF PASSAGE": THE MANAWAKA NOVELS
AS *KÜNSTLERROMANE*

Like the autobiographical novels of major modernist writers, such as D.H. Lawrence's *Sons and Lovers* (1913) and James Joyce's *A Portrait of the Artist as a Young Man* (1916), all the Manawaka texts are *Bildungsromane*, or novels of development (often delayed). The last two books – *A Bird in the House* and *The Diviners* – are also *Künstlerromane*, chronicling the development of an artist, as both narrators become writers, like Laurence herself. Both texts are, thus, metafictional, presenting the creative process in a self-reflexive manner, as defined in Linda Hutcheon's influential study, *The Canadian Postmodern* (1988), where she claims "The traditional *Bildungsromane* takes on different forms and emphases when its subject is female" (132). These texts are not only autobiographical metafiction, however, but *meta-autobiography*, because an examination of Laurence's juvenilia and the manuscripts of her novels demonstrate that the stories Vanessa and Morag write are the same stories Laurence wrote. In *A Bird in the House* both actual and fictional authors write a story about pioneers titled "The Pillars of the Nation," and both write a tale about the fur trade set in nineteenth-century Quebec. Tracing Vanessa's development as an artist, as the chapter on "'Death and Love': Romance and Reality in *A Bird in the House*" does, can therefore reflect Laurence's own creative growth, for her artistic alchemy may be illuminated by exploring the meta-autobiographical aspects of *A Bird in the House*. Similarly, in *The Diviners*, the stories the young Morag writes correspond to the stories the young Margaret wrote. For example, Laurence recycles her story *"Tal des Walde"* as "The Mountain" in her typescript of *The Diviners*. But, because her Knopf editor required her to excise such embedded fictions, she reduced this story, and many others, to a brief summary, as the chapter on "'(W)Rites of Passage': A Portrait of the Writer in *The Diviners*" demonstrates. Therefore, it is essential, in exploring the development of her oeuvre, to consider her juvenilia, collected in *Embryo Words* and *Colors of Speech*. The chapter on her "Embryo Words," her early works, explains how her early life – the loss of both parents in her childhood and the outbreak of war in her adolescence – influenced her writing and how her early writing developed her artistry.

Laurence allows each of her heroines to tell her own story: not only Vanessa and Morag, but also Hagar, Rachel, and Stacey narrate their own life-stories either in first-person confessionals or in a complex combination of first- and third-person narrative, often combined with a dual time scheme of past and present connected by memory. In "Time and the Narrative Voice," Laurence affirms, "Most of the fiction I have written in recent years has been written in the first person, with the main character assuming the narrative voice. Even when I have written in the third person, as I did in part of my novel *The Fire-Dwellers*, it is really a first-person narrative which happens to be written in the third person, for the narrative voice even here is essentially that of the main character" (157). Brenda Beckman-Long observes in "Authorizing her Text: Margaret Laurence's Shift to Third-Person Narration," "Both [Cameron sister] novels portray female experience from the point of view of the protagonist, but Laurence adapts the confessional form by adopting the third person for an ideological purpose: the authorization of the female voice" (65). Thus, not only the first-person narrators, but each of Laurence's protagonists may be viewed as a writer in her own right.

"TRUE NARRATIVE VOICE": NARRATIVE METHOD AND TIME STRUCTURE

Narrative voice and time structure are inextricably connected for Laurence. In her 1972 essay "Time and the Narrative Voice," she emphasizes "the relationship between the narrative voice and the treatment of time – it is the character who chooses which parts of the personal past, the family past and the ancestral past have to be revealed in order for the present to be realized and the future to happen" (160). In this same essay she explains, "it is so desperately important to discover the true narrative voice – which really means knowing the characters so well that one can take on their past, their thoughts, their responses, can in effect for awhile [*sic*] *become* them" (157). For example, she recalls, while writing *The Fire-Dwellers*, "I truly felt I was living two lives, Stacey's and my own ... I was so involved with her life, there were times it felt like I actually had six children, two of mine and four of hers" (*DE* 189). She had to stop writing an hour before her children returned from school so that she could extricate herself from her fictional space and return to the real world.

Command of "true narrative voice" constitutes one of Laurence's greatest talents as a novelist. As New states, "Perhaps more than any other writer of her time, she seemed to have mastered the rhythms and cadences of the Canadian speaking voice" (*MLWC* 1) – arguably because she first faced the challenge of reproducing African voices. Developing her own voice through the ventriloquism of translating Somali folk literature enhanced Laurence's gift for capturing her characters' idiom. She claims, "Our task is not to reject the past but to assimilate it, to take the language and make it truly ours, to write out of our own familiar idiom and out of our deepest observations of our people and our place of belonging on this planet" (IT 255). Laurence's fiction is distinguished by her gift for capturing her characters' individual idiom – from the child, Vanessa, through the housewife, Stacey, to the matriarch, Hagar. Speaking of Hagar, Laurence writes to Jack McClelland on 29 June 1963, "I think now that I can't ever again be content to write in anything except this idiom, which is of course mine" (quoted in King 184). Riegel writes, "Laurence showed Canadian readers and writers that one could legitimately write about 'home' and do so with a voice particularly Canadian" (xi). Lennox applauds her "distinctively Canadian sense of history, place, and idiom, and above all a gathering of unforgettable characters" (4). Laurence lamented the fact that it took her so long to discover her true voice as a woman writer, but she did so in her Manawaka novels.

"OUTER AND INNER TERRITORY": PEOPLE AND PLACES

Laurence affirms, "For me, fiction is primarily a matter of portraying individual characters as faithfully as I am able to do. These characters, however, do not live in a vacuum. They live in specific places" (IT 251). Paradoxically, authors achieve universality, Laurence believes, via particularity: "The most important thing about writing, to my mind, is what it is able to convey about the human dilemma, and in this sense one must always be concerned with themes which are not local and particular. But these themes can only be conveyed through the local and particular" ("Geography"). Her writing is rooted in real landscapes, with vivid verisimilitude. Laurence, who loathed cities, represents the rural-urban conflict vividly in her African and Canadian fiction, as her characters migrate from family farm or small town to the big city. Nathaniel Amegbe, in *This Side Jordan*, is divided between his tribal past in an Ashanti village and his present at Futura Academy in the city Accra. Hagar, Rachel, Stacey, and Morag all leave their small hometown of Manawaka for the metropolis of Vancouver, "jewel of the Pacific Northwest" (*FD* 10), just as Laurence did.

Laurence's greatest genius is for recreating the Canadian prairie, as Kristjana Gunnars claims: "Margaret Laurence has been a founding mother of Canadian literature. She has given voice to the Manitoba prairie. She has raised the value of all sectors of society by showing the full humanity of the most neglected and forgotten among us. From her example we have learned the value of Canadian literature and culture, the importance of art to that culture; the necessity of honesty in a dangerous time in history; the truth of fiction and poetry. Perhaps her greatest gift has been the way in which she showed us the depths and passions of the place in which we were living: Manitoba, through her, had taken full part in the human drama. We no longer needed to look elsewhere" (viii).

Laurence affirms, "Writing, for me, has to be set firmly in some soil, some place, some outer and inner territory" (*HS* 9). That "soil" generates a rich lode of symbolism in the work of a writer who is deeply entranced by nature. For example, water symbolism is the undercurrent that flows through all of her fiction – from the River Jordan that Nathaniel Amegbe hopes his son Joshua will cross in *This Side Jordan* (282), through the Wachakwa River, modelled on the Whitemud River of Neepawa, where Rachel comes to life by learning to love in *A Jest of God*, to the river beside which Morag, like Laurence, writes her novel, *The Diviners*. Both Hagar and Stacey escape from the metropolis of Vancouver to seek rest and peace by the sea, where they find salvation of a sort in *The Stone Angel* and *The Fire-Dwellers*. "The river [that] flowed both ways" (11) in *The Diviners* is "the river of life" (Kroetsch 50) itself that flows through all of Laurence's fiction.

"VEHICLE OR VESSEL": MYTH AND METAPHOR

Laurence is a great Canadian writer and also a significant author of African texts. But her genius extends beyond the borders of nationality. In *Long Drums and Cannons*, she claims that "Nigerian writers have already built up a body of work which is of interest and value not only in Africa but everywhere in the world where there are people who find in literature one way of discovering more fully the reality of others and of exploring the mystery of themselves" (*LDC* 203). Laurence, too, is a writer whose characters and themes "reach out beyond any national boundary" (*LDC* 13) to capture any reader interested in the human heart. Laurence was a highly educated, well-read writer familiar with writers of "the great tradition," as F.R. Leavis labelled it. She affirms, "Anyone who writes in the English language is in some way an inheritor of Shakespeare and Milton, of Fielding and Jane Austen, of Dickens and Thackeray" (IT 255). Laurence was greatly influenced by the modernist novelists she admired, such as Joyce Cary, E.M. Forster, James Joyce and D.H. Lawrence, many of whom also composed *Bildungsromane* or *Künstlerromane*, a distinctively modernist mode.

Laurence's education at Viscount Collegiate in Neepawa and at United College in Winnipeg introduced her to modernist poets T.S. Eliot, G.M. Hopkins and Robinson Jeffers. Her skilfull use of myth and metaphor, symbolic patterns and word play, reflects the influence of the modernist poets she admired. Just as modernist writers renewed and revised ancient myth, so Laurence "had an intuitive understanding of the power of myth" (*SL* 4), as Lennox and Panofsky assert. Laurence employs myth and metaphor to reveal her protagonists' true identity to the reader in undercurrents of symbolism that flow through each novel, often unbeknownst to the narrator herself, thus creating an ironic gap between the self-deceived protagonist and the reader – a gap that Laurence portrays her heroines ultimately bridging as they learn to know themselves.

Laurence is an artist who employs myth and metaphor to limn the cultural context of Africa and Canada, and her innovative artistry places her on the cusp between modernism and postmodernism. She claims, in "Gadgetry or Growing: Form and Voice in the Novel," "Form, in writing, concerns me more than it once did, but only as a means of conveying the characters and their particular dilemmas" (89). She insists, "I have always found the whole question of form not only fascinating but incredibly difficult" (Sullivan 76). Her experimentation with narrative structures placed her in the vanguard of innovative and experimental postmodernist fiction – notably in *The Fire-Dwellers* and *The Diviners*. In *The Fire-Dwellers*, she employs a complex typography, including dashes to convey Stacey's inner thoughts, indentation to convey her memories of the past, italics to convey her fantasies, and capital letters to convey the way Stacey is bombarded by the media. Chapter four, set at breakfast in the MacAindra kitchen, reads like a film script, complete with sound effects of telephone ringing and television blaring. In "Ten Years' Sentences," she explains that this form includes "third-person narration as well as Stacey's idiomatic inner running commentary and her somewhat less idiomatic fantasies, dreams, memories" (22). In *The Diviners*, Laurence employs cinematic techniques of "*Innerfilms*" describing Morag's fantasies of the future, such as her vision of her death (138), and "*Memorybank Movies*" of her memories of the past, such as "*Down in the Valley, the Valley So Low*" (139) about her first close encounter with Jules Tonnerre, to convey her complex mental processes. We can see a development in her post-modernist use of form to convey her protagonists' developing self-realization and self-empowerment.

Laurence says that what she is aiming for in her choice of form is "the kind of vehicle or vessel capable of risking that peculiar voyage of exploration which constitutes a novel" (GG 89). Indeed, she has taken her readers on a fascinating journey into "those strange lands of the heart and spirit" (*HS* 3) that we call the Manawaka cycle. As Paul Comeau concludes, in *Margaret Laurence's Epic Imagination*, "Margaret Laurence helped to give us our place to stand on" (144). Aritha van Herk writes, in "Margaret Laurence: The Shape of the Writer's Shadow," "The shape of Laurence's shadow is the shape of this country" (140).

CHAPTER 2

"Embryo Words":
Laurence's Early Writings

Few events are more exciting for the lover of literature than the discovery of new works by a familiar and beloved author. When those texts are early works that reveal the baby steps of a great artist, the discovery is even more valuable. Margaret Laurence began writing when she was just a child. Always canny about destroying drafts, she covered her early tracks as carefully as she could, but she could not destroy all her juvenilia, since several items had been published in her high school newspaper, *Annals of the Black and Gold*, when she attended Viscount Collegiate in Neepawa, Manitoba, 1940–44; in her college magazine, *Vox*, at United College in Winnipeg, where she was a student from 1944–47; and in the *Manitoban*, the University of Manitoba's newspaper.[1]

Laurence's juvenilia are collected in two volumes: *Embryo Words* (1997) and *Colors of Speech* (2000). *Embryo Words* includes nearly two dozen works – three stories and nineteen poems – and *Colors of Speech* includes another story, additional lyrics, and a previously unpublished long narrative poem about Winnipeg entitled "North Main Car." This early writing is valuable because it prefigures her Manawaka fiction in her hatred of war and love of nature, her vivid characterization and idiomatic dialogue, and the rich vein of metaphor, myth, and musicality that renders her a poet in prose. It also reveals how Laurence's own life informs her writing. Indeed, she recycles her early writing in the mature fiction that chronicles the development of a writer, *A Bird in the House* and *The Diviners*. A consideration of her early life will help to provide a context for these works and demonstrate how her early writing was essential to Laurence's development as one of Canada's greatest novelists.

Margaret Laurence, born Jean Margaret Wemyss in Neepawa, Manitoba, on 18 July 1926, began to compose stories before she was old enough to write them down. Her mother, Verna Simpson Wemyss, recorded the literary bent of Peggy, as she was known, in "Mother's Record of Baby": "A great imagination. Speaks a lot of her 'funny' house, where Paper Slim, and Mr. and Mrs. Slim live, also sister Polly, of whom she speaks, and plays Three Bears a lot, with herself as Tiny, her mummy as Mammy Muff, and her daddy Father Bruin. Starts her stories always, 'Once upon a time'" (*DE* 40). Verna's entries in this baby book stop at her daughter's fourth birthday. Peggy received a tricycle for her birthday and remembers her Aunt Marg helping her take it upstairs to show to her mother, who lay sick in bed. She never saw her mother again. Verna Wemyss died in 1930, two days after her daughter's fourth birthday, at age thirty-four, of an acute kidney infection. Laurence records, "This memory is my first conscious one, my own memory rather than the imagined memories of infanthood and early childhood that were based on what was told to me later on" (*DE* 24).

"I was always a writer," Laurence told her first biographer, Joan Hind-Smith. When asked what affected her writing most, she replied, "I think it was the number of deaths in my family" (9). Hind-Smith noted, "Laurence's creative drive increases whenever she suffers serious loss and, sadly for her, there were to be several such losses in her life" (7). As Laurence acknowledges in *Dance on the Earth: A Memoir*, "Only deaths in the family seemed real" (62).

Creation was an antidote to death for Laurence, as she constructed characters to people the darkness. After the death of her mother, she created a character named "Blue Sky." Morag Gunn of *The Diviners* also creates a character named "*Blue-Sky Mother*" (*D* 20) after the death of her mother and father. Morag, like Peggy with her imaginary

Mr and Mrs Slim, fabricates *"my spruce-house family"* (D 20). Again like Peggy with her imaginary sister Polly, Morag imagines a friend named *"Peony"* and an *"alter ego"* named *"Rosa Picardy"* (D 20–1).

Sylvia Fraser, in her Afterword to *The Fire-Dwellers*, writes that people who lose a parent early in life are called "'blood' children because that shocking severance of the blood tie creates a psychic wound that time never heals" (286). Phyllis Ralph, one of Peggy's playmates, recalls that Peggy was easily frightened after the death of her mother. Children liked to scare her by telling her "spook stories" at the deserted fairgrounds because "she'd scream blue murder," Ralph recalls in her 1984 interview with Greta M. Coger in the *Margaret Laurence Review* (2/3, 40).[2] Viriginia Sanburn, another childhood playmate, recalls: "Peggy was a great fantasizer. Pretend this, pretend that ... she was a great one for pretending" (Coger 2/3, 38).

Peggy's play was always creative: even her toys encouraged her imaginative child's play. While other little girls were playing with dolls, Peggy's favourite toys included a first-aid kit inspired by the fact that her Aunts Ruby and Velma were nurses, a tool bench inspired by the fact that her father was a gifted carpenter, and a microscope for examining the world – all focuses for imaginative play for her community of friends, including Mona Spratt, Phyllis Ralph, and Virginia Shore (DE 60).

Peggy had private places to pursue her fantasies. Her father, Robert Wemyss, town lawyer and amateur carpenter – recreated as Vanessa's father, Ewen MacLeod, the town doctor, in *A Bird in the House* – constructed a playhouse that would enchant any child. No doll's house, this was a life-size shed, equipped with real furniture and dishes, where Peggy could act out her fantasies.

Laurence's childhood was indeed a moving experience: every time there was a death in the family, they would move house. After the death of her mother, Robert, Marg, and Peggy moved to the Wemyss family home in 1934. So her playhouse became her most permanent home during her childhood because, wherever the family moved, they always took Peggy's playhouse along (DE 63–4).

Peggy's playhouse became even more important after the death of her father when she was nine years old, when she moved with her stepmother Marg and half-brother Bob from the "Little House" on Vivian to the Simpson home on First Avenue, known as the "Brick House" or the "Big House": "At the Big House, my play-house changed its function. It became my study, my refuge, my own private place. Even in winter, although the little shack wasn't heated, I used to go there to brood upon life's injustices, to work off anger, or simply to think and dream. In summer, I would climb up to the roof and lie there, hidden from view by the big branches of the huge spruce trees that bent over the gently sloping roof, and read for hours" (*DE* 64).

Peggy found another private place in the loft over the garage where her grandfather stored his McLaughlin-Buick. Vanessa MacLeod also hides in Grandfather Connor's old McLaughlin-Buick in order to write. Laurence records, "There was an outside staircase to this loft, and I had discovered that I could hide away better there than in the play-house. It was more inaccessible to the adult eye. I used to cheat on my violin practice and whip up to the loft, where I kept my five-cent scribblers" (*DE* 67). Her mother had been a pianist, and her stepmother wanted her daughter to study music – first piano and then violin. But Peggy did not want to be a martyr to music: she believed "my music [would be] made with words" (*DE* 42): "Writing was where she could help me the most and, over many years, she did. The end of my music lessons marked the beginning of her realization that writing might be the important area of my spirit" (*DE* 67). The last Christmas before he died, Peggy's father fashioned her present: a desk where she could write (*DE* 55).

Peggy's favourite pastime was writing. Ralph recalls, "She always carried these scribblers. She was always jotting something down" (Coger 2/3, 42). James King records, "By Grade 3, Peggy the writer came into being, when she began writing stories down; by Grade 5 she had scribblers filled with both prose and verse" (21). A photograph of a shy, frightened Peggy on her first day of school portrays her clutching a scribbler to her chest like a protective shield (*DE* 48–9). Laurence recalls, "I was writing all the time. Clumsy, sentimental poetry, funny verses, stories" (*DE* 61).

Peggy also liked to write plays: "The loft became a kind of forbidden theatre" (*DE* 67), she recalls. Sanburn records: "We used to do a lot of pretending to be this and that and it was always Peggy who wrote the script. We used to dress up and act out all the plays. But it was Peggy who ... invented the story that we were about to act out that day" (Coger 2/3, 33). The loft became the headquarters for her gang, who formed a secret society with a private code and hand-made book. Later, Peggy built her own doll's house, a dwarf house inspired by the Disney movie *Snow White and the Seven Dwarfs*, complete with miniature furniture and dishes, including bedspreads that she stitched herself. These miniature houses may have inspired her fiction writing by allowing her to stage domestic dramas with imaginary characters. Whereas the playhouse constructed by her father allowed her to *become* other people, the dwarf house that she built herself allowed her to *create* other characters whose destinies she could control – so she could play God the Creator, perhaps.

A writer must be a reader. Laurence affirms, "I was an insatiable reader. [I had] the immense good fortune to be born into a family of readers, and our house contained a great many books" ("Books" 239). The most important book, of course, was the Bible, and Laurence records that she kept the Bible that her Grandmother Simpson gave her all her life (*DE* 11–12). She considered the King James Bible one of the most eloquent texts in the English language, and all her writing demonstrates its influence – from her first novel, *This Side Jordan*, to her last novel, *The Diviners*. In *A Bird in the House*, Vanessa MacLeod mentions reading the Bible to find inspiration for her own creative writing. Perhaps Peggy did the same. Her favourite authors were Charles Dickens, Rudyard Kipling, Arthur Conan Doyle, Robert Louis Stevenson, and Mark Twain, as well as female writers Willa Cather and Lucy Maud Montgomery. While other teenage girls were swooning over new pop idol Frank Sinatra, Peggy preferred Kim, Alan Breck, and David Balfour. "Were there no women writers who spoke to my childhood? Not many" ("Books" 240). So Peggy composed her own adventure stories. Wes McAmmond, her grade seven teacher, recalls Peggy's early writing: "She'd bring in a scribbler. One time it was a play ... about knighthood" (Coger 4/5, 32). Laurence recalls, in an unpublished essay entitled "Geography – Outer or Inner": "My mother's advice when I was about 12 and had written a play about dukes and earls, 'Write what you know.' It took a long time to filter through to my consciousness" (np). Clearly, this was a lesson she took to heart.

Peggy's stepmother Marg, her beloved *Mum*, encouraged her daughter to read and discussed her reading with her while they washed the dishes. They even held contests to see who could quote the most poetry. A bibliophile, Marg served as Neepawa's first librarian. Together the two would study *Quill and Quire* to select new books for Neepawa's public library, including Canadian books. "Canadian books then? You bet," Laurence asserts. She calls her mother "an early evangelist for Canadian writing. She did not, of course, realize that her daughter would one day write out of our land and townspeople and that tradition, but perhaps she suspected it, for she gave me a serious critique of everything I wrote" (*DE* 285). *As For Me and My House* (1941), Sinclair Ross's novel set on the prairies in the Dirty Thirties ("Books" 243), had a powerful impact on Peggy: "I learned from that book that one could write about where one was, even a small prairie town" (*DE* 286). She records her reaction in her 1968 introduction to *The Lamp at Noon and Other Stories*: "When I first read his extraordinary and moving novel *As For Me and My House*, at about the age of eighteen, it had an enormous impact on me, for it seemed the only completely genuine one I had ever read about my own people, my own place, my own time" (7).

"THE LAND OF OUR FATHERS": LAURENCE'S FIRST STORIES

At thirteen, Laurence wrote her first novel, "The Land of Our Fathers," a pioneer epic in which a young wife constructs a birch-bark cradle to let her husband know that she is pregnant. This was Laurence's first Canadian story and the first instance of the name "Manawaka." Laurence recycled this story in *A Bird in the House*, where heroine Vanessa MacLeod writes *The Pillars of the Nation*, an "epic on pioneer life" (68), set "in the early days of the fur trade" (165), in which the heroine, Marie, builds a birch-bark cradle to announce her pregnancy to the prospective father.

As Laurence records in *Dance on the Earth*, "'The Pillars of the Nation' got an honourable mention and I was ecstatic. A few months later, a story of mine called 'The Case of the Blond Butcher' was actually printed in the young people's section of the Saturday *Free Press*" (73). "Land of Our Fathers" did indeed receive honourable mention in the *Winnipeg Free Press* Junior Writers' Contest in the 28 September 1940 Young Authors section, but was never published: "Results Announced of Annual Summer Serial and Short Story Competition: The above mentioned stories will appear in print as fast as we can manage it, and some of these stories too: The Land of Our Fathers by Jean Margaret Wemyss [*sic*]."³ "The Case of the Blond Butcher: A Wanted Man" appeared in the Young Authors section of the *Winnipeg Free Press* in two installments, on 18 and 25 January 1941, when Peggy was fourteen. The story is addressed to "Dear Diary," a conventional form for girls of the era. Laurence likely kept a formal journal throughout her life, if we can judge by the Somali diaries that provided the basis for her African travel journal, *The Prophet's Camel Bell*, or the journal she kept in her sixty-first and final year. The first-person narrator, Nancy Grayson, addresses her diary as a confidant, recording exciting incidents and realistic dialogue in a highly dramatic manner. "The Case of the Blond Butcher" is a detective story featuring two "detective-minded youngsters" appropriately named Nancy and Dick – recalling Nancy Drew, the amateur sleuth of popular girls' fiction, and the comic-strip detective, Dick Tracy. But this is "a murder story in which it turned out that no murder had been committed after all" (*DE* 73), Laurence explains.

"With 'The Blond Butcher,'" Laurence recalls, "I also received my first fan letter. It was written in purple ink and it was from a boy in Winnipeg. I was so embarrassed I didn't know what to do, so I threw it in the kitchen woodstove before Mum could see it and I never told a living soul" (*DE* 73-4). Peggy also had a poem printed in the *Winnipeg Free Press*, but they did not pay her the usual one-dollar fee, assuming that it would suffice to see her poem in print (Hind-Smith 10).

There is a fascinating footnote to "The Case of the Blond Butcher": the Young People's section of the *Winnipeg Free Press* for 18 January 1941 includes this Note from the Editor: "To Jean Margaret Wemyss: Thank you for what you say about our corrections in the stories and poems. You didn't give us much work on The Case of the Blonde [*sic*] Butcher. The few words we took out were almost all to save space and as well we made Dick's manners a little politer by lifting his, 'Say, listen here.' Perhaps it was more natural the way you had it! Do most young boys say, 'Listen here'? You do not need after this to be shy about sending in anything you like, Jean. The Case of the Blonde Butcher, for the effort of a fourteen-year-old author, does you great credit." Reading between the lines, one infers that the editor has tampered with the story by attempting to refine the story's style and the characters' idiom, as well as misspelling the title of the story and misrepresenting the author's name, and that Jean Margaret Wemyss has taken him to task for his interference. This was to be the first of Laurence's battles with editors.

"RECOGNITIONS AND REVELATIONS":
VISCOUNT COLLEGIATE

Peggy was planning to be a nurse, like her aunts, but at fourteen she had a revelation: "I can't be a nurse; I have to be a writer ... What I realized that day was that I had a life commitment and could do no other" (*DE* 74–5). Morag Gunn has a similar epiphany in *The Diviners*, when she realizes at fourteen her destiny as a writer (136). Peggy equipped herself for her new career by purchasing a second-hand Remington typewriter for $14 with money she earned at Leckie's Ladies Wear the summer before she entered Viscount Collegiate, when she learned they offered a typing course. She named this typewriter *Victoria* and a later model *Pearl Cavedweller*, a translation of her own Scots name, Margaret Wemyss – Margaret meaning "pearl" and Wemyss meaning "cave-dweller."[4]

High school provided opportunities to write: "The chief joys of high school ... were being able to work on the school newspaper and studying English literature" (*DE* 76), Laurence recalls. "Composition was a subject that, naturally, I enjoyed. We had to write either an essay or a story for the exam, and I always chose the short story. I took the precaution, though, of composing one in my head well before the exam and would, through nimble mental and verbal juggling, manage to connect it with one of the given titles" (*DE* 78). Mildred Musgrove, who taught Laurence English at Neepawa Collegiate, was the model for Miss Melrose, Morag Gunn's English teacher in *The Diviners*: "Morag worships her" (*D* 135). Reading poetry – especially Romantic poets Blake, Shelley, Keats, and Wordsworth; Victorians Tennyson, Browning, and Arnold; and Moderns Yeats, Brooke, Frost, and Sandburg – Laurence recalls, "I felt as though a whole series of doors were opening in my mind" (*DE* 77). She kept the *Pocket Book of Verse* that she used in Mildred Musgrove's English class all her life.

Peggy Wemyss participated in many activities at the Viscount School: she played violin in the orchestra, played sports, served on the Student Council, and acted as President of the Debating Club. But her main interest was the newspaper, *Annals of the Black and Gold*, which she edited for two years, cranking it out on an old Gestetner mimeograph machine that covered her in ink, under the guiding spirit of Mildred Musgrove.[5] Miss Musgrove recalls: "When [Peggy] was editor of the paper, she was very enthusiastic about that, and was racing here and there to get this write-up in or that or turn somebody on to do something. She wrote very little actually for herself in these *Annals of the Black and Gold*. It was wartime and the editorials she did were usually slanted toward war savings stamps or bonds" (Coger 4/5, 38–40). Besides editorials in each issue on the war effort, reviews of school concerts and plays, and a column titled "I am Nosy," Peggy also published creative work in the *Black and Gold*: a story, "Goodwill Towards Men" – printed in the Christmas issue of December 1943 and reprinted in *Embryo Words* 24–8 – and two poems: "Christmas Card" in the Christmas issue of December 1943 and "Song for Spring 1944" in the spring issue of 1944. *Annals of the Black and Gold* proudly proclaimed on its cover page Viscount Collegiate's heroic motto drawn from the last line of Tennyson's "Ulysses": "To strive, to seek, to find, and not to yield" – an appropriate motto for the idealistic and ambitious Peggy Wemyss.

Peggy wrote plays, as well as poetry and fiction, and earned a reputation as a playwright. A Sunday school teacher asked her to write a play for her kindergarten class, "The Sunbeams." Teenage Peggy wrote the play, providing a part for each Sunbeam (Hind 9). Peggy also acted in plays, including acting the lead in *Ada Gives Advice* in the school drama festival, and even directed a drama in high school. Reading Euripides' *Electra*, the drama of a heroic daughter who avenges her father, in Gilbert Murray's translation, was the high point of her final year, Laurence asserts (*DE* 77).

A SEPARATE PEACE: WARTIME WRITING

"My childhood could be said to have ended in 1939, the summer and autumn I was thirteen," Laurence recalls, for, "on September 5, 1939, my world changed out of all recognition, forever" (*DE* 71, 72). The war had a major impact on Peggy's adolescence: Don Straith, her first boyfriend, enlisted in the Royal Canadian Air Force upon graduation. Boys she knew in Neepawa were killed: the friend who told her war was declared died in a burning tank. So many Neepawa boys enlisted that in her final year there were no boys in her class. Many never returned. There were so few boys at the Saturday night dances at Neepawa's Pedlar's ballroom that girls had to dance with each other.

All that changed when an airfield was built near Neepawa, and "The RAF hit town" (*DE* 85). The first love of her life was a British aviator named Derek Armstrong, who introduced her to modern music and poetry. A "classy liar" (*DE* 86), Derek told Peggy his real name was Benjamin Britten. In *A Bird in the House*, Grandfather Connor tells Vanessa, in front of Michael, the soldier modelled on Derek, "I'll bet a nickel to a doughnut hole he's married" (184). Peggy's grandfather said the same of Derek. And he was right. Laurence recalls how "hurt and betrayed" (*DE* 88) she felt.

At age sixteen, on 19 August 1942, the day of Dieppe, Laurence learned the reality of war, when over 3000 Canadians, including a prairie regiment, the Queen's Own Cameron Highlanders, were killed, wounded, or captured (*DE* 83): "It runs as a leitmotif through all my so-called Manawaka fiction" (*DE* 84), she declares. She recreates her realization of war in Morag Gunn's experience of Dieppe in *The Diviners*. But the war influenced her early writing too: her 1944 Christmas story, "Goodwill Towards Men," is a war story that may be a response to the May 1941 flight of Hitler's deputy Führer Rudolf Hess from Augsberg to Scotland to negotiate a peace treaty. It may also be a response to Rudyard Kipling's chilling war story "Mary Postgate," in which Mary Postgate kills a German aviator, who has landed, his neck broken, under an oak tree, with the revolver of her dead young master, whose kit she is burning. Set in Scotland at Christmas, "Goodwill Towards Men" portrays young Robbie McDuff discovering a German aviator who has parachuted into an oak tree. Unlike vengeful Mary Postgate, Robbie McDuff, recalling his brother Sandy fighting in France and the "Good Man" whose nativity is being celebrated, takes the German soldier home for Christmas, making his own separate peace. Peggy's delightful sonnet, "Song for Spring, 1944," prophesies peace, portraying children who are free "To glance up, unafraid, at peaceful skies," and declares, "Nothing must blot that glory from their eyes" (*EW* 3).

Peggy, a patriot with wanderlust, tried to join the Women's Royal Canadian Naval Service. She planned to go to college, "but my country was calling, and so was life, experience, and adventure" (*DE* 89).

The navy was as far from home as a prairie girl could get, but, by the time the WRCNS reached her, they no longer needed recruits. So Peggy went to college instead of to war.

Laurence graduated from Neepawa Collegiate Institute in 1944 with the Governor General's Gold Medal for her 81% standing: "The citation ... praised her academic work, her participation in athletics and extracurricular activities and ... her leadership and initiative" (Hind 10). An article in *Annals of the Black and Gold* reports, "The most coveted award in the Neepawa Collegiate ... the Governor General's Medal [was] won by none other than our busy editor ... In awarding this medal, account is taken not only of academic work but also of athletic, extracurricular activities, leadership, initiative, and interest in school activities throughout grades X and XI." The article itemizes Peggy's work in the school orchestra, the drama and debating clubs, and, most of all, her editing of *Annals of the Black and Gold*. She was awarded a Manitoba Scholarship – fortunately, since her grandfather did not believe in advanced education for women. In *A Bird in the House*, Vanessa's mother sells the Limoges china to finance Vanessa's university education. Laurence's family made similar sacrifices. So, in 1944, Peggy entered United College, signing her letters "Peggy, alias Prairie Flower" (*DE* 106).

UNITED COLLEGE: "A BRAVE NEW WORLD"

"College was quite literally a brave new world," for "The doors to the world were opening" (*DE* 94, 90). English studies were again the high point for Laurence. Some of her teachers – such as Robert Hallstead, Arthur Phelps, and Malcolm Ross, later editor-in-chief of the New Canadian Library Series – became life-long friends. The English Club introduced her to modern writers such as Joyce Cary, Graham Greene, and T.S. Eliot and to Canadian authors Ethel Wilson, Sinclair Ross, and W.O. Mitchell; a real live writer, Morley Callaghan, actually visited the Club.

The Wemyss family gold seal ring with the cormorant emblem and the motto *Je pense*, which Peggy always wore, was right for this young idealist. Helen Warkentin, her roommate at Sparling Hall, reports, Peggy "seemed freer and more independent of mind than the rest of us" (ML 7). She recalls how Peggy declaimed poetry. Laurence records, "On one occasion, standing on the fire escape, I dramatically orated a few appropriate lines from Shelley only to receive a water-bomb treatment from the occupants of the floor above. It cured me of public oratory" (*DE* 92). After that, she confined her outpourings to the page. University offered new opportunities for writing because United College published a journal titled *Vox*, Latin for *voice*. Peggy served as assistant editor of *Vox* when Jack Borland was editor. Lyall Powers, who attended United College with Laurence and Borland, records, "she became both his sweetheart and his assistant in the literary endeavours of *Vox*" (*AH* 67). Peggy also published stories in *Vox*, including "Calliope" and "*Tal des Walde.*"

"COLORS OF SPEECH": LAURENCE'S EARLY STORIES IN *VOX*

"Calliope" (printed in *Vox* 18 in 1945 and reprinted in *Embryo Words* 29–35), a story about a boy lost in a carnival – "an aging slut without makeup" – may reflect her childhood terrors in the deserted fairgrounds and her summer visit to her friend Mona Spratt in Carman, Manitoba, where the two girls ran a hot-dog stand at a fair. Although she condemned "Calliope" as "sentimental," the story reveals her control of character, dialogue, and dialect in the person of German Joe, who dreams about a *schloss* on the Rhine and swears in German, reflecting the cultural influences of Winnipeg. "[Joe] copes with the reality of his bleak existence through alcohol and the creation of a mythical past," comments James King (56). The carnival characters, complete with snake charmer, prefigure later grotesques, like Morag's landlady Fan Brady, who, as Princess Eureka, performs a nightclub act with a python named Tiny in *The Diviners* (336).

"*Tal des Walde*" – printed in *Vox* 19 in 1946 and reprinted in *Embryo Words* 36–47 – the tale of Austrian Count Brueckner, who tries to recreate his family's feudal system in Canada, reflects a story Peggy heard as a child about an Austrian aristocrat who built a medieval estate near Riding Mountain.[6] Much later, Laurence recalls this story in a 12 February 1979 letter to Gabrielle Roy: "When I was a child, there was an isolated Ukrainian settlement somewhere near Riding Mountain … The local legend was that the settlement had been started by a Hungarian nobleman who had come to Canada, bringing all the Ukrainian peasants and serfs from his old-country estate … He had tried to impose a feudal system on 'his' people, until they discovered that they did not need to be serfs of his in the new land. I wrote a story about this when I was in college, long ago" (Socken 65). This sophisticated story embeds a tale in a narrative frame and creates character through dialogue and dialect. Laurence recycled the story in *The Diviners* as "The Mountain," a tale Morag writes in college (209). Recycling her juvenilia in her adult fiction thus reveals the autobiographical element of her Manawaka novels. Later, she regretted using a male narrator, but approved the moral: "The most interesting thing to me now about the story is that it does connect with all my subsequent writing in one way – a basic life-view that could say, even then, 'a man is never God, even in his own domain' and 'one should not mould the lives of others'" (*sic*, quoted in King 56–7).

"SONG'S SPLENDOUR": LAURENCE'S EARLY POEMS

Laurence also published in the *Manitoban*, the University of Manitoba's student newspaper. In her first year, she submitted poems under a male pseudonym. She explains in *Dance on the Earth*, "[W]hen I first submitted poems to the University of Manitoba student paper, *The Manitoban*, I sent them in under the name of Steve Lancaster. After the Lancaster bomber, and I had always liked the name Steve. I cringe with shame to recall it now. Later, I dared to use my own name, but it was J.M. Wemyss, I think, not Jean Margaret. In one of my early stories, published in the United College magazine *Vox*, I actually used a first-person narrative, but the narrator was a man" (*DE* 5). It is interesting to note how the name under each of her early works mutates from the impersonal "JMW" to "Jean Margaret Wemyss" to "Peggy Laurence" during her college career.[7] Laurence emphasizes the importance of names in her foreword to *Dance on the Earth*, where she laments the fact that "Women have no surnames of their own. Their names are literally sirnames" (*DE* 9).

Later, Laurence gained enough confidence to submit her poems under her own name and even to visit the *Manitoban*, where Jack Ludwig was editor. She recalls it was the fashion for aspiring poets to visit the office and dash off a poem on the typewriter. She crafted a poem for weeks and then typed it up in the office, as if on the spur of the moment. Impressed with its quality, the staff published it. She wondered if all "instant poetry" had the same origin. The *Manitoban* introduced her to Adele Wiseman, winner of a Governor General's Award for her novel *The Sacrifice* (1956) and the model for Ella Gerson in *The Diviners*. The two became life-long friends, concluding their letters to each other with the slogan *Corragio. Avanti*. Their meeting is recreated in the encounter of Morag with Ella Gerson at the *Veritas* office in *The Diviners* (194–5).

Although Laurence is famous for fiction, her early publications consisted primarily of poetry: "I was mainly writing poetry, not because my talent particularly lay in that direction but for the same reason that many undergraduates interested in writing tackle poetry or vignettes rather than longer prose: I didn't have enough time to concentrate on prose. Poetry isn't easier to write than prose, but many young writers think it is, and it's less daunting to undertake at that age than, say, a novel. As a short, intense form, it often appeals to young writers as being more in accord with youthfully intense, and usually intensely subjective, feelings" (*DE* 95–6). Her early poetry is intense indeed, reflecting preoccupations that persist throughout her career. Her 1944 poems express a loathing of war, "which runs through my whole life, in my hatred of war so profound I can't find words to express my outrage at these recurring assaults upon the human flesh, mind, and spirit" (*DE* 84). "Thought" – printed in the *Manitoban*, 13 October 1944, and reprinted in *Embryo Words* 4 – contrasts the pain of war with the peace of nature:

> I have need of wind and hilltops,
> Far away from the terror and brutality ...
> Where I am not forced by trivial minds
> To mouth trite nothings or explain insanities ...
> For my heart is sick with the heartsick world.

"The Imperishable" – printed in the *Manitoban*, 17 October 1944, and reprinted in *Embryo Words* 6–7 – portrays Nature redeeming death, as the earth embraces the bodies of the slain: "Forgiving all, she takes them to her breast." This lengthy, free-verse paean to Mother Nature seems to forecast her later maternalism: "Out of her dark womb is sprung / All the beauty and evil of the world." She also employs the trope of earth as the body of a woman, with its "furrows curv[ing] gently" – a trope she employs in her African novel and stories. This poem deifies a female nature as the source of all life: "This is earth, the mother, the maker and breaker / The sower and reaper, the beginning and the end."

"Pagan Point – Wasagaming – Approaching Night" – printed in the *Manitoban* on 3 November 1944 and reprinted in *Embryo Words 2* – also locates the divine in nature:

> This is a dim cathedral – full of rest,
> Remote from pain, where Man may find his God.
> This is the oldest chapel in the world.

The earliest existing poem by Laurence,[8] this eloquent free-verse poem also anticipates peace, as "splendid spruce / Uplift their arms to an untroubled sky." "Pagan Point" prophesies her story "The Loons," for "this peace is broken by the cry, / Raucous and heathen, of a far-off loon," symbolizing "unearthly paganism," as "Forgotten gods awake and claim anew / The temple that so long ago they knew." With the silencing of the loons, "The heathen gods [Neptune and Thor] are gone," and "the loneliness / Has blended with a reverence, a peace," as the lake becomes again the temple of nature.

"Poems" – a pair of brief lyrics printed in *Vox* 18 in 1945 and reprinted in *Embryo Words* 8-9 – also celebrate nature in "the wakening prairie" with these prophetic lines:

> Quietly I walk, wind-cloaked,
> Hearing the rain's promise
> That this land will be my immortality.

Another pair of brief lyrics, or twelve-line poems in rhyming quatrains, titled simply "Poems" – printed in the *Manitoban*, 10 October 1945, and reprinted in *Embryo Words* 13 – is also prophetic:

> Someday I shall make me a song for singing
> Shaped of laughter, and woven of pain ...
> We will tramp the fields, my song and I.

"Bus-Ride at Night" – printed in the *Manitoban* on 20 October 1944 and reprinted in *Embryo Words* 5 – reflects the young college student's commuting between Neepawa and "The City," as Manitobans labelled Winnipeg. This long, free-verse poem, with its reflections of Futurist poetry – poems like "The Express" by Stephen Spender, whose wartime poem "I Think Continually of Those Who Were Truly Great" is quoted by Vanessa in "Jericho's Brick Battlements" (181) – expresses alienation, as each rider is imprisoned in the cell of the self: "Apart we are, with no communication ... Locked in our own isolated minds." Such expressions of alienation validate Lyall Powers' view of Laurence as an "alien heart" (18). The poem concludes with enshrouding night, in which

> ... the wanderer knows himself alone and lost,
> With only his brave heart's shining to show the way
> Over rough furrows to the friendly fireside.

After VE Day, 8 May 1945, Peggy published comic verse in *Vox* 18 in the "Special Section of Children's Poetry." Her two short, rhyming "Chants" (reprinted in *Embryo Words* 12) portray mermaids counting Spanish doubloons. "Cabbages" (reprinted in *Embryo Words* 10-11), a lively ditty in rhyming couplets, depicts a butterfly conversing with a bumblebee about the advisability of living in a rosebush versus a cabbage and prefigures her children's fiction – especially *Jason's Quest*, a tale of a picaresque mole named Jason and his adventurous journey to London to seek a cure for his ailing city of Molanium.

Two sonnets published in 1945 are romantic. "Song" – printed in *Vox* 18 in April 1945 and reprinted in *Colors of Speech* 9 – begins, "Not now will I arise and come to you," and concludes with echoes of Robert Browning's "Prospice," written upon the death of Elizabeth Barrett Browning:

> Fearless, eternal, will we realize
> One integrated life, the barriers past,
> Soul fused in separate soul, no longer lost.

One wonders whether Peggy Wemyss was referring to her lost wartime love, Derek Armstrong. The second entry under "Poems" also suggests a lost love in the lines, "I shall bid you godspeed and set the memory of you free" and "stand at last alone, to meet / The phantom winds of night." "The Departure," a twelve-line sonnet, presents a woman addressing "Jesus, son of Joseph," saying, "I would have been your wife." As Powers writes, "The early voice of Peggy's Christian humanism, the poem anticipates her adult commitment to the social gospel" (64).

Poems collected in *Vox* 20 under the heading "Classical Framework" in December 1946 and reprinted in *Embryo Words* 14–15 reflect classical influences and prefigure Laurence's later literary allusiveness in their focus on Atthis and Sappho of Lesbos. "Song of the Race of Ulysses" – printed in *Vox* 20 in 1947 and reprinted in *Embryo Words* 16 – reflects the influence of both Homer and Tennyson: spoken by Ulysses, it concludes, "I would arise unquestioning and follow." "Thetis' Song about Her Son" – published in the *Manitoban*, 13 November 1946, and reprinted in *Colors of Speech* 10 – is a dramatic monologue spoken by Thetis, a Nereid, or divinity of the sea, and mother of Achilles. "'Bread hath he, but a man is weak in exile'" – published in *Vox* 20 in 1947, and reprinted in *Embryo Words* 17 – was inspired by Euripides' drama *Electra* and won a United College award in 1947. It concludes, "Let us sing songs against the impending shadows." Lyall Powers judges that this poem "reiterates the theme of alienation and lovelessness, the failure of human communication. The controlling voice in the majority of her poems," he concludes, "is that of the loner, one who has been alienated by the harshness of life and the inadequacies of human response to that prospect, and by the sadness of lost or unattainable love" (60).

These poems combine natural speech cadences, for which Laurence's mature fiction is most remarkable, with imaginative metaphor and a lyrical style marked by assonance and alliteration. The style is sometimes reminiscent, especially in its compound modifiers, of the idiom of Gerard Manley Hopkins, whose poetry she admired and whose style her final Manawaka heroine, Morag Gunn, defends in her husband, Professor Brooke Skelton's, honours seminar in *The Diviners* (243). Although Laurence's forte was fiction, her apprenticeship in verse made her prose poetic. We can observe the thematic and stylistic features of her mature fiction in these "embryo words."[9]

"Clay-Fettered Doors" – published in *Vox* in 1945 and reprinted in *Embryo Words* 20–2 – reflects Laurence's interest in the "religious and socio-political themes" (*DE* 99) that permeate her adult writing. A free-verse poem in five sections, reminiscent of Sandburg, "Clay-Fettered

Doors" anticipates Peggy's leftist leanings, expressing political satire in idiomatic speech:

> (Christ, man! Didn't you know that they're busy with
> Affairs of State
>   there, and even the C.C.F. can't tell you the right address?)(21)

All of her mature work questions "The nature of good and evil. Does God exist?" (*DE* 97). Like the derelict of "Clay-Fettered Doors," looking for "someone who answers to the name of God," all her protagonists – from Nathaniel Amegbe of her first published novel, *This Side Jordan*, to Hagar, Rachel, Stacey, Vanessa, and Morag of the Manawaka novels – search for God.

Peggy also published "The Earlier Fountain: A Study of Robinson Jeffers, his Early Poems and Philosophy" in *Vox*, 1947. It is impressive for its sophisticated perceptivity and stylistic sensitivity. She writes that Jeffers' characters are "superactive and violent, tense and turbulent embodiments of the dark potential of the human mind." She admires the forcefulness of Jeffers' Tamar, for example, but she is skeptical about the alienation of the characters: "Jeffers seems to desire to cast away humanity, to escape from the tangled network of human nerves into the freer life of nature. It is obvious that this morbid defeatism serves nothing." On a more humorous note, the Jeffers essay inspired this ironic blurb beside Peggy's graduation photo in *Vox*: "When Peggy was a little girl her mother inadvertently dropped her onto a volume of Robinson Jeffers on the floor. She has been writing poetry ever since. Seriously, she plans a career in journalism; after which, successful or otherwise, she will settle down, marry a man with at least a million dollars and raise an average Canadian family" (*Vox* 20, 3).

Laurence graduated from United College in 1947 with honours in English and a poetry prize that she attributed to her "gift of the gab" (*DE* 101). But other important events had occurred: she records, "At the time I graduated, I was also in love, seriously and deeply and, for the first time, realistically. I met Jack Laurence when both of us were living in an old rooming-house on Roslyn Road. I was in my final year at university … I said to myself, 'That's the man I'd like to marry'" (*DE* 102). "A handsome devil," Laurence says in the NFB film "First Lady of Manawaka," Jack was a war veteran studying engineering at the University of Manitoba. They embarked for England in December 1950, and thence for Africa, subject of her first four books, in January 1951. Laurence declares, "I was out there dancing on the earth" (*DE* 108).

Laurence's long narrative poem, "North Main Car,"[10] set in Winnipeg, foreshadows her famous fiction. As she later declared, "North Winnipeg in the 1940s decided a lot of my life" (*DE* 108). After her graduation from United College and her marriage in 1947, Peggy became a real resident of Winnipeg when the newlyweds moved into an apartment on Burrows Avenue across the street from Adele Wiseman. The Wiseman family, reflected in the Gersons of *The Diviners* (198-203), was an education for the Scots-Irish Peggy Wemyss. Adele's mother, a "wisewoman," took Peggy under her wing, teaching her about Judaic customs, Slavic traditions, and Socialist issues.

Laurence learned a lot about the city through her jobs: she worked first as a journalist for the *Westerner*, a Communist newspaper (she claims she was too naive to realize it was a Communist publication), for which she wrote book reviews in 1947. After the *Westerner* folded, she worked for the newly founded *Winnipeg Citizen*, Canada's only co-operative daily (*DE* 106–8), in 1948, writing a radio column and book reviews and covering the labour beat, about which, she adds, she knew nothing (*DE* 107). "It's in the Air," her radio column, influenced the budding writer by encouraging her to compose fiction in a dramatic manner employing dialogue. Laurence recalls, "Through high school and college I thought I would be a journalist" (*DE* 74), but she resigned from this newspaper when the managing editor informed her she was reputed to be a Communist. Newspapers figure in "North Main Car" too: "the ukrainian word and the canadian tribune? / or the ukrainian voice and the winnipeg free press" – "two voices, two sides of the great ravine." She learned more about Communism when she and Jack rented an apartment in a house belonging to Bill Ross, Communist Party organizer (*DE* 107). Later, she was registrar for the Winnipeg YWCA when the Japanese Canadians were released from the camps; when the YWCA formed a club for the young Nisei, or second-generation Japanese-Canadians, she learned more about their wartime internment (*DE* 108) which is recreated in Joy Kogawa's 1981 novel *Obasan*.

"A VAST FANTASIA": "NORTH MAIN CAR"

This urban experience is vividly reflected in the portrait of Winnipeg in "North Main Car." The poem opens with a paean to the city of Winnipeg, personified as "a lovely giant held by enticing night" in a combination of Wordsworth's rhapsody on Westminster Bridge and his apostrophe to Milton. But this city is female, and the "ungilding daylight" explores "her savagery and blemishes." Laurence's tribute to Winnipeg, apostrophized as "my city," reflects a celebration of Chicago, "Hog Butcher for the World," in "Chicago" from *Chicago Poems* (1916) by Carl Sandburg (1878–1967). Laurence admired Sandburg and used stanzas from his "Losers," from *Smoke and Steel* (1920), for the epigraphs for both *A Jest of God* and *The Fire-Dwellers*. "North Main Car" also contradicts Laurence's oft-expressed detestation of cities in her celebration of Winnipeg as "my city."

The style of the poem reflects the influence of the Modernists whom Laurence read as an honours English student and member of the English Club at United College (*DE* 94). In the manner made famous by ee cummings, she eschews capitals for names and the beginnings of lines in the framing sections, employing them only for the sections on the characters. The poem is written in free verse with the colloquial quality of real speech punctuated by passages of eloquence. The influence of the Imagist movement of the 1910s – seen in the poetry of Ezra Pound, Amy Lowell, William Carlos Williams, and H.D. – is evident in her evocative imagery: "tall gaunt houses, paint peeling, / crowd cottages like ancient swaybacks / among the young neat colts." The occasional brutality of her realism, illustrated in her description of the slaughterhouse – "The putridly-pungent blood, turning to withered rot; / Nostril-cutting brine; hides, new-peeled; guts but recently stilled" – recalls the violent verisimilitude of World War I poets Wilfred Owen, Isaac Rosenberg, and Siegfried Sassoon and of the Georgian poets in Edward Marsh's *Georgian Poetry* I-V (1912–22), examples of which Laurence read with Mildred Musgrove at Viscount Collegiate.

The title of the poem is appropriate, for she employs the streetcar as the structuring device for her exploration of North Winnipeg. The streetcar introduces the movement of the narrative, as "out of the north the streetcar crawls" – recalling the train that crawls "like a worm with a fiery head winding through the darkness" (117) in "A Painful Case" in James Joyce's *Dubliners*. As it travels along Main Street, "along the north town's spine," it takes us on an odyssey of Winnipeg, snaking through the ethnic ghettoes. The streetcar makes eight stops – at St John's Avenue, Mountain, Redwood, Alfred, Selkirk, Stella, and Henry – terminating at the CPR station, embarkation platform for voyagers and arrival point for immigrants.

Each time the streetcar stops, a character representing one of the ethnic groups of the poem – "jew and ukrainian, pole and english and negro" – steps aboard. The "streetcar's iron jargon" tells the people's stories. Seven characters are featured in "North Main Car," many of them immigrants: Steve, the slaughterhouse worker; Abraham Greenspan, the aging Jewish shop owner; Mrs Riley, the Irish cleaning woman; Ben, the Jewish labour organizer; Father Konarski, the Ukrainian priest; Nick Hrynchuk, the Ukrainian steel mill worker; and Takao Tamura, the Japanese artist. These characters represent the cultural mosaic of North Winnipeg. Two groups are conspicuous for their absence: the streetcar does not carry any Blacks because there was not a large Black population in North Winnipeg, although she mentions "the lithe negro girl" and "the negro lad" later in the poem; there are also no Aboriginal Canadians, even though North Winnipeg had a large native population, and even though she does feature the Métis family of Tonnerre in her Manawaka cycle. Curiously, only one of the passengers is female, although all her Manawaka protagonists are women. Laurence presents each character sympathetically, conveying their ethnic contexts accurately. Even though "North Main Car" is a poem, people predominate – appropriately for Laurence, for whom character was paramount. Ironically, we can see the budding novelist more clearly in the use of characterization, setting, and idiom in this poem than in her early prose fiction.

Steve, the slaughterhouse worker, is the first to board the streetcar. Steve has no surname, for he is "all names and all races." He is the prototype of the Winnipeg workman: "steve, your face is the face of my city." No-name Steve frames the entire narrative, for the author returns to him at the poem's conclusion. The conclusion of the poem, like its introduction, is prefaced by the emergence of the streetcar, as "out of the north town the car emerges." The streetcar, a symbol of separation, dividing Winnipeg like the proverbial railway track, the spine of the city, becomes an emblem of racial unity in the conclusion, as the poet appeals to the workers of Winnipeg to unite – just as "jew and ukrainian, pole and english and negro, / wait shoulder to shoulder at the streetcar stop."

The poet's thesis becomes explicit as she locates the common enemy in "the immaculate who live on the track's correct side": she is proselytizing for labour unification against management and big money – those who "lay up riches where neither moth nor rust / can corrupt, in the bank of montreal." She addresses each ethnic group, appealing to their common interests as working-class people, despite their differences, repeating the line, "you are betraying us," like a Greek chorus at the end of her appeal to each group to join her in an interracial dialogue embracing community.

Finally, as the streetcar reaches its last stop at the CPR Station, arrival platform for immigrants, she addresses her fellow-travellers, appealing to them to break down "the walls of race and creed" that divide them, so they may "see revealed the richness of our diversity, / the colors of speech and our song's splendor." This line, which provides the title for *Colors of Speech*, seems to sum up what Laurence terms in "North Main Car" the "vast fantasia" of postwar Winnipeg.

The concluding lines of the poem forecast a utopian vision of the future, as the speaker urges the disparate ethnic groups to work together to build "a fortress / founded on common creed, our bond as workingmen: / a base against oppression, our first bastion of tomorrow." Later, as a mature novelist, Laurence learns to dramatize her message implicitly in prose fiction, rather than proselytizing for her beliefs blatantly in poetry. As she writes to Adele Wiseman on 4 September 1951, "I've come to the conclusion that propaganda in any form is not for me" (*SL* 62). Nevertheless, her mature fiction retains the persuasive power of her early poetry, and it also retains its eloquence, earning her the reputation of a poet in prose, as Walter Swayze argues persuasively in his 1997 essay "Margaret Laurence: Novelist as Poet."

Readers are divided on the relative value of Laurence's early poems and stories. Powers judges, "Her poetry is markedly superior to her fiction" (59), but Barbara Pell disagrees: "the poems in [*Embryo Words*] are unremarkable, serious, student efforts that strain at metaphors and meaning and echo the modernists. The stories are better in that they display her innate gift for characterization and language, although she later recognized them as somewhat sentimental and contrived" (368). While her early stories anticipate her mature fiction in characterization and individual idiom, her best poems demonstrate remarkable eloquence, as well as a gift for metaphor and myth, lyricism and rhythm that distinguishes her best adult work, in my opinion. Both Powers and Pell agree, however, that Laurence's juvenilia anticipate her mature writing in both ideas and style: Pell judges that *Embryo Words* is clearly "an act of literary apprenticeship" that demonstrates her perennial interests in "nature, human love and war, religion and nationalism" (368).

Thus, an examination of Laurence's juvenilia can illuminate her mature fiction in many ways: it reveals how much her own life experience informs her fiction, it demonstrates how her early writing prefigures her famous Manawaka cycle in her favoured themes of war and nature, it shows how her early poetry prophesies the rich store of myth and metaphor in her fiction that renders her prose so poetic, it illuminates the *meta-autobiographical* elements of her *Künstlerromane*, and, finally, it reveals the origins of one of Canada's most revered writers.

CHAPTER 3

Heart of a Stranger:
Laurence's Life-Journey

Margaret Laurence had the heart of a traveller, and travel was closely connected to creativity, as she makes clear in *Dance on the Earth: A Memoir*. She records that one of her earliest stories was "a highly uninformed but jubilantly imaginative journal of Captain John Ball and his voyages to exotic lands, complete with maps made by me of strange, mythical places," and she recalls that she used her toy tool bench to create bread boards decorated with "gaily painted scenes from what I imagined to be life in other countries – a Dutch windmill, a Chinese pagoda – my imagination tearing around a world that I had not yet seen" (61). Laurence claims that she developed the heart of a traveller early, perhaps inspired by the travel books in her father's study – a fact that she transforms into fiction in "To Set Our House in Order," the second story in her autobiographical fiction, *A Bird in the House*.

None of her books exhibits this wanderlust so vividly as her 1976 collection of travel essays, *Heart of a Stranger*. Although it was the last major text published during her lifetime, *Heart of a Stranger* has been virtually ignored by critics – except for the rare writer like George Woodcock who shared her passion for travel and interest in travel writing – perhaps because critics have not perceived its importance to Laurence's oeuvre. As Sara Mills says, "There is a tradition of reading women's writing as trivial or as marginal to the mainstream, and this is certainly the attitude to women's travel writing, which is portrayed as the records of travels of eccentric and rather strange spinsters" (61). Mills adds, "One of the main current critical assumptions made about women's travel writing by feminists and others is that it is non-literary" (110). Such neglect is unfortunate in Laurence's case because her collection of travel essays is significant in three major ways.

First, at the literal level, *Heart of a Stranger* is a fascinating travelogue chronicling Laurence's journeys to lands like Egypt, Scotland, and Greece, in articles such as "Good Morning to the Grandson of Ramesses the Second," "Road from the Isles," and "Sayonara, Agamemnon." Even more intriguing is the opportunity it affords to witness a Canadian writer's response to other countries and cultures before postcolonial theory – which Laurence anticipates – became current. Therefore, this chapter will address what Laurence called "the many journeys of my life" (*DE* 25).

Second, *Heart of a Stranger* constitutes a concealed autobiography, for, in chronicling her literal life journey, Laurence also reveals her spiritual odyssey. In an unpublished paper entitled "Geography – Outer or Inner?", she insists, "Outer geography is not as important to me as the inner geography of the heart and mind." As Casey Blanton asserts in *Travel Writing: The Self and the World*, "the development of the genre we have come to call travel literature is closely aligned with the changing role of subjectivity in other kinds of literature, especially fiction and autobiography" (29) – a perception that is at the heart of Helen Buss's title trope in *Mapping Ourselves*. This approach applies very well to Laurence's text. In fact, she wrote a preface for *Heart of a Stranger* that was never published – unfortunately, because it illuminates the themes of her essays: "I saw, somewhat to my surprise, that they are all, in one way or another, travel articles. And by travel, I mean both those voyages which are outer and those voyages which are inner."[1] The majority of the journeys chronicled in these essays are psychological, with only a minority being travel essays. She organizes the nineteen essays – most previously published in various venues, including *Canadian Forum, Holiday, Maclean's, Mosaic, Vancouver Sun, Weekend Magazine* – to describe her travels as a circular life-journey that begins and ends in Canada, as her unpublished preface makes clear: "I have not arranged these essays in the order in which they were written. It seemed better to arrange them geographically, as travel articles, and this also includes a thematic arrangement, for they end, as most outer and inner journeys end, in a homecoming. My personal journeys seem to have been ones through many countries and cultures, including Scotland, land of my ancestors, and back to my ancestral home and then away from all of those places without ever repeating any of them, coming back to a final return to the land where I was born, Canada" (np). Patricia Morley employs Laurence's homecoming metaphor for the title of her study *Margaret Laurence: The Long Journey Home*, in which she also observes the circular pattern of Laurence's life: "Canada, Africa, England, Canada: full circle" (15). George Woodcock, in "Many Solitudes: The Travel Writings of Margaret Laurence," defines the essays in *Heart of a Stranger* as "an arrangement of personal myths in their order of relevance" (136).[2] Therefore, my exploration of *Heart of a Stranger* in this chapter will allow me to review Laurence's lifelong quest for her true place of belonging and thus to provide a context for an examination of her mature writings.

Third, since travel inspired Laurence's creativity, *Heart of a Stranger* can provide a key to her fiction. Morley observes the connection between travel and creativity in her 1980 preface to *Margaret Laurence: The Long Journey Home*: "Travel has played a major role in Laurence's life. It has helped to shape her literary vision, and provided her with a central metaphor: the psychic journey towards inner freedom and spiritual maturity" (np). Indeed, the nineteen essays collected in *Heart of a Stranger*, published between 1964 and 1976, the intense period of creativity in which Laurence wrote her Manawaka cycle, "deal with themes that I dealt with later in my fiction," as she explains: "Although I did not fully realize it at the time, in a sense I was working out these themes in a non-fiction way before I found myself ready to deal with them in the broader form of the novel" (*HS* 4).[3] Thus, certain essays anticipate her subsequent novels, especially *The Diviners*. Anthony Appenzell correctly notes in his essay "In the Land of Egypt: Margaret Laurence as Essayist," that the essays in *Heart of a Stranger* "provide us with many premonitory echoes of the contents of the novels: incidents, ideas, situations, facets of character, adumbrations of themes, which were eventually woven into the fabrics of her fiction" (277).[4] Therefore, an exploration of *Heart of a Stranger* can help to illuminate her fiction.

Laurence's arrangement of the nineteen essays is revealing: she frames the collection with two autobiographical essays: the first, "A Place to Stand On," and the last, "Where the World Began," both focus on her place of origin and are complemented by "Upon a Midnight Clear," all set in her home town of Neepawa, Manitoba. Four positioned early in the text focus on her sojourn in Africa: "The Poem and the Spear" celebrates the Somali leader, the Sayyid Mahammed 'Abdille Hasan, and "The Epic Love of Elmii Bonderii" celebrates the Somali poet. "The Very Best Intentions" is a more personal essay about her understanding of African cultures, and "The Wild Blue Yonder" records her flights to Africa. "Put Out One or Two More Flags" chronicles her years living in Elm Cottage in the village of Penn, Buckinghamshire, and "Road from the Isles" records her visits to Scotland. Three essays positioned later in the text address her return to Canada: "Down East," "The Shack," and "I Am a Taxi." Two essays concern her writings and promotional trips: "Inside the Idiot Box" and "Living Dangerously ... by Mail." The penultimate essays return to North America in a broader sense: "Open Letter to the Mother of Joe Bass" concerns racial violence in contemporary America, and "Man of Our People" celebrates the Métis leader Gabriel Dumont. Only a minority of her essays are travel pieces in the normal sense: "Good Morning to the Grandson of Ramesses the Second," "Captain Pilot Shawkat and Kipling's Ghost," and "Sayonara, Agamemnon" are included early in the text. Clearly, *Heart of a Stranger* was Jack McClelland's method of recycling some of Laurence's previously published journalism, but Laurence's genius renders the collection no mere miscellany of disparate items or occasional pieces, but a true odyssey of discovery.

Thus, an exploration of the sequence of articles can illuminate not only Laurence's travels, but also her circular life journey and the inspiration for her subsequent fiction, especially *The Diviners*.

Laurence takes the title and epigraph for *Heart of a Stranger* from the Pentateuch, which she read for the first time on her voyage through the Suez Canal, passing Mount Sinai, where Moses received the stone tablets of God's law, en route to Africa. In *The Prophet's Camel Bell*, she recalls, "[T]he verse that remained with me most of all, when at last and for the first time I was myself a stranger in a strange land, and was sometimes given hostile words and was also given, once, food and shelter in a time of actual need, by tribesmen who had little enough for themselves – *Thou shalt not oppress a stranger, for ye know the*

heart of a stranger, seeing ye were strangers in the land of Egypt" (18).[5]
This quotation from Exodus 23:9 inextricably connects the travel essays in *Heart of a Stranger* with her Somali travel memoir, *The Prophet's
Camel Bell*, and establishes the stance of the stranger that characterizes both her African and Canadian fiction. As Roseann Runte notes,
"travel writers were, and are, all strangers in a foreign land. Their attempt to define the environment which excludes them is essentially an
attempt to define themselves" (526). Laurence makes a revealing remark at the end of *The Prophet's Camel Bell*: "One can never be a
stranger in one's own land – it is precisely this fact which makes it so
difficult to live there" (249). Laurence did indeed have the heart of a
stranger, and she frequently writes about exile. No wonder Lyall Powers titled his biography *Alien Heart*.

Laurence began "Innocent Voyage," the first part of *The Prophet's
Camel Bell*, prophetically: "And in your excitement at the trip, the last
thing in the world that would occur to you is that the strangest glimpses
you may have of any creature in the distant lands will be those you
catch of yourself" (10). Laurence herself says of her travel memoir in
her unpublished essay, "Half War, Half Peace," "I wanted still to show
the process – the long gradual process of self-knowledge, a process
which never ends and which for me began in Africa, for it really was
Africa which taught me to look at myself" (5).[6] And Casey Blanton
judges, "the most culturally sensitive kind of travel writing has wres-
tled with the complexities of self and other and made that its subject"
(107). Michael Dixon puts the concept eloquently in his 1977 review
of *Heart of a Stranger*: "'Home,' as a locus of individual, social, and
mythic identity, is both the defining vision at the heart of Laurence's
'stranger' and the unifying focus at the core of this diverse collection
of personal anecdotes, travel reports and reflective essays"; he adds,
"Laurence becomes herself a kind of protagonist in these occasional
pieces, a guiding consciousness exploring the concept of home and the
strategies whereby estrangement is overcome" (477). Therefore, an exploration of the quest motif in *Heart of a Stranger* provides biograph-
ical background for an examination of Laurence's mature writings.

Heart of a Stranger begins at home in Canada. It opens with a personal essay titled "A Place to Stand On" – originally labelled "Sources"
and first published in *Mosaic* in spring, 1970 – in which Laurence acknowledges the importance of her puritanical Scots-Presbyterian ancestors in providing the vision that informs her fiction: "they had

inhabited a wilderness and made it fruitful. They were, in the end, great survivors, and for that I love and value them" (7). She acknowledges the value of her home town of Neepawa, Manitoba, in inspiring her mythical microcosm of Manawaka, her "town of the mind" (7). But Laurence was an escape artist, like so many of her heroines, and she was eager to shake the prairie dust off her feet.

Her husband, John Fergus Laurence, shared her wanderlust. After their marriage in 1947 and Jack's graduation from the University of Manitoba in Civil Engineering in 1949, the couple, keen to travel, moved to England and thence to Africa. Launched on her voyage of life, Margaret exults: "I was out there dancing on the earth" (*DE* 108). The newlyweds set sail from England in December 1950 on their voyage, via the Mediterranean, to a new continent, a new decade, and a new life.

Africa was their home for seven years – first Somalia and then Ghana – inspiring Laurence's first four books. As Fiona Sparrow observes in her study *Into Africa with Margaret Laurence*, "Travel as theme or metaphor acts as a framework for much of her African writing" (205). Laurence devotes four essays near the beginning of *Heart of a Stranger* to African topics, as previously noted: "The Poem and the Spear," "The Epic Love of Elmii Bonderii," and "The Very Best Intentions," with "The Wild Blue Yonder" giving a humorous account of her air travel to Africa.

"The Poem and the Spear" – called Laurence's "crowning achievement [and] a masterpiece of historical reconstruction" (478) by Michael Dixon – celebrates the Somali leader Mahammed 'Abdille Hasan, known as "the Sayyid" or "Noble Lord" by the Somalis and as "The Mad Mullah of Somaliland" (*PCB* 13) by the British because he led the Dervishes in their revolt against the British, using "the strangest of all military weapons – poetry" (*HS* 31). "The Poem and the Spear" was written in 1964, just after the publication of *The Stone Angel*, when Laurence still felt unready to return to fiction, but it was never published until it was collected in *Heart of a Stranger* in 1976. Laurence celebrates this "early nationalist leader" (*HS* 32) for both his idealistic leadership and the brilliance of his poetry. As Woodcock asserts in "Speaker for the Tribes," "[the Sayyid] was a bard of his people who turned poetry into a weapon as powerful as a rifle in rallying his followers" (31). This essay, by far the longest in the collection, demonstrates Laurence's sympathy with the Somali people faced with an imperialist invader equipped with technologically superior weaponry. It also demonstrates her passionate partisanship with the valiant but vanquished underdog. Laurence admires the Sayyid as a "nationalist leader" (32) – like Gabriel Dumont, the Métis leader whom she celebrates in "Man of Our People," the penultimate essay in *Heart of a Stranger*. In her introduction to "The Poem and the Spear" she notes that she emphasizes this same tribal theme in *The Diviners* (31). In her essay "Tribalism As Us Versus Them," she defines tribalism as "the social organization of an extended family group held together by common lineage, language, religion, social mores and ethical values" (*LDC* 223) – the very terms in which she values Dumont and the Sayyid.[7] Indeed, the concept of tribalism connects her view of African and Aboriginal Canadian peoples, as well as Scottish clans.[8] Laurence frequently referred to contemporary Canadian writers as her "tribe."

"The Epic Love of Elmii Bonderii," first published in *Holiday* in 1965 with the caption, "A fatal infatuation turned this Somali tribesman into a poet of awesome gifts," celebrates the romantic poet called "the Prophet of Love" (*HS* 65). In *The Prophet's Camel Bell* Laurence explains his plight: "Elmi Bondereii (Elmi the Borderman) was said to have died of love. He fell in love with a young girl named Hodan Abdillahi, but as he was not wealthy, she was married instead to Mohamed Shabel (Mohamed the Leopard). Elmi cherished his hopeless affection for five years" (105). He wrote poems, *belwo* and *gabei*, to celebrate his love. "This tale may be myth," she acknowledges in her introduction to the essay, "but myths contain their own truth" (*HS* 59). The concluding sentence of this introduction, excised from her typescript, adds, "I have always been fascinated by the ways in which man is a myth-making animal and how our myths express essential truths about us. Many years later, in *The Diviners*, I dealt with this theme in an entirely different circumstance and setting." Thus, Laurence emphasizes the correspondences between her travel writing and her fiction.

After their transformative sojourn in Somalia, the Laurences lived from 1952 to 1957 in the Gold Coast, soon to become Ghana, where Jack supervised the building of the new port of Tema that turned a small fishing village into the central port of the country. Ghana provided the setting for Margaret's first novel, *This Side Jordan* (1960), which depicts a cast of characters divided between Futura Academy, an African mission school, and Allkirk, Moore & Bright, an English textile firm, with Miranda Kestoe, a Margaret Laurence figure, caught in the middle. An idealistic liberal who desires to know the true Africa – like Adela Quested, in E.M. Forster's *A Passage to India*, who wants to know "the *real* India" (24) – Miranda makes a muddle when she meddles in racial matters. "The Very Best Intentions," a *Heart of a Stranger* essay about Laurence's own life in Ghana, reveals how Miranda reflects Margaret: like Miranda, Margaret rejects the role of *memsahib*. She wishes to appear "sympathetic, humanitarian, enlightened" (26) and to impress her African acquaintances with "not only my sympathy with African independence but also my keen appreciation of various branches of African culture – African sculpture, African literature, African traditions and proverbs" (24). "I still wore my militant liberalism like a heart on my sleeve," she comments ironically (24): "I found out that just having the heart in the right place is not enough," for "the small l liberal can, without meaning to, be incredibly condescending" (Sullivan 64, 63). Although this essay was the first Laurence published – in *Holiday* in 1964, with the caption, "In Ghana, as elsewhere, good will is not enough to make a friendship work" – she had already come to view her naive younger self from an ironic distance, as a novelist might view a character, and as the mature narrator views her childhood self in *A Bird in the House*. The friend whom she calls Mensah (echoing *mensa*, the Latin word for mind) is based on her real acquaintance Ofosu. In her introduction to this essay, she says that she changed Ofosu's name and profession to protect his identity and safeguard his security, since he was still living in Nkrumah's Ghana at the time (23). In her memoir she recalls, "I learned a great deal from Ofosu. One thing he taught me was that even if I were an anti-colonialist, I need not expect any communication with Africans at that point in history. I learned what it is to be a white liberal" (153).

"The Wild Blue Yonder" in *Heart of a Stranger* records Margaret's "air adventures" flying to Africa. Never a hardy traveller, she experienced every possible misadventure – from an attempted seduction by a travelling salesman to being locked in a lavatory on her journey to Ghana to participate, ironically, in Independence Day celebrations (106) – everything but being hijacked. She recalls reading an article on "Great Air Disasters of the Past Decade" (104) on one flight. The concluding sentence of her typescript, which is omitted from the published version, declares, "When I next return to Canada, I'm thinking of going by boat." Laurence employs a humorous, mocking tone in this essay, replete with amusing anecdotes, that belies the significance of these flights – when she flew home from Accra to the deathbed of her mother in 1957 or when the Somali government invited her, along with a few other colonials, to return from England to Hargeisa, all expenses paid, to celebrate the independence of the Somali Republic from Britain in 1966. This essay, first published in the *Vancouver Sun* in November 1973, employs a comic mask that provides protection for her private feelings in these essentially journalistic pieces.

The Laurences returned to Canada in 1957. "We both felt a need to return to our own land after having been away for nearly nine years" (*DE* 113), Margaret claims. But her travel to other lands, especially Africa, provided a new perspective on Canada. She explains in "A Place to Stand On": "I was fortunate in going to Africa when I did … because for some years I was so fascinated by the African scene that I was prevented from writing an autobiographical first novel. I don't say there is anything wrong in autobiographical novels, but it would not have been the right thing for me – my view of the prairie town from which I had come was still too prejudiced and distorted by closeness. I had to get farther away from it before I could begin to see it" (6). In *The Prophet's Camel Bell*, Laurence writes, "Our voyage began some years ago. When can a voyage be said to have ended? When you reach the place you were bound for, presumably. But sometimes your destination turns out to be quite other than you expected" (*PCB* 10). Indeed, Laurence's destination was her native Canada.

When the Laurences returned to Canada, however, it was not to Manitoba, but to Vancouver, where they lived from 1957 to 1962 – a period reflected in her 1969 novel *The Fire-Dwellers*, in which her heroine, Stacey MacAindra, a married mother like Margaret, recalls her childhood in Manawaka and experiences marital tensions that may reflect the Laurences' personal conflicts at that time. Curiously, Laurence does not include in *Heart of a Stranger* any essays describing their five-year sojourn in Vancouver – even though she wrote several articles there, published in the *Vancouver Sun* – perhaps because it was such a painful time in her personal life, marked as it was by the death of her beloved stepmother, Marg, and her separation from Jack.

This was not to be a permanent homecoming, however, for each Laurence had the heart of a traveller, and in 1962 they set off on a new round of travel. When Jack went to Pakistan in 1962, Margaret did not accompany him. Initially, the couple intended a geographical, not an emotional, separation. Margaret decided, however – after a visit to Calcutta with Jack in November 1963 that coincided with the assassination of John F. Kennedy – that she could not endure being a *memsahib* again or putting the children in boarding school, which living in Pakistan would necessitate. In *The Life of Margaret Laurence*, James King suggests that other factors may have affected her decision, including her pursuit to London of West Indian novelist George Lamming, with whom he suggests she had a brief affair (168–70). So, in 1962 Margaret left Canada again for London, where she hoped to find a literary community (*DE* 164), with her children, Jocelyn and David, in hand and Hagar in the mail (in the form of the manuscript of *The Stone Angel*) – her two kinds of offspring.

The Laurences lived for a year in a flat near Keats's house on Heath Hurst Road in Hampstead. From there they explored the labyrinth of London, inspiring Margaret's first children's book, *Jason's Quest* (1970), the saga of Jason, a picaresque mole who makes a pilgrimage to London on a quest for a cure for the mysterious illness that ails the city of Molanium.

Margaret rented Elmcot, a ramshackle labourer's cottage in Penn, Buckinghamshire, from her Macmillan editor Alan Maclean, launching a new decade of her life as an English villager, 1963–73. The "spirit of the house" was a portrait of Lady Maclean, who was Margaret's confidante (*DE* 169), perhaps inspiring Morag Gunn's "Saint Catharine," based on Catharine Parr Traill, in *The Diviners*. James King refers to "the spirit of creativity the house had unleashed within her" (314) because she wrote some her greatest works there, specifically her Manawaka books.

But Elm Cottage was not as remote from Canada as Laurence anticipated, for "Elmcot" became an unofficial Canada House, as she records in her *Heart of a Stranger* essay "Put Out One or Two More Flags": "I live on two-thirds of an English acre which appears to be the maple leaf forever. To put it bluntly, the place is crawling with Canadians" (108). She concludes: "Move over, High Commissioner, sir. The Low Commissioner is operating from Unofficial Canada House" (112). Canada, as it is represented in this essay, is not simply a place for Laurence, but a state of mind. When a friend reported that a student reading a Laurence novel in a Canadian literature course at home asked, "Doesn't she live in a castle or something in England?" (110), the Canadian colony nicknamed the cottage "Elm Castle." A friend sent a drawing of the New Elm Castle, designed by architect Everard Turnpenny Cetera, with a rope ladder, a moat with barracuda, and a reversible banner reading "*Moi Libre*: Me Free" on one side and "*Libre Moi*: Free Me" on the other (111). So many Canadians visited Elmcot that Margaret made signs for the rooms, lest people get lost in the night. At its best, the "agreeable anarchy" (111) reigning at Elmcot generated a sense of "extended family" (109). She dedicated *The Diviners*: "FOR the Elmcot people, past, present and future, and for the house itself, with love and gratitude," for she created her greatest works there. She employed the quotation from Al Purdy's poem, *Roblin Mills Circa 1842* – "*but they had their being once and left a place to stand on*" – as the dedication for *The Diviners* and as the title for the opening essay in *Heart of a Stranger*, "A Place to Stand On," linking her travel and fiction once again.

"Put Out One or Two More Flags," which was first published in the *Vancouver Sun* in 1972, retains the humorous tone of some of her other essays which originated as journalistic pieces. The title of the essay – a comic adumbration of the title of Evelyn Waugh's 1942 novel *Put Out More Flags*, which was intended as a call to arms during the phony war – suggests that Laurence felt besieged by Canadian travellers abroad, but it also belies the real pain that she suffered during her sojourn in Elm Cottage, including the dissolution of her marriage. In her introduction to the essay, Laurence writes, "This article is relatively frivolous, perhaps because any deeper feelings about our life in Elm Cottage ... seemed and still seem to be a private matter" (107). As Dixon observes, "The personal anecdotes on her life at Elm Cottage in Buckinghamshire and her 'shack' in Ontario are stylistically indistinguishable from those recounting experiences with taxis, television, and airplanes: all dance cheerfully along the mere surface of events as if written by a particularly charming and articulate correspondent to an acquaintance more casual than intimate" (278). Laurence's retrospective introductions to the essays resemble the retrospections by the adult narrator that conclude stories in *A Bird in the House* and replicate the duality of vision and narrative method that characterizes so much of her writing, from her Somali travel memoir to her Manawaka fictions.

Laurence returned to Canada in fiction a decade before she returned in the flesh, for it was at Elm Cottage that she wrote her Manawaka novels. *The Stone Angel* constituted a homecoming, for she explains, "I had to begin approaching my background and my past through my grandparents' generation, the generation of pioneers of Scots-Presbyterian origin, who had been among the first to people the town I called Manawaka" (*HS* 6). She writes, "I'm back in my own territory, in a sense, both geographically and spiritually" (*FL* 215): "I experienced the enormous pleasure of coming home in terms of idiom" (TYS 20). After she published *The Stone Angel* in 1964, she wrote her Cameron sister novels, *A Jest of God* (1966) and *The Fire-Dwellers* (1969), and then *A Bird in the House* (1970). Her *Heart of a Stranger* essay, "Living Dangerously ... by Mail," first published in the *Vancouver Sun* in 1972, records the urgent messages sent to her editors on her "typewriter transmitter" (145) regarding her titles: "I've had more trouble with titles than a prospective peer," she asserts, "And I've defended my titles more often than a middleweight boxer" (144). Her most strenuous battle involved the title of *The Stone Angel*, which her publishers suggested calling *Old Lady Shipley* (145). The mocking tone of this essay, first published in the *Vancouver Sun* in 1972, belies the real distress she experienced in battling with her publishers over her works, especially the question of whether or not she should transform *A Bird in the House* into a novel, as she recalls in *Dance on the Earth: A Memoir* (198).

A Jest of God forced Laurence out of her British ivory tower and launched a new phase of her travels by returning her to Canada for two brief trips – first, for a publicity tour to launch the book and then to accept the Governor General's Award for Fiction in 1966. This was appropriate for this novel about a spinster school teacher who emerges from her solipsistic existence, leaves her small prairie home town, and embarks on a new life.

Her *Heart of a Stranger* essay, "Inside the Idiot Box," first published in the *Vancouver Sun* in June of 1972 with the title "Hello Aunt Nelly; I'm on the Telly," chronicles her publicity disasters. Although a generous and gregarious individual, Laurence was an intensely shy and private person where publicity was involved. She recalls being led, "a lamb to the slaughter" (130), to a television interview about her first novel, *This Side Jordan*: the interviewer questioned her about Africa – "do you think Africa would be a better place if there were more people like you there?" (131) – leaving Laurence dumbfounded. Once she made a fool of herself by "fighting with a *flower*" (133) on camera: the director asked her to pick a flower that turned out to be a "Great Mullein of the Figwort family" (133). She omitted this typically self-mocking sentence from her typescript: "'Oh, great,' I said, 'Nature woman. The female Thoreau of Otonabee. That's me!'" The *Jest of God* publicity tour, a nightmare for this "babe in the literary woods" (*DE* 180), began disastrously. She landed in Toronto, dubbed "the Vile Metropolis," or "V.M." for short (*DE* 180), with no clothes because Air Canada had lost her luggage and no money because she could not cash her traveller's cheques in Toronto on a Sunday. She recalls, "I was thinking of Canada, my home and native land, as a foreign country and myself like the biblical Ruth, 'in tears amid the alien corn'" (*DE* 179). Any thought of returning to Canada as a permanent home was far from her mind at this point.

A Jest of God proved pivotal to Laurence's life when Paul Newman and Joanne Woodward took a film option on the novel to make the movie *Rachel, Rachel*, allowing her to purchase her beloved Elmcot. But she did not hide in her ivory tower at Elm Castle like the Lady of Shalott. She had the heart of a traveller, pursuing her life-journey to lands like Egypt, Suez, and Greece.

"We had travelled to England and Africa, and travel no longer seemed strange – it seemed to be the natural way of life for me, the way I had always wanted," Laurence wrote in an unpublished section of "Jericho's Brick Battlements," the last story in her collection *A Bird in the House*.[9] But Laurence was uncomfortable in the role of tourist, as she explains in her introduction to "Sayonara, Agamemnon," her *Heart of a Stranger* essay about her tour of Greece, first published in *Holiday* in 1976: "I had so seldom been a tourist and found the role a difficult one at first. In East and then West Africa, where we had lived a total of seven years, we had been outsiders, strangers, but not tourists" (11). She begins the essay by explaining, "A tourist is not merely any traveller in a land unknown to him or her. A tourist, strictly speaking, is one who goes on tours. We have lived in England, Somaliland, and Ghana. We had visited various places in Italy and in India ... We had travelled most of Canada. But we had never gone on a tour.[10] For us, the Four Day Ultra Classical was a *rite de passage*, an initiation into the world of genuine tourism" (11). After visiting Olympus, Delphi, and Parnassus in the company of American, Swiss, and Japanese tourists, whose individual and national personalities she captures perfectly and whose polyglot talk she recreates dramatically, she sees "Today facing Yesterday" (17). Visiting the Lion Gate at Mycenae, where "Agamemnon, king of men" (20), was murdered upon his return from the Trojan War by his wife Clytemnestra to avenge his ritual sacrifice of their daughter Iphegenia, she realizes "the actuality of the past" (19).[11] She concludes, "*Sayonara*, Agamemnon ... The initiation was over. We were qualified tourists" (21). Laurence positions this essay after "A Place to Stand On" and before her essays on Africa – probably in order to distinguish between being a tourist and being "a stranger in a strange land."[12] Positioning it after her African essays and before her essays chronicling her tours of Egypt would, however, make that point more clearly, as well as being chronologically more accurate.

Holiday magazine commissioned Laurence to write two travel articles on Egypt and the Suez. She travelled with her two young children in Egypt in January 1967 and wrote the articles on her return home to London. "Good Morning to the Grandson of Ramesses the Second" describes her visit to Luxor, where her guide called himself "the King of Luxor and the grandson of Ramesses II" (70). Again, her fascination with the past is gratified as she tours the temples of the gods: "In Luxor one is always having to make the mental shift between the world of the living and the world of the dead. Sometimes the present seems tawdry in comparison with the past, and yet it is a relief to come back, because living disorder is better than dead order" (72) – a sentiment that presages some of her later fictions, including the story "To Set Our House in Order." In the next essay, she writes, "The near past is often painful, but the past beyond living memory has had its thorns trimmed" (*HS* 99). She stayed in the Old Winter Palace where she imagined, wrongly, as it turned out, Lord Carnarvon lived when he opened the tomb of Tutankhamen in the Valley of the Kings in 1922. Her fascination with female pharaoh Hatshepsut – (74) a monarch referred to in *The Fire-Dwellers* as "an ancient Egyptian queen [who] ruled as pharaoh in her own right" (172) – may have fed her feminism, as her interest in the necropoli may have encouraged her emphasis on death and embalming in *A Jest of God*. She concludes her essay with sentiments reminiscent of Shelley's "Ozymandias": "I know quite well that it is useless to interpret the past through one's own concepts, just as it is useless to try to interpret oneself through these much-too-old stones. Yet I persistently keep trying to do both. Something about the magnificence and futility of these structures, something about the tenacity and the ultimate vulnerability of the kings, men who built them in an attempt to defeat the undefeatable, time and death – this will haunt the mind always, as the jackals haunt the temples, for it contains all there is of human paradox" (83).

"Captain Pilot Shawkat and Kipling's Ghost" describes Laurence's trip along the Suez Canal – "A slender blue spear of water improbably piercing the desert" (85), which she calls "a long sigh for the past or a prayer for the future" (85) – on a boat appropriately named the *British Traveller*. As they sail through the desert, past Mount Sinai, where Moses led the children of Israel, she wonders, "how can we be sailing through the desert?" (87), and she recalls Kipling's "Road to Mandalay": "Ship me somewheres east of Suez" (86). She describes the ships waiting to pass through the canal, "grotesquely beached, like great dead whales washed ashore or Noah's arks left perched on land after the floods receded" (89), one of them carrying a load of red double-decker London tour buses. Again, she recalls Queen Hatshepsut, who sent her ships to Africa through this canal around 1495 BCE (90). She recalls the modern construction of the canal by Ferdinand de Lesseps nearly a century ago and the political conflicts over its ownership. Laurence, an "anti-imperialist from a long way back" (100), is struck by the irony: "Once the canal epitomized a world of Victorian opulent trade and the self-righteous certainties of colonialism. Now it exists in a world seared with uncertainties, and in a Middle East feverish with rival Arab nationalisms" (100). In contrast, after the voyage, at Port Said's opulent Casino Palace, she meets several exiles, "expatriates in their own country" (98), who "play games, for reality is too harsh and their dilemmas cannot be solved" (99). These lost souls call themselves "the Wanderbirds" (96), a name that could well apply to the Laurences.

After completing "Good Morning to the Grandson of Ramesses the Second" and "Captain Pilot Shawkat and Kipling's Ghost" back in London, Laurence was relaxing in the bathtub when her daughter told her Egypt and Israel were at war. *Holiday* magazine never published the essays, since the Seven-Day War made tourism in Egypt and the

United Arab Republic an impossibility. Laurence writes in her preamble to the Suez essay, "They seem now to have taken place in some other and distant world" (67). Consequently, these two 1967 essays, the latter intended to celebrate the centenary of the Suez Canal, appeared for the first time in *Heart of a Stranger* (DE 182–3).[13]

Most important for her personal odyssey were her visits to Scotland, recorded in "Road from the Isles" in *Heart of a Stranger*. The Wemyss family hailed from Fifeshire in the Lowlands, but in her introduction to this essay she insists, "I always felt my spiritual ancestors were Highlanders" (113). She treasured her family Scots trophies as "religious relics," especially the silver plaid pin with the family crest and motto, "*Je Pense* – 'I think'" (114) – although Peggy Wemyss preferred the Cameron war cry, "'Sons of the hound, come here and get flesh!'" (114). She travelled in 1965 on the Royal Highlander, the night train to Inverness, passing Culloden, where the Highland clans were broken in 1746.[14] Laurence was deeply moved by this tragedy and compared the slaughter of the clansmen by the Sassenach to the invasion of the Canadian Aboriginals' territories by the Selkirk settlers who were driven to the New World by the Highland Clearances and who became her own ancestors. She draws a parallel: "the Highlander today is in somewhat the same position as the North American Indian." In her introduction, she comments, "I came to a greater understanding of the Scots' clan system through a certain amount of knowledge of the tribal system in Africa" (113).

"Road from the Isles" was first published in *Maclean's* in May 1966 under the title "In Pursuit of My Past on the Road from the Isles," with the blurb, "She'd been raised on the Canadian prairies, with the brave legends of a Scotland she'd never seen. Then the author went in search of a dream – and found the reality." It is the last piece in *Heart of a Stranger* that can be accounted a travel essay in the usual sense. Bred up on Scottish songs like Harry Lauder's "Road to the Isles" (113) and the novels of Sir Walter Scott, Laurence was deeply disillusioned by what she terms the "mock Scots" (122) of "the tartan dolly trade" (120) in modern Scotland. Clearly, Laurence's period as a tourist is over because she finds herself utterly antipathetic to the very concept of tourism. So "Road from the Isles," situated at the centre of the book, constitutes a significant turning point in her life journey. Interestingly,

Laurence, at one point, employed "Road from the Isles" as the title for the collection.

Her trips to Scotland taught her more about Canada than Scotland, for she says, in "Road from the Isles," "my first view of Scotland was in some strange way also my first true understanding of where I belonged, namely the land where I was born" (113). In "A Place to Stand On," Laurence writes, "Other past generations of my father's family had lived in Scotland, but for me, my people's real past – my own real past – was not connected except distantly with Scotland" (6–7). In "Road from the Isles" she says, "for the first time Scotland had become real to me, both in its past and in its present," but "I still did not feel any personal sense of connection with its history" (121). In fact, she says, "The Highlands of Scotland struck a chord in me because they reminded me of Clear Lake in Manitoba," so "some kind of ironic historical wheel had now come full circle" (122). The fact that she changes the title of the popular song, "Road *to* the Isles" to "Road *from* the Isles" suggests that she is turning away from the Highlands. As she explains in "Where the World Began," the final essay in *Heart of a Stranger*, "My long-ago families came from Scotland and Ireland, but in a sense that no longer mattered so much. My true roots were [in Canada]" (173).

Laurence recreates her "pilgrimage to the land of the ancestors" (113) in *The Diviners*, where Morag Gunn, the girl from Manawaka, visits Scotland to search for her heritage, only to realize that it lies in Canada, her true heartland – "Christie's real country. Where I was born" (415). Morag recalls Thomas Wolfe's maxim, "You Can't Go Home Again," and responds, "You have to go home again" (324). In her introduction to "Road from the Isles," Laurence notes, "this article now seems to me to be an early working-out, in non-fiction, of a theme I would later, in *The Diviners*, express in fiction, namely the feelings a person has when making the pilgrimage to the land of the ancestors" (113). She comments, "It is as though in my fiction I knew exactly where to go, but in my life I didn't, as yet" (*HS* 113). She explains that, like Morag, "when I went to Scotland, making the obligatory pilgrimage to the town in Fifeshire where my people had come from, I knew then where I belonged, which was in that small prairie town in Manitoba" (Sullivan 70). As Dixon concludes, "Estrangement between past and present, here and there, is overcome in each case by an act of interpretive imagination that implicitly defines history as both a context of individual identity and a species of fiction. Home is not a place but an idea; not a fact but a fiction" (478).

Laurence first returned to Canada as a visitor in 1969 as writer-in-residence at the University of Toronto, where she called herself "the Ann Landers of Massey College" (DE 195), during Robertson Davies' tenure as Master. She was named writer-in-residence at the University of Western Ontario in 1973 and in 1974 at Trent University, where she was appointed Chancellor in 1981. Although 1969–70 was a painful season for Margaret personally, since she was separated from her children and divorced from Jack, it was an important one professionally, as she published three books that year: *The Fire-Dwellers, Jason's Quest*, and *A Bird in the House*. The last constituted a fictional homecoming because she recreates her childhood and her family in these stories.

Her first year as writer-in-residence proved pivotal, for it was a prelude to a permanent return to her homeland. She maintained Elmcot as a family home, but she needed a "foothold in Canada" (DE 196). She found that foothold in a cedar cabin on the Otonabee River near Peterborough, described in "The Shack," originally titled "The Beloved Place," the *Heart of a Stranger* essay that celebrates her return to Canada: "The most loved place, for me, in this country has in fact been many places" (147), for the cabin recalled her family cottage at Clear Lake. She published this essay in *Weekend Magazine* under the title "Loneliness Is Something That Doesn't Exist Here," the final phrase of the essay. She also wrote her last Manawaka novel overlooking the Otonabee River. In her final essay, "Where the World Began," she recalls, "the river seemed to be flowing both ways. I liked this, and interpreted it as an omen, a natural symbol" (173). "The river [that] flowed both ways" (D 11) is the current of inspiration that flows through *The Diviners*. In fact, a typescript version of this essay at York University is titled "The River Flows Both Ways." As a symbol that she had come home, she raised a sign at the Shack saying *Manawaka*.

Divining a well inspired her last and arguably greatest novel, *The Diviners*, composed over three summers in the Shack overlooking the Otonabee River. The well-driller, who divined the water with a willow wand, said, "Lard, woman, you got enough water there to supply half a Trona" (127) – a far cry from her fictional diviner, Royland. Her "Boss" at "McStew," Jack McClelland, had a poster made for the Shack declaring, under a parody of Ontario's coat-of-arms: "No Visitors Allowed: By Order of the Government of Ontario; By Authority of J.G. McClelland, Servant & Publisher" (147). Thus, the Shack is mythologized, as Elmcot was. *The Diviners* won the Governor General's Award in 1975. Laurence held a unique launching party for the novel – "a divining contest" (129).

The Shack gave the Manitoba native the chance to shed her "prairie chip" (124) against eastern Canada. Although she declares in "A Place to Stand On," "I always considered southern Manitoba very beautiful, and I still do" (7), in her essay "Down East" in *Heart of a Stranger*, she celebrates Ontario towns with their "sense of history" and revels in "the scarlet flames of trees" (125), which defeat even the skillful wordsmith. She admires the colours that the Group of Seven captured with paint: no wonder so "many Canadian writers couldn't see the people for the trees" (125), she quips. She celebrates the land of Susanna Moodie and Catharine Parr Traill, Morag's "Saint Catharine." "Scratch a Canadian, and you find a phony pioneer" (173), she mocks, but in "Down East," first written for the *Vancouver Sun* in 1971, her appreciation of Canadian landscapes emerges strongly: "The land still draws me more than other lands. I have lived in Africa and in England, but splendid as both can be, they do not have the power to move me in the same way as, for example, that part of southern Ontario where I spent four months last summer in a cedar cabin beside a river" (173). As Marni Stanley observes in "Travelers' Tales," "As a general rule the best ... travel writers seem to be the ones who had the most contact with the land" (58) – a point that is very true for Laurence.

In viewing Canada's situation "under the huge shadows of those two dominating figures, Uncle Sam and Britannia" (172), Laurence considers the escalating violence in the United States and its involvement in Vietnam. She positions an essay entitled "Open Letter to the Mother of Joe Bass,"[15] which she wrote for Purdy's 1968 collection *The New Romans*, near the end of *Heart of a Stranger*. She focuses on two newspaper photographs: first, Joe Bass, a twelve-year-old boy accidentally shot by police; then the picture of a North Vietnamese woman trying to wipe napalm from the face of her child.[16] Although she despairs of the current "descent into lunacy" in contemporary America, she acknowledges, "I am a North American – I cannot exclude myself from the dilemma. I cannot say *them*. It is forced upon me to say *us*" (159) – a concept she explores in "Tribalism As Us Versus Them." Although she is a stranger to both children's mothers, she feels a deep empathy with them. Echoes of these sentiments surface in *The Fire-Dwellers*, which she was composing as she wrote this article, for Stacey, mother of four, fears the gloom and doom of a world on fire.

When she was ready to return to Canada for good, it was not to the Prairies. Instead, she settled in an Ontario town that closely resembled her hometown of Neepawa, even to the river flowing through the town. She purchased a brick house in Lakefield – home of pioneer Susanna Moodie, author of *Roughing It in the Bush*, and her sister, botanist Catharine Parr Traill, author of *The Backwoods of Canada* – that resembled her grandfather's house in Neepawa. In her introduction to "Down East," Laurence notes, "When I wrote about Lakefield in this article I didn't imagine that within a few years one of its old brick houses would be mine and that I would be settled in a small town not unlike the one in which I grew up" (123). When she found the house had been an undertaker's parlour like the Simpson funeral home, she was amused at the irony.

Although Laurence had the heart of a traveller, she was no driver, so she took taxis between her cabin and her Lakefield house. In the *Heart of a Stranger* essay "I Am a Taxi," a slight piece written for the *Vancouver Sun* in 1970 that separates "Inside the Idiot Box" from "Living Dangerously ... by Mail," she recalls chatty taxi drivers from Cairo to Athens and claims that Toronto drivers are the gabbiest. She connects travel with fiction again: "I collect taxis and the life stories of taxi drivers in precisely the same way as taxis themselves collect a multitudinous variety of fares" (135).

Laurence continued to be productive in Lakefield, despite attacks from fundamentalist sects in her own county of Peterborough. She published four books during those years – *Heart of a Stranger* and three children's books: *Six Darn Cows* (1979) about six cows that are lost and then found, *The Olden Days Coat* (1979) about time travel, and *The Christmas Birthday Story* (1980), a text that was lost and then returned (*DE* 217–20). But she never completed another novel, despite repeated attempts to write one titled *Dance on the Earth* about two sisters closing up their summer cottage for the season and recalling their family history.[17] In a 9 February 1973 letter to Harold Horwood, she predicted that *The Diviners* "will be the last Manawaka fiction, as all the threads are tied in this novel, or the wheel comes full circle" (*VLS* 97). In her interview with Sullivan, she affirms, "I do have, both in my own life and in my life view, a sense of the wheel coming full circle, that kind of journey, where we end up in the place where we began, but with a different perspective" (69). The wheel had come full circle in Laurence's life as well as her fiction. In a cancelled statement from the typescript of the introduction to "The Shack," she announces, "I was coming home."

Heart of a Stranger is Laurence's record of that long journey home – the return of the native. In her published foreword to *Heart of a Stranger*, in referring to the biblical source of her title and the epigraph to the volume, she explains how her travels ultimately brought her home:

> That verse from Exodus has always meant a great deal to me. I have spent a good many years of my adult life as a stranger in strange lands, in some cases as a resident, and in others as a traveller. I have met suspicion and mistrust at times, and I have also met with warmth and generosity. The process of trying to understand people of another culture – their concepts, their customs, their life-view – is a fascinating and complex one, sometimes frustrating, never easy, but in the long run enormously rewarding. One thing I learned, however, was that my experience of other countries probably taught me more about myself and even my own land than it did about anything else. Living away from home gives a new perspective on home. I began to write out of my own background only after I had lived some years away, and when I finally came back to Canada to stay, nearly ten years after I had returned in my fiction, I knew for certain that it was where I belonged, and I knew why. (*HS* 3)

She concludes: "These ... essays are very much interwoven with that process. ... I see them as travels and entertainments, but they are also a record of the long journey back home" (*HS* 4).

Heart of a Stranger celebrates that homecoming to her "heartland" (*DE* 275), bringing her life journey full circle. After travelling through many distant lands in *Heart of a Stranger*, she returns to Canada in three of the last four essays: "Upon a Midnight Clear" recalls her Christmas traditions. "Man of Our People" celebrates the Métis leader Gabriel Dumont, balancing "The Poem and the Spear," her essay on the Somali leader Hasan. Finally, she takes us home to Neepawa, Manitoba, "the microcosm of a prairie town" (173), in her last essay, "Where the World Began," which mirrors her first essay, "A Place to Stand On," thus framing the entire collection.

"Upon a Midnight Clear," first published in *Weekend Magazine* under the title "The Greatest Gift of All," describes this "festival of faith" (151) as it was celebrated in her childhood home. In her preamble to the essay, she explains, "This article was published in December 1974, just before our first Christmas in my Lakefield house, which is now establishing some of its own traditions, while as always carrying over some of those from the past" (151). In the article she recalls the Christmas traditions that she replicated in England, but she affirms, "what Christmas celebrates is grace, a gift given from God to man" (151), clarifying the significance of her original title. "Those Christmases at Elm Cottage had a feeling of real community. For me, this is what this festival is all about – the sense of God's grace, and the sense of our own family and extended family, the sense of human community" (156). She shows that that community can be recreated no matter where one travels.

"Man of Our People" was originally published in *Canadian Forum* for December 1975 under the title "Man of Honour," a review essay on George Woodcock's 1975 study *The Métis Chief and His Lost World*. Laurence draws parallels between the plight of Canada's Métis under the leadership of Louis Riel and Gabriel Dumont and that of the Somali people under the leadership of the Sayyid, and she notes their relevance to *The Diviners* in this excised passage from her introduction to "Man of Our People" in which she justifies including the review essay in *Heart of a Stranger*:

This review article does include many of my own feelings and views about this period and about a nomadic tribal society clashing with an incoming colonialist power, the aftermath of which is still with us, and cannot be shelved or shrugged off. The spirits of Dumont and Riel, of Big Bear and Poundmaker, after the long silence, are speaking once again through their people, their descendants. Will we ever reach the point where it is no longer necessary to say Them and Us? I tried to approach this subject in terms of Nigerian writers in *Tribalism As Us Versus Them* and indeed in many other places in my writing. I believe we must reach that point or perish. Canadians who, like myself, are the descendants of various settlers, many of whom came to this country as oppressed or dispossessed peoples, must hear native peoples' voices, for they speak not only of the soul-searing injustices done to them but also of their re-discovered sense of self-worth and their ability to tell and teach the things we all need to know. (222)

The legends of Gabriel Dumont inspired the myths of Jules Tonnerre in *The Diviners*, linking *Heart of a Stranger* with Laurence's Manawaka fiction. Laurence affirms her admiration for Dumont: "Dumont was not only a very romantic kind of character, but was also a genuinely heroic person" (Sullivan 77) – just as she viewed Hasan. This celebration of Gabriel Dumont near the end of her collection reflects her celebration of the Sayyid in her earlier essay, "The Poem and the Spear." Thus, these two essays, like the first and last of the volume set in her home town, frame the volume. Dixon links this group of essays: "Thus, in a third group of essays, Laurence marshals the artist's powers of discernment, empathy, and imagination to bridge the primal estrangement between herself and individuals of different race and culture: a Somali poet, a Black mother in Detroit whose son has been shot by police; a Ghanaian lawyer; the Métis leader, Gabriel Dumont" (478). Dixon concludes his review eloquently: "Each of these struggles for insight into the heart of a stranger brings Laurence, and her readers, a complementary revelation of our common humanity, our ultimate 'home.' Such insight is rare, and the collection is at once a gloss on Laurence's fiction and an implicit apologia for fiction itself: we are all 'strangers' but, alas, we are not all artists" (478–9).

"Where the World Began" was originally published in *Maclean's* in December 1972 with the subtitle, "A small prairie town as an aspect of myself." In the essay, Laurence explains the ways her home town has become internalized as part of her psyche and her artistic vision. In her introduction to the essay, she explicitly connects her travel writing with her Manawaka fiction: "I wrote this article in 1971, when I was beginning my novel *The Diviners*. I see now that I used it as one more means of working out a theme that appears in the novel, that is, the question of where one belongs and why, and the meaning to oneself of the ancestors, both the long-ago ones and those in remembered history. Until I re-read these articles, I didn't realize I had written so much on this theme before I ever dealt with it fictionally. I didn't realize, either, how compulsively I'd written about the river, the same river that appears in the novel" (169). But she omitted this interesting passage in her typescript from the introduction to the essay: "[E]very writer of fiction writes out of the place where, for them, the world began, and most writers of fiction also in some way write out of the land of their ancestors, which in the end is the same world as where the writer's own sight was formed. The journey takes us a long way, and the land of our distant ancestors may be a long way off. But I suspect that where we have finally chosen to live matters a whole lot. It may be a homecoming, as it happened to be in my case. Or it may be putting one's new roots into a different soil ..." (224). Laurence writes in a 14 November 1972 letter to Harold Horwood regarding Morag Gunn of *The Diviners*, "being a writer is really only a means of getting at the ways in which our ancestors stalk through our lives, the ways we make myths of our parental figures and even of our own lives, the ways in which we see ourselves turning into ancestors and myths" (*VLS* 96). As Angelica Maeser Lemieux writes in "The Scots Presbyterian Legacy," "There is a sense in which the private journeys frequently extend into fictional ones and create a conflation of myth and reality" (165). After describing the topography, architecture, and eccentricities of Neepawa, Laurence explains, "This was my territory in the time of my youth, and in a sense my life since then has been an attempt to look at it, to come to terms with it" (*HS* 172). "This is where my world began," she concludes, "A world which formed me, and continues to do so." (174). She moved this homecoming essay from its previous position to the concluding spot in *Heart of a Stranger* to emphasize her decision to return to her native land. In a cancelled sentence from her typescript, she writes, "I came to the conclusion that the land of my birth was the true land of my knowable ancestors, a conclusion I also arrived at with Morag in *The Diviners*" (222), connecting her travel essays and her Canadian fiction once again.[18]

Laurence ends with her origins, recalling Mary of Guise's motto, "In my end is my beginning" and T.S. Eliot's *Little Gidding*: "The end of all our exploring / Will be to arrive where we started / And know the place for the first time." In a sentence omitted from the typescript of her introduction to "Down East," Laurence observes, "endings often have a remarkable resemblance to beginnings" (213). So *Heart of a Stranger* describes a Möbius strip, just as *The Diviners* does, because the last essay, "Where the World Began," reflects the first, "A Place to Stand On," for she affirms in both the importance of her birthplace in inspiring her artistic vision.

Laurence made her last trip to her "heartland" (*DE* 275) in the final year of her life to visit her brother Bob, who was dying of cancer – recorded in "VIA Rail and Via Memory" (*DE* 275) in the Afterwords to *Dance on the Earth*. Soon after celebrating her sixtieth birthday in July 1986, she was diagnosed with terminal lung cancer. She had planned to attend a conference on *The Stone Angel* in Norway in November, but she was forced to cancel her trip. Foreseeing her final voyage, she wrote to the organizer that she fears this last "passage" (Seyersted 213, *SL* 407), although she calls herself a Christian with faith in the Holy Spirit, for "[n]o one can tell about that last voyage" (*DE* 120).

Laurence ended her life in Lakefield on Epiphany Sunday, 1987. Despite her youthful rebellion, she chose to have her ashes buried in the family plot in the Neepawa cemetery. In *The Diviners*, she quotes Psalm 39:12, "*For I am a stranger with thee, and a sojourner, as all my fathers were*" (426). Later, her admirers purchased the old Brick House as a monument. Laurence's life is indeed the story of "the long journey back home" (*HS* 4).

Heart of a Stranger takes us on a journey of discovery through Laurence's travels to distant lands that ultimately illuminates our country of Canada. But Laurence also saw her fiction as an exploration. In her published foreword to *Heart of a Stranger*, she explains, "The whole process of fiction is a mysterious one, and a writer, however experienced, remains in some ways a perpetual amateur, or perhaps a perpetual traveller, an explorer of those inner territories, those strange lands of the heart and spirit" (3). As Woodcock asserts in "Many Solitudes," "Her novels are all in a sense travel books, vividly descriptive in terms of environment, involving a great deal of journeying, both

inner and outer, and coming at the end to those self-transforming realizations that are the destinations of all internal voyagings" (135).
Laurence claims that "Each novel is a kind of voyage of discovery"
(Gibson 192): what she terms "the kind of vehicle or vessel capable of
risking that peculiar voyage of exploration which constitutes a novel"
(GG 89) can take us on a far more fascinating journey than any travelogue, for it leads us into the psychic landscape of the human heart
and mind.

PART TWO

The African Texts
"A Seven Years' Love Affair with a Continent"

CHAPTER 4

"A Labour of Love": *A Tree for Poverty: Somali Poetry and Prose*

Laurence's experience of Africa contributed to making her a great Canadian writer. She learned about Africa not only from observing and interacting with Africans in Somaliland and Ghana during her seven-year sojourn there, 1951–1957, but she also learned significant lessons from reading, or hearing, African literature – notably Somali oral folk literature and Nigerian literature. In fact, she possessed an extensive library of African literature, including 148 books, many underlined and annotated, now collected at McMaster University. The texts that are most valuable for a study of how Laurence's Canadian fiction was influenced by her knowledge of African literature are *A Tree for Poverty: Somali Poetry and Prose* (1954), the first translation and publication of Somali folk literature, and *Long Drums and Cannons: Nigerian Dramatists and Novelists, 1952–1966*. These two literary studies, her first and last African texts respectively, frame her five African books. *The Prophet's Camel Bell* (1963), called *New Wind in a Dry Land* in its American edition – a travel memoir based on the journal she kept in Somaliland during her 1951–52 sojourn there – is also valuable for this enterprise, especially the chapter titled "A Tree for Poverty," in which Laurence discusses her translations of Somali folk literature.

SOMALI POETRY AND PROSE

Examining *A Tree for Poverty: Somali Poetry and Prose* can reveal how translating Somali folk literature influenced Laurence's creative writing. Useful discussions of these translations have been written by Fiona Sparrow – both in the chapter entitled "Something More Than Nothing" (45–69) in her excellent study *Into Africa with Margaret Laurence* (1992), and in her article "Margaret Laurence of Hargeisa" (1997) – and by Donez Xiques – in her introduction to the 1993 edition of *A Tree for Poverty*, her essay, "Margaret Laurence's Somali Translations" (1992), and her book, *Margaret Laurence: The Making of a Writer* (2005). Xiques asserts, "Laurence's own literary skills must have been enhanced as a result of her work with the richly imaginative and carefully crafted tales of the Somalis" (*TP* 13).[1] I argue that translating Somali oral folk literature, both poems and stories, influenced Laurence's Canadian fiction significantly.

A Tree for Poverty, first published by Eagle Press in Nairobi in 1954, includes thirty poems and excerpts, with extensive commentaries, and thirty-six stories of Arabic and Somali origin, again with commentaries, plus an introduction combining anthropology, cultural commentary, and literary criticism that James King calls a "crisp and concise explanation of an oral literature" (92). As Fiona Sparrow asserts, in *Into Africa with Margaret Laurence*, "*A Tree for Poverty* bears the mark of literary excellence not only in the standards set for the translations, but in the visionary concept that gives unity to a varied collection of songs and stories" (68–9).[2]

When Margaret accompanied Jack to Somaliland in 1951, she was in an anomalous position as a Canadian woman married to an engineer in the employ of the Department of Public Works. Jack was employed to build *ballehs*, or reservoirs, to preserve the rains through the *jilal* (drought) in the desert of the Haud, but Margaret found her own form of conservation. Not having any job of her own, Margaret was elated to discover a project. After discussing Somali literature with Polish poet and Somali linguist Dr Bogomil Andrzejewski and his assistant, poet Musa Galaal, at Sheik, she recalls, "I was filled with enthusiasm": "I knew that I had found what I would like to work at" – namely, translating Somali folk literature. "But I could not do it alone. Would I be able to find people who would help me? I was certain that I would" (*PCB* 46).

Dr Andrzejewski, known as Gus, an eminent linguist and specialist in Cushitic languages at the London School of Oriental and African Studies, was the most fluent speaker of Somali in the European community. Gus and Musa worked together with Margaret, who was studying Somali, to translate Somali poetry. She explains their collaborative method in *The Prophet's Camel Bell*: "It was a three-way process. Musa knew a great many *gabei* and *belwo*, and had a wide knowledge of the background and style of Somali poetry, but while his command of English was fluent, he had to discuss the subtler connotations of the words with Gus in Somali. Gus and I then discussed the lines in English, and I took notes on the literal meanings, the implications of words, the references to Somali traditions or customs. I would then be able to work on this material later, and attempt to put it into some form approximating a poem, while preserving as much as possible of the meaning and spirit of the original" (*PCB* 113). Translation was not always a painful process: in *The Prophet's Camel Bell*, Margaret recalls that, while Jack courted sun-stroke unloading bulldozers on the docks of Djibouti (132), "I sat in the cool depths of the Consul's bathtub and worked on translations of desert poetry" (130).

In her 1970 preface to *A Tree for Poverty*, Laurence labels her translations "amateurish" and acknowledges, "I am neither a literary critic nor an anthropologist" (19).[3] Critics disagree with these modest disclaimers: Donez Xiques claims that Laurence is "a diligent and gifted translator" (*TP* 15); Fiona Sparrow judges, "her translations have an elegant literary style that compensates for any slight loss of accuracy" (53). She adds, "She spoke with affection for her first published book, but with modesty about the value of the translations it contained. Yet their value has never been questioned by the acknowledged authorities on the subject" (69). Moreover, Laurence did considerable research for her African texts: British novelist Mary Renault, in her review of *This Side Jordan*, calls Laurence "a scholar and translator of African folklore and poetry" (24), and Fiona Sparrow notes, "Considerable research lies behind *A Tree for Poverty*, which has an authority that is based on first-hand knowledge of the Somalis, their country and its traditions. The book also derives its strength from Laurence's admiration for the people and their literature" (69).

Laurence asserts, "My translations are, in most cases, by no means literal, but they do remain true to the thought and imagery of the original" (*TP* 25). As she explains in a 4 September 1951 letter to Adele Wiseman, "I have tried all along to be as true as possible to the original, and yet not to be too hidebound and thereby lose the implied meaning in the original" (*SL* 63). Professor Andrzejewski confirms these assertions: "What is astonishing is that in spite of the language barrier, she developed such empathy with the Somalis that even though her translations are sometimes not very close to the original she conveyed their spirit and atmosphere with a high degree of accuracy" (*TP* 12). In her 1970 preface (19), Laurence acknowledges the superiority of Gus's translations in his *Somali Poetry* (1964), but critics compare her translations favourably with his. In "Margaret Laurence of Hargeisa," Fiona Sparrow judges, "the elegant English of her translations is as true in its way to the Sayyid's art as Andrzejewski's faithful rendering" (132), for "the translations are finely done and they testify to the beauty of the original as well as to the excellence of Margaret Laurence's craft" (130). African writer Micere Gitae-Mugo judges that Laurence "succeeds in leaving her translations as Somali as possible in content and flavour" (12), although David Richards considers Laurence's translations too westernized. Sparrow states in *Into Africa with Margaret Laurence*, "In Laurence's version the imagery, imaginatively and skilfully translated and interpreted, has a pleasing effect" (56). Adele Wiseman calls Laurence's translations "very fine and sensitive lyrics in English" (610) in her review, and Donez Xiques asserts, "Laurence has succeeded in producing translations that are themselves poems" (*CL* 38). She concludes, "These translations show Laurence's appreciation of complex poetic techniques and an ability to employ her own considerable skill in producing a book of lasting value and significance" (*CL* 40).

Laurence explains in her preface to *A Tree for Poverty* that her purpose in translating and publishing Somali poetry is to record and thus preserve poems which, existing only in the oral tradition and in the memories of the poets, would otherwise be lost (25). Donez Xiques notes, "For the thousands of Somali refugees who have sought asylum in English-speaking countries, this volume could well be a cherished link with their history and culture, as well as a beacon of hope for a brighter future" (8). In her 1973 preface, Laurence asserts, "I think it was a good thing that the translations in *A Tree for Poverty* were done, partly because they constituted the first collection to be translated into

English and partly because I think they do convey some sense of the life and concepts of the Somali nomadic people" (19). Curiously, she never considers cultural appropriation as an issue, assuming it is correct to record and publish Somali oral folk literature, just as Jack assumes it is right to build roads and ports in Somaliland. Post-colonial studies of the last few decades have questioned such common mid-twentieth-century assumptions.

A Tree for Poverty was published in 1954 with the assistance of the colonial Administrator. It was highly ironic for Laurence, who loathed imperialism, that it was "an 'imperialist' who would make the publication of these translations possible" (*PCB* 47). When Laurence discovered to her joy that she was pregnant, she moved to the *megala*, or town, of Hargeisa, where she worked "at the Secretariat, as the Administrator's Secretary" (*PCB* 245) – that is, as secretary to the Chief Secretary of the Protectorate Government, James Shirley. When Shirley read the manuscript of *A Tree for Poverty*, with its description of the harsh life of the Somali Bedouin, known as "the people without a pillow," he committed himself to seeing it published. Eventually he succeeded in his aim, and *A Tree for Poverty* was published in Nairobi in 1954 with funds provided by the Government of the British Protectorate of Somaliland. The author was then known as "Margaret Laurence of Hargeisa" in the British Library General Catalogue (Sparrow 46).

Since all remaining copies of this original imprinting had been bought up by the Peace Corps for distribution to the volunteers going to the Somali Republic, William B. Ready, Librarian and Professor of Bibliography at McMaster University, elected to republish the text in a photographic facsimile of the original edition, as Laurence explains in her preface to that 1970 edition. She asserts, "although I am neither a literary critic nor an anthropologist, I would still stand behind most of what I said in the [1954] Introduction. My main reservation now about those remarks would be that I was in places unwittingly condescending, in the manner of white liberals, out of pure ignorance, for Somaliland was my first contact with a culture other than my own, and I had much to learn about the validity of human differences. I still do, but at least I know it now" (*TP* 19). In 1993, ECW republished *A Tree for Poverty*, including an introduction by Donez Xiques and both Laurence's introduction to the original 1954 edition and her preface to the 1970 edition. Only recently has this valuable text begun to receive the attention it deserves, as scholars begin to appreciate Laurence's African, as well as her Canadian, texts.

Initial reviews by British reviewers such as V.H.W. Dowson – who claims, "Mrs Laurence is to be heartily congratulated not only for being the first to undertake the publication of so large a collection of translations from the Somali, but also for the felicity of her verse" (52) – and also by Canadian reviewers like Adele Wiseman – who concludes, "Mrs. Laurence and her collaborators are to be commended for giving us a glimpse of more light from not so dark Africa" (611) – were positive. But the book, with its limited printing and circulation, was not widely read. Laurence cared deeply about *A Tree for Poverty* and lamented in a 4 September 1951 letter to Adele Wiseman that it was so largely ignored. But she was outraged to discover that passages from *A Tree for Poverty* had been plagiarized and published without acknowledgment by John Buchholzer in his 1959 book *The Horn of Africa: Travels in British Somaliland* (SL 63). Plagiarism may be the sincerest form of flattery, however, for it confirms the value of her text.

"Love and War": Somali Poetry

Laurence's translation of Somali poetry influenced her own development as a writer in terms of her command of language, metaphor, and music. It is appropriate that Laurence began her professional publications with translations of poetry because many of her early works were poems, as we observed in "Embryo Words," the chapter on her juvenilia. She could also be said to have concluded her writing career with poetry, because she selected several poems for the Afterwords of her last published text, *Dance on the Earth: A Memoir* (1989), such as "Old Women's Song" (225–8) and "For My Sisters" (293–6).

In her introduction to *A Tree for Poverty*, Laurence explains why poetry is so important to the Somali people. First, she claims, "the Somalis are a nation of poets" (23). Equally important are the circumstances of their life: there are very few materials for art in their barren landscape, in addition to the fact that the Muslim religion forbids the making of images or figures, whereas poetry requires no materials, but only memory. The Somalis are a nomadic people: only essential items can be carried on trek, but poems, unlike tangible artifacts, are portable. Poetry, with its delight in love and lovely women, provides relief from the harshness of Somali daily life during the desert drought. The Somali people are poor in possessions but rich in literary culture. Thus, poetry provides "a tree for poverty to shelter under," as the line from the Somali *gabei* which Laurence uses for the title and epigraph of her translation asserts. "It is almost inevitable, then," she concludes, "that literature should be the cultural medium of the Somali people" (24).

She quotes the lines *"On the plain Ban-Aul there is a tree / For poverty to shelter under"* as the epigraph for the chapter of *A Prophet's Camel Bell* titled "A Tree for Poverty." She begins the chapter thus: "This part of a Somali *gabei* always seemed to me to express Somali literature as a whole, which, in its way, was also a tree for poverty to shelter under, and so, when I had completed the translations, I took a title from these lines" (210). The rest of the chapter, as she explains, is taken directly from *A Tree for Poverty*, including passages from her introduction, one *belwo*, extracts from two *gabei* – "To a Friend Going on a Journey" by Mahammed 'Abdullah Hassan, and "To a Faithless Friend" by Salaan Arrabey – and two stories about 'Igaal Bowkahh and Ahmed the Woodseller. She wished to include more material from *A Tree for Poverty* in *The Prophet's Camel Bell*, but her publishers refused her request.

Translating Somali poetry was a challenging task, in part because the language is so difficult in itself,[4] but also because it was an exclusively oral language with no actual orthography until 1972. Moreover, although Somali is a "language well suited to poetry" (*PCB* 45), "the extreme difficulty of the Somali literary language" (*TP* 26) poses a problem because the prevalence of portmanteau words and metaphors in Somali poetry, with their wealth of connotations, makes it difficult to translate: for example, the word *marooro*, the name of a plant that tastes acrid in the morning but sweet in the evening, may be a metaphor for a woman. Laurence annotates her text with commentaries on her translations. She explains in a 1951 letter to Wiseman, "often a Somali word is very compressed and there is no single counterpart for it in English. ... so the process of putting it into more or less literary English lies in the choice of words" (*SL* 63). Much of her commentary on her translations of poetry focuses on the appropriate choice of words.

Thus, the work of translation honed Laurence's linguistic skills, inciting her to discover *le mot just*. The "wordsmith" (33) of *The Diviners*, for example, searches for the precise words to describe the "liquid bronze" (33) colour of the river that "flowed both ways" (11).

The demanding nature of the forms of Somali poetry added to the difficulty of translation. "Somali poetry is formal and governed by strict rules" (*HS* 36) and "set literary conventions" (*SL* 63). Alliteration is a major structural method in Somali poetry, especially in the *gabei*, where a number of words in every line are alliterated, with a caesura in the middle of the line, rather like Anglo-Saxon poetry. Laurence makes considerable use of alliteration and assonance in her own prose – not only in Nathaniel Amegbe's monologues in *This Side Jordan*, such as his dream of the Nazarene as an Ashanti king (77), but also in her Manawaka cycle. Hagar compares her girlhood self to "prissy Pippa as she passed" (*SA* 5). Portraying the forest in *This Side Jordan*, she writes, "Death and life meet and mate. ... And at night the silence of the snake" (105).

There are several types of Somali poetry: the lyrical *belwo*, the demanding *gabei*, the *giiraar* or war song, and the *hes*, a song accompanying a dance. In *A Tree for Poverty*, Laurence focuses on "the epic *gabei* and the lyrical *belwo*" (*PCB* 46), the oldest and the newest forms and also the most popular and accessible forms. She includes an extract from a *girraar* – "The Bond between Kings" by Sultan Wiil Waal: "if thy kingdom is lost to thee, / I tremble for my own" (55).

Laurence learned there was also a considerable body of women's poetry, poetry by women for women: "women have all their own gabei" (*TP* 27), as she was informed. "However, since Somali women are very shy with Europeans and since few of them speak any English, it has been impossible so far to obtain any examples of women's poetry" (*TP* 27), she confesses. Consequently, and ironically, she does not include any poetry by women in *A Tree for Poverty*. Women are writ large in men's poetry, however, where love and beauty are praised. But love, like beauty, does not last long after marriage: "Like the flowering desert after the drought, love was of a season, not for ever. While it flourished, therefore, let the songs be made and the beauty of young girls remarked upon, for soon enough they will enter their own *jilal*" (*PCB* 103–4).

The Belwo: *"Short Lyric Lovesongs"*

The *belwo*, whose name means "a trifle" or "a bauble" (*TP* 28), is sung to familiar tunes. The form was invented in 1944 by 'Abdi Deeqsi when his truck broke down (Sparrow 57). As Laurence explains to Wiseman, the *belwo* are "short lyric lovesongs, which are set to music and sung, mainly by the young men. When sung, they have a rhythmic syncopated beat, very similar to American jazz. The old men affect to scorn the belwo, in much the same way as older chaps at home will scorn jazz. These belwo are usually not more than 3 or 4 lines long, altho' they are often sung in ballad form, with 10 or 15 put together, and a chorus" (*SL* 63).

The *belwo* is a brief lyric love-poem developed around a single image – rather like the *haiku* translated by Ezra Pound from the Japanese or the imagist poems of modernists such as Hilda Doolittle or Amy Lowell. The *belwo* is composed by a man to praise the beauty of the woman he loves and wishes to marry, and to persuade the woman to return his love: "Woman, lovely as lightning at dawn, / Speak to me even once" (48). The love lyric is a universal form: "He who has lain between her breasts / Can call his life fulfilled. / Oh, God, may I never be denied / The well of happiness" (*TP* 52) is a lyric outcry recalling the Middle English poem, "Oh Western Wind." The *belwo* comparing the lover separated from his beloved to a dhow or boat adrift in a "gray and empty sea" (*TP* 48) recalls the Anglo-Saxon poem "The Seafarer"; Ezra Pound's translation conveys the outcast "care-wretched, on ice-cold sea" (18). "The curving of your breasts / Like apples sweet and small" (*TP* 51) suggests the Song of Solomon: "Thy two breasts are like two young roes that are twins" (7:3).

The *belwo* was close to the heart of many of the Laurences' team: "Mohamed [their cook] was always singing *belwo*" (*PCB* 179), Laurence recalls. Once at Sheik, when Musa was reciting some of his own love poetry, Hersi Jama – their translator and a reputed poet, Laurence's "Teller of Tales" (*PCB* 169) – responded, "You have opened a wound that had healed" (*PCB* 171).

Most *belwo* centre on one theme, such as the *Carpe Diem* topos of Renaissance poems, as in Robert Herrick's "To the Virgins," a trope that is burlesqued in Andrew Marvell's "To His Coy Mistress" and echoed in these *belwo*: "Turn not away in scorn. / Some day a grave will prove / the frailty of that face, / And worms its grace enjoy. Let me enjoy you now – / Turn not away in scorn" (50); "Your body is to Age and Death betrothed, / And some day all its richness they will share: / Before your firm flesh goes to feed their lusts, / Do not deny my right to love you now" (51). As Laurence asserts, "The 'belwo,' the short love-poems, have a freshness and a lyricism that cannot fail to be observed. Many of the images used are original, apt, and lovely. There is a wealth of imagination, and an appealing candour and frankness. The best Somali belwo have a simplicity that is graceful and moving, in the same manner as our own folk-song verses" (26).

Translating poems developed Laurence's literary skills and taught her the craft of writing. Adapting *belwo*, which centre on an image, developed her mastery of metaphor in particular, one of the most distinctive aspects of her writing. In *This Side Jordan*, she writes of the jaundiced Cora Thayer, a kind of psychic cripple, "She began to unfold like some pale graveyard peony in the charitable sun" (*SJ* 126). The insomniac Rachel Cameron views the night as "a gigantic ferris wheel turning in blackness" (24), to which she is glued in *A Jest of God*, while Stacey MacAindra imagines herself "held underwater by her hair, snared around auburn-rusted anchor chains" in *The Fire-Dwellers* (34). And who could forget Hagar's epiphanic metaphor in *The Stone Angel*: "Pride was my wilderness, and the demon that led me there was fear" (292)?

The musical elements of Somali poetry, especially the *belwo*, which is sung to popular tunes, taught Laurence the importance of rhythm and sound in writing. Amegbe's monologues are especially rhythmical – "When I was a little boy in my mother's womb … When I was a little boy in my father's tomb" (75) – but so are her Manawaka texts, earning her the reputation of a poet in prose. Even an incidental description in *The Fire-Dwellers* is evocative, rich with metaphor and music: "In the lobby of the Princess Regal Hotel, some yawning yellow-toothed fishwife, fleshwife, sagging guttily in a print dress sad with poppies, is sweeping up last night – heel-squashed cigarette butts, Kleenex blown into or bawled into, and ashes" (10). One could select almost any passage from her novels and render it as poetry simply by dividing it into lines. Walter Swayze observes, in "Margaret Laurence: Novelist-as-Poet," that the opening of *The Stone Angel* is only considered prosaic because it is printed as prose: if read aloud, it sounds like poetry (5).

The Gabei: "A Long Narrative Poem"

The *gabei* is the second type of poem Laurence translates in *A Tree for Poverty* – alliterated narrative poems, rhythmic but unrhymed, and chanted rather than sung. Laurence says, "There are numerous types of poetry, but the one which is most highly regarded and the most difficult to compose is the *gabay*, a long narrative poem, highly alliterative and containing many allusions to Islamic theology, Somali genealogy, history, and legend" (*HS* 36).[5] She explains its significance: "The Somali gabei is considered to be the highest literary form in the culture. Gabei may be on any topic, but the rules of gabei-making are strict and difficult. A gabei poet must not only have an extensive vocabulary and an ability to express himself fluently and in terms of figures of speech. He must also possess considerable knowledge of the country, its geography and plant-life, Somali medicine and animal husbandry [as well as] Muslim theology and religious history" (*TP* 32). Laurence tells Wiseman in her 1951 letter: "the gabay are the long, semi-epic poems, dealing with every subject from love to war, altho' the emphasis is generally on war or politics or philosophy. These poems are written in literary Somali ... a language which has its own vocabulary, much of which is unknown to the average young Somali, unlearned as yet in gabay composing. They are not sung, but are chanted, in a sort of monotonous but rhythmical way ... very boring if you can't understand Somali, but highly interesting when translated" (*SL* 63–4).

Poets progress from *belwo* to *gabei*: "The young men who continue their interest in poetry grow gradually into gabei poets, guided by the older established poets" (34), because "The gabei requires more depth of thought, a more complete treatment of subject, broader subject matter, more complexity of style, and much more poetic discipline than the belwo" (34), Laurence explains. Men gather in tea shops to recite and critique each other's poems. In *Heart of a Stranger*, she writes, "Simple love songs are fine for those who are young in years or mentality, but the poems of the elders are the *gabay*, long and intricate, following complex rules of composition, full of theological and genealogical allusions. These are the vehicles of political persuasion, personal invective, admonition, philosophical speculation. Through the *gabay*, a man can express what is closest to his heart and mind – his grief, his rage, his faith, his love, his resolution" (*HS* 60).

Although the *gabei* may contain references to many subjects, the most popular topics are "love and war" (*TP* 33). War *gabei* are popular because some of the best *gabei* poets were leaders whose fame ensured the survival of their poems. Love poetry may be sensual, but must be tasteful: Laurence mentions a *gabei* contest in which poets had to describe the vagina without using the word itself and without offending public morality (*TP* 35).

In *Heart of a Stranger*, Laurence includes essays on two poets celebrated for their *gabei* on each of these two subjects: "The Poem and the Spear" celebrates one of Somalia's most revered warrior poets, Mahammed 'Abdille Hasan, and "The Epic Love of Elmii Bonderii" celebrates the romantic poet known as "the Prophet of Love" (65). Hasan was a warrior leader known as "the Sayyid" or "Noble Lord" by the Somalis and as "The Mad Mullah" by the British because he led the Dervishes in their revolts against the British early in the twentieth century, using "the strangest of all military weapons – poetry" (*HS* 31). As Michael Dixon states in his review of *Heart of a Stranger*, "The Poem and the Spear" "illuminates the factual record with epic poetry to generate vivid comprehension of the feelings, values, and cultural perspectives motivating Mahammed 'Abdille Hasan, the warrior-prophet-poet who led a tribal insurrection against British rule in Somaliland nearly a century ago" (478). Laurence admires Hasan as a "nationalist leader" (*HS* 32) and admires the brilliance of his poetry: "His poems show a firm grasp of the intricacies of Somali literary style, and his own passionate beliefs give strength and carrying power to the lines even in translation" (*HS* 36). His fame as a great leader preserved his poems for posterity. Laurence includes in "The Poem and the Spear" part of his *gabei* "The Path of Righteousness," in which he catalogues the virtues of the good Muslim:

He who devotes himself to the holy war and is garlanded
with flowers,
He who turns against the English dogs
And who wins the victory and glory and the songs of praise.
(*HS* 36–7)

She also includes part of his *gabei* "To a Friend Going on a Journey" in *A Tree for Poverty*:

> To all the blessings I bestow on you,
> Friend, yourself now say a last Amen. (*TP* 53).[6]

"The Epic Love of Elmii Bonderii," first published in *Holiday* in 1964, and later collected in *Heart of a Stranger*, describes this "poet of epic love" (63), who reputedly "died of love" (59). Elmii Bonderii, meaning "Elmii the Borderman, because he had been born near the Ethiopian border" (60), was an unlikely poet, an ordinary man who was suddenly inspired to compose brilliant *gabei* by his love for a young girl named Hodan Abdilahi. Her family refused his suit because he had no money, but when he returned from Djibouti seven years later with the *yarad*, or bride-wealth, Hodan was already married to Mohamed Shabel, or Mohamed the Leopard (62). Elmii Bonderii, literally lovesick, died of grief at age thirty-five, even though dozens of young women reputedly visited his sickbed in hopes of healing him. Laurence includes in *A Tree for Poverty* Elmii Bonderii's love-*gabei* "Quaraami," meaning "passion," in which he extols the beauty and domestic accomplishments of the woman named Baar:

> A proud grace is her body's greatest splendour.
> My heart leaps when I see her walking by,
> Infinite suppleness in her body's sway. (*TP* 58)

"Drama and Excitement": Somali Stories

The Somalis are "natural poets *and* storytellers" (*TP* 23, my emphasis), Laurence asserts, and she likely learned as much from translating their stories as she did from translating their poems. "Somali folk-literature is extremely rich ... In a country as barren as this, where the population is almost entirely nomadic and where the actual process of survival demands so much effort and tenacity from each tribesman, it seems remarkable that there should be such a large body of unwritten literature, containing such a high degree of dramatic sense, vivid imagination and wit" (*TP* 47). "The Somalis excel in story-telling" (*SL* 64), Laurence claims, and they have "a great emotional need for drama and excitement … vividness of imagination and expression and a keen sense of the dramatic in word, timing and gesture" (*TP* 41). This need is most easily met, given their barren landscape and harsh way of life, by the spoken word, with which Somalis are highly skilled. These qualities are reflected in their folk tales, which are recounted around the campfire.

Laurence includes in *A Tree for Poverty* three dozen stories composed of two main types – Somali tales and stories that are Arabic in origin. It is not surprising that many tales originate in Arabia because the Somalis are Muslims, and Arabia is the centre of their religion and culture, and many make the pilgrimage to Mecca. Darod and Ishaak, the legendary founders of Somalia, originated in Arabia. Nine of her paraphrased stories are Arabic, while seventeen are Somali.

Laurence explains that these stories were translated by two different methods: some were translated literally by Musa Haji Ismail Galaal and Bogomil Adrzejewski and then paraphrased by Laurence, while others were recounted to her mainly in English by Hersi Jama and Ahmed Nasir, gifted storytellers whose dramatic presentation vividly conveyed the spirit of the stories and influenced Laurence's own gift for storytelling. "Voice" is one of the most frequently used words in Laurence's vocabulary: for example, she entitles the section on emerging writers in *Long Drums and Cannons* "Other Voices," and she changed the title of her story "The Spell of the Distant Drum" to "The Voices of Adamo." She has an excellent ear for the individual voices of her characters, an ear she no doubt developed from listening to these dramatic narrators. Later, she recreates the idiom of that king of storytellers, Christie Logan, memorably in *The Diviners*.

In both Somali and Arabic stories, the essential element, according to Laurence, is *character*. Arabic stories demonstrate particularly interesting characterization, including the tales of Amed Hatab, the "little man" (37) who is both pathetic and sympathetic, foolish and clever, unlucky and fortunate at the same time – a kind of Eastern Everyman. Stories featuring the gentle, pious Nebii Hhudur, "the eternal 'good shepherd'" (38), who represents the "idealization of poverty" (38), contrast sharply with the tales of Haroun Raschid, who personifies power and riches. Such paradoxes are, in Laurence's opinion, natural in a country where poverty dominates: thus, wealth and power are desired, but the "'poor but good and brave' person is admired" (*TP* 43).

Characterization is equally important in Somali folk tales and can take different forms. Many stories feature historical figures, such as Darod or Ishaak, the legendary founders of the Somali people. Again, paradox is paramount, as exemplified by the stories about the Sultan Wiil Waal, the generous but cruel, wise but vain, ruler. For example, in the tale of "Wiil Waal and the Silver Ring," the Sultan demands the impossible – that his wife deliver a child in his absence on pain of death, although infidelity would also be punishable by death. Only her wits save her. Laurence says, "His wife is the only person consistently able to match wits with the Sultan, and in her we see all the features a Somali values in a wife. She is clever, but she is also gentle and womanly. And for all her beauty and sharpness of wits she is still obedient and faithful to her husband"(39).

The character of 'Igaal Bowkahh contrasts sharply with that of Wiil Waal. Laurence writes, "With the character of 'Igaal Bowkahh, the modern Somali is portrayed, almost caricatured. 'Igaal is a humorous character and there is something in his essential toughness, his way of laughing in the face of disaster, his pride and jauntiness, even in the most discouraging of circumstances, that remind one very much of the pride, courage and humour of the ordinary bush Somali. Perhaps his most typically Somali characteristic is his staunch individualism" (39). She adds, "Individualism and independence are a necessary step to survival [and] 'Igaal Bowkahh, in a humorous way, illustrates this individualism and independence extremely well" (*TP* 40).

Somali folk tales feature male protagonists. The only female protagonists are wicked women or monsters, such as the grotesque figure of Deg-Der, the cannibal woman, and Arawailo, the man-hating queen – suggesting a fear of women on the part of Somali storytellers, who are male. Deg-Der, meaning "Long Ear," becomes a man-eater after bearing three daughters but no sons; eventually she is killed by her own daughters. Laurence includes two stories about Arawailo. "Arawailo and the Climbing of Mil-Milac" (126) tells how an ancient magician helps the people outwit the cruel queen's commands. "The Death of Arawailo" (128) dramatizes her murder at the hands of her own grandson, whose castration she has commanded. Women throw flowers and green branches on her grave, while men throw stones. Legend has it that this accounts for the numerous cairns of stones scattered throughout Somalia. It is ironic that both these characters were realized for Laurence by Hersi's fine acting: "when he told me of Arawailo, he made me see the barbaric splendour and the cruelty of that fabled queen" (*PCB* 177). Clara Thomas connects these characters with Hagar Shipley, Laurence's "Canadian Grotesque" (*MWML* 31). Such a category could include other poignant Manawaka characters, such as Christie Logan's simple, obese wife, Prin, in *The Diviners* and Buckle Fennick's blind, obese mother in *The Fire-Dwellers*.

"Hersi-Half-tongue," as he was called by the Somalis because of his speech impediment, was the Laurences' translator. His translations were dramatic but ungrammatical: so "His English had a grotesque lyricism about it" (*PCB* 170), Laurence recalls. But he was also an orator and a poet, known for his early love poems. Educated in a Quranic school, he was a *mullah*, or lay priest, who had read the Quran four times and discussed the *Kitab*, or The Book, with Margaret. When she asked him about Somali tales, she recalls in *The Prophet's Camel Bell*, he was noncommittal, saying, "We are not having such things presently times" (176). Once he accepted her interest in Somali folklore, he exclaimed, "Stories – if we are speaking of stories, who is knowing more of these considerations than I?" (176). So Hersi gathered tales from elders and recounted them to Margaret in English in her brushwood hut, acting them out in a dramatic fashion, "transforming himself by some alchemy of expression or stance into whatever he chose – a saint or a sultan ... taking on the characters like cloaks" (*PCB* 177) – a "Method" storyteller, in fact.

Characterization is crucial to Laurence's own fiction, as she emphasizes in numerous essays and interviews. Even in her Somali journal, *The Prophet's Camel Bell*, character is all-important, for Laurence devotes an entire chapter to each member of Jack's team: Mohamed, their cook; Arabetto, their driver; Abdi, "The Old Warrior"; and Hersi, "A Teller of Tales" – capturing their character and recording their voices. Her African fiction is filled with memorable characters, from Nathaniel Amegbe and Victor Edusei of *This Side Jordan*, to Kofi, Adamo, Tetteh, and Mammii Ama of *The Tomorrow-Tamer and Other Stories*. Characterization is also crucial to her Canadian fiction: Hagar may be the most famous character in Canadian literature, and numerous critics praise her gallery of portraits of female protagonists in her Manawaka fiction.

A second feature of Somali literature emphasized by Laurence that parallels her own fiction is the importance of moral or ethical elements. There are two main types of Somali story: the moral tale, with a strong element of religion and faith, that is intended "to instruct as well as to entertain" (42), and "'the crime *does* pay' type of story" (42), featuring the quick-witted thief. Tetteh, the central figure in Laurence's story "The Pure Diamond Man," who tries to outwit Hardacre, the Englishman who wants to witness the old African ways, is a good example of the latter type. Laurence explains that "the apparent paradox is not a real one" (44), for "characteristics of guile and craftiness plus generosity and piety can exist here within the individual person with no lack of harmony" (42). This apparent contradiction does not suggest any moral confusion, Laurence insists; rather, the contrast merely represents "a realism that recognizes the presence of both good and evil in the world and in the individual" (43) – a realism that distinguishes Laurence's own fiction and that is frequently celebrated by critics. Such contrasts, Laurence affirms – "aggressive avarice versus generosity, guile and cheating versus honesty and piety, cruelty versus kindness and wisdom, the 'poor and good' versus the 'rich and clever,' the beautiful versus the grotesque – exist in almost all folk-tales found in countries where life is hard and insecure but where religious faith flourishes" (44). Laurence compares such paradoxical tales with those of Chaucer, Boccaccio, and the Bible. "There is no real paradox except the basic one found in countries where poverty and insecurity have corrupted people but have, miraculously, been unable to stamp out their humanity – warm, hospitable, humorous, and of an amazing courage" (*TP* 45). She affirms that her goal, in her own fiction, is to "present the living individual on the printed page in all his paradox" (Cameron 103). Laurence's Manawaka characters, like Hagar Shipley and Christie Logan, realize this goal brilliantly.

Two elements in Somali folk tales that are closely related to the moral aspect are religion and magic. Wiseman notes in her review, "Often biblical in tone and quality, they are at other times filled with a primitive blend of reality and magic" (611). These two subjects are not unrelated, since the religious aspects of a tale may involve miracles. Most moral concepts have a religious base, including generosity to the poor and hospitality to strangers. The word "Islam" means literally "submission to God," and acceptance is one of the tenets of Somali religion. Laurence explains, for an inhabitant in a land where life is insecure, "complete faith in and submission to God is the only thing that saves his sanity" (45). Laurence read the Quoran in English translation and discussed the *Kitab*, The Book, with Hersi. But during the *jilal*, or drought, she was unable to emulate the Somalis' fatalistic attitude: "for myself, it did not apply, this faith, perhaps because I had never needed it the way they did. I viewed it from the outside. As far as I was concerned, God was deaf. If we did not hear the sound of each other's voices, no one else would" (*PCB* 64). Religion, however, is central to all her African and Canadian fiction. In *This Side Jordan*, Nathaniel Amegbe is torn between the old gods of his ancestors' Ashanti religion and the new God of the Christian mission that educated him. In her Cameron sister novels, *A Jest of God* and *The Fire-Dwellers*, Rachel and Stacey carry on dialogues with God that are central to their development. Hagar's epiphany is catalyzed by the hymn "*All people that on earth do dwell*" (*SA* 291).

Two other features of Somali folk tales that Laurence isolates for comment are a sense of the dramatic and a sense of humour. Regarding the dramatic, Laurence notes the importance of timing to build up suspense by delaying the revelation, plus the use of repetition as a ritual to intensify suspense and dramatic effect, as well as the use of surprise, as in "The Great Surprise." She explains how the dramatic effect of these stories is intensified by the talent of the storyteller, for every good Somali storyteller is also an accomplished actor. Laurence acquired a sense of the dramatic from storytellers Hersi Jama and Ahmed Nasir, and her own fiction is highly dramatic. Even her Somali journal is composed of vivid vignettes filled with suspense, such as the story of the wounded cheetah or the tribesmen held at bay only by the rifle that Margaret was incapable of firing. She employs dialogue as well as dialect to dramatize events in her African and Canadian fiction. For example, the fourth chapter of *The Fire-Dwellers*, set in the MacAindra kitchen at breakfast time, is written like a film script with sound effects but no narrative signifiers (86–9).

Humour is also prevalent in Somali prose, and it may take one of three forms – the humour of the ridiculous or fantastic, the humour of the stupid and absurd, or the humour of cleverness and sharpness of wit. The last type is illustrated by the thief story, a kind of humour that may be used to convey the moral of the tale. One of the qualities that distinguishes Laurence's own fiction (and that has been almost totally ignored by critics) is humour: Archipelago and Doree, the delightful denizens of "The Perfume Sea," are humorous examples from her African tales. Her Manawaka fiction is also filled with humour: Stacey MacAindra of *The Fire-Dwellers* has a good sense of humour, as did her creator, and even the life story of Hagar Shipley, that "holy terror" (304), tragic as it is, has comic elements that intensify, rather than diminish, its pathos.

"A Labour of Love"

Laurence labelled *A Tree for Poverty* "a labour of love" (*PCB* 248), the fruit of what she called a "seven-years' love affair with a continent" (*TYS* 18). As Fiona Sparrow affirms, "*A Tree for Poverty* is a work that Laurence thought of with affection. She would also have been entitled to think of it with pride" (69). In fact, it was because of *A Tree for Poverty*, which Laurence terms "a small book of Somali poetry and prose translations" (*HS* 106), that she was invited to Mogadishu for the Somali Independence Day celebrations in Hargeisa on 1 July 1966 – as recorded in her *Heart of a Stranger* essay, "The Wild Blue Yonder" (101–6). Although the Somali Republic had broken off diplomatic relations with Britain, it invited ten individuals to fly out from England, all expenses paid, to participate in the celebrations. Clearly, the affection that inspired her translation was reciprocated by the Somalis.

Wendy Roy concludes "'I Was Against It': Margaret Laurence and British Imperialism in Somalia," in *Maps of Difference: Canada, Women, and Travel* (2005), with these words: "Laurence's legacy in Somalia thus is not her short-termed administrative support work for the British colonial government as it prepared for independence but, rather, her translations and transcriptions of Somali orature and the thoughtful, often complicated, and conflicted mapping of issues of imperialism and gender evident in her travel narrative" (209). Indeed, *A Tree for Poverty* became a source for future translations and studies of Somali folk literature. As Micere Mugo asserts in her review of *A*

Tree for Poverty, "Metaphorically, Laurence's voice in *A Tree for Poverty* is the voice of the forerunner 'crying in the wilderness' pointing out 'the way'" (87).

These Somali translations also helped to point the way back to Canada for Laurence: as she explains in "Ivory Tower or Grassroots?: The Novelist as Socio-Political Being," "I had come back home to Canada via Africa, both physically and spiritually" (157). She could have added "creatively," for these translations also enriched her creative writing. Clearly she learned much about language and metaphor, characterization and dramatization from translating Somali folk-literature, both poetry and prose, that enhanced her own writing, both African and Canadian. Thus, her exploration of Somali oral literature is also the voice of the forerunner of her fiction pointing out the way to the fascinating world of her African and Canadian novels and stories.

CHAPTER 5

"The Sleeping Giant":
Long Drums and Cannons: Nigerian Dramatists and Novelists, 1952–1966

In "Margaret Laurence and Africa," Craig Tapping claims, "Canadian literature is the sleeping giant behind the description of Nigerian literature in *Long Drums and Cannons*," for "Laurence's critical endeavours on behalf of African literature determine what it is she will attempt on returning to Canada" (73). *Long Drums and Cannons: Nigerian Dramatists and Novelists, 1952–1966* (1968), Laurence's fifth and final African text, like her first book, *A Tree for Poverty: Somali Poetry and Prose* (1954), reveals the connections between her African and Canadian writing. The parallels between the aspects of Nigerian literature that she praises and the aspects of her Canadian fiction that readers admire are striking. These parallels are no coincidence, for Laurence composed her African critique while writing her Manawaka cycle. Moreover, she was drawn to writers who shared her values and was influenced by them in turn. Thus, Nigerian literature can be seen to have influenced her Canadian fiction. It will be valuable to demonstrate the truth of Tapping's sleeping giant metaphor. But first, a review of the origins, purpose, and value of Laurence's Nigerian critique will be useful, since this text, out of print from 1968 to 2001, is unfamiliar to many readers.

Laurence composed *Long Drums and Cannons* to bring the new wealth of Nigerian literature in English to the attention of Western readers. It covers the period from 1952 to 1966 – the fifteen years in which Nigerian writers created "a kind of Renaissance," as she claims (11).[1] She locates the origins of this literary renaissance in the new Nigerian universities, especially the University of Ibadan, founded in 1948; in the MBARI writers' and artists' club, founded in 1954; and in literary journals such as *Black Orpheus*, founded in 1957 and edited by such distinguished scholars as Ulli Beier, Jahnheinz Jahn, Wole Soyinka, Ezekiel Mphalele, and Ronald Dathorne (11). Laurence dates this renaissance from 1952, when Amos Tutuola's *The Palm-Wine Drinkard* was the first novel in English by a Nigerian to be published outside Nigeria and widely read in the West: "Since then there has been an outpouring of plays and novels, a kind of renaissance, the flourishing of a new literature which has drawn sustenance both from traditional oral literature and from the present and rapidly changing society" (11). She concludes her study with Soyinka's experimental novel *The Interpreters*, Clark's *Ozidi*, Ekwensi's *Iska*, and Achebe's *A Man of the People*, all published in 1966 – some of them, especially Achebe's novel, reflecting the conflict that was already beginning in Nigeria.

In *Long Drums*, she devotes one chapter to each of five outstanding Nigerian writers of fiction and drama: "Voices of Life, Dance of Death" celebrates the plays of Wole Soyinka; "Rituals of Destiny" focuses on the plays of poet John Pepper Clark; "The Thickets of Our Separateness" praises the novels of Chinua Achebe; "A Twofold Forest" explores the fiction of Amos Tutuola; "Masks of the City" examines the novels of Cyprian Ekwensi; and "Other Voices" introduces six promising new writers – T.M. Aluko, Elechi Amadi, Nkem Nwankwo, Flora Nwapa, Onuora Nzekwu, and Gabriel Okara – almost all of whom validated Laurence's prophecy of literary achievement. As G.D. Killam claims, "Margaret's book remains one of the surest ways into an understanding of the writing she reviews, especially into Achebe, Soyinka, and Clark, authors whose writing is progressively more studied in the world beyond, as well as in Africa" (1987, 33).

Interestingly, Laurence chooses not to address Nigerian poetry in *Long Drums* because, as she explains in her introduction, "this field is now extensive enough to require a separate commentary" (13). This choice seems ironic in light of her passionate interest in translating Somali oral poetry for *A Tree for Poverty*. But it does reflect the fact that fiction dominated her creative interests during the sixties, and it also suggests the importance of the dramatic element in her novels.

Laurence introduces each author with a brief biography, as well as information about the cultural background that might be unknown to a Western audience unfamiliar with African tribal traditions. She provides à commentary on the major works of each author that is clearly intended to introduce a reader to new material, for it consists primarily of summaries that are studded with insights, as she comments intepretively and contextually on the artistry of these writers. As Clara Thomas affirms in *The Manawaka World of Margaret Laurence*, *Long Drums and Cannons* "is a work of expository scholarship and careful background research into tribal rites and customs" (189). Fiona Sparrow judges in *Into Africa with Margaret Laurence*, "Laurence locates each new text within its regional context, but she never denies it a place within a wider field of reference, within a world where boundaries are recognized, but only because they can be crossed" (204). And Tapping concludes, "She gets it right every time, and with each writer she discusses" (70).

Long Drums and Cannons began with a request to write four scripts on Nigerian literature for the BBC, which wanted an impression of Nigeria as seen through the eyes of its contemporary writers (King 220). Laurence, who had taken a passionate interest in African affairs after her seven years in Somalia and Ghana, and who had already published four texts about Africa, embraced this project enthusiastically. Residing in England from 1962 to 1972 – first in Hampstead, London, and then in Elm Cottage in Penn, Buckinghamshire – she had the advantage of the cultural opportunities of London. The 1965 Commonwealth Festival gave her a chance to see plays by Soyinka and Clark. Her Macmillan editor Alan Maclean recalls that Laurence had an affair with Jamal, an ambassador from an African country to the court of St James (Duncan 15) – a married man with seven children, whom she dubbed "the old lion" (King 224) – who introduced her to African artists. As she reports, "I had met a number of young Nigerian writers, including Wole Soyinka and the poet Christopher Okigbo, through mutual friends in London, and had begun to read other works by Nigerians" (*DE* 184–5). Laurence's numerous annotated and underlined African texts bear witness to her familiarity with African literature, as does her extensive index to *Long Drums* (187–8).[2]

On 16 January 1966, she wrote to Adele Wiseman: "After about 4 months reading and thinking about Nigerian writing, traditional and contemporary, I feel I've taken a do-it-yourself course in contemporary African writing, and I have so much material it nearly breaks my heart, as there isn't anything I can do with it, but maybe I'll write a book, which would be no hell critically as I am no academic critic and don't even know the jargon, but it might be interesting in an amateur way" (York). She resolved to collect her scripts on Nigerian writers into a book, writing to Wiseman on 7 July 1966, "I want to know about Africa," and "I've always wanted to do some really close literary criticism" (*SL* 210–11). On 2 May 1967, she reported, "I finished the *final* work on the Nigeria book yesterday, and handed it over last night to Alan Maclean" (*SL* 216). Thus, she composed *Long Drums and Cannons* while writing *A Jest of God* (1966) and *The Fire-Dwellers* (1969).

Laurence was a novelist, however, not an academic, and she was apologetic about her limitations as a critic and scholar. In a sentence from her typescript that was excised from *Long Drums and Cannons*, she acknowledges, "I do not delude myself that this is a work of literary criticism. It is a commentary, written from the point of view of a reader and a writer."[3] This writerly approach allows Laurence to include her own insights into Nigerian authors' creativity and artistry and to produce a readerly text that eschews jargon. In *Dance on the Earth: A Memoir*, she recalls, "I continued to work on a survey I was writing of contemporary Nigerian writers ... *Long Drums and Cannons* was never intended to be a deep analysis. It was, rather, a survey and an interpretation, from the viewpoint of a reasonably skilled reader who stood outside the culture and who hoped to make these works better known and more accessible" (*DE* 184–5). Fiona Sparrow judges, "the value of her work as a pioneering analysis is considerable, and her line by line commentary is not without many well-argued and perceptive judgments, which, more than twenty years later, have lost none of their point and value" (162). Laurence wished to make those literary giants Wole Soyinka and Chinua Achebe, whom she calls "one of the best novelists now writing anywhere" (*LDC* 222), better known to Western readers. She succeeded in her mission.

In "Margaret Laurence and Africa," Tapping recalls that introducing himself as a Canadian to a university class in Eastern Nigeria in 1979 was greeted by an enthusiastic chant: "Canada, Canada." When he asked the source of the enthusiasm, one student explained, "one Canadian had done more than any other person to promote Nigerian writing internationally and, in so doing, had examined the crucial role writers play in building a culture. And that Canadian was Margaret Laurence in her book *Long Drums and Cannons*" (66).

Long Drums and Cannons, the first study of Nigerian literature, was hailed as a pioneering work by reviewers when it was first published by Macmillan in Britain in 1968 and by Praeger in America in 1969. The critics who reviewed it most enthusiastically were Canadian – probably as a result of Laurence's reputation in Canada as a novelist because she had published her first Manawaka novels, *The Stone Angel* in 1964 and *A Jest of God* in 1966, before she published *Long Drums and Cannons* in 1968. Moreover, many Canadian readers were less familiar with African literature and cultural studies at that time. Therefore Clara Thomas judges, in her 1969 review "Ascent and Agony," that "*Long Drums and Cannons* is an important guidebook and commentary on Nigerian literature" (92). James Dale of McMaster University, which purchased the typescript of *Long Drums and Cannons* in 1969, concludes, "Laurence has done a great service in making Nigerian literature better known ... for this is much the best and fullest account yet provided of Nigerian prose writing in English." Dave Godfrey judges in "*Piquefort's Column*," "The newcomer to this part of the jungle [*sic*] will find her an intelligent and understanding guide; her own fans will find in this study an explanation for some of the depths of *The Stone Angel*" (249). Ironically, *Long Drums and Cannons* was not published in Canada until the following century.

International reviewers – such as Alistair Niven, who calls *Long Drums and Cannons*, in the *Legon Observer*, "perhaps the best book relating to Nigerian literature in English that has been produced" (17); Lewis Nkosi, who deems it, in "A Question of Literary Stewardship" in *Africa Report*, "a modest book written with admirable clarity and simplicity" (70); and Eric Sellin, who, in the *Journal of Modern Literature*, considers it most valuable for the novice – are generally positive. The anonymous author of "Ways into Africa" in the *Times Literary Supplement* claims Laurence "eminently succeeds in her aim: even those who have had little knowledge of Nigerian writers before reading her book will be convinced by her perceptive analysis that this is indeed now a significant part of world literature." John Povey states, in the *Journal of Asian and African Studies*, "If I had to advise a reader of one book that would be the most useful introduction to this new writing I think it would be Margaret Lawrence's [sic] volume. I would recommend it for the precise and common-sense explanations it gives concerning writings which have too often been treated by critics not as works of literature but as anthropological, linguistic or political evidence of contemporary African conditions" (110). He writes, "Margaret Lawrence [sic] brings us back to the recognition that these are authors as well as racial and national spokesmen and it is a valuable and healthy reminder" (110).

The most balanced reviews come from Canadian Commonwealth literature specialists: G.D. Killam applauds Laurence's study: "Her arguments are exact and convincing" (1970, 110). Anthony Boxhill judges, "Quite apart from its content, this book is very significant because it is written by a Canadian about Nigerian writing. As a Canadian it is easier for her to be disinterested than a Nigerian critic, or a British critic, whose countrymen were the colonizers mentioned in so much of the writing" (106).

Unfortunately, *Long Drums and Cannons* did not receive the circulation or the recognition that it deserved, although Chinua Achebe singled it out for special praise in his 1975 study, *Morning Yet on Creation Day* (18), largely because it was outdated before its publication by the outbreak of civil war in 1967 in Nigeria – "Africa's wounded giant," as Laurence labels it in her unpublished introduction to *Long Drums and Cannons*.[4] In her 1968 "Author's Note" (13) to *Long Drums and Cannons*, she laments the death of Christopher Okigbo, whose poem "Heavensgate" provided the title and epigraph for her study: "long drums and cannons: / the spirit in the ascent": "The title of this book, taken many months ago from one of his poems, now seems cruelly ironic" (13).[5] Thomas concludes her review, "Ascent and Agony" thus: "The cost of the ascent has always been great: now, literature cannot begin to measure its agony" (93). In 1969 Laurence wrote "Tribalism As Us Versus Them" (*LDC* 223–32), a previously unpublished essay that forms, in effect, an afterword to *Long Drums and Cannons*, and which is therefore included as an appendix to the 2001 edition. Beginning with the statement, "Tribalism would seem to be central to the present civil war in Nigeria and Biafra" (*LDC* 223), the essay is an analysis of tribalism in Africa and its relevance to contemporary Nigerian literature.

Recently, Canadian critics have re-evaluated *Long Drums and Cannons*, concluding that it is still relevant three decades later. Killam judges, "*Long Drums and Cannons* is still a source of enduring insight into the origins and strengths of Nigerian writing" (*LDC* x). He also claims, "[Laurence] has left an important and enduring legacy in *Long Drums and Cannons*. The book is as valid today as when it was published in 1968" (1987, 33). Sparrow concludes, "*Long Drums and Cannons* is still a valuable work and essential reading for those embarking on a study of Nigerian literature since it explains its beginnings with thoroughness and sensitivity" (163). Tapping asserts, "*Long Drums and Cannons* cannot but astonish the reader granted the hindsight of the present. The book is historically significant ... What is striking is just how exact and scrupulous, and therefore undated, Laurence's judgments, insights and explanations are" (70). And King concludes, "*Long Drums* is a good critical book, especially if it is seen as the work of a professional writer of fiction passing judgment on the works of her peers and, in the process, revealing to herself and her readers some of the controlling ideas in her own writing" (221).

Laurence's study of Nigerian literature still has significance for a contemporary reader, but its significance has reversed. No longer do Western readers need any introduction to Nigerian writers, especially Chinua Achebe and Wole Soyinka, who have long since achieved international acclaim, as the 1986 awarding of the Nobel Prize for Literature to Soyinka illustrates. Rather, Laurence's critique illuminates not so much Nigerian literature as the author's own values. *Long Drums and Cannons* now has reflexive value as a historical document chronicling the perspective of a Western writer and as a means of revealing Laurence's own artistry.

Canadian critics have observed parallels between Laurence's fiction and the African writers she discusses in *Long Drums and Cannons*. Patricia Morley asserts, in *Margaret Laurence: The Long Journey Home*, "Because she feels a sympathetic identification with many Africans, her comments on their work reveal many of her own attitudes towards writing" (35). James King judges in *The Life of Margaret Laurence*, "It is obvious that in the work of Wole Soyinka, Chinua Achebe, Amos

Tutuola, Flora Nwapa and their contemporaries Margaret Laurence also saw reflected many of her own themes" (221). Paul Comeau states, in *Margaret Laurence's Epic Imagination*, "she recognized the tremendous influence of Africa as the crucible for such central themes in her later work as survival, exile, independence, tribalism and communication, to name but a few" (15). Craig Tapping claims, in "Margaret Laurence and Africa," *Long Drums* "sheds further light on Laurence's literary mission in Manawaka and environs," for "the critical terms with which Laurence describes Achebe's early achievement prefigure her own Manawaka cycle" (70, 73).

The fact that Laurence wrote *Long Drums and Cannons* during the decade when she composed her Manawaka cycle is relevant. Thomas judges, in "'Morning Yet on Creation Day': A Study of *This Side Jordan*," "She was particularly influenced then, I believe, by her recent work in *Long Drums and Cannons* on the Nigerian writers, especially Achebe, Soyinka and Okigbo" (104). In "'Canada, Africa, Canada': Laurence's Unbroken Journey," Morley concludes: "*Long Drums and Cannons* (1968), published in the middle of the decade in which her Manawaka works were produced, is as much a spiritual autobiography as is her earlier travel memoir, *The Prophet's Camel Bell*. Through an analysis of Nigerian dramatists and novelists, Laurence reveals her own way of seeing, a vision which proves to have surprisingly close parallels with those of modern Nigerian writers" (81–2).

While several scholars have noted parallels between Laurence's fiction and her commentary on African writers, these parallels have not yet been examined fully. Examining the features of Nigerian authors' work that she praises in *Long Drums and Cannons* can reveal how African writing influenced Laurence's Canadian fiction: first, the emphasis on individual character and the protagonist's dilemma; second, themes of respect for the gods of the ancestors and the necessity of freedom and communication; and third, the use of myth and metaphor, individual idiom and poetic prose to convey these universal themes. She concludes *Long Drums* in this way: "Nigerian novelists and dramatists have constantly expressed in their work themes which are not confined to one place or one time – the individual's effort to define himself, his need to come to terms with his ancestors and his gods, his uncertainties in relation to others, his conflicts in the face of his own opposed loyalties, the dichotomy of his longing for both peace and war, his perpetual battle to free himself from the fetters of the past and the compulsions of the present" (181).

Laurence praises Nigerian writers, especially Achebe and Soyinka, for their characterization: "[Achebe's] ability to create memorable and living characters place[s] him among the best novelists now writing in any country in the English language" (89); and "[Soyinka's] people are never ciphers or symbols, always persons speaking in their own voices" (15). She concludes "Voices of Life, Dance of Death," her discussion of Soyinka's writing, with this eloquent encomium: "Soyinka's writing is life-filled, overflowing with energy, capable of realizing human personalities and catching the sound of one particular voice, at times intensely comic, coloured with rhythm and dance, with drums and masquerades. But underneath, there is a concern with the inner territory of the spirit, a painful appraisal of the usually hidden parts of the mind. This strong undercurrent in his writing places him, ultimately, among the chroniclers of the areas of darkness within us all" (69).

Laurence praises portraits of women in Nigerian literature. She admires the eponymous heroine of Flora Nwapa's *Efuru* (1966), which "takes place almost totally within the minds and society of women" (169), for, "although Flora Nwapa's women belong in an Ibo village, they convey insights which are valid anywhere" (169). She also praises female protagonists portrayed by male novelists, such as Ihuoma, the heroine of Elechi Amadi's *The Concubine* (1966), which portrays "the mystery at the center of being," the "the age-old conflict of man with his gods" (163). She says, "Ekwensi's women come alive and step from the printed page much more often than his men do, and he has created a few really memorable women characters" (133), including the eponymous protagonists of *Jagua Nana* (1961) and *Iska* (1966): "In *Jagua Nana* he has created a magnificent and fully alive character" (136–7), who will "remain alive for a long time" (140); Filia is nick-named Iska, meaning "wind," suggesting "Africa's wind of change" (149).

In numerous essays and interviews, Laurence affirms the paramount importance of character to her own writing. In fact, she says she is possessed by her protagonists – like the dancers who are possessed by the spirits of the ancestors in Nigerian masquerade drama or the storytellers whose tales she translates in *A Tree for Poverty*. Laurence has created powerful female individuals in her Manawaka cycle: Hagar,

Rachel, Stacey, Vanessa, and Morag comprise the most memorable gallery of portraits of women characters in Canadian literature.

She also emphasizes the importance of the character's dilemma, torn between loyalty to the past and the exigencies of the present, a dilemma that is vividly represented by Achebe's protagonists: Okonkwo in *Things Fall Apart* (1962), Obi Okonkwo in *No Longer at Ease* (1963), and Ezeulu, the priest of Ulu, in *Arrow of God* (1965). For Nigerian writers, such dilemmas or conflicts include "the clash between generations, the social and individual disturbances brought about by a period of transition, the slow dying of the destructive aspects of tribalism, [and] the anguish and inadequacy of uncompromising individualism as an alternative to tribalism" (12). Laurence views tribal conflict as Nigeria's major dilemma in her essay "Tribalism As Us Versus Them," where she inquires, "How does tribalism appear in the writings of Nigerian novelists and dramatists in the period between 1952 and 1966?" (223), the same period she covers in *Long Drums and Cannons*. She praises Nigerian literature in her introduction to *Long Drums* for "the insight it gives not only into immediate and local dilemmas but, through these, into the human dilemma as a whole" (13) because, as she affirms in her conclusion, "their dilemma is not theirs alone. It is very profoundly all mankind's" (231).

Laurence frequently emphasizes in essays and interviews the importance of her protagonists' dilemmas: "I like to think that my books basically deal with human dilemmas which could be understood by somebody in Africa or New Zealand" (Gibson 193). In her 1978 essay "Ivory Tower or Grassroots? The Novelist as Socio-Political Being," she writes, "Fiction ... speaks first and foremost of individual characters, and through them it speaks of our dilemmas and our aspirations" (259). Her emphasis on the individual's dilemma reveals her interest in conflicting themes of past and present, individualism and tribalism, freedom and ancestry, communication and denial: "Certain themes recur throughout contemporary Nigerian writing. There is a strong desire to reassess the historical past, to revalue the life of the village and the traditional forms of society, to rediscover roots which were severed. Many Nigerian writers have been concerned with an attempt ... to reunite with a past which was for several generations lost or despised ... a past composed of real and vulnerable people, their ancestors, not the figments of missionary and colonialist imaginations" (178). Laurence felt so strongly about the mission of Nigerian writers to redeem their ancestral past that she revisits it a decade later in "Ivory Tower or Grassroots?: The Novelist as Socio-Political Being":

> In Nigeria, as in many parts of Africa, people lost their own self-value, their own distinctive voices, throughout three generations of colonialism. They were taught as children to despise their ancestors and the old gods, and the result was, of course, that they learned to despise themselves. Chinua Achebe's generation of writers (which includes very many writers of distinction such as Wole Soyinka, John Pepper Clark, Cyprian Ekwensi, T.M. Aluko, Elechi Amadi, Flora Nwapa, and Gabriel Okara) has drawn on their relatively newfound sense of self-worth and on their people's past, and has tried consciously to impart these values to their own people, to combat the psychic damage done during the years of domination by British imperialism. (IT 253)

Laurence, as we know from her Somali memoir, *The Prophet's Camel Bell*, was passionately anti-imperialist: "my feeling about imperialism was very simple – I was against it" (*PCB* 25). And in *Heart of a Stranger* she identifies herself as "anti-imperialist from a long way back" (*HS* 100). She applauds Nigerian writers' mission to express the forgotten voices of their gods and ancestors. In her preface to *Long Drums and Cannons*, she explains the mission of Nigerian writers in these words:

> Modern Nigerian literature interprets Africa, both past and present, from the inside. Africa was interpreted and misinterpreted by outsiders for long enough. Now its own writers are engaged in reassessing their past, in rediscovering their inheritance, in interpreting themselves both to their own people and to the rest of the world. This process has been of enormous value, both inside and outside Africa. To several generations of West Africans, educated in mission schools and brought up with a view of Africa which was superimposed upon them from the outside, the work of writers such as Chinua Achebe and Wole Soyinka must surely have done much to restore a true sense of their own past, a

knowledge of a tribal society which was neither idyllic, as the views of some nationalists would have it, nor barbaric, as many missionaries and European administrators wished and needed to believe. (12)[6]

Laurence also explains in her 1969 essay, "Ten Years' Sentences," that Nigerian writers created a renaissance by "drawing upon their cultural past and relating it to the present, seeking links with the ancestors and the old gods in order to discover who they themselves were" (30).

Laurence sees the ancestral past haunting the present in Nigerian writing and in her own work too, because she believes "the past and the future are both always present" (TNV 157). As she affirms in "A Statement of Faith," "the ancestors in the end become everyone's ancestors" (122). In "A Place to Stand On" in *Heart of a Stranger*, she discusses the "attempt to understand one's background and one's past, sometimes even a more distant past which one has not personally experienced" (*HS* 6): "This sort of exploration can be clearly seen in the works of contemporary African writers, many of whom re-create their people's past in novels and plays in order to recover a sense of themselves, an identity and a feeling of value from which they were separated by two or three generations of colonialism and missionizing. They have found it necessary, in other words, to come to terms with their ancestors and their gods in order to be able to accept the past and be at peace with the dead, without being stifled or threatened by that past" (*HS* 6). This is precisely Laurence's own approach in her fiction, as she explains in *Heart of a Stranger*: "Oddly enough, it was only several years ago, when I began doing research into contemporary Nigerian writing and its background, that I began to see how much my own writing had followed the same pattern – the attempt to assimilate the past, partly in order to be freed from it, partly in order to try to understand myself and perhaps others of my generation, through seeing where we had come from" (*HS* 6). When she created her first Canadian heroine, Hagar Currie of *The Stone Angel*, she returned to an ancestral past: "I had to begin approaching my background and my past through my grandparents' generation," for Hagar "incorporates many of the qualities of my grandparents' generation" (*HS* 6-7) – just as Achebe began with his grandparents' generation in his first novel, *Things Fall Apart*.

We can see similar conflicts recreated in Laurence's African fiction, especially *This Side Jordan*, where her central character, mission-educated Nathaniel Amegbe, trapped between the tribal past of his father, the *Kyerema*, or drummer, in an Ashanti village and his own present in the city of Accra, is helpless to pursue the future: "I belong between yesterday and today" (106), he laments. Ironically, he teaches "African Civilizations of the Past" (22) at "Futura Academy." Amegbe hopes the future will resolve the conflicts between past and present in the person of his newborn son, as he exhorts him to "Cross Jordan, Joshua" (282). In her Manawaka cycle, the need to respect ancestors, while freeing oneself of the past in order to go forward into the future, can be seen in all her Canadian heroines, especially Vanessa MacLeod's rebellion against her patriarchal grandfather in *A Bird in the House*.

Laurence says, "My writing, then, has been my own attempt to come to terms with the past. I see this process as the gradual one of freeing oneself from the stultifying aspect of the past, while at the same time beginning to see its true value" (*HS* 8). She explores Nigerian writers' progress toward independence in terms of the protagonist's "perpetual battle to free himself from the fetters of the past and the compulsions of the present" (*LDC* 181). The theme of freedom is closely connected to the value of the past, for one must appreciate the past while freeing oneself from its fetters.

Freedom is central to her own African fiction, as she dramatizes the process of independence: *This Side Jordan* employs epigraphs drawn from the Akan proverb, "Oh God, there is something above, let it reach me," as well as "Slogans from African 'mammy-lorries'" demanding freedom. *The Tomorrow-Tamer* ends with Mammii Ama chanting "Free-Dom" in the final story "A Gourdful of Glory" (242). Laurence cites the "quest for freedom" as central to her own fiction (*IT* 258), for all her protagonists seek freedom from the shackles of the past.

Clearly, the theme of communication is closely related to that of freedom. In "The Thickets of Our Separateness," her chapter on Achebe in *Long Drums and Cannons*, Laurence emphasizes his focus on communication as he "seeks to send human voices through the thickets of our separateness" (112): "Achebe's writing also conveys the feeling that we must attempt to communicate, however imperfectly, if we are not to succumb to despair or madness" (112). G.D. Killam, in his introduction to *A Jest of God*, claims, "the problem of communication is central in Margaret Laurence's novels" (np). In *Heart of a Stranger*, Laurence writes, "if we are really to know the reality of another, we must communicate with what is almost the only means we have – human speech" (159). Rachel Cameron must learn to communicate or perish, and the breakdown of communication in Stacey's family is represented by the fact that her youngest child, Jen, cannot or will not speak. Recalling her friendship with Achebe in *Dance on the Earth: A Memoir*, Laurence writes, "Knowing that, in our different ways, Achebe and I have been trying to do much the same sort of thing all our writing lives, I recognized that communication [between African and Western writers] could be possible" (153).

Laurence claims, "The best of these [Nigerian] writers have also chosen themes which are at once universal and able to carry their particular experience" (*LDC* 178). Paradoxically, authors achieve universality, in her view, via vivid particularity. She admires writing that is rooted in real landscapes – from Tutuola's jungle, through Soyinka's swamps, to Ekwensi's city – that paints the forests and deserts of Nigeria as vividly as her own writing portrays the Canadian prairies.

Nigerian characters are often torn between a rural past and an urban present, and Laurence represents that conflict vividly in her African and Canadian fiction, as her characters migrate from family farm or small town to the big city. For example, Nathaniel Amegbe moves from an Ashanti village to the busy city of Accra in *This Side Jordan*, and Adamo abandons his village for the military band of the colonialist army in "The Voices of Adamo" in *The Tomorrow-Tamer and Other Stories*. Hagar, Rachel, Stacey, and Morag all leave Manawaka for the metropolis of Vancouver.

Laurence praises Nigerian writers for their *form* as well as their content, particularly for their ability to embody their themes in suggestive symbolism, lively dialogue, and eloquent, stylish prose. Laurence admires the symbolic richness of Nigerian writers, especially Soyinka. She is particularly interested in his use of the Yoruba *abiku* and the Ibo *ogbanje*, the talking drums and dancing masks. Both are important to her own creative writing: her first published short story, "The Drummer of All the World" (1956), opens her collection of stories, *The Tomorrow-Tamer* (1963), set in the emergent nation, Ghana. Metaphorical masks pervade her work, notably in the story "The Mask of the Bear" in *A Bird in the House*, where she writes of "the Bear

Mask of the Haida Indians": "before it became a museum piece, the mask had concealed a man" (*BH* 86). Water symbolism is the undercurrent that flows through all her fiction: just as the river is central to Soyinka's *Swamp Dwellers* and Clark's *Raft*, so "The river [that] flowed both ways" (*D* 11) is crucial to *The Diviners*. Killam concludes, "Margaret Laurence's artistic and moral fastidiousness is nowhere more certain than in her essays in *Long Drums and Cannons*" (1987, 33).

Laurence praises Nigerian writers' adaptation of English to communicate an African reality – from the eloquence of Soyinka through the quirkiness of Ekwensi to the bitter irony of Achebe: "Soyinka's ability to translate into English words the rhythms and the beliefs of Yoruba drumming and mask dancing; J.P. Clark's terse and formal lines which are so effective in dealing with the rituals he is exploring; Okara's use of Ijaw speech patterns in order to create a prose which is also a kind of poetry; Ekwensi's knack of catching the tone of the city dweller's speech with its jazziness like highlife music; the precision of Aluko's writing when he mimics a newspaper article which is a hybrid English, combining Yoruba oratory with mission-school sloganising – all these are ways in which Nigerian writers have made of English a language which is specifically their own" (*LDC* 178). Laurence quotes Achebe's essay on "English and the African Writer": "The African writer should aim to use ... an English which is at once universal and able to carry his peculiar experience" (177). Achebe succeeds. Laurence's own fiction is distinguished by her ability to capture her characters' individual idiom – from the child Vanessa, through the housewife Stacey, to the matriarch Hagar: "The main concern of a writer remains that of somehow creating the individual on the printed page, of catching the tones and accents of human speech, of setting down the conflicts of people who are as real to him as himself. If he does this well, and as truthfully as he can, his writing may sometimes reach out beyond any national boundary. The best of these Nigerian plays and novels reveal something of ourselves to us, whoever and wherever we are" (13). And that is what distinguishes Laurence's own fiction, as well as Achebe's novels. As W.H. New states, "Laurence mastered the rhythms and cadences of the Canadian speaking voice" (*ML* 1).

Long Drums and Cannons has value as a pioneering study of Nigerian literature that illuminates its subject *and* as a historical document chronicling the perspective of a Western woman writer long before post-colonial studies became current. Laurence recalls in her memoir, "I found it exciting that African writers were producing what I thought I and many Canadian writers were producing: a truly non-colonial literature" (*DE* 185). No longer can we view Laurence simply as a Canadian writer. Rather, she is a post-colonial writer who, as Killam claims, was "a forerunner of … 'cultural studies'" (*LDC* viii). Nowhere is this made clearer than in *Long Drums and Cannons*, called by Chinua Achebe an "important book by a great ambassador of literary culture" (*LDC* back cover). Killam claims, "[T]he wisdom and comprehensive humanity which inform all of Margaret's writing remains in this last – and perhaps by her own account, the best – of her 'African' books" (1987, 33). Christian Riegel states, "*Long Drums and Cannons* establishes Laurence as a post-colonial writer" (*LDC* xii). And Abdul-Rasheed Na'Allah claims, "*Long Drums and Cannons* retains its first and forever relevant position to the cross-cultural paradigm encouraged in Elaloro discourse. … When Laurence's melodious drums beat for Nigerian writing, our rhythmic steps roll across her Canadian prairie into the world's scholarly spaces" (*LDC* lviii, lxi). Equally important, *Long Drums* now has reflexive value as a reflection of the influence of Nigerian literature on one of Canada's greatest novelists. In introducing Nigeria's "Other Voices" to Western readers in *Long Drums and Cannons* and in translating Somali folk literature for *A Tree for Poverty*, Laurence discovered her own voice.

Laurence concludes *Long Drums and Cannons* by claiming, "Nigerian writers have already built up a body of work which is of interest and value not only in Africa but everywhere in the world where there are people who find in literature one way of discovering more fully the reality of others and of exploring the mystery of themselves" (181). In her foreword to *Heart of a Stranger*, she explains the connection between her experience of other cultures and her own creative processes in terms of exploration of uncharted territories, both literal and figurative (3). Thus, *Long Drums and Cannons* can not only illuminate Nigerian literature and reflect Laurence's post-colonial perspective; it can also illuminate our exploration of those uncharted territories we call the Manawaka cycle.

"The Face of Africa": *The Prophet's Camel Bell, This Side Jordan,* and *The Tomorrow-Tamer*

Laurence learned about Africa not only from translating Somali oral literature for *A Tree for Poverty* and critiquing Nigerian literature for *Long Drums and Cannons.* She also learned about Africa from living in African countries, observing and interacting with the people, and recording her impressions in the Somali diaries that produced her travel memoir, *The Prophet's Camel Bell* – "that best of Canadian travel books" (30), as Woodcock labels it in "Speaker for the Tribes."

The Prophet's Camel Bell conveys Laurence's impressions of the Somalis and her awareness of her own anomalous role in Africa in ways that prophesy her portrayal of her African characters in her Ghanaian novel, *This Side Jordan,* and Ghanaian stories collected in *The Tomorrow-Tamer.* Her emphasis on self-empowerment for her Canadian heroines has its roots in her depiction of the struggle for independence in the two African countries in which she lived, Somalia and Ghana.

THE PROPHET'S CAMEL BELL: "A STRANGER IN A STRANGE LAND"

The Prophet's Camel Bell – or *New Wind in a Dry Land* in the American edition – is judged by George Woodcock, in his afterword to *This Side Jordan,* to be "arguably the best travel book ever written by a

Canadian" (*SJ* 284). Patricia Morley claims simply, in *Margaret Laurence: The Long Journey Home*, "This is one of the finest and most evocative travel books ever written" (60).

When Jack was employed by the British colonialist Department of Public Works, Margaret was initially not allowed to accompany him because the DPW did not provide accommodation for married British couples. When Jack described Margaret as "a hardy *Canadian* girl," however, "an accomplished woodswoman, a kind of female Daniel Boone,"[1] they relented and allowed her to go with him. And so Margaret accompanied her husband to Somaliland in January 1951.

Laurence began her "Innocent Voyage," in *The Prophet's Camel Bell*, thus: "And in your excitement at the trip, the last thing in the world that would occur to you is that the strangest glimpses you may have of any creature in the distant lands will be those you catch of yourself" (10). Perhaps we do understand others through knowing ourselves and comprehend ourselves through understanding the Other. Mannoni capitalized the word "Other" in his study *Prospero and Caliban: The Psychology of Colonization* (1956), where he defines the "Prospero complex" (110): "What the colonial in common with Prospero lacks is awareness of the world of Others, a world in which Others have to be respected" (108). In her memoir, *Dance on the Earth*, Laurence affirms, "That book was a revelation. Mannoni said things about colonialism and the people who had been colonialized that struck me deeply" (155). In *The Prophet's Camel Bell*, she claims that reading Mannoni after her sojourn in Africa inspired a "shock of recognition": "Among the most perceptive and undeniable insights are those of Mannoni, in whose study of the psychology of colonization every European who has ever lived in Africa cannot fail to see something of himself" (208, 249). In recording her view of Somalis, Laurence reveals herself. In "Half War, Half Peace," she asserts, "It was really Africa which taught me to look at myself." Morley says, "The quest for self-knowledge provides a subtext for the book" (52). Barbara Pell writes in "The African and Canadian Heroines: From Bondage to Grace," "*The Prophet's Camel Bell* is less a travelogue than a story of spiritual growth ..." (37).

Laurence had a habit of writing about one place while living in another because she required the perspective provided by time and distance. As G.D. Killam claims in his introduction to *This Side Jordan*,

"Margaret Laurence achieves a distance and objectivity that no other expatriate has managed and thus she is, so far as I am concerned, the best expatriate writing about Africa."[2] Laurence revisited her Somali diary a decade later in a break from writing *The Stone Angel*, as she recalls in *Dance on the Earth: A Memoir*: "I got out all my old diaries from Somaliland and wrote *The Prophet's Camel Bell*" (157). She predicts to Wiseman on 29 March 1961, "This will be a kind of labour of love" (*SL* 133), the very same phrase she used for her Somali translations. Laurence expressed her ambitions for *The Prophet's Camel Bell* to Wiseman in the same letter: "One other thing I want to do some time, although it's not likely to amount to much, and that is to see what I can do with the voluminous diaries I kept while we were in Somaliland. Perhaps they wouldn't be of interest to anyone except ourselves." She adds, "I'm glad I didn't try to do this years ago, as the thing would then have been filled with pompous theories about colonialist administration, etc., and now I only want to include the things that actually happened" (*SL* 132). She conveys her doubts concerning her Somali memoir in a 5 August 1962 letter to Wiseman: "My reservations are concerned with the book itself, which (a) doesn't seem to me to count, really, as it is non-fiction, and (b) does not seem at this point to be what I wanted to write at all, anyway by which I mean that I think the material was there but I did not do justice to it." She adds, "The script isn't terrible – just mediocre. I think it is too nice – I feel it will offend no one. ... I think the whole thing is too bland. But I do not feel I can re-write it ... I wrote it as honestly as I could, and worked on it obsessively for 8 months, but I've had it now, even though I now feel it is too superficial" (*SL* 142). Later, she writes to Wiseman on 29 August 1962, "It was my last painful breaking of ties with Africa" (*SL* 149).[3] Still later, Laurence writes to Wiseman on 17 August 1963, "'The Prophet's Camel Bell' came out here about a week ago. So far no reviews. Let us hope it gets one or two. I am not very impressed with it, as a book, but the photographs are nice. I am kind of disenchanted, as it were, where it is concerned, as I think it is not honest enough" (*SL* 165). On 20 September 1963, she writes, "Some of the reviews in the provincial papers are good for the laughs, if nothing else. One said something like 'What she lacks in writing skill she makes up for in her determination to say nothing which will damage East-West relationships!!'" (*SL* 168). Later, she destroyed the diaries: "Seen from a distance, the details in my notebooks begin to take on a new meaning" (188), she notes. In *The Prophet's Camel Bell* we see an older and wiser author looking back on her naive self and ironizing the self-portrait with her habitual self-mockery – "the naive liberal mocked by an older, wiser self" (33), as Morley puts it.

The Prophet's Camel Bell portrays two Margarets – before and after, innocence and experience – just as *A Bird in the House* presents two Vanessas – the naive child actor and the wiser adult narrator. For example, when Abdi, the Laurence's driver, said to Jack, "Your memsahib – a queen" (200), Margaret recorded in her diary that being courteous gains one "popularity" with Somalis, but, years later, she scribbled the word "*Bosh*" (201) in the margin, demonstrating her dual perspective. Morley notes, *The Prophet's Camel Bell* is "both a spiritual autobiography ... and a portrait of a people" (45), for Laurence's sense of her self and her role in Somalia greatly influenced her perception of the Somali people and vice versa. Therefore an exploration of her self-presentation should precede an examination of her portrayal of Somali men and women.

Laurence's position in Somaliland was an anomalous one composed of contradictions and conflicts. Married to an engineer in the employ of the British government, she was a part of the colonialist community but, as a citizen of a country, Canada, that had been a British colony, she disapproved of British colonials: "I believed that the overwhelming majority of Englishmen in colonies could properly be classified as imperialists, and my feeling about imperialism was very simple – I was against it. I had been born and had grown up in a country that once was a colony, a country that many people believed still to be suffering from a colonial outlook, and like most Canadians I took umbrage swiftly at a certain type of English who felt they had a divinely bestowed superiority over the lesser breeds without the law" (25). Just as her role as a Canadian enabled her to accompany her husband to Africa, so her Canadian perspective allowed her to view the colonialist regime differently from the British community. Mohamed, the Laurences' cook, expressed it perfectly: "Canadian peoples different" (31).

"Every traveler sets foot on shore with some bias" (25), Laurence acknowledges, and she admits that she is no exception, but her bias is directed at the Europeans, rather than, as was the case with most Western newcomers, at Africans. She asserts, "I found the sahib-type English so detestable that I always imagined that if I ever wrote a book about Somaliland, it would give me tremendous joy to deliver a withering blast of invective in their direction" (226). Nevertheless, she felt empathy with individuals, however prejudiced she felt toward groups. As Constance says to her husband Brooke about their servant Love, in Laurence's story "A Fetish for Love" in *The Tomorrow-Tamer*, "That's – people. This is a person. It's not the same thing" (173). Despite her distaste for imperialists, Laurence writes with admiration of the Administrator of the Protectorate and his wife in her chapter "The Imperialists" in *The Prophet's Camel Bell* (222–6).

Alf, a foreman in charge of building roads, is the exception that proves the rule: "how could you possibly think of a man as an imperialist when he told you, sorrowfully and in perplexity, that he tried to start a football team, but the Somalis didn't seem to take to the game?" (28). Laurence judges, "in trying to turn camel herders into truck drivers, desert tribesmen into town-dwelling mechanics, [Alf] was trying to construct a bridge that would cross centuries and oceans in a single span" (28) – like the literal bridge that crosses the river in "The Tomorrow-Tamer," linking the Ghanaian village with the modern world. Despite the "lunatic comedy" (28) that results from this near-impossible task, however, the roads did get built. Interestingly, Margaret never questions the colonialist enterprise of building roads across Africa – perhaps because Jack was involved in the same enterprise. We should remember, however, that the events recorded in *The Prophet's Camel Bell* took place in the fifties, decades before post-colonial theory became current.

Laurence's position in Somaliland was an anomalous one because as a white Canadian woman she did not fit into any group. As the wife of an employee of the Department of Public Works, she was part of the colonialist enterprise, but as an anti-imperialist, she was odd woman out. As Jack's wife, she was part of his team but, as the only woman in the camp, she was an outsider. Sparrow notes, "As a Canadian she belonged neither to African nor European society" (99). As a Canadian, she did not fit in with the British wives; as a Westerner, she was excluded from the company of the closely guarded Somali women. In short, by virtue of her race, gender, class, and nationality, she did not belong anywhere. She was "neither flesh, fowl, nor good salt herring" (*BH* 108–9), as Vanessa's Grandmother MacLeod put it. She was indeed "a stranger in a strange land" (18).

First she did not fit in with the British sahibs at the Hargeisa Club, where her rebellious comments drove colonial "dinosaurs" (*DE* 153) right out of the club. She recalls an episode when she unwittingly caused a scandal: she set out on foot to visit the market in the *magala*, or town, of Hargeisa, only to discover that she had been tailed by police. "European women did not go to the Somali town alone, and no European ever went on foot" (34), she learns. Later, she recorded in her diary, "'much ado about nothing'" (34).

She felt little sympathy with the British colonial wives, the memsahibs of the Hargeisa Club:

> Their explanation of me was in essence the same as Mohammed's. I was from another country. They shrugged and smiled, a trifle stiffly, perhaps, but politely. Later, it seemed to me that in those early days of our tour quite a few memsahibs must have looked upon me with a greater generosity than I afforded them. At the time, I only saw the distance which they put between themselves and the Somalis, whom they tended to regard either patronizingly or with outright scorn. I did not appreciate then the really desperate boredom of some of these women, the sense of life being lived pointlessly and in a vacuum. Nor did I perceive the need many of them felt to create a small replica of England here in the desert and the enormous effort they put into a task that must inevitably fail. (32)

Laurence later dramatized this desperate boredom in Cora Thayer, wife of the manager of the British textile firm of Allkirk, Moore & Bright, in her Ghanaian novel, *This Side Jordan* (1960).

On the other hand, she could not get close to Somali women, who were closely protected and who viewed European women as "hybrid creatures" (55) because they wore trousers. Once, when she was in the garden in slacks, she noticed some Somali women gawking at her and talking. She understood enough Somali to comprehend what they were saying: "Is it man or beast?" one asks, and the other answers, "Allah knows. Some strange beast"(56). Margaret retreated at once to the bungalow and changed into a skirt: "Never again did I wear slacks in Somaliland, not even in the desert evenings when the mosquitoes were thick as porridge, not even in the mornings when the hordes of glue-footed flies descended" (56).

Although she was part of Jack's team and grew fond of Abdi, their driver, and Hersi, their translator, she saw things very differently from them. One striking example is her reaction to the baiting of a wounded cheetah: when she begs the men to put the beast out of its misery, they decline, until Jack is fetched and dispatches the beast with a crowbar (147). She realizes, "It was not a matter of intelligence but of viewing the whole of life through different eyes" (93).

Although as Jack's wife she was part of the paternalist structure, as a woman Margaret was not accepted as Jack would be by the Somalis, for her gender contradicted her colonialist connection. When some elders visited the Laurence bungalow to speak with Jack, Margaret entertained them in Jack's absence. One of the elders commented that never had he known "such a fine memsahib," leading Margaret to think, "*I handled that pretty well, I think; yes, I'm sure I did*" (40). Later, Mohamed informed her that she committed "a terrible breach of etiquette" (41) that outraged the elders: they would never discuss serious matters with a woman, but were too polite to let on.

Laurence thought, because her intentions were good, the Somali people must like her: "I did not then know how much the Somalis resented the Christian conquerors, or if I suspected it, I felt somehow that I would be immune from their bitterness, for did I not feel friendly towards them? Surely they would see it. But they looked at me from their own eyes, not mine" (34–5). In a 20 September 1963 letter to Wiseman, she says, "Inscribe it on my tomb – she meant well" (*SL* 168).

In short, Margaret was a memsahib who condemned colonialism: "I could not face the prospect of being called 'Memsahib,' a word which seemed to have connotations of white man's burden, paternalism, everything I did not believe in" (23). Later, in Ghana, as she notes in her memoir, "I began to realize that, as I had been in Somalia, I was going to have to be a memsahib, a concept I hated and despised" (*DE* 143). After her children were born, the conflict between her personal life as a wife and mother and her professional life as a writer made her feel she "was attempting an impossible juggling act" (*DE* 157), an act that led her, reluctantly, to accept a role she despised: "I looked after the children myself, but I had a great deal of help with domestic chores. I accepted this with enormous guilt. I didn't want to be privileged, I rejected the label of memsahib, and yet Shira, the wife of Grey, our cook, washed my children's diapers and clothes while Grey planned and made the meals. This helped me more than I can say in terms of my writing, but I still felt ambivalent. How could I justify it? I couldn't, but I accepted it, not only because it was the line of least resistance but also because I badly needed that time to do my writing" (*DE* 152). In "Anti-imperialism and Feminism in Margaret Laurence's African Writings," Wendy Roy discusses the conflicts between Laurence's feminist views and her anti-imperialist attitudes. In "'I Was Against It': Margaret Laurence and British Imperialism in Somalia," she concludes, "Laurence's feminist principles are sometimes at odds in her African texts with her anti-imperialist beliefs" (193). In a 23 January 1964 letter to Ethel Wilson, Laurence vents her outrage at being called a memsahib: "I had a very good visit in Pakistan with Jack, in November, and enjoyed leading a truly indolent life – for a month. I'm afraid it isn't a life which I could happily lead in any permanent sense any longer, and this creates great difficulties, naturally, as work abroad is certainly the right thing for Jack. ... Anyway, re: Pakistan – how odd it was to be called 'memsahib' again! I am afraid that the European communities in such places are almost as isolated as they ever were, and although I always resolve firmly not to argue, I find myself slipping into the old sense of *anger*. There are, of course, really notable exceptions ..."4

Two Margarets are at war, then, in *A Prophet's Camel Bell*: the mother who reluctantly accepts the role of memsahib and the liberal who was influenced by the social gospel and by Winnipeg's "Old Left." The journey recreated in this memoir is the journey from naive idealist to conscious realist. As Morley judges, "Africa cauterized Laurence's youthful naivete and liberal optimism" (45). Laurence concludes, "Yet something of the real world did impinge upon our consciousness, and portions of the secret empire of the heart had to be discarded, one by one" (251).

Africa has long been a metaphor for the unknown, the shadow self, the heart of darkness. In *The Prophet's Camel Bell*, Laurence quotes Graham Greene in his 1961 memoir *In Search of a Character: Two African Journals*: "Africa will always be the Africa of the Victorian atlas, the blank unexplored continent the shape of the human heart" (249). As Sir Thomas Browne wrote in his *Religio Medici*, "We carry with us the wonders we seek without: there is all Africa and her prodigies in us" (17). "Africa is still today a place of wonder" (9), Patricia Monk judges in "Shadow Continent."

Laurence opens *The Prophet's Camel Bell* with this idea of wonder: "May they not just be true, the tales of creatures as splendidly strange as minotaurs or mermaids?" (9). She exudes, "Nothing can equal in hope and apprehension the first voyage east of Suez, yourself eager for all manner of oddities, pretending to disbelieve in marvels lest you appear naïve, but anticipating them just the same, prepared for anything, prepared for nothing, burdened with baggage – most of it useless, unburdened by knowledge, assuming all will go well because it is you and not someone else going to the far place (harm comes only to others), bland as eggplant and as innocent of the hard earth as a fledgling sparrow" (9). Her journey in Africa is a journey from innocence to experience. The "wily pamphleteer" who warned newcomers about "wooly bears, a ferocious cloth-eating insect" (12) deflected the fears of strangers from actual difficulties to "mythical beasts" (12). Laurence follows Sir Richard Burton's footsteps into East Africa – although she is critical of his low opinion of the Somalis as "stupid, dirty, and most damning of all, poor Muslims" (25) – as he writes, "Of the gladest [*sic*] moments in human life, methinks, is the departure upon a distant journey to unknown lands."

Laurence employs the second person to draw the reader into the journey of discovery that she is about to chronicle: "There you go rejoicing, as so you should, for anything might happen and you are carrying with you your notebook and camera so you may catch vast and elusive life in a word and a snapshot" (9). Indeed, Laurence was equipped with notebooks in which she captured her experiences in words and a camera with which she caught images that are reproduced in her text.[5] In "Shadow Continent," Monk notes, "Metaphorically speaking, the stereotype vision of Africa acts as a mirror showing part of ourselves that we cannot see until it is bounced off the reflecting surface – and that part of us is the Shadow" (9). Laurence discovered her shadow self reflected in the mirror of the faces of African men and women.

"THE FACE OF AFRICA"

Arriving in Aden as the naive idealist portrayed in "Innocent Voyage," Laurence searches for "the face of Africa" (24). Upon leaving Somalia, an older and wiser Laurence considers the complex character of their driver, Abdi: "Trying, by writing it out, to unearth something of his meaning, I put in my notebook – 'He is an exaggeration of all the qualities he possesses. He is courage and pride and anger writ large. Perhaps his is the face of Africa – inscrutable to the last.' My feeling at this time was that I would never understand" (207). Ultimately, she acknowledges the difficulty of knowing the Other. Initially, however, she is confident, as she describes Somali men as tall, gaunt, and proud, "their features a cross between negroid and Arabian" (21). Somali women appear to be "meek and gentle creatures" (22) – in contrast to the "pride and dignity" of "the assertive men" (*SL* 48) – but eventually she learns they are "meek as Medea" (22). Her journey to perception involves the ability to penetrate appearances in order to perceive reality.

Although Laurence was excluded from the company of Somali women because of Somali customs and because of the language barrier, she was interested in their situation. She reports, "women's lives were harsh, and after marriage they changed from girls to lean and leather-skinned matrons in the space of a few years" (75). She adds, "After marriage, Somali women, especially those in the desert, led lives of continual heavy work and drudgery. ... Not surprisingly, most women lost their beauty within a few years. Not surprisingly, also, they frequently became irritable and nagging" (103). In *A Tree for Poverty* she notes, "Both tribal and religious traditions place women's status as infinitely inferior to that of men," for "The double standard is extremely strong. The Somali wife is expected to be faithful to her husband, but fidelity is not expected of him" (30). Thus, "the status of women was low, according to both tribal and religious traditions, and a woman's wits and her sharp tongue were often her only protection" (103). Therefore, "A man who treated his wife with unusual thoughtfulness would be laughed at and scorned by the rest of the tribal group" (*TP* 30).

Consequently, men treat their wives harshly, and wife-beating is common, for a "husband who was unusually considerate of his wife would be thought weak and would be mocked at by his fellow tribes-men" (103). Somalis think that, in not beating Margaret at all, Jack is "carrying consideration too far" (197), for they perceive a connection between wife-beating and fertility. Somali members of the camp were concerned about the Laurences' childless state, praying, "Allah send you a son" (200). They took it as a good omen when Jack and Margaret acquired an ostrich egg as a keepsake, for it was considered to be "a powerful fertility charm" (145). "To my great joy, I became preg-nant" (245), Laurence records near the end of her Somali memoir.

Laurence writes wife-beating into "A Fetish for Love" in *The To-morrow-Tamer*. When Love, the young wife of Constance and Brooke's aging houseboy, Sunday, proves to be barren, like her predecessors, Sunday beats her mercilessly: "Constance found Love at the side of the bungalow and knelt beside her. The blood on the girl's face had dried, leaving dark rivers like cooled lava on her skin" (170). When Con-stance interferes by taking Love to her own "ju-ju man" (180), white doctor Guy Bennington, he gives her a green syrup – a placebo in-tended more for Constance than Love (179). But Love remains bar-ren, and the beatings continue unabated. Whiskey, the Kestoes' cook, in *This Side Jordan*, also beats his new "small wife" (133) largely be-cause, like his old wife, she is barren: Laurence describes "Whiskey's hoarse and irascible muttering as he cursed at his two wives for his own sterility" (*SJ* 235). Laurence felt strongly about such child-brides, and Sunday's child-wife reflects Hawa, a young bride that Laurence encountered in Somalia (56–7).

Like any tourist, Laurence was curious to learn about the Somali people, especially the women: "I felt I must discover everything about Somali beliefs, customs, traditions. … What did the Somali bride-price actually involve? Did men love their wives or merely regard them as possessions? Could a woman divorce her husband for infidelity? … Did the cliteridectomy make it impossible for Somali women to enjoy sex?" (47). She learned the answers to some of these questions, includ-ing the last, but she was dismayed by her new knowledge. As the only woman in the camp, she was put in charge of the medicine kit. Ironi-cally, a first-aid kit was her favourite toy as a child, as she explains in *Dance on the Earth: A Memoir*, because two of her aunts were distin-guished members of the nursing profession (60). In Somalia she be-came a kind of medicine woman, happily handing out aspirin, but when it came to real suffering – a Somali herdsman dying of thirst – she was humbled by her own helplessness: "What had I known of life here at all? I recalled the faith-healing of the Illalo's ear, and the simple boracic treatment of Abdi's eyes. It seemed to me that I had been like a child, playing doctor with candy pills, not knowing – not really knowing – that the people I was treating were not dolls. Had I wanted to help them for their sake or my own? Had I needed their gratitude so much?" (74). This confrontation with the dehydrated Somali herdsman catalyzed crucial realizations for Laurence: "For a while, after that day, I could not stand to look at my toy potions and powders. I shoved the tin box under a camp cot. I would have no more to do with it. Then I saw that this way, too, was an exaggeration. Would I do nothing simply because I could not do everything? The searching sun of the *Jilal* exposed not only the land but the heart as well" (74).

FEMALE GENITAL MUTILATION: THE WOUND THAT WILL NOT HEAL

One of the wounds she could not heal was genital mutilation: "Somali girls underwent some operation at puberty. ... The operation was either a removal of the clitoris, or a partial sewing together of the labia, or perhaps both. But whatever was done, apparently a great many women had considerable pain with menstruation and intercourse, and the birth of their children was frequently complicated by infection" (75). The rite of *gudniin* can range from removal of the clitoris alone to removal of the clitoris and minor labia and sewing together of the major labia to create a surface "smooth as the breast of a pigeon," as one Somali woman put it. Infibulation, the most extreme form, can cause urinary infections that can lead to divorce, ostracism, or even death. "That infibulation plays an important role in the life of females in Islamic northeastern Africa is clear," Esther Hicks affirms in *Infibulation* (2). Infibulation is a traditional custom practised for four thousand years and in at least twenty-eight African countries, "cutting a brutal swath through the center of the continent – from Mauritania and the Ivory Coast in the west, to Egypt, Somalia and Tanzania in the east," as Rogaia Mustafa Abusharaf asserts in "Unmasking Tradition" (23).

Efuru (1966) by Flora Nwapa – the only novel by a woman included in Laurence's study of Nigerian literature, *Long Drums and Cannons:*

Nigerian Dramatists and Novelists, 1952–1966, simply because it was the only novel published by a woman by the time Laurence published her study in 1968 – is the first text by a woman to enter the African canon and the first to discuss clitoridectomy. In fact, the rite opens the novel: Efuru, described as "a remarkable woman" (1), marries Adizua. Because Efuru is motherless, Adizua's mother, Omeifeaku, visits Ugwunwa to arrange for Efuru to have her "circumcision" (8) or "bath" (10) before pregnancy, lest her baby die. The operation is not described, but Nwapa writes, "Efuru screamed and screamed. It was so painful" (10). The neighbours comment, "Efuru is having her bath. Poor girl, it's so painful" (11). Ironically, Adizua "felt all the pain. It seemed as if he was the one being circumcised" (10).

Thirty years later Somali fashion model Waris Dirie described her "circumcision" graphically in "Becoming a Woman," chapter four in her autobiographical memoir, *Desert Flower* (1998): "The prevailing wisdom in Somalia is that there are bad things between a girl's legs, parts of our bodies that we're born with, yet are unclean. These things need to be removed – the clitoris, labia minora, and most of the labia majora are cut off, then the wound is stitched shut, leaving only a scar where our genitals had been" (37). After *gudniin*, Dirie fainted from pain and awoke to find the ground soaked with her blood and her sex drying on a rock in the sun. Her genitals became infected, and she ran a high fever as she lay in bonds for forty days. Urinating was excruciating. She feared she would die, like her sister. When she recovered, she recalls, "I discovered a patch of skin completely smooth except for a scar down the middle like a zipper. And that zipper was definitely closed. My genitals were sealed up like a brick wall that no man would be able to penetrate until my wedding night, when my husband would either cut me open with a knife or force his way in" (45). Dirie ran away when her father planned to marry her to a rich old man. Her sealed vagina was as good as gold to her father, for her suitor was to pay him many camels for her. As a proverb quoted by Hersi, the Laurences' translator, says, "*The daughter of a poor man has no vagina*" (169). As a result of *gudniin*, Dirie suffered pain with menstruation, was unable to enjoy sexual relations, and required corrective surgery before she could bear a child. It is estimated that ninety-eight per cent of Somali women have been sexually amputated thus. Dirie's prominence as one of "Revlon's Most Beautiful Women" gracing the covers of fashion magazines enabled her to become a spokeswoman for the rights of African women. The United Nations appointed her as an ambassador for its international campaign to end female genital mutilation.

Laurence writes, "In the opinion of an educated Somali friend of ours, this operation was one custom which would take a very long time to die, for the old women would never agree to its being abandoned, he believed, even if the men would" (75). How right he was: fifty years later, clitoridectomy is still practised in Africa and has even followed women to North America.

Only recently has female genital mutilation, circumcision, clitoridectomy, or infibulation been discussed publicly in conferences on African and women's rights and publicized in studies such as *Infibulation* by Esther Hicks, *Cutting the Rose: Female Genital Mutilation: The Practice and Its Prevention* by Efua Dorkenoo, *Warrior Marks: Female Genital Mutilation and the Sexual Blinding of Women* by Alice Walker and Pratibha Parmar, and *Female Genital Mutilation: A Call for Global Action* by Nahid Toubia, as well as studies by Yael Tamir, Olayinka Koso-Thomas, Fran Hosken, Renee Saurel, Jacqueline Smith, and Lilian Passmore Sanderson.

But Canadian writer Margaret Laurence publicized this subject decades earlier in her Somali journal, *A Prophet's Camel Bell*, and also in her Ghanaian novel, *This Side Jordan*.

When Somali women asked Margaret to give them something to help their pain, she thought, "the lunatic audacity of shoving a mild pill at their total situation was more than I could stomach" (76). Humbled by her helplessness, torn between her desire to assist the women and her fear of imperialist intervention, she felt paralyzed and replied, "I have nothing to give you. Nothing" (76).

But Laurence did not do nothing. She did what she did best: she wrote, writing female genital mutilation into her first novel, *This Side Jordan*, which reflects her five years in the Gold Coast.[6]

THIS SIDE JORDAN: "A HUMAN SACRIFICE"

Johnnie Kestoe, the racist and sexist protagonist of the novel, has felt a "curious itch of desire" (4) to have sex with an African woman – from the opening scene, where "Johnnie Kestoe, who didn't like Africans, was dancing the highlife with an African girl" (1) named Charity

Donkor at the Weekend In Wyoming nightclub, under the jealous eyes of his pregnant wife, Miranda, and Charity's escort, Victor Edusei. He flirts with the temptation to indulge a "disgust that beckoned almost as much as it repelled" (11) with "Saleh's serpent-eyed daughter, [who] laugh[s] at his unacknowledged desire" (228), and with the "small wife" of his cook, Whiskey (134–5). Finally, he indulges this urge, arranging to have sex with a prostitute at the Weekend In Wyoming. The girl, a young virgin from the north, is offered as "a human sacrifice" (227) by the "Highlife Boy Lamptey" (212) to appease the white man's wrath – to deflect Johnnie Kestoe's anger from Lamptey's friend, "Wise-Boy" (213), Nathaniel Amegbe.

"She lay spreadeagled, sheeplike, waiting for the knife. ... Her slight spasm of fear excited him. She was a continent and he an invader, wanting both to possess and to destroy" (231). The trope of the land as a female and the invader as a male, or of colonialism as the rape of a culture, is a familiar one, recalling John Donne's "The Sun Rising": "She is all States, and all Princes I, / Nothing else is." Anne McClintock opens *Imperial Leather: Race, Gender and Sexuality in the Colonial Contest* with Rider Haggard's map of King Solomon's mines in the anthropomorphic shape of a woman's body – a "conflation of the themes of gender, race and class" (4). But Johnnie is dismayed, when "Emerald," as she is named by the pimp, Joe-boy, bleeds copiously after coitus. The omniscient narrator explains: "Among certain peoples, the clitoridectomy was performed at puberty. By a bush surgeon – some fetish priestess perhaps. Some of them were said to use the long wicked acacia thorns as needles. The wounds often became infected and did not heal for a long time. ... The scars had opened when he savaged her" (233). "Savaged" is a strong word, and an ironic one, for Johnnie has viewed "Emerald" as a savage, but it is he who best deserves the label, as he re-enacts the rape of Africa on her body.

Strangely, however, this hemorrhage, the emblem of "the clot of blood on a dirty quilt" (232), recalls "the clot of blood on a dirty quilt" (59) that signaled the death of Johnnie's Irish mother, Mary, in a London slum as a result of a self-inflicted abortion. Even the child prostitute's name, "Emerald," reflected in her green cloth, recalls not only the forests of the north where she was sold into slavery, but also the Emerald Isle from which the Kestoes hail – just as the "emerald trail of sea weed" (185) makes the sea-bird girl a symbol of Ireland in James

Joyce's *A Portrait of the Artist as a Young Man*. This connection with his childhood trauma, the loss of his mother, instigates an epiphanic realization that brings the girl to life for him, individualizing her in his eyes: "She was herself and no other. She was someone, a woman who belonged somewhere and who for some reason of her own had been forced to seek him here in this evil-smelling cell, and through him, in-dignity and pain" (233).[7] Johnnie viewed the girl from a colonialist perspective, but she defeats his expectations, evading the stereotype to emerge as a living individual – a feat that Laurence achieves in all her fiction. Astonishingly, after this indelible scene, a redemptive moment is achieved, as the girl reaches out her hand and touches his, smiling to reassure him, and he takes her hand and spreads her green cloth gently over her damaged body in a gesture of atonement. This power-ful scene ends with Johnnie parking alone by a lagoon and sobbing as he has not done for nearly twenty years, as he is finally released into his mourning for his mother. Laurence's use of the girl to effect her hero's epiphany, however, seems like another sacrifice.

This powerful rapprochement proves to be the prelude to a recon-ciliation between two sides. *This Side Jordan* is constructed schemat-ically with two casts of characters: the "Whitemen," the English colonialists who run the Textile Branch of the firm Allkirk, Moore & Bright – including accountant Johnnie Kestoe, manager James Thayer and Bedford Cunningham – and the Africans, including Nathaniel Amegbe and his family and colleagues at Futura Academy, where he teaches African History. In her essay "Gadgetry or Growing: Form and Voice in the Novel," Laurence recalls, "When I wrote my first novel, *This Side Jordan*, I had very little consciousness of form. The novel is cast in a traditional mould, with a straightforward third-person nar-ration, and the chapters alternate between the viewpoints of the African teacher, Nathaniel Amegbe, and the Englishman, Johnnie Kestoe. ... The chapters, I think, did need to be alternating, especially since the African viewpoint and the European were so different" (81–2). Clara Thomas notes, "there is an insistence on symmetry ... that seems some-times to be contrivance" (*MW* 50). The two sides finally meet formally in chapter nine – when Miranda visits Futura Academy and Nathaniel visits Allkirk, Moore, & Bright – in the middle of this well-made novel. From that point on, the two groups intermingle in increasingly fraught incidents until the final reconciliation.

The prejudice against imperialists that Laurence acknowledges in *The Prophet's Camel Bell* – "I have never in my life felt such antipathy towards people anywhere as I felt towards these pompous or whining sahibs and memsahibs" (228) – is evident in *This Side Jordan*, where she portrays the British cast of Allkirk, Moore & Bright and their wives as pathetic, and the African characters, especially Nathaniel Amegbe, as sympathetic. She wrote to Wiseman on 20 January 1979, "I had to re-write all the sections of my first novel that dealt with the Brits in W. Africa because I had treated them so unsympathetically" (*SL* 353). As Killam notes, Laurence "had to overcome an anti-imperialist attitude which was in danger of turning her white characters into caricatures" (*SJ* x). Even Laurence's stepmother, Marg, who read the second draft of *This Side Jordan* on her deathbed, "felt I had put my heart and soul into a portrayal of the African characters and had, unconsciously or deliberately, made stereotypes of the whites" (*DE* 117), as Laurence recalls: it was "her final gift to me" (*DE* 117). So she dedicated *This Side Jordan* "*In Memory of my Mother, Margaret Campbell Wemyss.*"

One manuscript assessor said he was "only reasonably nauseated" by her passages of purple prose. In "Ten Years' Sentences," Laurence reveals the revision process for *This Side Jordan*: "More revision, I thought, was out of the question. I had already rewritten half the book from scratch when I decided, after leaving Africa and getting a fresh perspective on colonial society, that I'd been unfair to the European characters. More work I couldn't face. A quick cup of hemlock would be easier. However, as we were a little short on hemlock just then, I got out the manuscript instead. I hadn't looked at it for months, and I saw to my consternation that the gent with the upset stomach was undeniably right in some ways. I managed to cut out some of the more emotive prose (although not enough) and lived to bless him for his brutal criticism" (17). After such readers' responses, Laurence revised her manuscript yet again, and it won the Beta Sigma Phi first novel award in 1960 (*DE* 155), after it was published simultaneously in 1961 by Macmillan in England, St Martin's in the United States, and McClelland and Stewart in Canada. Woodcock judges, "*This Side Jordan* was the best of a number of novels published during the 1960s by Canadians who had lived and served in West Africa, and it can still be read as a valuable fictional document of the times" (*SJ* 287).

Reviews, however, were mixed: although Kildare Dobbs opines of the Amegbes, "these people don't need Free-dom [sic]; they need a marriage counselor" (62), and the anonymous reviewer for the *Times Literary Supplement* titles his review "Muddling into Maturity,"[8] Mary Renault praises *This Side Jordan*: "A scholar and translator of African folklore and poetry, Miss Laurence has written a first novel of rare excellence" (104). Laurence says, "I not only had at that point a number of Ghanaian friends, but I had read enormously widely, books of anthropology and books written by Ghanaians too about their own culture" (*PS* 64).

Laurence did extensive research on Ashanti culture – as her acknowledgment of scholars R.S. Rattray, J.H. Nketia, Eva Meyerowitz, and J.B. Danquah in the flyleaf of the novel indicates – to achieve what Killam calls a "re-creation of a cultural reality" (xviii) in Amegbe's monologues, which form the heart of the novel. Nathaniel is torn between the Akan religion of his tribal background and the Christian religion of the mission where he was educated, unable to choose between "Nyame's Tree and the Nazarene's Cross" (32). Laurence writes, "He has rejected the old gods and the old tribal ways of his people, but the past still exercises a strong influence over him" ("SJ"). His most rhetorical soliloquy portrays the Nazarene as a "King of Ashanti" (77) – "King Jesus came riding on a milk-white horse, and he crossed the river of Jordan" (76) – prophesying Danso, in "The Merchant of Heaven," who portrays Jesus as an African (*TT* 75). Woodcock says Amegbe's monologues materialize ancient tribal beliefs "as visions and voices in what seems to be a bicameral mind in the process of detachment from a world of myth" (*SJ* 286).

The true hero of *This Side Jordan* is not the unsympathetic Kestoe, or even the sympathetic Amegbe, however, but Ghana itself. Independence, as suggested by the mammy-lorry slogans that Laurence employs as epigraphs for the novel – "The Day Will Come – Authority Is Never Loved – Flee, Oh Ye Powers Of Darkness – Rise Up, Ghana" – is the theme. Laurence writes in "This Side Jordan," her précis of the novel, "The keynote of this novel is change and growth" (3): "Set in the Gold Coast, the new Ghana, some months before that country became the first British colony in Africa to gain its independence, *This Side Jordan* is a novel about a society in transition. In the social and spiritual ferment of a country that is emerging both from the colonial rule and from its own old tribal patterns of life, people must change not only their ways of living but their ways of thinking. But the changes within the individual involve as many conflicts and struggles as do any national political changes" (SJ 1). She charts the progress of the policy of Africanization in the firm of Allkirk, Moore & Bright, whereby Africans will replace British employees: "This firm has decided recently to expand their Africanization programme and they want to train local staff to take over from expatriates" (186). But the staff – the squire James Thayer, the knight Bedford Cunningham, and accountant Johnnie Kestoe – are opposed to Africanization. Johnnie sabotages the squire, however, by treacherously undermining him with Cameron Sheppard, the envoy from the firm's head office in London.

Laurence encountered the same resistance to Independence for Ghana on the part of colonials:

They used to say, "Independence will never come. If it does, they'll be asking for us back in five minutes." I believed the opposite, which did not make me popular. I saw around me a collection of well-meaning human dinosaurs, old colonialists who couldn't recognize that their time was over in Africa and who, I suspect, were terrified to go back to their own countries. They had advantages in Africa that none of them would ever have had in England, among them power, power given to people who were, some of them, mediocre, who wouldn't have got very far in Britain, but who imagined themselves to be totally necessary to Africa. They couldn't see or accept that they had become, historically, totally redundant, and that their years of privilege and arrogance were swiftly coming to an end. There were times when old colonials walked out of a cocktail party on account of remarks I had made. I *was* tactless. I was tactless, though, because I believed profoundly in what I was saying. (*DE* 153)

Laurence portrays this attitude poignantly in the Thayers and Cunninghams in *This Side Jordan*. In *The Prophet's Camel Bell* she writes, "Every last one of these people purported to hate Africa, and yet they all clung to an exile that was infinitely preferable to its alternative – nonentity in England" (228). The Laurences, however, were pleased about Africanization: Jack agreed to be replaced by a trained Somali as engineer in charge of building *ballehs*. When they visited the Balleh of the Camels and found that herdsmen resented their presence as foreigners, Jack and Margaret were more pleased than offended. When they left Somalia, they took their treasures – the ostrich egg and the camel bell given to Jack by Ahmed Abdillahi, a young Eidagalla chieftain (159), to commemorate his title as "*odei-gi- rer-ki*, the old man of the tribe" (135). This camel bell inspired the title of Margaret's memoir and the epigraph from James Elroy Flecker's "The Gates of Damascus": "God be thy guide from camp to camp, / God be thy shade from well to well. / God grant beneath the desert stars /Thou hearest the prophet's camel bell."

Laurence is not sanguine about the future of Ghana following independence, however. She voices her skepticism through Victor Edusei, a "been-to" journalist and graduate of the London School of Economics, who reflects Laurence's friend Ofosu. As Victor Edusei mocks Nathaniel Amegbe, who teaches African History at Futura Academy, so Mensah/Ofosu mocks Margaret's interest in African history by declaring, "Africans have no history" (*HS* 25). Victor – whose surname begins with the first three letters of the word "education" and whose given name suggests victory – addresses his friend Nathaniel Amegbe – whose surname suggests an existential "am" and "be" (like E.M. Forster's character, Dr Aziz, in *A Passage to India*) and whose African first name has been replaced by the Christian mission with a biblical name:

You put your faith in Ghana, don't you? The new life. Well, that's fine, boy. That's fine for you. But as far as I'm concerned, it's a dead body lying unburied. You wait until after Independence. You'll see such oppression as you never believed possible. Only of course it'll be all right then – it'll be black men oppressing black men, and who could object to that? There'll be your Free-Dom for you – the right to be enslaved by your own kind. You can see it happening already. We've been ruled too long by strangers, Nathaniel. We've got the slave mentality. I don't mean we're humble. Slaves aren't humble; they're ruthless. They don't want freedom for everybody – all they want is to be the man who holds the whip. Maybe we'll learn differently, in a hundred years or so. Maybe we'll have civil war, and maybe we'll need it. Who knows? But I'm afraid I haven't got your optimism. You can keep Ghana. (*SJ* 117–18)

A portrait of Nkrumah with the caption "Freedom" (229) above the bed where Johnnie Kestoe "savaged" Emerald provides a tacit ironic comment on Ghana's independence.[9] As Woodcock notes in his afterword, many Africans "looked to the future with a naïve optimism" (287), but Laurence prophesied "with remarkable accuracy" (288) the plight of liberated African states: "*This Side Jordan* and the two other books I wrote which were set in Africa, *The Prophet's Camel Bell* and *The Tomorrow-Tamer*, were written out of the milieu of a rapidly ending colonialism and the emerging independence of African countries. They are not entirely hopeful books, nor do they, I think, ignore some of the inevitable casualties of social change, both African and European, but they do reflect the predominantly optimistic outlook of many Africans and many western liberals in the late 1950s and early 1960s" (TYS 18).

Rather than portraying political optimism, then, Laurence presents hope for humanity through personal relations. Killam claims that *This Side Jordan* "reveals a quest for understanding at the individual level" (xviii). The good will of Nathaniel Amegbe and Miranda, the Laurence figure in the novel, ultimately overcomes awkwardness and embarrassment. Miranda naively wishes to see the true Africa – like Adela Quested, who wants to see "the real India" (24) in E.M. Forster's *A Passage to India*, and like Laurence herself, who felt "I must discover everything about Somali beliefs, customs, traditions" (47), only realizing later, "People are not oyster shells, to be pried at" (51). Miranda, meaning "marvelous," recalls the daughter of Prospero, that archetypal colonizer, who discovers a "brave new world" of strangers in Shakespeare's *Tempest*. Laurence writes that Miranda "was crazy about quaint customs – she collected them like postage stamps" (SJ 196–7). Miranda's desire to impress Nathaniel with her interest in ancient African customs recalls Margaret's desire to appear "sympathetic, humanitarian, enlightened" (26) to her African friend, Mensah, in "The Very Best Intentions." Ultimately, however, Laurence portrays mutual empathy as Amegbe realizes that Miranda is also vulnerable: "Miranda's eagerness to know, her exaggerated politeness, her anxiety to please, her terrible kindness – none of it had moved him at all. Only, now, the sudden knowledge that she could feel humiliation and anguish like himself" (262–3) touches him, just as Emerald's anguish touches Kestoe. As Laurence explains in "This Side Jordan," "Nathaniel, who has deeply resented Miranda's determined kindness, finally understands that she, too, can feel humiliation and pain like himself" (2). While Laurence employs male protagonists in most of her African fiction, she also portrays their recognition, as a result of their realization of the vulnerability of women, that women are individuals, like themselves.

Laurence concludes this schematic narrative, with its counterpointed chapters alternating between the African and European casts of characters, by a double childbirth. Both Miranda and Aya, Amegbe's wife, give birth to a first child, Mary and Joshua, at the same time and place – reflecting the fact that Margaret gave birth to a son at the same time as Honour, the wife of her African friend, Ofosu, as she recalls in her essay, "The Very Best Intentions": "Mensah's son was born about the same time as ours and in the same hospital" (HS 27). In "Outside Africa," his 1961 review of This Side Jordan, Kildare Dobbs writes scathingly of this double childbirth: "In their female functions all women are equal. 'All same like Queen Victoria' as Bombay pimps assure one. The new generation arrives in all the messy pangs of labour, the uncontrollable mystery on the colonial floor. For hospital read Ghana, for birth-pangs read birthpangs: the figure is trite, the allegory too willed" (63).[10] But the blood that signals the birth of Johnnie's child redeems the blood that signaled the death of Mary Kestoe, Johnnie's mother. As a sign of this redemption, he asks Miranda to name their daughter Mary.

Amegbe voices the author's hope in his injunction to his baby boy: "Cross Jordan, Joshua" (282). These final words of the novel recall the Lord's injunction, "Cross Jordan, Joshua" (245), quoted by the preacher, and the hymn, *"Joshua crossed the river to the Promised Land"* (247), that is sung at the evangelical church that Amegbe attends with Aya before the birth of their child. The injunction also reflects the title, *This Side Jordan*, and the epigraph: "Until the Lord hath given your brethren rest, as he hath given you, and they also have possessed the land which the Lord your God giveth them; then ye shall return unto the land of your possession, and enjoy it, which Moses the Lord's servant gave you on this side Jordan towards the sunrising" (Joshua I:15). Fiona Sparrow concludes, "Nathaniel's final vision is an intertwining of faiths that promises a new inheritance across Jordan and the possibility of hope" (130). Morley claims that all Laurence's writing is a quest for "the Promised Land of inner freedom" (45). In "Ten Years' Sentences," Laurence writes, "In *This Side Jordan* ... victory for the side of the angels is all but assured. Nathaniel holds up his newborn son, at the end, and says, 'Cross Jordan Joshua.' Jordan the mythical *could* be crossed; the dream-goal of the promised land *could* be achieved, if not in Nathaniel's lifetime, then in his son's. This was the prevailing spirit, not only of myself but of Africa at that time" (19). She adds, "Things have shifted considerably since then. ... I now find this novel out-dated and superficial and yet somehow retrospectively touching" (19).

Later, Laurence recalls, "In my first novel, *This Side Jordan*, published in 1960, I described the birth of Miranda Kestoe's child from the point of view of Johnnie Kestoe, the child's father. How could I have done? How could I have been so stupid, so self-doubting?" (*DE* 5–6). If she had written this novel later, she might have written from the point of view of Miranda, the Laurence figure in the novel. Later, she was appalled that she had dared to write from the point of view of Nathaniel Amegbe, the central consciousness in *This Side Jordan*. If she had written *This Side Jordan* still later, she might have made Miranda the protagonist and possibly the narrator of the novel. In her Manawaka cycle, she writes exclusively from the female viewpoint.

Laurence did write one African narrative from a female point of view. "Uncertain Flowering" portrays Karen Aynsley returning home from school in England to Bor Mado, a thinly disguised version of Hargeisa, in Somaliland. Discovering that both her parents are engaged in adulterous affairs, and tired of being a "kid," she plots to lose her virginity. Fabricating an affair in England, she encourages Lieutenant Howard Tavershaw to "let all his young longing for a woman take her as its object" (33). Her "uncertain flowering" proves an abortive de-flowering – aborted when he discovers that she is, in fact, a virgin: "She lay there on the bed, still as stone, her body rigid. Her eyes were open, but they saw only the wall" (34). This climactic scene prefigures the scene when Johnnie Kestoe rapes Emerald, who is also said to be "not more than sixteen" (229) and a virgin. Tavershaw, like Johnnie, covers the girl's body with a spread, and Karen, like Emerald, reaches out to touch his hand. The portrait of their English social club, with its drinking and decadence, reflects Laurence's experience at the Hargeisa Club. She wrote to friends in 1951, "We were so glad to get away from Hargeisa, with all its constant and unvarying drink-parties, its bed-hoppers and its gossip!" (King 89). "Uncertain Flowering," published in *Story Magazine* in 1953, was the first story Laurence ever published, although she credits "The Drummer of All the World" with that distinction in *Dance on the Earth* (110). "Uncertain Flowering" is a significant story, though little known, because it was also her only published piece of fiction set in Somaliland.[11]

Although Laurence attempted to write a Somali novel and did write stories set in Somalia, she actually published only non-fiction works about Somalia and only fictional works set in Ghana. Perhaps that is because she did not reside long enough in Somalia to enable her to see Somalis from within, as she sees Nathaniel Amegbe in *This Side Jordan*. "Uncertain Flowering," while set in Somaliland, focuses almost exclusively on British expatriates. The one exception is Karen Aynsley's bond with Yusuf, the Somali servant who had been a marksman in the Camel Corps during the Mullah Campaigns (16) – reflecting Abdi, "the Old Warrior" of *The Prophet's Camel Bell* (198) – and who taught her to speak Somali. Laurence's Somali sojourn lasted only eighteen months, whereas she resided in the Gold Coast for five years. Furthermore, Laurence was able to meet and converse with numerous Ghanaians who were Western-educated and fluent in English, like Mensah/Ofosu of "The Very Best Intentions," whereas her knowledge of the Somali language was necessarily limited, limiting her familiarity with Somali people. Thus, it is understandable that virtually all her published African fiction is set in Ghana.

CHILD PROSTITUTION: "A LIFETIME OF BONDAGE"

Female genital mutilation is not the only atrocity experienced by women that Laurence writes about. She also deplores the prevalence of child prostitution in Africa. In *The Prophet's Camel Bell*, she explains, "For many men and women, princes and commoners from the distant forests and from the lands as far away as the Niger, Somaliland was the end of a bitter journey and the beginning of a lifetime of bondage, for here the Arab slave routes had emerged at the sea, and from there the dhow-loads of slaves had once been shipped across the Gulf of Aden to be sold in the flesh markets of Arabia" (13). In *The Prophet's Camel Bell* she describes her tacit friendship with the eight-year-old girl Asha, a child prostitute in the *jes*, or "tea-shop-cum-brothel" (156), that situates itself next to Jack's camp. "The *jes* provides amenities of one kind and another" (157), so Jack allots them a ration of water, thereby making the Laurences complicit in Asha's exploitation. Called by the Somali word that means literally "a small opening" (157), Asha sits silent at Margaret's feet while she writes in her hut: "We did not talk much, Asha and I, for I did not know what to say to her. I never asked her about her life. My knowledge of Somali was too limited, and who would I get to translate?" (157). At sundown, when Jack's men finish work and repair to the *jes* for refreshment, Asha leaves quietly, murmuring, "*Nabad gelyo*. ... May you enter peace" (157), but Margaret is unable to return the traditional response, "*nabad diino* ... the peace of faith" (157). Dismayed by Asha's plight, she feels helpless, as she did in the face of the pain of the mutilated Somali matrons. She hesitates to meddle, fearing that interference might exacerbate Asha's situation: "I did not know what to do. ... So, whether out of wisdom or cowardice, I did nothing" (157-8). "In this part of the world," Jack advised, "you have to learn that, if you can't change something, you might as well not worry about it" (20). King writes, "Peggy felt silenced. She had not yet found a voice to deal with such agonies" (87). But, again, Laurence did not do nothing. She did "slightly more than nothing" (75): she wrote.

She wrote child prostitution into one of the short stories in *The Tomorrow-Tamer*. She said, "Asha's half-wild half-timid face with its ancient eyes will remain with me always, a reproach and a question" (*SJ* 158). The vision of the child haunted her, and Asha is reborn as Ayesha, the beloved "child" of Violet Nedden, the British exiled narrator of "The Rain Child."[12] Miss Nedden, English teacher, loves her "forest children" (106), but bears the sign of Africa in the form of an ulcerated sore that has lamed her, "like any ulcerated beggar of the streets" (107). When the sensual Kwaale – who is at home in Africa, and who resents the doubly exiled Ruth Quansah, an African-born girl raised in England – tells Miss Nedden that Ruth struck Ayesha, the teacher reminds her of the saying from Exodus that Laurence quotes in *The Prophet's Camel Bell* and that provides the title for Laurence's travel essays: "Thou shalt not oppress a stranger, for ye know the heart of a stranger, seeing ye were strangers in the land of Egypt" (114). Later, Violet, the aging and crippled English "queen," seated on her mock throne, with her ebony cane as a scepter, lifts Ayesha from the stool at her feet and cradles the damaged child in her arms: "my small Ayesha, whose childhood lay beaten and lost somewhere in the shanties and brothels of Takoradi or Kumasi, the airless upper rooms of palm-wine bars in Lagos or Kaduna" (130). Miss Nedden explains to Ruth Quansah, "She must have been stolen, you see, or sold when she was very young. She has not been able to tell us much. But the Nigerian police traced her back to several slave-dealers. When they discovered her she was being used as a child prostitute. She was very injured when she came to us here" (117). She adds, "There are many like her, I'm afraid, who are not found or heard about" (117) – many like Emerald, another young girl sold into slavery. Child prostitution was prevalent in many African countries, but, like female genital mutilation, the issue was not acknowledged until recently. Laurence brought the subject to public attention in her African fiction and non-fiction long before the issue was publicized.

THE TOMORROW-TAMER: "THOU SHALT NOT OPPRESS A STRANGER"

Indelible as these individuals are, no one character dominates this collection of ten separate stories. Rather, the hero of *The Tomorrow-Tamer and Other Stories*, as in *This Side Jordan*, is Ghana itself, as it emerges from colonization into independence. Laurence's collection reflects this development in its structure: the first story, "The Drummer of All the World," features a European male narrator, Matthew, named for Christ's disciple,[13] and the last story, "A Gourdful of Glory," features an African woman, Mammii Ama, whose name suggests "Mother Love." The first story begins with the words, "My father," in the opening sentence, "My father thought he was bringing salvation to Africa" (1), and the last story ends with a description of Mammii Ama as an Earth Mother: "Like a royal palm she stood, rooted in magnificence, spreading her arms like fronds, to shelter the generations" (244). When Matthew makes love to Afua, he comments, "Possessing her, I possessed all earth" (12), echoing the imperialist trope when Johnnie Kestoe rapes Emerald, whereas, in the final story, Mammii Ama "spread her arms wide, as though she would embrace the generations. ... She was an opening moonflower, filled with the seeds of life everlasting" (237). As Barbara Pell judges in "The African and Canadian Heroines: From Bondage to Grace," "In the cultural upheaval of the new Africa on the verge of independence ... Laurence also saw images that she associates with the end of the heroine's pilgrimage out of bondage, freedom, dignity, and spiritual grace" (36–7). This independence is reflected in Laurence's Canadian fiction also, where all her Manawaka novels delineate the developing self-empowerment of her female protagonists – from the stifled Hagar, through the repressed Rachel and conflicted Stacey, to the rebellious child Vanessa and the self-liberating adult writer Morag.

This movement from European to African, white to black, and male to female is a gradual one, as Laurence subtly delineates the process of Africanization. Initially, in "The Drummer of All the World," Matthew is suckled by Yaa, mother of Kwabena, leading him to believe that he and Kwabena are brothers (3), until Independence (17) comes and the process of Africanization (17) continues, whereby Matthew's post is to be given to an African (18). The African woman in this story is relegated to the role of nurse, giving her nourishing milk to the European conqueror, "because her love, like her milk, was plentiful" (4). But by the last story, "A Gourdful of Glory," the African mammy is viewed as a Colossus: "Mammii Ama lifted the gourd vessel high above her head, and it seemed to her that she held not a brittle brown calabash but the world" (242).

Africanization creates a happy ending to "The Perfume Sea,"[14] as the delightful flotsam and jetsam (20), Archipelago and Doree, are reprieved when Mercy Tachie requests a makeover "in the new way" (46), as portrayed in *Drum* magazine. "By an act of mercy ... we are saved" (47), exults Archipelago. The sign over their barber shop *cum* beauty salon undergoes Africanization when it changes from advertising "English-Style Barber – European Ladies' Hairdresser" (30) to "All-Beauty Salon – African Ladies A Specialty" (42). A serious form of Africanization provides the epiphanic conclusion of "The Merchant of Heaven," when Brother Lemon's commission of a painting for his Angel of Philadelphia Mission inspires Danso's portrait of the Nazarene as an African (76) – recalling Amegbe's rhapsodic vision of Jesus as an Ashanti king on a white horse crossing the River Jordan in *This Side Jordan* (77).[15]

Laurence is not always sanguine about the future of Africanization, however. Kofi is a victim of colonization in the title story "The Tomorrow-Tamer," when the "bridgeman" plunges to his death: "The bridge, clearly, had sacrificed its priest in order to appease the river" (103).[16]

Like Icarus, Kofi dared to look at the sun and, blinded, lost his footing on the bridge. Patricia Morley writes, "Kofi's fall from grace in a moment of exulting self-deification suggests the Icarus myth and the concept of hubris from classical Greek tragedy. Kofi's act is also a betrayal of the values of his own people. His proud ambition is ironically fulfilled when his people weave both his death and the new bridge into their myth" (25). Laurence comments on the cause of his death:

> [Kofi] has a vision of a world which includes his own and yet goes far beyond it. He dies because he does not really know the rules of survival in any world except his own. He achieves in death something which he could not have achieved in life – in some way, he does tame tomorrow for his people, although they interpret his death in terms of their own concepts. They feel he was the sacrifice made by the bridge to the river, and they say "a man consumed by the gods lives forever." Kofi is both scapegoat, unintentionally, and messiah, also unintentionally. He himself is the bridge, not between better and worse cultures, but simply between different cultures, between people who do not understand one another, and who, at some point, must try.
> ("Author's Commentary" 72–3)

In "The Voices of Adamo," first titled "The Spell of the Distant Drum,"[17] Adamo is devastated to learn from Captain Fossey – who is being posted back to Britain, to be replaced by an African – that he is discharged from his post as regimental drummer. The regiment has become his family since the death of his own family. Clearly, this story echoes *Mister Johnson* by Joyce Cary, one of Laurence's literary heroes. She comments, "I wrote what I think is my best short story, 'The Voices of Adamo,' after I read Mannoni's book" (*DE* 155), implying that Mannoni's "Prospero Complex" (110) is the concept she aims to dramatize in this story of a drummer and his master. In "Godman's Master," Laurence's allegory of colonialism, Godman, freed by Moses Adu from the box in which he was forced to play a priest's oracle, repeats his role in a circus, because that is all he knows (157). The story ends with Godman going up "to take his place with the other performers on the broad and grimy stage" (160) – "the human comedy – African style" (Morley 20). The story dramatizes the desirability of freedom and the security of bondage, for freedom can be frightening. When Moses Adu remonstrates, "There is more to freedom than not living in a box," Godman responds, "You would not think so if you had ever lived in a box" (155).[18]

In "A Gourdful of Glory,"[19] Laurence ironizes independence: Mammii Ama believes all the market women will ride the bus free after independence; the jaundiced, skeletal white woman with a face like a skull laughs at Mammii Ama's illusion. When independence comes, Mammii Ama boards the bus hopefully, but is disillusioned to learn that she must still pay her fare (241). Her coin resounds in the hollow metal fare box as resonantly as the coin that concludes Joyce's *Dubliners* story, "Two Gallants," with its biblical implications of betrayal (60): "The clank of the coin in the fare-box echoed again and again in her head, drowning the heart's drums" (*TT* 243). Laurence is hopeful but not optimistic about Ghana's independence. As James King concludes, "A glimmer of hope surrounds the conclusion to the novel whereas the short stories are much more about the impossibility of any significant understanding between black and white" (125).

"The Mask of Beaten Gold," inadvertently omitted from *The Tomorrow-Tamer and Other Stories*, is not affirmative in its portrayal of miscegenation.[20] Laurence includes an albino child and a chameleon to highlight the issue of colour. The story portrays a mixed marriage between a British doctor, Philip Thrane, and Candace, his African wife educated as a nurse in London, Laurence's only female "been-to" – that is, an African educated abroad. Their child, Jeremy, is suddenly afflicted by cerebral malaria and dies. His death is foreshadowed by the scene in which he buries himself in sand (34), by the albino boy with his "pilgrimage of pain" (33), and by the eyeless "death mask of King Kofi Kakari" (31) referred to in the title. After the boy's death, his father "looked at the golden death mask of Kofi Kakari for a long time, the smooth and sightless eyes, the perfection of the features, the portraiture so skillfully done in metal that Jeremy had imagined it to be the photograph of a living man" (39). Thus, the death of Jeremy Thrane appears to result from the curse of King Kofi Kakari on miscegenation.

Clearly, Laurence learned a great deal about Africa during her sojourn there.[21] In the process, she also learned much about herself. She views this process as a journey of self-discovery: at the outset of *The Prophet's Camel Bell*, she said, "Our voyage began some years ago.

When can a voyage be said to have ended? When you reach the place you were bound for, presumably. But sometimes your destination turns out to be quite other than you expected" (10). She ends her memoir by acknowledging, "And yet the voyage which began when we set out for Somaliland could never really be over, for it had turned out to be so much more than a geographical journey" (260). Indeed, it proved to be a journey into "the secret empire of the heart" (251).

One of the secrets of the imperial heart that she discovers is her own desire to be respected, admired, and, yes, loved as a sympathetic liberal. Finally, however, she must acknowledge that she, too, has been part of the imperial project: "This was something of an irony for me, to have started out in righteous disapproval of the empire-builders, and to have been forced at last to recognize that I, too, had been of that company" (251).

The understanding of the Other that Laurence acquired through observing Africans, especially women, inspired the self-knowledge that she needed to create living individuals in her fiction. In *Heart of a Stranger*, she acknowledges the need "to understand those others who are our fictional characters" (3). Laurence believed the time for outsiders to write about Africa was over, but she used the comprehension of the human heart that she had gained from her experience in Africa and applied it to her native land of Canada. Her hatred of colonialism and love of independence translated into her depiction of Canada as a postcolonial nation, and her sympathy with the plight of African women translated into her portrayal of the self-empowerment of Canadian women in her Manawaka cycle. Pell concludes, "Laurence's Canadian heroines were born in Africa" (46).

PART THREE

The Canadian Texts

"A Small-Town Prairie Person"

CHAPTER 7

"A Town of the Mind":
Laurence's Mythical Microcosm
of Manawaka

Margaret Laurence's five Canadian fictions are all set in her mythical microcosm of Manawaka:[1] "A strange place it was, that place where the world began. A place of incredible happenings, splendours and revelations, despairs like multitudinous pits of isolated hells. A place of shadow-spookiness, inhabited by the unknowable dead. A place of jubilation and of mourning, horrible and beautiful. ... It was, in fact, a small prairie town" (*HS* 169).[2] This passage introduces "Where the World Began," the concluding essay in Laurence's collection of travel essays, *Heart of a Stranger*. The "prairie town" described here is Neepawa, Manitoba.[3]

Neepawa is the model for Manawaka. In her "Sources," retitled "A Place to Stand On," the opening essay in *Heart of a Stranger*, Laurence clarifies connections and delineates differences between her factual, individual hometown and her fictional, universal "town of the mind": "Manawaka is not my hometown of Neepawa – it has elements of Neepawa, especially in some of the descriptions of places, such as the cemetery on the hill or the Wachakwa valley ... In almost every way, however, Manawaka is not so much any one prairie town as an amalgam of many prairie towns. Most of all, I like to think, it is simply itself, *a town of the mind* [my italics], my own private world, which one hopes will ultimately relate to the outer world which we all share" (7). Laurence metamorphoses her actual hometown of Neepawa into the microcosmic Manawaka, the setting of her famous Manawaka cycle of five Canadian fictions. The parallels between these literal and figurative towns underscore the way Laurence's early experience informs her fiction. The way she transfigures Neepawa as Manawaka also illustrates her artistic alchemy. As Patricia Morley observes, "Laurence has turned the town of her youth into a metaphor of universal human experience" (18). Nothing can traverse national boundaries so easily as the human imagination, and the artist uses fiction to recreate a private kingdom for every reader to inhabit.

Many great writers have created a mythical microcosm based on their birthplace: we recall Walter Scott's Waverley, Thomas Hardy's Wessex, William Faulkner's Yoknapatawpha County, and Sherwood Anderson's Winesburg, Ohio. Canadian fiction is famous for its regional richness: "A 'Dictionary of Canadian Mythology' would contain a very large entry under 'Small Town,'" (173–4), Clara Thomas declares in *The Manawaka World of Margaret Laurence*. One thinks of Stephen Leacock's Mariposa, Sinclair Ross's Horizon, Robertson Davies's Deptford, and Alice Munro's Jubilee. But Thomas insists that Manawaka is the most famous of these microcosms: "But no town in our literature has been so consistently and extensively developed as Margaret Laurence's Manawaka. Through five works of fiction, it has grown as a vividly realized, microcosmic world, acting as a setting for the dilemmas of its unique individuals and also exercising its own powerful dynamic on them. Manawaka is also specifically, historically, and geographically authentic, dense with objects and true to its place and its development through time" (MW 173–4). A visitor to Neepawa may be surprised because Neepawa is identical to Manawaka in particulars: from the Brick House to the Little House, from the Regal Café to the Roxy Theatre, from River Street to Mountain Avenue, from the cemetery on the hill to the river in the valley – it is all there, exactly as in the novels. But the actual town has none of the fiction's power. Neepawa is just an ordinary town, no different from any other prairie town or small town anywhere, entirely lacking the mythic power of Manawaka. Then the visitor may see the trestle bridge, where John Shipley is killed in *The Stone Angel*, except that the train tracks are gone, leaving only the two earthen supports with a gap in the middle – Canada's answer to Tintern Abbey perhaps. Thus the visitor realizes that Neepawa/ Manawaka is both an ordinary little town *and* a town of mythic power – just as our birthplace appears small to our adult eyes, yet still retains the magical power it had for us as children. That is the miracle that Margaret Laurence, the myth-maker, recreates in Manawaka.

THE CHILD IS MOTHER OF THE ARTIST

The child may be mother of the artist, for both view the outside world through magical lenses. Laurence's mythologizing of Neepawa as Manawaka is essentially a child's view of reality. She uses this quotation from Graham Greene's *Collected Essays* to introduce "A Place to Stand On": "'The creative writer perceives his own world once and for all in childhood and adolescence, and his whole career is an effort to illustrate his private world in terms of the great public world we all share'" (*HS* 5). Laurence responds, "If Graham Greene is right – as I think he is – in his belief that a writer's career is 'an effort to illustrate his private world in terms of the great public world we all share,' then I think it is understandable that so much of my writing relates to the kind of prairie town in which I was born and in which I first began to be aware of myself" (*HS* 9). She begins "Where the World Began" by explaining how her childhood home created her adult vision: "Because that settlement and that land were my first and for many years my only real knowledge of this planet, in some profound way they remain my world, my way of viewing. My eyes were formed there" (*HS* 169). And she concludes her personal essay with this manifesto: "This is where my world began. A world which includes the ancestors – both my own and other people's ancestors who became mine. A world which formed me, and continues to do so, even while I fought it in some of its aspects, and continue to do so. A world which gave me my own lifework to do, because it was here that I learned the sight of my own particular eyes" (*HS* 174).

Greene's perception of a golden age of childhood, as well as Laurence's metamorphosis of Neepawa into the microcosm of Manawaka, illustrates Selma Fraiberg's theory of *The Magic Years*, the title of her study of early childhood, introduced in this passage from her Preface:

The magic years are the years of early childhood ... These are "magic" years because the child in his early years is a magician – in the psychological sense. His earliest conception of the world is a magical one; he believes that his actions and his thoughts can bring about events. Later he extends this magic system and finds human attributes in natural phenomena and sees human or supra-human causes for natural events or for ordinary occurrences in his life. Gradually during these first years the child acquires knowledge of an objective world and is able to free his observations and his conclusions from the distortions of primitive thought.

By "magic" I do not mean that the child lives in an enchanted world where all the deepest longings are satisfied. It is only in the minds of adults that childhood is a paradise, a time of innocence and serene joy. The memory of a Golden Age is a delusion for, ironically, none of us remembers this time at all. At best we carry with us a few dusty memories, a handful of blurred and distorted pictures which often cannot even tell us why they should be remembered. This first period of childhood ... is submerged like a buried city, and when we come back to these times with our children we are strangers and we cannot easily find our way.

But a magic world is an unstable world, at times a spooky world, and as the child gropes his way toward reason and an objective world he must wrestle with the dangerous creatures of his imagination and the real and imagined dangers of the outer world, and periodically we are confronted with his inexplicable fears or baffling behaviour. Many of the problems presented by the child in these early years are, quite simply, disorders created by a primitive mental system that has not yet been subdued and put into its place by rational thought processes. (ix–x)[4]

Fraiberg's description of the child as magician sounds like a definition of the creative artist, and her distinction between the imaginative and rational methods reads like a distinction between the artistic and scientific modes of thought, as delineated by C.P. Snow in his Rede Lecture on *The Two Cultures and the Scientific Revolution*.

We could extend Fraiberg's argument from early childhood to ancient or primitive cultures, if we consider myth as defined by M.H. Abrams in the following passage:

In classical Greek, "mythos" signified any story or plot, whether true or false. In its central modern significance, a myth is one story in a mythology – a system of hereditary stories which were once believed to be true by a particular cultural group, and which served to explain (in terms of the intentions and actions of supernatural beings) why the world is as it is and things happen as they do …

A mythology, we can say, is any religion in which we no longer believe. Poets, however, long after having ceased to believe in them, have persisted in using the myths of Jupiter … and Jonah for their plots, episodes, or allusions; Coleridge said, "still doth the old instinct bring back the old names." (111–12)

In "Literature and Myth," Northop Frye defines literature as a "developed mythology" (35), explaining how "the typical forms of myth become the conventions and genres of literature": "We saw that one important social function of a mythology is to give a society an imaginative sense of its contract, of its abiding relations with the gods, with the order of nature, and within itself. When a mythology becomes a literature, its social function of providing a society with an imaginative vision of the human situation directly descends from its mythological parent. In this development the typical forms of myth become the conventions and genres of literature, and it is only when convention and genre are recognized to be essential aspects of literary form that the connexion of literature with myth becomes self-evident" (35). Myth, as defined by Abrams and Frye, informs Laurence's microcosmic world of Manawaka.

Paradoxically, myth may tell a greater truth than so-called reality. Perhaps that is why Plato exiled poets from his republic. Frye argues that "myth [is] a disguise for the real truth" (37). Bruno Bettelheim argues in *The Uses of Enchantment* (1976), "fairy tales make such great and positive psychological contributions to the child's inner growth" because "our cultural heritage finds expression in fairy tales, and through them is communicated to the child's mind" (12). And Bettelheim quotes Aristotle as saying, "The friend of wisdom is also a friend of myth" (35).

Morag Gunn declares in *The Diviners*, "The myths are my reality" (415); Laurence writes, "myths contain their own truth, their own strong reality" (*HS* 59). And in a metaphysical sense, Manawaka *is* more real than Neepawa. Laurence affirms in her interview with Geddes, "I think that the fiction comes to have its own special reality," for "the fictional town of Manawaka often seems as real to me as my own town of Neepawa" (806). Occasionally, she refers to Neepawa accidentally as "Manawaka." She raised a sign reading "Manawaka" at The Shack (*HS* 147), her cabin on the Otonabee River where she wrote *The Diviners*. Michael Dixon observes in his review of *Heart of a Stranger*, "Home is not a place but an idea; not a fact but a fiction" (478). The National Film Board documentary on Laurence is titled *First Lady of Manawaka* (1979).

Laurence's Manawaka, like Scott's Waverley, Hardy's Wessex, or Faulkner's Yoknapatawpha County, universalizes the human experience through mythologizing it. Laurence may mythologize reality compulsively, for she allegorizes not only Manawaka, but Neepawa itself. In "Where the World Began" she views her birthplace through the magical lenses of childhood, describing Neepawa in apocalyptic terms, "the Northern Lights flaring across the sky, like the scrawled signature of God" (*HS* 170), suggesting the end of the world and the day of judgment.

But myth must be rooted in reality. In "A Place to Stand On," Laurence explains the necessity for employing the individual to convey the universal: "Writing, for me, has to be set firmly in some soil" (9). The rich "soil" of reality is what gives Laurence's fiction its vivid verisimilitude. As Clara Thomas writes in "The Town – Our Tribe," in *The Manawaka World of Margaret Laurence*, "Margaret Laurence's world is Everyman's and Everywoman's, but its particularities are emphatically Canadian. Grounded in a small western town, her people move out into the wider world, but they carry Manawaka with them, its constraints and inhibitions, but also its sense of roots, of ancestors, and a past that is living still, both its achievements and its tragic errors" (177). Particularizing fiction is, paradoxically, precisely what universalizes it. Laurence immortalizes the Canadian prairies in Manawaka. She delineates the dual importance of her roots to her writing: "When one thinks of the influence of a place on one's writing, two aspects come to mind. First, the physical presence of the place itself – its geography, its appearance. Second, the people. For me, the second aspect of environment is the most important, although in everything I have written which is set in Canada, whether or not actually set in

Manitoba, somewhere some of my memories of the physical appearance of the prairies come in [... for] these are things I will carry inside my skull for as long as I live, with the vividness of recall that only our first home can have for us" (*HS* 7). Laurence's mythologizing of Neepawa as Manawaka involves two types of metamorphosis – first, a moralized landscape and, second, legendary characters.

METAPHORICAL MAPPING

Laurence makes Manawaka into a moralized landscape in the great tradition of Paul Bunyan's *Pilgrim's Progress* (1684), where features of topography symbolize social or moral values. She may be influenced in her use of the *paysage moralisé* trope by the African religions she considers in *This Side Jordan* and *The Tomorrow-Tamer*, wherein natural phenomena, such as groves and rivers, are sacred to the gods – like Kofi, the bridgeman, being sacrificed to the god of the river in "The Tomorrow-Tamer." Consider her use of the river, from the River Jordan to the Wachakwa River, in both her African and Canadian fiction. Manawaka's Wachakwa River Valley, modelled on Neepawa's Whitemud, is a natural setting for passion, a trysting spot for lovers like Rachel Cameron and Nick Kazlik in *A Jest of God*. In winter the frozen river is a source of delight for skaters or a fatal attraction, as it is for Daniel Currie, when a black hole, "a deep wound on the white skin of ice" (*SA* 23), is a window out of this world in *The Stone Angel*. And, of course, the river represents the current of memory that flows through *The Diviners* (11).

Manawaka is dominated by two prominent sites, both denoting death. First is the cemetery on the hill, where Hagar begins her life story in *The Stone Angel*. Manawaka's graveyard parallels Neepawa's Riverside Cemetery, where Laurence's ashes are buried in the family plot, beneath the gaze of the stone angel that guards the graves, under a tablet reading *Wemyss* on one side and *Laurence* on the other, marking the end of her "long journey back home" (*HS* 4).[5] Neepawa's graveyard faces a golf course across the river, a sharp contrast between the quick and the dead. But the dead do live. In her essay "Where the World Began," Laurence includes the dead in her community: "The dead lived in that place too ... My own young mother lay in that graveyard, beside other dead of our kin, and when I was ten, my father, too, only forty, left the living town for the dead dwelling on the hill" (172). The second repository for dead things in Manawaka is the nuisance grounds, or the town dump, which is next to the graveyard – "all the dead things together," as Morag Gunn puts it in *The Diviners*. The cemetery serves as the symbolic setting for Laurence's first Manawaka novel, *The Stone Angel*, while the nuisance grounds serves as the symbolic setting for her last Manawaka novel, *The Diviners*, framing the entire Manawaka cycle. This kingdom of garbage is ruled by that scavenger of souls, Christie Logan, a scapegoat or Christ figure who takes away the sins of the world in the form of empty bottles and aborted babies. Morag, as an orphan, is a nuisance, *white trash* in the town's eyes, and so naturally she is cared for by the keeper of the Nuisance Grounds, becoming one of his "salvage operations" (*D* 26). Neepawa also terms the town dump the "nuisance grounds" – "a phrase fraught with weird connotations, as though the effluvia of our lives was beneath contempt but at the same time was subtly threatening to the determined and sometimes hysterical propriety of our ways" (*HS* 171), as Laurence observes in "Where the World Began."

"Yet the outside world had its continuing marvels" (*HS* 170), Laurence recalls, and so she extends her moralized landscape to the terrain around the town, as she recreates her childhood kingdom in her Canadian fiction. Beyond Manawaka lie "Diamond Lake," based on Clear Lake, where Laurence's family summered, and "Galloping Mountain," modelled on Riding Mountain. Whenever Stacey MacAindra needs to escape from the urban rat race in *The Fire-Dwellers*, she recalls Diamond Lake, where her happiest memories are set. At the end of *The Diviners*, Pique embarks for Galloping Mountain, where she will rejoin the remnants of the Tonnerre family in order to care for the orphaned children. Laurence's romanticization of Manitoba place-names in her Manawaka fiction seems ironic if we recall Vanessa MacLeod's remark in "The Loons" that "Galloping Mountain was now a national park, and Diamond Lake had been re-named Lake Wapakata, for it was felt that an Indian name would have a greater appeal to tourists" (*BH* 119).

But the actual place names are romanticized too. Consider this passage from *Neepawa, Land of Plenty*, a 1958 publication commemorating the seventy-fifth anniversary of the town of Neepawa, reportedly incorporated as a town in 1883 by Laurence's grandfather, John Wemyss, a lawyer: "'NEEPAWA' comes from the language of the Crees and signifies 'plenty' or 'abundance.' Thus, the town adopted as its emblem the Cornucopia, full to overflowing with the fruits of the earth. The word 'Manitoba' is a combination of two Indian words, 'Manitou' – the Great Spirit, and 'waba,' the narrows of Lake Manitoba. It has also been translated as 'The Great Spirit's Voice,' probably reminiscent of the roar of the ocean-like surf on Lake Winnipeg" (10).⁶ Just as the name *Manitoba* may be an amalgam of *Manitou* and *waba*, so the name *Manawaka* seems an amalgam of *Manitoba* and *Neepawa*.

Neepawa and Manitoba are Cree names, then, meaning "Land of Plenty" and "God's Country," but that is not how they appeared to the young Margaret Laurence growing up on the prairies, when "the Drought and Depression were like evil deities" (*HS* 170). An escape artist, like most adolescents, the young Peggy Wemyss longed to be out there "dancing on the earth" (*DE* 64). In "A Place to Stand On," the opening essay in *Heart of a Stranger*, Laurence acknowledges that, as an adolescent, "my view of the prairie town from which I had come was still too prejudiced and distorted by closeness. I had to get farther away from it before I could begin to see it" (6). But in "Where the World Began," the concluding essay in the collection, she acknowledges, "When I was eighteen, I couldn't wait to get out of that town, away from the prairies. I did not know then that I would carry the land and town all my life within my skull, that they would form the mainspring and source of the writing I was to do, wherever and however far away I might live" (*HS* 172).

As Michael Dixon states in his review of *Heart of a Stranger*, "[Laurence] needed the distance, the perspective of time and travel, to perceive the elements in her home town of Neepawa that could be selected and ordered into the fictional Manawaka, 'a town of the mind,' an amalgam of setting, atmosphere, and characters that transcends the personal and specific to distil reality from actuality" (478). And, as Alan Bevan states in his introduction to the 1973 NCL edition of *The Fire-Dwellers*, "Manawaka is more than a place: it represents its creator's point of reference. It is a world from which each of the three protagonists tries to escape, but which is always there" (viii).

THE WRONG SIDE OF THE TRACKS

For Laurence's protagonists, as for the author herself, the railway is the great escape from the small prairie town, the link with the rest of Canada. The haunting voices of the trains summon all her fictional heroines away to farflung lands. Laurence enjoyed "a life-long love affair with the railways," for "[t]he long steel was what would carry us out of innumerable ruts in small towns during the Depression, into what we imagined to be the vast glamour and ease of other places, other lives" (*DE* 61–2). For Stacey Cameron, the "small-town girl" who has "shaken the dust of Manawaka off herself at last" (*FD* 11–12), the train whistles beckon her to the big city. For the mature Laurence, "the train is always moving / west," as she writes in her nostalgic 1983 poem "Via Rail and Via Memory":

> because a train
> of consequences binds me
> like long-ago binder twine
> twining lives and land together (*DE* 275).

This "train" of thought makes an ideal transition from the first of the influences of Laurence's birthplace on her creation, "the place itself," to the second significant influence, "the people." The railway did bind the dominion together but also provided the proverbial social divide. The population of Manawaka, with its suggestion of *Man awaken*, is divided morally by the tracks into "upright" and "downright" (16), as Vanessa MacLeod puts it in *A Bird in the House* – just as surely as the train track over the trestle bridge separates life from death for John Shipley in *The Stone Angel*. This passage from *Neepawa, Land of Plenty*, illustrates this intrinsically moral view: "Because the country surrounding Neepawa was populated with industrious, courageous, God-fearing citizens, Neepawa became a *good* town; a *good* place in which to live because it was the centre of a number of *good* districts. The relationship has been *good*" (140–1 my italics).

Laurence recalls Neepawa's class barriers: "All of us cast stones in one shape or another. In grade school, among the vulnerable and violet girls we were, the feared and despised were those few older girls from what was charmingly termed 'the wrong side of the tracks.' Tough in talk and tougher in muscle, they were said to be whores already. And may have been, that being about the only profession readily available to them" (*HS* 172). Manawaka replicates Neepawa's class barrier. In *A Jest of God*, Rachel Cameron, resident of Japonica Street, draws this definite distinction:

"This is known as a good part of town. Not like the other side of the tracks, where the shacks are and where the weeds are let grow knee-high and not dutifully mown, and where a few bootleggers drive new Chevrolets on the strength of home-made red biddy" (*JG* 17). Even death respects this great divide. Rachel, living in the Cameron Funeral Home, declares, "No one in Manawaka ever dies, at least not on this side of the tracks ... Death is rude, unmannerly, not to be spoken to in the street" (*JG* 19–20). So death is banished by the proper Scots Presbyterians. Rachel reveals the ethnic origin of this class barrier: "Half the town is Scots descent and the other half is Ukrainian. Oil, as they say, and water. Both came for the same reasons, because they had nothing where they were before. That was a long way away and a long time ago. The Ukrainians knew how to be the better grain farmers, but the Scots knew how to be almightier than anyone but God" (*JG* 71). Laurence depicts the railway as the backbone of the nation, uniting the country but dividing the classes.

Unlike the Cameron sisters who live on the right side of the tracks, like Margaret Jean Wemyss herself, Morag, adopted daughter of the town scavenger in *The Diviners,* lives on the wrong side. Like James Joyce recreating the streets of Dublin in *Ulysses* from his self-imposed exile in Zurich, the middle-aged Morag reruns mental films mapping Manawaka in *The Diviners*: "*I can smell the goddamn prairie dust on Hill Street, outside Christie's palatial mansion*" (36):

> *Hill Street, so named because it was on one part of the town hill which led down into the valley where the Wachakwa River ran ... Hill Street was the Scots-English equivalent of The Other Side of the Tracks, the shacks and shanties at the north end of Manawaka, where the Ukrainian section-hands on the CPR lived. Hill Street was below the town; it was inhabited by those who had not and never would make good. Remittance men and their*

draggled families. Drunks. People perpetually on relief. Occasional labourers, men whose tired women supported the family by going out to clean the big brick houses on top of the hill on the streets shaded by sturdy maples, elms, lombardy poplars. Hill Street – dedicated to flops, washouts and general nogoods, at least in the view of the town's better-off. (36–7)

Everyone knows his place in the social hierarchy of Manawaka, symbolized by its moralized cityscape, with the "upright" at the top of the hill and the "downright" (*BH* 16) at the bottom. The Hill Street blues bottom out into the river valley, where the shacks house the people literally beyond the pale – including the Métis family of Tonnerre modelled on Neepawa native Pate Chaboyer (*AH* 18) – an area only recently eliminated from Neepawa, where fatal fires, like the one that tragically kills Piquette Tonnerre in *The Diviners*, occasionally occurred.

"THAT HOUSE IN MANAWAKA"

The architecture of Manawaka's social hierarchy emblematizes the status of its inhabitants. As Vanessa recalls in the opening sentence of *A Bird in the House*, "That house in Manawaka is the one which, more than any other, I carry with me" (11). She refers to the Brick House as "part dwelling-place and part massive monument" (11) for her Grandfather Connor. Just as Laurence insists, "the Big House was my grandfather's stronghold and he ruled it like Agamemnon ruling Mycenae or Jehovah ruling the world" (*DE* 63), so Grandfather Connor's Brick House resembled "some crusader's embattled fortress in a heathen wilderness" (*BH* 11). At the conclusion of *A Bird in the House*, Vanessa recalls: "Twenty years later, I went back to Manawaka again. … I did not go to look at Grandfather Connor's grave. There was no need. It was not his monument" (190–1). The implication is that the Brick House, not his gravestone, is his true memorial.

So houses are memorials or coffins in Manawaka. In *The Stone Angel*, Hagar notes, "At the Shipley place the rusty machinery stood like aged bodies gradually expiring from exposure," and the warped porch "wore a caved-in look, like toothless jaws" (169), reflecting the dying derelict Bram Shipley within. In *The Diviners*, the Scavenger

Christie Logan's house, full of discarded items – *good rubbish* (D 51) – from the town dump, is an extension of the Nuisance Grounds.

Some of Laurence's houses in Manawaka, as in Neepawa, are literally mortuaries. Rachel and Stacey Cameron live over the mortuary where their father Niall Cameron reigned in his basement underworld as king of the dead, anaesthetized by his special embalming fluid, in the Cameron Funeral Home, which has less life than the real Riverside cemetery. Similarly, the Simpson house in Neepawa, where Laurence spent her adolescent years, served as a funeral parlour: because her Grandfather Simpson was a cabinet maker, he also fashioned the town's coffins, and during the Depression he once gave a workman a child's coffin in payment for services rendered. Young Peggy Wemyss must have cowered in her bed at night, thinking of bodies awaiting burial in the basement. When the mature Laurence learned that the mellow old yellow brick house she bought in Lakefield, Ontario had served as a funeral parlour, she almost died laughing. Ironically, the Simpson House in Neepawa, referred to as the Brick House, is now the Margaret Laurence Home, maintained by a friendly staff as a memorial to the creator of the Manawaka cycle.

Laurence extends her architectural analogy to the house of God, drawing class distinctions between different churches in Manawaka modelled on Neepawa's own church denominations. Neepawa boasts a complete complement of religious establishments, including a Roman Catholic Church, an Orthodox Church, the United Church attended by the Wemyss family, where Margaret Jean Wemyss herself was christened and married, the Presbyterian Church which held out against Church Union, and the Anglican Church which displayed a comic sign warning, "*Drive carefully. The person you hit might be an Anglican.*"[7]

In *A Jest of God*, Rachel Cameron describes the Presbyterian Church that the Camerons attend religiously, contrasting it with The Tabernacle of the Risen and Reborn in both religious and social terms. Comparing ecclesiastical architecture, Rachel says, ironically, of the Presbyterian Church, "The wood in this church is beautifully finished. Nothing ornate – heaven forbid. The congregation has good taste ... The Tabernacle has too much gaudiness and zeal, and this has too little" (47). The Tabernacle, which Noreen attends in *A Bird in the House*, resembles the proverbial haunted house, with its turrets and curlicues and its crimson neon sign advertising resurrection. Thus, the various church establishments reflect the taste in decor, and the social class, of the parishioners.

LEGENDARY CHARACTERS

The moralized landscapes and monumental mansions of Manawaka are peopled by larger-than-life characters, heroes and monsters, like the bogeys that children create out of pathetic derelicts, recalling Fraiberg's magic world. Laurence insists, "The oddities of the place were endless," as she recreates her child's view of Neepawa's eccentrics in "Where the World Began": "An old man lived, deranged, in a shack in the valley ... a wild Methuselah figure shambling among the under-brush ... muttering indecipherable curses or blessings, a prophet who had forgotten his prophesies ... kids called him Andy Gump, and feared him. Some sought to prove their bravery by tormenting him. They were the mediaeval bear baiters and he the lumbering bewildered bear half blind, only rarely turning to snarl" (*HS* 171). Laurence writes in "Where the World Began," "I had known all along in the deepest and often hidden caves of the heart that anything can happen anywhere, for the seeds of both man's freedom and his captivity are found everywhere, even in the microcosm of a prairie town" (*HS* 173), for "Everything is to be found in a town like mine. Belsen, writ small but with the same ink" (171). Laurence was familiar with the cruelty, as well as the kind-ness, of small-town people. Peggy Wemyss was called "Piggy" by cruel children, and the adult Margaret was sometimes referred to as "the Squaw" by townspeople in a racial slur based on her aboriginal ap-pearance, as recalled by the older residents of Neepawa. As Lyall Pow-ers writes, "racial prejudice flourished, hypocrisy was vibrantly alive, cultural and religious bigotry festered" (*AH* 48) in Laurence's home town. As Linda Hutcheon writes, in *The Canadian Postmodern* (1988), referring to the small town in fiction, "Occasionally these small towns were presented as idyllic places of rural felicity or as refuges from urban madness. But most frequently and most powerfully, the small town in Canadian fiction came to represent a limited and limiting society from which protagonists yearned to escape" (197).

The denizens of Manawaka are as mythic as the childhood bogey-men of Neepawa. Laurence's characters are legendary figures – not just Piper Gunn, the hero of Christie Logan's Scots Tales, but Christie him-

self, the town Scavenger, diviner of rubbish, who declares in his prophetic seer's voice, "By their garbage shall ye know them" (48). Many
characters in Laurence's "microcosm of a prairie town" (*HS* 173) are
types – from Ewen MacLeod, the town doctor, to Brampton Shipley,
the town drunk. Some of Laurence's characters achieve heroic status
– "self-made man" Jason Currie (named for the warrior of the golden
fleece), who "had pulled himself up by his boot straps" (*SA* 7), parallels Laurence's own Grandfather Simpson, who walked the fifty miles
from Winnipeg to Portage La Prairie as a young man.

Just as Laurence acknowledges idolizing and devilizing[8] Grandfather Simpson in *Dance on the Earth*, so Vanessa demonizes Grandfather
Connor fuming in his basement dungeon with its whiff of brimstone.
Stacey views her husband as "Agamemnon king of men" (*FD* 8), and
she envisions his boss Thor Thorlakson (actually Vernon Winkler) as
"Mephistopheles" (44) and as the "God of thunder" (244). Rachel
Cameron views the new undertaker Hector Jonas, named, ironically,
for two legendary figures, Hector and Jonah, as a "Comic prophet,
dwarf seer" (*JG* 131). Rachel even allegorizes her lover, Nick Kazlik,
and herself as "The milkman's son. The undertaker's daughter" (73).
Many Laurence characters, such as Rachel and Hagar, are loaned legendary status by their biblical namesakes. Indeed, Hagar is one of the
most famous figures in Canadian fiction. John Lennox explains this
phenomenon in "Manawaka and Deptford: Place and Voice":

> Manawaka's mythologies are those of Scots-Irish Canada – the
> small town, mercantile Calvinism and the Old Testament world
> associated with both.They are the mythologies of heroes and self-
> made men like Jason Currie and Vanessa MacLeod's Grandfather
> Connor whose foot journey of one hundred miles eventually
> assumes epic meaning in her mind. They are the legends of dis-
> possessed newcomers like Piper Gunn. They are the stories of
> another ancient, wandering people seeking deliverance in a new
> land: Hagar, Abraham, Jacob and the angel in *The Stone Angel*;
> Rachel and Jonah in *A Jest of God*; Jericho's walls in *A Bird in
> the House*; Sion in *The Diviners*. They are the history of the new
> land itself – Louis Riel and Batoche in *The Diviners*. (29)

Therefore, Lennox concludes "Place and Voice" thus: "There is a way
in which Laurence works out from her particular place and its times

to touch what they, and we, represent universally ... Given this special skill and perception ... it is ultimately the Manawaka voices which articulate the accents and places of the Canadian imagination with the most authentic resonance" (29).

Manawaka and its people were so real to Laurence that, when she completed *The Diviners*, the last novel in the Manawaka cycle, she wrote to Al Purdy on 3 February 1973, "Actually, for me this is a bit worse than the usual withdrawal symptoms at the end of a book, because in fact this is the end of a 12-year involvement with Manawaka and its inhabitants, and as the wheel comes full circle in this novel, it will be the last of those. There will, if this one is published, be 5 books concerning the town and its people. Little did I think, when writing THE STONE ANGEL, that it would all work out like this. So I feel a bit odd, and empty, as though part of my inner dwelling place has now been removed from me. I don't know where to go now – this is why I've always said this would likely be my last novel" (*FL* 270). So closely was the cabin on the Otonabee River where she wrote *The Diviners* associated with her Manawaka microcosm that, after completing her final Manawaka novel, Laurence sold it.

Manawaka is indelibly etched on the minds of both reader and writer. Laurence acknowledges in "A Place to Stand On," "I may not always write fiction set in Canada. But somewhere, perhaps in the memories of some characters, Manawaka will probably always be there, simply because whatever I am was shaped and formed in that sort of place, and my way of seeing, however much it may have changed over the years, remains in some enduring way that of a small-town prairie person" (*HS* 9). She affirms, in "Where the World Began," "The town of my childhood could be called bizarre, agonizingly repressive or cruel at times, and the land in which it grew could be called harsh in the violence of its seasonal changes. But never merely flat or uninteresting. Never dull" (*HS* 169–70). She extends her focus on the small town to encompass the entire dominion: "The same ... could be said for Canada in general. Why on earth did generations of Canadians pretend to believe this country dull? We knew perfectly well it wasn't. Yet ... for many years we valued ourselves insufficiently, living as we did under the huge shadows of those two dominating figures, Uncle Sam and Britannia. We have only just begun to value ourselves, our land, our abilities. We have only just begun to recognize our legends and to give shape to our myths" (*HS* 172). Margaret Laurence is one of those Canadian writers who have made truth of myth and shaped the legend of our land. By mythologizing Neepawa as the microcosm of Manawaka, Laurence has opened Canada to the world.

CHAPTER 8

"A Holy Terror": Hagar, Hero(ine)
of *The Stone Angel*

The Stone Angel, Laurence's first Manawaka book, has been lauded as the great Canadian novel. In 1982 critics named *The Stone Angel* the best of the top hundred Canadian novels.[1] Since then, it has been praised by many critics as one of the greatest novels of the century. In 2002 the CBC *Canada Reads* survey rated *The Stone Angel* among the top five Canadian novels. Hagar may be the most famous figure in Canadian fiction. Constance Rooke claims, "In Canadian literature, Hagar is reigning still as Queen of all the characters" (25).

Certainly Hagar inspires powerful responses: Laurence reports that one British reviewer called *The Stone Angel* "'The most telling argument for euthanasia' which he had ever read" (*DE* 166), while in Canada Hagar was just "everybody's grandmother" (*DE* 166). Laurence herself is ambivalent about Hagar: "I both loved and deplored her" (*G* 2). Readers are also ambivalent: Hagar is the character we love to hate and hate to love. Still, Hagar haunts us.

Laurence claims, "The character of Hagar in *The Stone Angel* seemed almost to choose me" (*HS* 6). She explains in a 1961 letter to Adele Wiseman how Hagar took her by surprise: "I made two false starts on 2 separate novels that I'd had in mind for some time and found I could not write either one. Very nicely plotted they were, but dead as door-nails. Then this daft old lady came along, and I will say about her that she is one hell of an old lady, a real tartar. She's crabby, snobbish, dif-ficult, proud as Lucifer for no reason, a trial to her family, etc. She's also – I forgot to mention – dying" (*SA* 312).[2]

But Hagar must come to life before she can die. She must climb the great chain of being from stone to angel in order to release her spirit, to give up the ghost, to death. Before she can die, however, she must acknowledge herself as a woman. Educated by her father, the proud patriarch Jason Currie, motherless Hagar tries to be the strong son he never had. So she rejects her womanhood. She learns contempt for women, especially her mother, who died in giving birth to her. Afraid to be a woman or mother, she refuses to join the family of woman and rejects the female familial roles of wife, mother, daughter, sister, and the roles of lover and friend. Haunted by her father after his death, Hagar becomes a patriarch in petticoats.

She must discover her identity as a woman through her roles in re-lation to the men in her life. Initially, she laments, "Oh, my lost men" (6); ultimately, she acknowledges her role in their deaths: "Oh, my two, my dead. Dead by your own hands or by mine?" (292). The drama of *The Stone Angel* is the development of Hagar's sense of respon-sibility for the deaths of her husband and son. Now "rampant with memory" (5), Hagar's retrospective narrative allows her to relive the rejections that led to their deaths and to atone for her crimes of the heart.[3] Only when she has redeemed herself is she free to die. She must also acknowledge herself as mother to her firstborn son, Marvin. Her deathbed is her childbed, as she finally gives birth to herself as a woman and a mother. Finally, the angel is freed from the stone. Adele Wiseman says in her afterword, *The Stone Angel* is a "Pygmalion tale, without the external Pygmalion figure, in which the old lady, in her continu-ous monologue, discovers herself, carves out and completes the shape of her own life, comes fully alive at last before she dies" (*SA* 310).

Hagar virtually created the novel, as Laurence recalls in *Dance on the Earth: A Memoir*: "An old woman had come into my mind. I sup-pose she had been there for a while, but all at once she became insis-tent. That novel became *The Stone Angel*" (155). Writing the novel was like taking dictation from a determined ghost: "It was as if the old woman was actually there, telling me her life story, and it was my responsibility to put it down as faithfully as I could" (156). So much did she dominate the novel that Laurence originally titled it simply *Hagar.*

Hagar narrates the novel: "The story demanded to be written in the first person," Laurence asserts: "Hagar was an old lady telling me her own story. I attempted to put it down without manipulating it" (Fabre 199). After completing *Hagar*, as it was called in embryo, Margaret suffered doubts when Jack advised her to rewrite it in the third person and in chronological order. Margaret declared, "Impossible, however – [Hagar] is speaking; that is simply a fact" (315). She decided to "stick to the first draft, come hell or high water. The old lady knew what she was doing when she told me her life story" (314). Laurence asserts, "I felt when I was writing *The Stone Angel* an enormous conviction of the authenticity of Hagar's voice" (GG 82). In fact, Hagar has a dual voice: "Hagar's description of places and events and her inner feelings were emerging in a kind of poetic, even rhythmic, prose, whereas her speech to others was brusque, down-to-earth, testy and cranky" (DE 156).

Hagar also dictated the form of the novel, for Laurence vouchsafes her characters some autonomy. In "Time and the Narrative Voice" Laurence explains "the relationship between the narrative voice and the treatment of time," for "it is the character who chooses which parts of the personal past, the family past and the ancestral past have to be revealed for the present to be realized and the future to happen" (TNV 160). Laurence chose "to record Hagar's life in time present and encompass her long past in a series of dramatic memories by having each one of her memory sequences triggered by an event in her present" (DE 156).

So powerful was Hagar that she actually broke up their marriage, Margaret claims: "When I wrote the first draft of *The Stone Angel*, Jack wanted to read it. I didn't want him to. I think I knew his response would be pivotal in our marriage ... I allowed him to read it in the end, and he didn't like it much, but for me it was the most important book I had written, a book on which I had to stake the rest of my life" (DE 158). Following this artistic disagreement, the couple had a serious argument in which Margaret rebelled – perhaps like Morag rebelling against Brooke's judgment of her writing in *The Diviners*. In 1962 Margaret went to London with her two children and "the old lady" – her two kinds of offspring – while Jack went to Pakistan: "Strange reason for breaking up a marriage: a novel. I had to go with the old lady, I really did, but at the same time I felt terrible about hurting him" (*DE* 158). This masterpiece was almost lost forever when the only copy of the manuscript was sent by surface mail, which took weeks to deliver it: "This was the novel for which I had separated from my husband and embarked on who knew what, uprooting and dragging along my two children, and I almost seemed to be trying to lose it" (*DE* 159). But Hagar proved irrepressible.

Laurence calls Hagar "an archetypal figure" representing her "Scots Presbyterian prairie background" (Hutchinson 75) – a Canadian archetype: "*The Stone Angel* is the first book that I had written about my own country of the heart" (Arnason 33). When she finally returned to her own people in her fiction, however, it was to her grandparents' generation: "I had to begin by approaching my background and my past through my grandparents' generation, the generation of pioneers of Scots-Presbyterian origin who had been among the first to people the town I called Manawaka." She adds, "Hagar, in *The Stone Angel*, was not drawn from life, but she incorporates many qualities of my grandparents' generation. Her speech is their speech, and her gods their gods" (*HS* 6–7).[4]

Hagar's archetypal stature is reinforced by parallels with her biblical namesake *Hagar*, the Egyptian handmaid who is driven into the wilderness with her son Ismael by Sarah, Abraham's wife, in Genesis 16.[5] Laurence says the novel "parallels the story of the biblical Hagar who is cast out into the wilderness" (Sullivan 68), although "in the case of my Hagar the wilderness is within" (Fabre 198). As Joan Coldwell observes, "Incorporating many biblical allusions, the novel offers a modern version of the archetypal quest for spiritual vision" (*OCCL* 1098).

Most important, Hagar is the archetype of the dying woman. Laurence affirms, "If Hagar in *The Stone Angel* has any meaning, it is the same as that of an old woman anywhere, having to deal with the reality of dying" (*HS* 9). *The Stone Angel* is a novel about death, and the subject of mortality gives the text its power. That Hagar begins her narrative in a cemetery – like Pip, who achieves self-awareness in a graveyard, as he contemplates the graves of his parents and siblings, in Dickens' *Great Expectations* – telegraphs her topic to the reader.

The death of the powerful individual is the stuff of tragedy and the greatest literature of our culture – from the classical drama of Sophocles and Aeschylus, through the Renaissance drama of Marlowe and Shakespeare, to the modern drama of Eugene O'Neill and Tennessee Williams. W.H. New calls Hagar's story "an essentially tragic one" (MLWC 138), and critics have compared her to tragic heroes. Claudette Pollock argues that Hagar's story "parallels Lear's tragic tale of misplaced parental affection" (267).[6] The tragic inevitability derives from the fact that Hagar, like all mortals, must die. But she denies the facts of death. She must descend to a figurative hell, Miltonic in its darkness visible, where she is "exposed to the core" (116), while physicians penetrate the mystery of her being before she realizes, "Something threatens me, something unknown and in hiding, waiting to pounce" (117).

But she cannot name the last enemy. Like many tragic figures, Hagar has a tragic flaw: pride that cannot accept the inevitable. Critics have noted that pride is both Hagar's strength and her weakness. Laurence labels it "spiritual pride," chief of the seven deadly sins, and calls Hagar "proud as Lucifer" (Fabre 194).[7] In "Hagar in Hell: Margaret Laurence's Fallen Angel," Paul Comeau argues that Laurence uses "Milton's Satan as the prototype for her own proud, rebellious angel [as] *The Stone Angel* represents Margaret Laurence's vision of Hell, with Hagar Shipley manifesting the characteristics of the most notorious fallen angel" (11). Calling herself "Proud as ... Lucifer" (191), the rebel angel, Hagar tries to outface death.

Hagar knows from the outset that she is dying, but, like all unpleasant truths, she denies the fact of death. Laurence chooses as epigraph the lines from Dylan Thomas's villanelle addressed to his dying father – "*Do not go gentle into that good night, / Rage, rage, against the dying of the light*" – to suggest Hagar's rage against death *and* her rage for life – unlike her brother Matt: "He didn't fight his death as some do ... He let himself slip away" (60).[8] Hagar does know that she is going to die, however much she refuses to acknowledge the fact: "*Listen. You must listen. It's important. It's – quite an event*" (282), Hagar shrieks in italics: *Someone really ought to know these things*" (296). She promises, "I'll have a word or two to say, you can depend on that, before my mouth is stopped with dark" (139), and she is as good as her word. The true drama of *The Stone Angel* lies in Hagar's acceptance of death.

Laurence's fascination with age and death was inspired by the death of her stepmother in 1957. She wrote to Wiseman in 1957, "I would like to write a novel about an old woman ... I picture a very old woman who knows she is dying, and who ... is moving with tremendous excitement – part fear and part eagerness – towards a great and inevitable happening, just as years before she experienced birth" (311). Laurence parallels birth and death: "I think birth is the greatest experience of life, right until the end, and then death is the greatest experience. There are times when I can believe that the revelation of death will be something so vast we are incapable of imagining it" (311). Laurence's friend Budge Wilson confirms that she "thought of death as a second birth – a delivery into a second unknown territory" (13). Laurence recalls the birth of her son in 1955: "I felt as though I were looking over God's shoulder at the moment of the creation of life" (*DE* 149). Her parallel of birth and death is apt: just as the mother's body labours to deliver the new life, so the aging body must labour to deliver the spirit. To "give up the ghost" means literally to liberate the spirit. Thus, in dying, Hagar gives birth to, or mothers, her self. She connects birth and death when, on her deathbed, she recalls the birth of John: "When my second son was born, he found it difficult to breathe at first. He gasped a little, coming into the unfamiliar air. He couldn't have known before or suspected at all that breathing would be what was done by creatures here. Perhaps the same occurs elsewhere, an element so unknown you'd never suspect it at all, until – Wishful thinking. If it happened that way, I'd pass out with amazement. Can angels faint?" (307).

That such a young woman would aspire to write a novel about an old woman facing death is not surprising when one realizes that death brought Laurence back to Canada 1957, when her stepmother Marg, her beloved "Mum," lay dying of cancer in Victoria. The deathwatch Margaret held by her bedside is indelibly described in *Dance on the Earth: A Memoir*, where she calls those months "among the most difficult and anguished of my life" (113).

The person who inspired the character of Hagar, however, was her patriarchal Grandfather Simpson – memorialized as Timothy Connor in *A Bird in the House*. James King records that "Margaret admitted to Budge Wilson that her Grandfather Simpson was the real model for Hagar" (160). Laurence was haunted by hatred of her grandfather – "a stern old autocrat much like a male Hagar Shipley" (Cameron 4), she asserts. Elsewhere, she confirms, "the character of Hagar in *The Stone Angel* is strictly a fictional character … although some of her characteristics are similar to those of my grandfather" (Hutchison 75).[9]

Laurence states, "A title should, if possible, be like a line of poetry – capable of saying a great deal with hardly any words. The title of a novel should in some way express the whole novel, its themes and even something of its outcome. It should all be there in a phrase" (*HS* 144). But her editors disliked her working title *Hagar*, suggesting *Old Lady Shipley* instead (*HS* 145). Desperate, Laurence reread the Psalms, seeking a title and coming up with *Sword in my Bones*, which sounded, she realized, like "a tale of pirates and buried treasure" (*HS* 145). Finally, she looked at the manuscript, and there it was in the very first sentence: "Upon the hill brow, the stone angel used to stand" (3); "The title, the real and true and only possible title had been there all the time, in the first line of the book" (*HS* 145).[10]

The Stone Angel was the perfect title, for, as Laurence observes, "it does dominate the book like an imposing symbol" (Fabre 199). The stone angel broods over the entire novel, from the opening page, where Hagar reflects, "I wonder if she stands there yet, in memory of her who relinquished her feeble ghost as I gained my stubborn one, my mother's angel that my father bought in pride to mark her bones and proclaim his dynasty for ever and a day" (3). When she leaves Manawaka, shocked at "how small the town was and how short a time it took to leave it, as we measure time," she passes "the dump grounds and the cemetery on the hill": "I could see on the hill brow the marble angel, sightlessly guarding the gardens of snow, the empty places and the deep-lying dead" (142). Hagar consigns her lost men to the angel's guardianship. Finally, she recalls her last visit to the cemetery: "The angel was still standing there, but winters or lack of care had altered her. The earth had heaved with frost around her, and she stood askew and tilted. Her mouth was white. We didn't touch her. We only looked. Someday she'll topple, and no one will bother to set her upright again" (305).

Hagar, of course, is the stone angel:[11] she is "stone blind" (58), just as the stone angel is "doubly blind – not only stone but unendowed with even a pretense of sight. Whoever carved her had left the eyeballs blank" (3).[12] Hagar feels angry – "at God, perhaps, for giving us eyes but almost never sight" (173). She recalls, "The night my son died I was transformed to stone and never wept at all" (243). You cannot get blood, or tears, from a stone. But this petrified woman must weep and bleed: "Rigid as marble" (146), Hagar must be made flesh.

The stone angel is a brilliant symbol, spanning, as it does, the spectrum of creation, from inanimate matter to pure spirit. The "great chain of being" stretched from base metal through vegetation and animal life to human beings and ultimately to the pure spirit of the angels who sit at the throne of God, for, as the Psalm states, "thou hast made him a little lower than the angels" (8:5). Hagar must climb this cosmic ladder from earth to angel. As E.M.W. Tillyard explains in his *Elizabethan World Picture*, "The chain of being is educative both in the marvels of its static self and in its implications of ascent" (28). Hagar does have feet of clay, but, ultimately, she will transcend the "ashes to ashes, dust to dust" of death to emerge as pure spirit when she gives up the ghost. As Woodcock says, "The stone angel [is] hewn out of the earth and blind as creatures that live in earth, and as such is an appropriate symbol for Hagar Shipley, the choleric earthy mother who inhabits *The Stone Angel*" (57). The titular symbol thus provides a cryptic paradox that condenses God's whole creation and the novel's entire action into two little words.

Women were referred to as angels in Hagar's Victorian era. A wife and mother was "the Angel in the House," the title of Coventry Patmore's 1854–63 sequence of poems in praise of married love: "Her children arise up, and call her blessed; her husband also, and he praiseth her" (Proverbs 31:28). Prostitutes were called "fallen angels." The widowed Hagar feels like a snow angel (81), suggesting the angel of death.

Hagar, the woman of stone, is as good as dead already. Laurence affirms, "part of Hagar has been dead for years through pride and her strict sense of dignity even before she was old and sick" (Fabre 193). Hagar, calling herself "the Egyptian" (92) and "Pharaoh's daughter" (43), compares herself to a mummy: at Silverthreads, she wonders, "Is it a mausoleum and I, the Egyptian, mummified with pillows and my own flesh, through some oversight embalmed alive? ... I won't look at a thing, not one, on the conducted tour of this pyramid. I'm blind. I'm deaf" (96–7). Later she wonders, "Perhaps when I'm let out, launched into wind and sun, I may disintegrate entirely, like the flowers found on ancient young Tutankhamen's tomb, which crumbled when time flooded in through the broken door" (111).

Hagar's narrative contains many symbols of rebirth. Hagar is "the egg woman" (132) who saves the money for her escape by selling eggs to the citizens of Manawaka, including Lottie Dreiser and her daughter, Arlene. "The damn chickens were a godsend," she acknowledges, even though she detests chickens. Hagar is revolted by a pile of fertilized eggs: "The chicks, feeble, foodless, bloodied and mutilated, prisoned by the weight of broken shells all around them, were trying to crawl like little worms, their half-mouths opened uselessly among the garbage" (27). While Hagar can only "gawk and retch," refusing to put them out of their misery, Lottie, "light as an eggshell herself, ... took a stick and crushed the eggshell skulls" (27). Hagar must also emerge from her shell at last. She is packed into the car with pillows, "like an egg in a crate" (93), for the journey to Silverthreads, suggesting rebirth.[13]

The Stone Angel is a novel about a metamorphosis. Numerous images suggest transition. Hagar pictures herself "lying on my Afghan cocoon like an old brown caterpillar" as she lies, "[p]aralyzed with embarrassment" (208), on the sofa, eavesdropping on John and Arlene's lovemaking. Later, in hospital, she says, "I lie in my cocoon" (306) and, on the last page, she longs to return to "my sleek cocoon" (308). These images suggest the metamorphosis of the *psyche*, the Greek word for "butterfly" and for "soul," from its earthly chrysalis.

Hagar shows signs of coming to life. Her tell-tale heart beats frantically in the bonehouse of her body like a bird trying to escape from its cage: "My heart is pulsing too fast, beating like a berserk bird. I try to calm it. I must, I must, or it will damage itself against the cage of bones. But still it lurches and flutters, in a frenzy to get out" (95). Later, in hospital, in her "canvas cage" (286), she feels "the pain beating its wings against my rib cage" (256).

What will free her heart? Telling "the heart's truth" (292). Before she can come to life, she must acknowledge herself as a woman. She sees "the hairy triangle that still proclaims with lunatic insistence a nonexistent womanhood" (77). Her "nonexistent womanhood" is not just a feature of her old age, but a symptom of her life-long denial of her true femaleness.

Hagar is afraid to be a woman. Why? Because her mother, who "relinquished her feeble ghost as I gained my stubborn one" (3), died in giving birth to Hagar: "she'd not died when either of the boys was born, but saved her death for me" (59). So, when her first son is born, Hagar is sure she will not survive: "I believed I was going to die" (100).

That is why Hagar cannot don her mother's plaid shawl, treasured by her brother Dan ever since their mother's death, when her brother Matt asks her to comfort the dying Daniel: "I can't. Oh Matt, I'm sorry, but I can't, I can't. I'm not a bit like her'" (25). She explains: "But all I could think of was that meek woman I'd never seen, the woman Dan was said to resemble so much and from whom he'd inherited a frailty I could not help but detest, however much a part of me wanted to sympathize. To play at being her – it was beyond me. 'I can't, Matt.' I was crying, shaken by torments he never even suspected, wanting above all else to do the thing he asked, but unable to do it, unable to bend enough" (25). Thus, we see, early in her narrative, that she rejects the role of sister in refusing to comfort her dying brother. This is the first of many female roles that she will refuse to fill. She rejects the mantle, or shroud, of "thankless motherhood" (59) in fiction by refusing to impersonate her nameless mother and also in fact by refusing to acknowledge her firstborn son.

We can understand why Hagar is afraid to be a woman and afraid to perform female roles, if we recall the female virtues of the Victorian era: selflessness, submission, self-sacrifice – virtues illustrated by Agnes Wickfield in Charles Dickens's novel *David Copperfield*, defined in the guidebooks to womanly behaviour of the era, and cited by Mary Poovey in *Uneven Developments: The Ideological Work of Gender in MidVictorian England* (7–8) – qualities that contradict the virtues of the Puritan work ethic that Hagar was raised to respect.

Brought up by her father, patriarchal "self-made man" (7) and pioneer of commerce Jason Currie – named both for the heroic Argonaut leader who rescued the Golden Fleece and for the Anglo-Indian spice that symbolizes temper – Hagar tries to be the son her father wanted. For his sons, Matt and Dan, are weaklings, like their mother: "My brothers took after our mother, graceful unspirited boys who tried to please him but rarely could. Only I ... was sturdy like him and bore his hawkish nose and stare that could meet anyone's without blinking an eyelash" (7–8). With no mother to teach her to be a woman, Hagar is her father's daughter and his would-be son: he declares proudly, "You take after me ... You've got backbone" (10). "Jason Currie's black-haired daughter" (6), she agrees, "I did take after him" (10).[14] Though she despises his snobbish values and rebels against them, she absorbs his pride and prejudice and repeats his maxims to her son John. She bequeaths John the Currie plaid pin (124), with the crest depicting a

castle and a sword, along with the war cry, "*Gainsay Who Dare!*" (15).
John trades the plaid pin for the Tonnerres' hunting knife, like the one
Bram used to feed him honey (125), thus preferring his father's severing instrument to his mother's connecting one. "The plagues go on from
generation to generation" (284), Hagar finally acknowledges.[15]

Educated by her father, Hagar views herself in male terms. She calls
herself "handsome" – not "beautiful" like a woman, but "handsome"
like a man: "Not beautiful, I admit, not that china figurine look some
women have, all gold and pink fragility, a wonder their corsets don't
snap their sparrow bones. Handsomeness lasts longer" (60). She describes herself as "tall and sturdy and dark" (27) and feels "surly" toward Lottie Dreiser's fragile femininity.

Hagar despises women, calling them cows and sows: her daughter-
in-law Doris "strains like a calving cow" (31), and Hagar grunts "like
a constipated cow" (92). Critics have noted Hagar's abundant nature
imagery, especially her references to animals, but not the derogatory
nature of these pejorative comparisons. She absorbed this contempt
from her father's attitude to his housekeeper, Aunt Dolly, to "No-name
Lottie Dreiser's mother" (18), and to his dead wife – "the brood mare
who lay beneath because she'd proved no match for his stud" (43).

So Hagar rejects her womanhood in an attempt to be the son her
father always wanted. The ghost of Jason Currie haunts Hagar Shipley, just as John Simpson haunted Margaret Laurence. Hagar con-
ceals her female body under masculine garments. Seeing her reflection
in a mirror, she is shocked: "I was wearing, I saw, a man's black over-
coat. ... The face – a brown and leathery face that wasn't mine. Only
the eyes were mine, staring as though to pierce the lying glass and
get beneath to some truer image, infinitely distant" (133). Hagar has
to discover that distant identity, her female self so long overlaid by
masculine traits.

Her female identity seems buried in the black trunk stamped with
her maiden name, "*Miss H. Currie*" (140) – prototype of the "wooden
box" (185) in which she expects to be carried out of life – the maiden
identity she reverts to when she packs her trunk to leave Bram (140).
"Yet now I feel that if I were to walk carefully up to my room, approach the mirror softly, take it by surprise, I would see there again
that Hagar with the shining hair" (42).

Mirror metaphors abound in *The Stone Angel*, as Hagar searches for her true reflection: "I am past ninety, and this figure seems somehow arbitrary and impossible, for when I look in my mirror and beyond the changing shell that houses me, I see the eyes of Hagar Currie, the same dark eyes as when I first began to remember and to notice myself" (38). Only her eyes, those windows of the soul, are still Hagar, but her eyes are blind, like the stone angel. Thus, *The Stone Angel* is a study of perception, as Hagar gradually learns to see clearly. Wiseman applauds "the power of her sightless stone angel as metaphor, since the story is, on a profound level, the account of how her stone angel gains sight" (310).

Metaphors of prison also abound in *The Stone Angel*, for Hagar is imprisoned in her own mortifying flesh. But Hagar's pride is her prison, her fortress. Like all strongholds – including Grandfather Connor's Brick House, like "some crusader's embattled fortress in a heathen wilderness" (*BH* 11) – it protects inhabitants from intruders, but also prevents the inhabitants from escaping. Paranoid from childhood, Hagar sees people as potential threats. She fears to make herself vulnerable, for the weak perish, like "gutless" Regina Weese, whose gravestone she views with contempt (4). "Stifling my laughter and my tears" (10), she refuses to express emotion – except "choler" (245) – like Grandfather Connor, or Simpson. Her constipation is a grotesque metaphor for her inability to express herself: "the windy prison of my bowels belches air, sulphurous and groaning" (58), like damned souls in hell – "Job in reverse" (40). "I'm locked like a bank vault, with no key" (191), she declares; "My mind's locked" (146). She is "choked with it now, the incommunicable years" (296). Hagar is entombed in the prison of her pride: Laurence affirms, "a part of Hagar has been dead for years through pride and her strict sense of dignity even before she was old and sick" (Fabre 193).

To come to life Hagar must accept her identity as a woman. To enter the family of woman, she has to accept her female roles as sister, daughter, wife, and mother. Her names emphasize the issue of roles. Her father never called her by her name: "He called me 'Miss' when he was displeased, and 'daughter' when he was kindly disposed toward me. Never Hagar" (14). Marvin calls her "Mother" (130) – ironically, since she refuses to fulfill that role for him. Only Bram calls her by her Christian name: "You know something, Hagar. There's men in Manawaka call their wives 'mother' all the time. That's one thing I never done" (80). She reflects, "It was true. He never did, not once. I was Hagar to him, and if he were alive, I'd be Hagar to him yet. And now I think he was the only person close to me who ever thought of me by my name, not daughter, nor sister, nor mother, nor even wife, but Hagar, always" (80).

Hagar is unwilling to fulfill woman's natural roles as wife, mother, daughter, and sister. Indeed, she fails in each of these functions, rejecting the roles. First, she refuses to be the daughter her father desires her to be, when she rebels against his domination by marrying the socially unacceptable Bram: "drunk with exhilaration at my daring" (49), she flings his family war-cry, "*Gainsay who dare*" (15), in his face. She snubs the namby-pamby suitors he parades before her, and selects the most unsuitable, and the most blatantly sexual, spouse to spite her father, who disinherits her in revenge in this Freudian family romance.[16]

The hints of an incestuous impulse of the widower toward his chatelaine daughter may explain Hagar's urge to escape his domination. He gives her lozenges with sugary messages: "*Be Mine, You Beauty, Love Me, Be True*" (13). After beating her palms with a ruler in this war of wills, he throws his arms around his daughter: "He held me so tightly I was almost smothered ... I felt caged and panicky" (10). Later, when she returns from the ladies' college in Toronto – "Pharaoh's daughter reluctantly returning to his roof, the square brick palace so oddly antimacassared in the wilderness" (43) – he looks at her possessively, "as though I were a thing and his" (43).[17] When she threatens to teach at the South Wachakwa school house, he grips the newel post "as though it were a throat," and says, "You think I'd let you go to the kind of dances they have there, and let all the farm boys paw you?" (44). Whispering, "Men have terrible thoughts," he squeezes her hand so hard it hurts, as he begs, "Stay" (44). "How I feared his hands" (44), Hagar acknowledges. When she announces that she intends to marry Bram, "he reached out a hand like a lariat, caught my arm, held and bruised it," commanding, "You'll not go, Hagar" (49) – the only time he ever calls her by her name. "Armored" (44) in her "bottle-green costume" (43), she defies him. When she refuses to stay and be his chatelaine, he disinherits her. Appropriately, he donates his wealth to create Currie Memorial Park, where cultivation will control the wild tendencies of nature, and his immortality will be blazoned in the pink frilled petals of petunias (64).

Marrying Bram, whom her father declares "common as dirt" (48) and "[l]azy as a pet pig" (46), is the ultimate act of rebellion. That, of course, is his major source of attraction. Just as Jason Currie is connected with the urge to cultivate nature, symbolized by the portly peonies that Hagar despises, so Brampton Shipley represents the wildness of nature, "the hot rush of disrespectful wind" (5) that blows through the cultivated cemetery gardens. As proprietor of Manawaka's first general store, Jason Currie is the "fledgling pharaoh in an uncouth land" (3), while Bram is the uncouth citizen of that uncultivated country. Bram's cursing, drinking, and association with "half-breeds girls" (47) make him the ideal foil to her proud, puritanical father, while his sexual experience as a widower and womanizer attracts the virginal Hagar.

Hagar relishes Bram's earthiness: "I reveled in his fingernails with ingrown crescents of earth that never met a file. I fancied I heard in his laughter the bravery of battalions. I thought he looked a bearded Indian, so brown and beaked a face. The black hair thrusting from his chin was rough as thistles" (45) – recalling the thistles that threaten the cemetery posies (5). The vital, virile farmer is everything her urban, capitalist father is not – "so hey-day, go-day, God-send-Sunday" (168), in contrast to Currie's proud puritanism. Meeting Hagar at a dance, Bram dares to "press his outheld groin against my thigh" (47) in an unbridled suggestion of sexuality. Mortified, Hagar nevertheless accepts his subsequent invitation to dance.

Hagar and Bram are an ideal example of the attraction of opposites: he is Dionysian to her Apollonian. She is college-educated, while he reads Eaton's catalogue "to improve his mind" (113). She revels in her lover's link with the land, in his "smelling of sweat and sun" (113), while he likes her to be a lady: either he aspires to rise socially, or he is challenged to pull her off her pedestal. But the attraction of opposites soon degenerates into a war of attrition, as the attributes that first attracted them to each other become the very qualities they abhor: "here's the joker in the pack – we'd each married for those qualities we later found we couldn't bear, he for my manners and speech, I for his flouting of them" (79). Here the battle of the sexes is exacerbated by the class war: while Hagar is respectable, Bram is uncouth: "I could have been proud, going to town or church with him, if only he'd never opened his mouth" (70), Hagar acknowledges, for "He couldn't string two words together without some crudity" (79).

Ironically, however, Hagar, a schoolmistress *manquée*, has an impulse to cultivate Bram, to "imagine him rigged out in a suit of grey soft as a dove's breast-feathers" (45). She wants to convert Bram in order to impress her father: "Father would soften and yield when he saw how Brampton Shipley prospered, gentled, learned cravats and grammar" (50). But Bram proves a reluctant pupil to her schoolmarm's tutelage, and he resists her refashioning.

Hagar, unfamiliar with the birds and the bees, with no mother to teach her the facts of life, is shocked when she is "deflowered": "I had not known, and when he'd bent, enormous and giant, I could not believe there could be within me a room to house such magnitude. When I found there was, I felt as one might feel discovering a second head, an unsuspected area. Pleasure or pain were one to me, meaningless. I only thought – well thank the Lord now I know, and at least it's possible, without the massacre it looked like being" (52). The wedding gift of a silver-topped decanter that Bram gives her as he initiates their marital relations is a potent symbol of sexuality (51). Later, long after Bram's death, Hagar says, "I never thought much of that decanter at the time, but now I wouldn't part with it for any money" (62).

Her reaction, the next morning, is to scrub the kitchen, "as though I'd been driven by a whip" (52). She "worked like a dray horse" (112) to make the Shipley place ship-shape, for, in the Victorian code of ethics, "cleanliness was next to godliness." Thus, she attempts to control the chaos of nature by elbow grease. Still the "dainty-nosed czarina" (27), Hagar recalls her girlhood self: "How anxious I was to be neat and orderly, imagining life had been created only to celebrate tidiness, like prissy Pippa as she passed" (5).

Hagar envisions love in the image of courtly love portrayed by Pre-Raphaelite painter Holman Hunt in his medieval portrait of "the knight and lady's swooning adoration" (82). "Love, I fancied, must consist of words and deeds delicate as lavender sachets, not like the things he did sprawled on the high white bedstead that rattled like a train" (80). Later, she finds her school copy of Barrett Browning's *Sonnets from the Portugese* in her black trunk, "annotated with violet ink – 'n.b.

passion' or 'plight of women' scribbled by a nincompoop who'd borne
my Christian name" (126). She realizes, "*His banner over me was love
...*[18] His banner over me was only his own skin, and I no longer know
why it should have shamed me" (80–1). She has been too sexually and
emotionally inhibited to acknowledge to herself or to her husband how
"I sucked my secret pleasure from his skin" (80), for "I prided myself
upon keeping my pride intact, like some maidenhead" (81). An old
woman facing death, she says, "My bed is cold as winter" (81): she
imagines she is lying in the snow and, when she arises, "there would
be the outline of an angel with spread wings" (81) – a snow angel.

Bram seeks solace in his stallion Soldier and in drinking red biddy
with his buddy, Charlie Bean. Hardly a knight on a white charger, Bram
is still "strong as a horse," Hagar affirms. Hagar frequently refers to
herself in equine terms, as she recalls flirting with young men: "Oh, I
was the one all right, tossing my black mane" (46). As an old woman,
she thinks, if she approaches her mirror quietly, "I would see there
again that Hagar with the shining hair, the dark-maned colt off to the
training ring, the young ladies' academy in Toronto" (42). It is curious that Hagar, married to a man who loves horses, views herself in
equine terms.

One of the most poignant points in their marriage, when Hagar
fails her husband most, involves the death of Soldier. "Bram was crazy
about horses" (83), she recalls. Hagar likes Rosa Bonheur's *The Horse
Fair*, where "the great-flanked horses strut eternally" (83). She is attracted to the potent virility represented by those horses, recalling D.H.
Lawrence's use of horses to symbolize male sexuality in *St. Mawr*. But
she is terrified of them in the flesh: as Bram says, "You never gave a
damn for living horses, Hagar" (83). She agrees: "He was quite right
that I never cared for horses. I was frightened of them, so high and
heavy they seemed, so muscular, so much their own masters – I never
felt I could handle them" (83). Bram, like Chris in "Horses of the
Night," dreams of owning saddle horses. When his gray stallion, Soldier, follows the black mare into the night, recalling Bram's pursuit of
the black-maned Hagar, and he fails to find him in the blizzard, Hagar
says, "I'm sorry about it, Bram. I know you were fond of him" (87).
Bram erects a rock to mark Soldier's grave, recalling the stone angel
that Jason Currie raised to memorialize "the brood mare" (43) who
was his wife. Hagar thinks, "I felt so gently inclined that I think I might

have opened to him openly" (87–8). But Bram, unaware of her secret, thinks the kindest thing he can do is to leave her alone, and she is not anxious to enlighten him. So, like Scarlett and Rhett, they miss their moment. Hagar's failure to express her love leads to a stalemate.

Again, at the point of the birth of their first child, she acknowledges, "In that moment when we might have touched our hands together, Bram and I, and wished each other well, the thought uppermost in my mind was – *the nerve of him*" (100–1). Communication is impossible between the puritanical bourgeoise and elemental farmer who make such strange bedfellows. As a result of their hostility, Bram "changed, put away the laughter he wore and replaced it with a shabbier garment" (113).

Their marital relations eventually degenerate into a martial state: "Twenty-four years, in all, were scoured away like sandbanks under the spate of our wrangle and bicker" (116). She confesses, "I'd be the last one to maintain that marriages are made in heaven, unless, as I've sometimes thought, the idea is to see what will happen, put this or that unlikely pair together, observe how they spar" (167) – recalling "the brutal joker" (48) of *The Jest of God*.

The nadir of Bram's Dionysian descent is the night the Mountie sees him relieve himself against the steps of Currie's Store (115), leading the children to label him "Bramble Shitley" (131). When Hagar encounters Bram buying stale donuts and vanilla extract for his buddy Charlie Bean, she says, "We walked out of the store together ... and that was the last time we ever walked anywhere together, Brampton Shipley and myself" (135).

This deadlock causes Bram to degenerate into a derelict. Eventually he shrinks, literally, under the weight of her disapprobation. When Hagar returns for his death, she is shocked to see how the big, bear-like Bram has shrunk to "an ancient child" (183). His "land that was never lucky" (29) is an extroversion of his decay, resembling a cadaver that has given up the ghost: "At the Shipley place the rusty machinery stood like aged bodies gradually expiring from exposure, ribs turned to the sun [and] the front porch ... had been given a final pliers twist by frost, and wore a caved-in look, like toothless jaws" (169). After his death, the "gray shell of a house" (208) is like a corpse from which the soul is departed. Small wonder that Marvin, who works for "Britemore Paint" (166), is so "mad on paint" (153).

Ultimately, Hagar fails as a wife, leaving her husband's home just as she left her father's house twenty years earlier: "Each venture and launching seems impossible until it becomes necessary, and then there's a way, and it doesn't do to be too fussy about the means" (135). Ironically, she moves to the west coast to work as housekeeper in Mr Oatley's stone house, recalling her father's housekeeper, Aunt Dolly Stonehouse.[19]

Just as she has failed as a wife, so she also fails as a mother. Her son Marvin lives to please his mother, but she disowns him: "I almost felt as though Marvin weren't my son" (62). When he leaves, at age seventeen, for the Great War, she does not have a word to say: "I didn't know what to say to him. I wanted to beg him to look after himself, to be careful, as one warns children against snow drifts or thin ice or the hooves of horses, feeling the flimsy words may act as some kind of charm against disaster. I wanted to hold him tightly, plead with him, against all reason and reality, not to go. But I did not want to embarrass either of us, nor have him think I'd taken leave of my senses. While I was hesitating, he spoke first" (129). She merely tells him to hurry, lest he miss his train. When Marvin prompts, "Mother," "I realized I was waiting with a kind of anxious hope for what he would say, waiting for him to make himself known to me" (130). Hagar always waits for the other person to speak, not realizing her own responsibility to speak. Hagar is unable to express her emotions or to say what she feels. Like Vanessa's Grandfather Connor, the only emotion she can express is anger: choler is indeed her essential humour, as George Woodcock observes.[20] Of course, Hagar blames Marvin, for nothing is ever her fault: "he was never a quick thinker, Marvin. Words would not come to his bidding, and so the moment eluded us both" (130). Marvin has no "facility with words" (34), unlike his flamboyant brother John, with his facile fabrications. When Hagar says she has "two sons ... I mean, I had two. One was killed – in the last war" (104), she may suggest that she wishes Marvin, not John, had died. Marvin is "the unknown soldier, the one whose name you never knew" (182),[21] just as Bram is the "unknown man" (183), the man she never knew: "I couldn't speak nor reach to him in any way at all" (100).

Hagar mythologizes her sons, decreeing that Marvin is a Shipley who takes after Bram, while John will provide the dynasty her father desired and be the son to Jason Currie that she herself could never be, "a boy after his own heart" (123): "Jason Currie never saw my second son or knew at all that the sort of boy he'd wanted had waited a generation to appear" (64). Even John knows she's wrong: "You always bet on the wrong horse ... Marv was your boy, but you never saw that, did you?" (237). While she sees her favourite, John, as a fanciful boy, forever "spinning his spiderwebs" (157), she views Marvin as "a stolid soul" who "lives in a dreamless sleep" (58). Hagar, named for the biblical figure, views John in Messianic terms: calling herself "a stout Madonna" (122), she "prayed to him as though he were some infant and relentless Jesus" (54). As Bram, his name echoing "Abraham," swears by "Judas Priest," John swears by "jumping Jesus" (128). Bram brags he was born in a barn – "Me and Jesus" (125), believing his barns will rise "miraculous as Jesus from the tomb" (114). No Messiah, Marvin is a disciple: "High day or holiday or Judgment Day – no difference to Marvin. He would have put his elbows on the table if he'd been an apostle at the Last Supper" (34).[22]

"Oh my lost men" (6), Hagar laments at the outset of her retrospective, for she has lost her father, her husband, and her son, but she rejects all thought of her responsibility for their loss: "No, I will not think of that" (6); "I can't change what's happened to me in my life, or make what's not occurred take place. But I can't say I like it, or accept it, or believe it's for the best. I don't and never shall, not even if I'm damned for it" (160). Guilt incites retrospection, for she is compelled to confess, to make restitution, and to seek redemption. "Now I am rampant with memory" (5), she declares, as she relives her life in this *Vollendungsroman*, or "novel of winding up" (31), in Constance Rooke's phrase.[23] Like a drowning woman, whose whole life flashes before her eyes, "Hagar's life flashes before her, demanding justification" (499), as Kertzer argues in "*The Stone Angel*: Time and Responsibility," for "She reviews her life in order to pronounce a verdict on it" (501). Later she laments, "Oh, my two, my dead. Dead by your own hands or by mine? Nothing can take away those years" (292), as she begins to accept responsibility for their demise.

Sorry is the "magic word" in *The Stone Angel*, just as in *A Bird in the House* (90): everyone but Hagar says it: Bram when he makes love to her (116), Marvin when Bram lies dying (182), John when he lies dying (241), and Lees when he summons Marvin (253). Only Hagar cannot apologize. But she must learn to say the magic word before she can be forgiven: she apologizes to John for her complicity in his death and Arlene's through the proxy Lees (257). So eased is she by her atonement that she thinks, "I could almost ask God's pardon ... for thinking ill of him" (248). She tells Lees that she is "sorry about your boy" (253), and she has "the grace" to apologize when she is rude to a nurse (275).

Hagar, however, is the classic unreliable narrator. Determined, in her rage at fate, to lay the blame on someone else, she attempts to justify her "stone heart" (4) and her ungenerous actions. Critics continue to take her words at face value, crediting her vilification of her daughter-in-law Doris, when, in fact, Doris must be a saint to tolerate this mother-in-law from hell. Hagar is as self-deceived as any Austen heroine, and Laurence's narrative skill lies in allowing Hagar to unwittingly reveal herself to the reader in this ironic retrospective.[24]

Laurence reconstructs Hagar's past life through flashbacks conveyed in chronological order, triggered by events in her present. Although Laurence believed this form was a flaw in the novel, her orchestration of Hagar's life is psychologically and artistically successful.[25] Past and present merge finally when Hagar, "remembering furiously" (6), relives her betrayal of John, effectively bringing her reminiscence to an end.

Hagar betrays her beloved son John by her possessive love just as surely as she betrays her son Marvin by lack of love. When she leaves Bram, Hagar takes John with her, saying, "I'll have a man in the house" (141), suggesting a secret desire to make her son her lover. This possessive love echoes the incestuous urge that drove her from her father's house – Freud's Oedipal complex reversed. Indeed, *The Stone Angel* is almost a re-vision of D.H. Lawrence's *Sons and Lovers* in which the mother rejects the father and cleaves to the son – except that the mother, rather than the son, is the centre of consciousness here.[26]

Hagar is uncomfortable with the thought of her son's sexuality: when she eavesdrops on him tumbling a girl in the garden or overhears "the stifled storming of his breath in the night" (159), she acknowledges, "I didn't care to dwell on the thought of his manhood" (159). When Hagar lies in her Afghan cocoon eavesdropping on her son's lovemaking with Arlene, she is jealous – jealous because she has no lover and because she wants to keep John for herself.

When John calls Hagar back to the Shipley farm as Bram lies dying, she makes John take her to the Manawaka cemetery to check the Currie memorial. "The marble angel lay toppled over on her face, among the peonies, and the black ants scurried through the white stone ringlets of her hair" (178) – a symbol of Hagar's fear of falling. While John laughs, saying, "The old lady's taken quite a header," Hagar, horrified, shames him into righting the statue against his protest: "That would be great, to break your back because a bloody marble angel fell on you" (179). Hagar abstains from strain because "I was afraid for my heart" (179). She admits, "I wished he could have looked like Jacob then, wrestling with the angel and besting it, wringing a blessing from it with his might. But no. He sweated and grunted angrily" (179). John's feet of clay are all too visible here. When he rights the statue, Hagar is appalled to see it defaced: "Someone had painted the pouting mouth and cheeks with lipstick" (179). The reader suspects that it is none other than John himself who has desecrated the memorial – suggesting his contempt for the Currie clan or for his mother, whom he calls "Angel" (172).

Hagar *is* the fallen angel – like Lucifer to whom she compares herself. She fears falling, recalling Dan's fatal fall through the ice. But she does fall, and it is this fall that prompts her son to suggest Silverthreads Nursing Home, impelling her escape to Shadow Point. There, she falls again. Laurence constructs a Manichean cosmos in *The Stone Angel* that reinforces the spiritual dimensions of the narrative. Even the swear words reinforce this concept, with Hagar praying "for heaven's sake" and Bram not giving "a good goddamn" (70).

Throughout *The Stone Angel*, Hagar portrays herself waiting: "Stonily, I wait" (290). But what she is waiting for she does not know: "It was a becalmed life we led there, a period of waiting and of marking time. But the events we waited for, unknowingly, turned out to be quite other than what I imagined they might be" (160). What they are awaiting here is the death of John, just as, later, Hagar awaits her own demise: "And here am I, the same Hagar, in a different establishment once more, and waiting again" (160). Once again, Hagar awaits death. Or, like Beckett's tramps, she may be waiting for God. Hagar's "Pilgrim's Progress," in Clara Thomas's phrase, is her life-journey to death.

Hagar runs away to escape not only from Silverthreads, but from the fact of death. She escapes to "*Shadow Point*" (147), for she is in the shadow of death. She recalls Psalm 23, "The Lord is my shepherd ... though I walk through the valley of the shadow of death," but she identifies with Keats's Scottish gipsy Meg Merrilies, quoting the line,

"Her book [was] a churchyard tomb" (152) – like Hagar and her stone angel – and the last lines: "God rest her aged bones ... She died full long agone" (163).[27] The angel of death awaits Hagar too.

The old fish cannery, "like the sea-chest of some old and giant sailor" (215), is filled with symbols of death, like Hagar's "junkyard of my memory" (213). She is struck by the skeleton of the "ghost vessel" (215), reminiscent of a death ship for the "Viking dead" (216), waiting to waft her to death. The place is "filled with shadows" (218), just as she herself is "an angry ponderous shadow" (159). She considers death: "Perhaps I've come here not to hide but to seek. If I sit quietly, willing my heart to cross over, will it obey?" Hagar wonders, "Although the place is right, the time may not be, and I can see as though in a mirror of never-ending depth that I'd not willingly hasten the moment by as much as the span of a breath" (192).

Hagar is not ready to die: before she is released, she must be redeemed. She discovers a scale (154), a symbol of justice. Water is a symbol of absolution, but Hagar has forgotten to bring water when, like Persephone, she descends the stairs – "the steps that lead down and down" (148), to a "pit and valley" (185), a purgatory. Her guilt is suggested in her allusion to *The Ancient Mariner* as she quotes the line, "*Water water everywhere nor any drop to drink,*" addresses herself as "old mariner," and asks, "What albatross did I slay, for mercy's sake?" (186).[28] As "queen of moth-millers, empress of earwigs" (216), she imagines "a judicial owl holding court," with "sparrows as jurors": "they'd condemn me quick as a wink" (192). As Jon Kertzer writes, "Hagar puts herself on trial and argues for both prosecution and defence," for "she has a fierce thirst for justice" (25–6). Her "parched flesh" (186) requires redemptive water. "What would a fortress be without a well?" (153), she wonders. "A raucous gang of sparrows" (186) leads her to her "well in the wilderness" (187) – alluding to Genesis 16:7: "And the angel of the Lord found her by a fountain of water in the wilderness" – suggesting that Hagar will meet God's messenger there. In her escape, she is drawn to the sea (224), symbol of salvation and of the unconscious into which she will descend.

Clearly, Hagar is also escaping from guilt, again, for this is her third removal: "To move to a new place – that's the greatest excitement. For a while you believe you carry nothing with you – all is cancelled from before, or cauterized, and you begin again and nothing will go wrong this time" (155). But, as Laurence insists, we carry our "mental baggage" with us. Hagar blames others for her lonely state: "Every last one of them has gone away and left me. I never left them. It was the other way around. I swear it" (164). Her "room with a view" (155) in the abandoned house allows her to perceive her own guilt at last.

Hearing the call of "the plaintive voices of the drowned," Hagar imagines her own sea change: "Now I could fancy myself there among them, tiaraed with starfish ... waiting until my encumbrance of flesh floated clean away and I was free and skeletal and could journey with tides and fishes" (162). Terrified by her own death wish, she chastizes herself smartly: "Stupid old woman, Hagar, baggage, hulk, chambered nautilus are you? Shut up" (162).

The cannery is filled not only with images of death, but also sacramental symbolism.[29] Christ was a fisherman and a fisher of souls: Hagar makes her bed on fish nets, far from the hoses uncoiled like serpents (215). The seagull, a figuration of her albatross, is a scapegoat, or scapegull, saving her from the marauding dogs, "the hounds, the hunters" (185). The gull is a symbol of death, but also a symbol of salvation, like Noah's dove, for it attracts a special messenger. Alone and frightened in her wilderness, Hagar sings a hymn of appeal to God:

Abide with me,
Fast falls the eventide,
The darkness deepens,
Lord with me abide – (218)

Salvation comes in the unlikely guise of Murray Ferney Lees, salesman for Dependable Life Assurance (221). Hagar's wounded gull saved him from the vicious dogs. An unlikely confessor figure, Lees communes with the old woman over a mock-eucharist of wafers and wine. Drunk, he confesses his guilt for his own loss: grandson of an evangelist preacher in Blackfly, he became a Redeemer's Advocate, and attended the Tabernacle, where a banner proclaimed, "*All Now Living Can Be Saved,*" and they sang, "*Dip your hands ... in the blood, / The pure and living Blood of the Lamb*" (226). Now "drunk as a lord" (230), Lees confesses his guilt for his loss: ironically, in attending a vigil at the Tabernacle called by "Pulsifer," an obvious play on "Lucifer," for the end of the world, he fails to save his son from a house fire. Re-

sponding to his tacit cry, "*Listen. You must listen*" (232), Hagar does
a remarkable thing: she reaches out and touches his hand in sympathy
and encouragement – the first time we witness her reach out to anyone. Her words of shared sympathy, "I had a son ... and lost him"
(234), counter her conversation with Mr Troy: when she declared, "I
had a son ... and lost him," Troy responded, "You're not alone," and
she replied, "That's where you're wrong" (121). Finally, she can acknowledge a community of suffering with Lees.

In a trance induced by both alcohol and illness, Hagar relives the
death of her son John. Mistaking jealousy for indignation, she plots
with Lottie Dreiser to send her daughter East to prevent the lovers'
marriage. When John threatens to foil their plan by impregnating Arlene, Hagar warns him, "You have to avoid not only evil but the appearance of evil" (238). So she forbids John to bring Arlene to what,
since the death of Bram, is now her house, driving the lovers to ditches
and to death: "They never played at house again in the Shipley place"
(237). Drunk for the first time in months, John accepts a bet from
Lazarus Tonnerre and dies, with Arlene, after his truck collides with
a special freight train bringing relief to Depression victims. Arlene is
killed and John fatally wounded on Manawaka's trestle bridge – a con-
vergence of the twain that forms a graphic symbol of conflicting im-
pulses in the novel.[30]

"No one's fault. Where do causes start, how far back?" (240), Hagar
wonders. Praying, "*If he should die, let me not see it*" (241), echoing
the biblical Hagar's prayer for Ismael, "Let me not see the child's death,"
Hagar lies to John about Arlene. While she waits, speechless, he reaches
out to touch her hand to comfort her, calling her "Mother" and saying, "I'm sorry" (241) – sorry for his fatal foolishness, until his pain
grips him with its "demoniac possession" (241). "And then he died.
My son died" (242). She blames him for her inability to say what she
feels: "I'd had so many things to say to him, so many things to put to
rights. He hadn't waited to hear" (243). After the funeral she refuses
to visit the cemetery: "I didn't want to see where he was put, close by
his father and close by mine, under the double-named stone where the
marble angel crookedly stood" (243).

Hagar recalls, "The night my son died, I turned to stone and never
wept at all" (243). She refused to cry before strangers, so she has never
mourned her son's death, because mourning would require her to

acknowledge her responsibility for his loss: "I found my tears had been locked too long and wouldn't come now at my bidding" (243). In the present, she weeps at the slightest thing – when a doctor speaks to her with sympathy or when a girl gives up her seat on the bus. She is amazed "that I should have remained unweeping over my dead men and now possess two deep salt springs in my face over such a triviality as this" (92). She admits, "I didn't waste long in mourning" (164): when Bram died, "It was John who cried, not I" (184); she has never mourned her mother, but viewed her weakness with contempt; and she was "too angry with Father ... to mourn his death" (63).

Hagar longs to mourn, but cannot – until she atones for the death of her son. The trauma of John's death, which turned her to stone, also marks the end of her memories. Only when she has apologized to John can she move forward toward death. She relives and revises her rejection of John by proxy, and her father-confessor figure, Lees, offers her absolution. The confessional is thus a turning point for Hagar, as it finally releases her into her mourning. Following that, she can apologize and atone, repent and make restitution – even to God: "I could even beg God's pardon this moment, for thinking ill of Him some time or other" (248).

Once she has apologized to John and atoned for her crime by proxy, she can accept his death: "The dead's flame is blown out and ever more shall be so" (250). Moreover, she can finally begin to accept the reality of her own impending death, as well as her true identity: "They can dump me in a ten-acre field for all I care, and not waste a single cent on a box of flowers, nor a single breath on prayers to ferry my soul, for I'll be dead as mackerel. Hard to imagine a world and I not in it. Will everything stop when I do? Stupid old baggage, who do you think you are? *Hagar*. There's no one like me in this world" (250).

Hagar has always been proudly self-reliant and has rejected the role of passive victim. Kertzer claims, "It is only when she accepts her powerlessness – a difficult penance for her proud spirit – that she ... can be redeemed" (26). Hagar resents her helplessness: "I lie here passively, hating my passivity" (250). But helplessness is her salvation, for it forces her to acknowledge her part in the human community. Saying, "I can't bear to feel indebted" (258), she refuses to pardon Lees for betraying her. When Doris points out, "Mr. Lees saved your life" (253),

Hagar reaches out to touch his hand, apologizes for her crankiness, and expresses sympathy for the first time: "I'm sorry about your boy" (253). After her atonement, she is able to mount the steps out of her purgatory and back to the world of human community. Hagar wished that John could resemble Jacob wrestling with the angel, but it is Marvin – who "sweats and strains, teeters me aloft" (253), as he struggles to help his mother, the stone angel herself, to mount the steps up from limbo and back to reality – who is truly Jacob.

Entering the hospital forces her into acknowledgment of her imminent death: "Only now do I see that what's going to happen cannot be delayed indefinitely" (254). "Lord, how the world has shrunk," she exclaims: "The world is even smaller now. It's shrinking so quickly. The next room will be the smallest of all" (282) – a coffin, like the black box stamped with her name. She wants to cry, "*Listen. You must listen. It's important. It's – quite an event*" (282). Realizing its magnitude, she needs to communicate: "I'm choked with it now, the incommunicable years, everything that happened and was spoken or not spoken. ... Someone should know. This is what I think. *Someone really ought to know these things*" (296).

Entering the hospital also plunges her into the family of women, as she lies "surrounded by this mewling nursery of old ladies. Of which I am one. It rarely strikes a person that way" (264). Hagar is beginning to be able to see herself from the outside, as others see her, just as she is able to see others from inside, as they see themselves. In short, she is growing up at last. The ward is "bedlam" (255), and "the voices flutter like birds caught inside a building" (256). She recalls, "*A bird in the house means a death in the house*" (217). Hagar can "feel the pain beating its wings against my rib cage" (256), like the spirit caged in its bonehouse.

Appalled at first by the litany of beseeching voices like a Greek chorus, Hagar is horrified to discover that hers has been one of them, as she calls out to John (261). Finally she hears her own voice cry, "*Bram!*" (275), and longs to hear him answer, "*Hagar*" (284). Seeing an elderly man in the Silverthreads summerhouse and thinking he is Bram, the "doubly-blind" Hagar is suddenly "gifted with sight" (105): "If I speak to him ... will he turn to me with such a look of recognition that I hardly dare hope for it, and speak my name?" (106). In truth, she has regretted the loss of Bram and repented her rejection of him for a long time. Beset by "the image of Bram's heavy manhood" and awakening to find the bed empty, "I'd be filled with such a bitter emptiness it seemed the whole of night must be within me" (160), she says. Alone in a bed as "cold as winter," she imagines herself as "an angel with spread wings" (81). "The icy whiteness covers me, drifts over me, and I could drift to sleep in it like someone caught in a blizzard, and freeze" (81) – like Bram's beloved stallion, Soldier.

Hagar had wished Bram gone: she told Mr Oatley her husband was dead: "That's the only mention I ever made of Bram" (158). In a gesture of atonement, she has him buried in the Currie plot and has his name carved on the red name-stone beside the stone angel – "so the stone said *Currie* on the one side and *Shipley* on the other" (184).[31] The "Currie-Shipley stone" (306) is ironic: it memorializes Hagar and Bram's marriage in rock, appropriate for Hagar, the stone angel, but it also recalls Tom Brangwen's belief that "an Angel is the soul of man and woman in one: they rise united at the Judgement Day as one Angel" (138) in D.H. Lawrence's novel *The Rainbow* (1915).

Hagar demands a semi-private room, but when Marvin manages to secure one in the new wing, she is disappointed: "That's all I need ... A new wing" (280), she snaps. The nighttime voices that threatened her translate into suffering women: Mrs Dobereiner prays, in German, to be released from her pain; Mrs O'Reilly is a "mountain of flesh" (259), but "the voice of the mountain" (267) is sweet, tinged with an Irish lilt. Annoyed by Elva Jardine – whose name suggests Eve and the Garden – Hagar comes to care for and feel for Elva, finally reaching out to touch her hand and express a sense of community with the Freehold woman (273).

In her semi-private room, Hagar first affronts and then assists her young roommate, Sandra Wong. Hagar notes that Sandra is a "celestial" (286), and perhaps the aid she renders her is a small attempt to redeem Mr Oatley's crimes against such "celestials" (156). Hagar, incensed on the girl's behalf at the unfairness of her suffering, struggles to reach her "destination" – a mere bedpan, but to Hagar it is a "grail" (301) – at considerable inconvenience to herself. This is a momentous effort, because it is the first time we see Hagar put herself out to help or ease another human being. Later, she is released into laughter with

Sandra: "Convulsed with our paining laughter, we bellow and wheeze. And then we peacefully sleep" (302). This is also the first time we see Hagar laugh, really laugh, freely and joyfully.

Hagar, like all Laurence's Manawaka heroines, has a combative relationship with God: "Can God be One and watching? I see Him clad in immaculate radiance, a short white jacket and a smile white and creamy as zinc oxide ointment, focusing His cosmic and glass eye on this and that, as the fancy takes Him" (93). She stops going to church: "I preferred possible damnation in some comfortably distant future, to any ordeal then of peeking or pitying eyes. But now, when time has folded in like a paper fan, I wonder if I shouldn't have kept on going. What if it matters to Him after all, what happens to us?" (90). "No mercy in heaven" (250), Hagar declares, but she often swears "for mercy's sake." If people swear by what they most respect, then it is telling that so many of Hagar's expletives involve God. After her confession, she understands "God is Love" (228). She reflects, "I've often wondered why one discovers so many things too late. The jokes of God" (60) – paralleling *A Jest of God*.

Just as death frames Hagar's story, which begins in a graveyard and ends with her demise, so hymns also frame Hagar's narrative. At the outset, she recalls attending church as a child, with her father, Jason Currie, and singing the hymn that prophesies her ultimate salvation:

> *Unto the hills around do I lift up*
>   *My longing eyes.*
> *Oh whence for me shall my salvation come,*
>   *From whence arise?*
> *From* GOD *the* LORD *doth come my certain aid,*
>   *From* GOD *the* LORD *who heaven and earth hath made.* (16)

But Hagar's eyes are blind, and so she cannot lift them up to God. A rebel angel, she cannot acknowledge God: "God might have created heaven and earth" (17), but she believes Jason Currie is "a self-made man" (17). Likewise, Hagar is too proud to acknowledge her creator. Therefore, she has not been able to acknowledge her mortality. Finally, as she confronts her imminent death, she can acknowledge God. She asks Mr Troy to sing the "Old Hundredth"[32]:

All people that on earth do dwell,
Sing to the Lord with joyful voice.
Him serve with mirth, His praise forth tell;
Come ye before Him and rejoice. (291–2)

Hagar is "a sleepwalker wakened" (285), as the "Old Hundredth" catalyzes her epiphany:

> I would have wished it. This knowing comes upon me so forcefully, so shatteringly, and with such a bitterness as I have never felt before. I must always, always have wanted that – simply to rejoice. How is it I never could? I know, I know. How long have I known? Or have I always known, in some far crevice of my heart, some cave too deeply buried, too concealed? Every good joy I might have held, in my man or any child of mine, or even the plain light of morning, of walking the earth, all were forced to a standstill by some brake of proper appearances – oh, proper to whom? When did I ever speak the heart's truth?
>
> Pride was my wilderness, and the demon that led me there was fear. I was alone, never anything else, and never free, for I carried my chains within me, and they spread out from me and shackled all I touched. Oh, my two, my dead. Dead by your own hands or by mine? Nothing can take away those years. (292)

Finally, Hagar is released into her mourning and can weep – "I'm crying now" (244) – so that she can at last begin the process of atonement and redemption.[33]

Finally, Hagar accepts her mortality. As proof, she leaves a legacy to her granddaughter: she bequeaths her sapphire ring, an heirloom inherited from her own mother,[34] to Christina, confirming her acceptance of death, affirming her acknowledgment of her mother, and symbolizing her link in the matriarchal chain of being (279). She asks Doris to bring her the *Lily of the Valley* perfume that Tina gave her (263), knowing that lilies of the valley were woven into wreaths for the dead (33). Marvin and Doris bring her roses, "pale buds just beginning to open" (277), suggesting rebirth, like the seed in her *Sweet Pea Reader* (13).

Hagar has never been able to speak "the heart's truth" (292). Whenever she wishes to say something kind, frogs and toads leap from her mouth: "Oh, I am unchangeable, unregenerate. I go on speaking in the same way, always" (293). For the first time, we see Hagar speak true. When Marvin visits and asks how she is, she eschews the conventional reply, "*I'm fine*," and involuntarily expresses her fear of death: "I'm – frightened. Marvin, I'm so frightened" (303). The eyes of the blind are opened as her "eyes focus with a terrifying clarity on him" (303).

Hagar's appeal prompts his apology: "If I've been crabby with you some times these past years … I didn't mean it" (304). His apology incites her realization, as he grasps her hand: "Now it seems to me that he is truly Jacob, gripping with all his strength and bargaining. *I will not let thee go unless thou bless me*. And I see I am thus strangely cast, and perhaps have been so from the beginning, and can only release myself by releasing him" (304).[35] Wishing to ask his pardon, she realizes that he awaits her blessing: "You've not been cranky, Marvin. You've been good to me, always. A better son than John" (304). Realizing "the dead don't bear a grudge nor seek a blessing. The dead don't rest uneasy. Only the living," Hagar sees that she must release the dead and recognize the living. Only when she acknowledges herself as mother to Marvin can she can be redeemed and released into death. "Marvin looking at me from anxious elderly eyes, believes me. It doesn't occur to him that someone in my place would ever lie" (304) – ironically, since it is not a lie. When the nurse admires her strong heart, he declares, "She's a holy terror" (304). Just as the title, *The Stone Angel*, condenses the whole of creation into a paradox, so Marvin's epithet encapsulates the paradox of Hagar's duality. "Listening, I feel like it is more than I can now reasonably have expected out of life, for he has spoken with such anger and such tenderness" (305). She could say – like Christie Logan, when Morag tells him, "you've been my father to me" – "I'm blessed" (*Diviners* 420).

Hagar freely exchanges the gift of love and thus frees herself from her chains of pride: "I lie here and try to recall something truly free that I've done in ninety years. I can think of only two acts that might be so, both recent. One was a joke – yet a joke only as all victories are, the paraphernalia being unequal to the event's reach. The other was a lie – yet not a lie, for it was spoken at least and at last with what may perhaps be a kind of love" (307).[36] As Laurence says, "the tragedy of [Hagar's] life has been that, because of her spiritual pride, she has been unable to give and receive the kind of love that she was capable of" (Fabre 193).[37]

Facing death, she has yet to reconcile herself with God: "Ought I to appeal? It's the done thing. *Our Father* – no. I want no part of that. All I can think is – *Bless me or not, Lord, just as You please, for I'll not beg*" (307). Still the same stubborn Hagar, she acknowledges, "I can't help it – it's my nature" (308).[38] But she dies a woman and a mother, repeating, as she holds the cup of water, a sacramental symbol, in her own hands, what she terms "the mother words" – "There. There" (308). Ultimately, Hagar gives birth to herself as a woman. Her last words, "And then" (308), suggest breathless anticipation. Can angels faint? Thus, although *The Stone Angel* concludes with death, the traditional ending of tragedy, the implications of redemption and rebirth suggest that Hagar's story is not a tragedy but a divine comedy. As Laurence writes of Hagar's story, "It, too, is a tragic-comedy – isn't life, generally?" (312).

"Sisters under Their Skins": A *Jest* of God and *The Fire-Dwellers*

A Jest of God (1966) and *The Fire-Dwellers* (1969) are sister novels, literally and figuratively. Laurence writes, "In *The Fire-Dwellers*, Stacey is Rachel's sister (don't ask me why; I don't know; she just is)" (TYS 21). Opposing personae of the author perhaps, Rachel Cameron, the narrator of *A Jest of God*, and Stacey Cameron MacAindra, the heroine of *The Fire-Dwellers*, could not be more different in personality or situation, even though they share a common Cameron heritage. Rachel seems a gawky, introverted spinster schoolteacher who has returned home to Manawaka from university in Winnipeg upon the death of her alcoholic undertaker father Niall Cameron to care for her hypochondriacal mother May.[1] Stacey appears to be a broad-beamed, hard-drinking, middle-aging extrovert who has escaped the clutches of the Cameron clan in Manawaka to live in the metropolis of Vancouver with her salesman husband Mac and their brood of four children.

Nevertheless, the family resemblance is obvious: their shared Scots-Presbyterian ancestry, which Laurence views as distinctively Canadian, provides an armour of pride that imprisons both sisters (like all Laurence's Manawaka heroines) within their internal worlds, while providing a defence against the external world.[2] To overcome that barrier between persons, both sisters must learn to understand and accept their heritage in order to liberate their own identities and free themselves for the future. Both women must also learn to love themselves before they can love each other or anyone else. Rachel and Stacey each receive a sentimental education through a brief love affair; as a result of learning to empathize with their lovers, they learn to love themselves and the people they live with. The sisters have not seen each other for seven years, but by the end of each novel they will be *en route* to reunion. Laurence's emphasis is, as always, on love in the sense of charity or empathy, as her solipsistic protagonists develop from claustrophobia to community.

A Jest of God and *The Fire-Dwellers* are sister novels in practical terms as well. Published in 1966 and 1969, the two novels were composed simultaneously, as Laurence interrupted work on *The Fire-Dwellers* to write *A Jest of God*[3]: "Stacey had been in my mind for a long time – longer than Rachel, as a matter of fact" (TYS 22). Laurence explains in *Dance on the Earth: A Memoir*: "I began writing *The Fire-Dwellers* before *A Jest of God*, but I destroyed about a hundred pages of that manuscript when I realized there were two novels in my head and I had begun the wrong one. The novels concerned two sisters, Rachel and Stacey, and took place within the same span of one summer. The books were self-contained but interrelated. Each sister envied the other for what each imagined was an easier life than her own. Rachel at thirty-four, an unmarried school-teacher looking after her supposedly frail mother, and Stacey, thirty-nine, mother of four children, struggling to communicate with a nonverbal husband. When I discovered that Rachel's story had to be told first, it was a revelation. Stacey's story would come later" (176). In their narratives, Rachel and Stacey endure parallel but opposing turning points in their lives. The simultaneity is best exemplified by the fact that the letter that Stacey writes to her mother in *The Fire-Dwellers* is the same letter that Mrs Cameron reads to Rachel in *A Jest of God*. In fact, three letters form a framework for the novels, structuring the sisters' relationship.

With classic sibling rivalry, each sister envies the other, thinking that the grass is greener on the other side of the Rockies. Rachel's reflection is ironic for the reader of both sisters' narratives: "It's all right for Stacey. She'd laugh, probably. Everything is all right for her, easy and open. She doesn't appreciate what she's got. She doesn't even know she's got it. She thinks she's hard done by, for the work caused by four kids and a man who admits her existence. She doesn't have the faintest notion. She left here young. She gave the last daughter my name. I suppose she thought she was doing me a favour. Jennifer Rachel. But they call her Jen" (*JG* 105). The two novels are an exercise in point of view, or the road not taken – perhaps two sides of the author – as each woman must learn to empathize with her sister, to view her with compassion and charity. "Only connect" is a tall order, but one that Laurence believes in.[4]

The artistic parallels between the sister novels are just as striking as the factual ones. The two primary fictional techniques Laurence employs to delineate the sisters' character development are symbolism and structure. Titles, epigraphs, nursery rhymes, names, and settings are all clues to the symbolism. The name Rachel connects the younger sister with her biblical namesake and "Stacey" with her elder, fertile sister Leah. The titles of both novels, *A Jest of God* and *The Fire-Dwellers*, are significant, generating central themes and motifs. Both sisters introduce their narratives with nursery rhymes – "The wind blows low, the wind blows high"[5] and "Ladybird, ladybird, fly away home"[6] – containing keys to their characters, and also to the patterns of imagery. The epigraphs for both novels are drawn from Carl Sandburg's poem "Losers": Rachel's archetype, Jonah, and Stacey's prototype, Nero, also provide crucial clues to their characters.[7]

Laurence interweaves structural with symbolic techniques to dramatize the sisters' identity crises, manipulating narrative method to convey the divisions between the characters' inner and outer life, subjective and objective reality. This manipulation of narrative method also structures the time sequence in a flashback technique, relating memory and desire, as the protagonists try to come to terms with the past in order to free themselves for the future. As Laurence explains in "Time and the Narrative Voice," "Rachel and Stacey are threatened by the past," for "the past and the future are both always present" (New 157). Both sisters are haunted by their living death in the mausoleum of the Cameron Funeral Home, and they must both lay the ghosts of the past to rest in order to survive for the future. While the polyphonic narrative structure dramatizes each protagonist's fractured psyche and the society's fragmented culture, the undercurrent of symbolism interweaves character and theme into an artistic unit.

Although *A Jest of God* and *The Fire-Dwellers* have been recognized as sister novels from the outset, the connections between them have not yet been fully explored.[8] I will examine first the structural and then the symbolic parallels between *A Jest of God* and *The Fire-Dwellers*.

"THE GIFT OF TONGUES": NARRATIVE STRATEGIES IN *A JEST OF GOD*

Even though *A Jest of God* won the Governor General's Award in 1966, early critical response to Laurence's first-person, present-tense narrative method was negative. In "Lack of Distance," Robert Harlow "applaud[s] with only one hand," judging, "this book is a failure" (190): Rachel's character is "carpeted wail-to-wail with her failures ... The reader, instead of identifying, finds himself (herself, too, I should think) silently shouting at her to get some eye-liner, save for a mink, strong-arm a man, kill her mother and stop bitching."[9] Clara Thomas judges that "artistically, as a novel, it slides out of balance. Because everything comes through Rachel's consciousness and because her mind is so completely, believably, neurotically obsessed, she cannot really see the world around her or the people in it" (*MW* 51). That, of course, is the point: Laurence shows us a schizophrenic character waking up to reality, as the narrative method recreates this development dramatically. Laurence defends her narrative method thus: "*A Jest of God*, as some critics have pointed out disapprovingly, is a very inturned novel. I recognize the limitations of a novel told in the first person and the present tense, from one view point only, but it couldn't have been done any other way, for Rachel herself is a very inturned person" (GG 84).[10]

Laurence's use of narrative method in *A Jest of God* mirrors Rachel's dilemma perfectly. The protagonist is her own narrator: "the thin giant She" (7) is both our "I" and our "eye." As she relates her inner and outer experience, the narrative forms an exercise in psychoanalysis, for Rachel is in dire need of therapy. Hanging on to sanity by her fingernails, she is obsessed with fear of madness: "Am I doing it again, this waking nightmare? How weird am I already? Trying to stave off something that has already grown inside me and spread its roots through my blood?" (24). Consciousness for Rachel is "*Hell on wheels*": she is bound to the clock's nocturnal circling as to a cosmic Catherine wheel (24). Oblivion is preferable, or at least the little death of sleep, for Rachel inhabits a nightmare world, which she describes in surrealistic pictures: "The darkening sky is hugely blue, gashed with rose, blood, flame pouring from the volcano or wound or flower of the lowering sun. The wavering green, the sea of grass, piercingly bright. Black tree trunks, contorted, arching over the river" (91–2). *A Jest of God* records Rachel's struggle to save her sanity and survive in a sometimes insane world.

Nick Kazlik is not the only character with a phantom twin, a brother who died, for Rachel is a "divided self," in the terms of R.D. Laing. The 1968 film version of *A Jest of God*, directed by Paul Newman, starring Joanne Woodward, was appropriately titled *Rachel, Rachel*, for there are indeed two Rachels, and they live in two different worlds, seen through opposite ends of a telescope:[11] "I have no middle view. Either I fix on a detail and see it as though it were magnified – a leaf with all its veins perceived, the fine hairs on the back of a man's hands – or else the world recedes and becomes blurred, artificial, indefinite, an abstract painting of a world" (91). Doubly divided, Rachel addresses herself as a separate person: "We have discussed this a long time ago, you and I, Rachel" (77). Her ultimate humiliation occurs when two adolescent aliens overhear her address her image in a washroom mirror: "Maybe it wasn't the sun" (159). She sees herself reflected in a glass window wearing her white hooded raincoat, like the negative of a photograph (35) – her own *döppelganger*.[12] Scarcely "a material girl," she is not sure if she is even alive.

Rachel hardly inhabits the real world, so threatening does it appear. In her paranoid state, she interprets a former student's innocent greeting as hostility (62). Her former "children," grown into adolescents, appear to her as Venusians, with their jewelled eyes and candyfloss hair, invading her planet earth, dispossessing her (18). Instead, she lives in her own imagination, in the "deep theatre" (97) of the mind, where "I dramatize myself" (10). But this inner theatre is dangerous too, for the paranoid Rachel imagines "an unseen audience ready to hoot and caw with a shocking derision" (101). Not even the star of her own drama, Rachel is an uneasy extra, fearing ridicule. Nor is she in control of her private theatre, for the masturbation fantasy of the "shadow prince" (25) gives way to the involuntary nightmare of the kingdom of death, where corpses powdered like clowns stare at her with glass eyes, their rouged lips twitching to mock her terror. Laurence's elision of the erotic fantasy with the dream of death suggests Rachel's father, the mortician, may be her shadow prince, the dead lover whose ghost she must lay to rest before she can come to life.[13]

Laurence wants to help women find their own voice, to give her heroines "the gift of tongues" (32), but Rachel's voice is stifled in interior monologues. Her only real outcries are silent screams like Münch paintings, rendered in emphatic italics: "*My God. How can I stand – *" (23). When she does speak, it is in artificial or borrowed voices: the "Peter-Rabbitish voice" of a simpering schoolmarm (11) or the "robot's mechanical voice" (54) of the dummy she feels she is, or, most insidious of all, an echo of "Mother's voice, lilting and ladylike" (84) – and false: "Whoever said the truth shall make you free never knew this kind of house" (106). Not until the turning point of the novel will Rachel's inner and outer voices unite, when she enters the real world. Meanwhile, the only person she can talk to is a God she claims not to believe in.

Repressed, Rachel is like a volcano ready to explode. Her own voice, long stifled in the crypt on Japonica Street, finally surfaces in cryptic cries in the Tabernacle of the Risen and Reborn (35), where the *"gift of tongues"* has been given to the congregation. Rachel's friend Calla Mackie explains, "We hold ourselves too tightly these days, that's the trouble. Afraid to let the Spirit speak through us. Saint Paul ... says *I thank my God I speak with tongues more than ye all*. And what about *the tongues of men and of angels*? What else does *the tongues of angels mean, if not glossalalia?*" (33). Rachel fears that Calla will "suddenly rise and keen like the Grecian women wild on the hills," but it is Rachel who finds her tongue: "Not Calla's voice. Mine. Oh my God. Mine. The voice of Rachel" (43). But the outburst is abortive, for Rachel rejects it as hysteria, along with Calla's kiss, proffering love (44).[14]

The voice of Rachel is "mourning for her children" (187), like the Rachel of Genesis and the Rachel of Jeremiah, who wept for her children "because they were not."[15] A childless spinster, Rachel calls her pupils "my children" (8), although she knows she should not. She mourns most for James Doherty, the creator of *splendid* spaceships, where astronauts ascend ropes "like angels climbing Jacob's ladder" (12).[16] Since Rachel has no right to touch James with tenderness, her repressed affections erupt in violence, as she strikes him across the face with her ruler, causing a river of blood, emblem of vitality, to stream down his face – prefiguring the Wachakwa River Valley where James plays hooky and where Rachel will come to life by learning to love (58–9).

In both sister novels, a love affair with a man of different ethnic background provides the catalyst for the heroine's development.[17] Rachel has a summer romance with Manawaka native Nick Kazlik,[18] a high-school teacher in Winnipeg who is back visiting his parents for the summer. The Scots-Presbyterian spinster from the right side of the tracks envies the indigent Ukrainians for having more fun – "Laying girls and doing gay Slavic dances," mocks Nick (94). Appropriately, "the milkman's son" awakens "the undertaker's daughter" (73), a modern sleeping beauty, on the banks of the Wachakwa River. "As private as the grave" (96), this tomb becomes a womb for Rachel, delivering her from the mausoleum of her Cameron Funeral Home. By making love to her, Nick gives Rachel "the gift of tongues," so that she can finally speak, touch, and love – even herself. Since Nick "inhabits whatever core of me there is" (153), Rachel learns to live in her own body at last, no longer wearing her hands "like empty gloves" (7).

Realizing that she can give houseroom to another creature, she says to Nick, "If I had a child, I would like it to be yours," echoing her biblical namesake's cry, "*Give me my children*" (154). His response, "I'm not God. I can't solve anything" (154) is a lesson to Rachel.[19] When he suddenly disappears, after showing her a shadowy boyhood snapshot, Rachel realizes, "He had his own demons and webs" (197). Driven by parental pressure to replace his dead brother by inheriting the dairy farm from his father, "Nestor the Jester," Nick quotes Jeremiah 12:8: "I have forsaken my house – I have left mine heritage – mine heritage is unto me as a lion in the forest – it crieth out against me – therefore have I hated it" (116). Rachel has a parallel problem: Laurence explains, "She tries to break the handcuffs of her own past, but she is self-perceptive enough to recognize that for her no freedom from the shackledom of the ancestors can be total" (TYS 21).

"A STRANGER IN THE NOW WORLD": NARRATIVE
IN *THE FIRE-DWELLERS*

Stacey's sense of identity is not as shadowy as Rachel's, but it has been badly bruised and battered in the marital wars. Somebody's wife, somebody's mother, somebody's daughter, and somebody's sister, Stacey has forgotten who she is – "I'm not myself" (156) – a common problem for women of her era, as Betty Friedan emphasized in her influential book *The Feminine Mystique* (1963).[20] Laurence dared to write a novel about the Housewife as Heroine. Male reviewers[21] were even more outraged by Stacey than by Rachel: Barry Callaghan dismissed Stacey's anguish as "the bleating of a dumb, starved and boring lady of neither the night nor the day but of limbo" (*FD* 284). Laurence responded, "Instead of writing a novel about a negro homosexual heroin-addicted dwarf, I had written a novel about a white anglosaxon protestant middle-aged mum – ye gods" [*sic*] (*FL* 87). But Stacey's schizoid plight is as real as Rachel's. Stacey asks, "Who is this *you?*" and replies, "I don't know" (159). She begins to doubt she even exists, "now that I'm not seen" (138). An invisible woman, she looks into the mirror "to make sure I'm really there" (132). She dreams she is carrying her severed head into the forest (115), suggesting the severing of her essence from her existence.

Caught between her past name, "Stacey Cameron," and her present label, "Mrs MacAindra," she addresses herself by various epithets – from "dream girl" (170) to "female saint" (231), from "clown" (122) to "doll" (189), from "idiot child" (177) to "mean old bitch" (27). She addresses herself in various voices, inquiring, "Who're you? One of your other selves" (106). Impatient with this Jiminy Cricket character, she exclaims, "Bugger off, voice" (189). Like Rachel, Stacey has no one but herself to talk to – except "God, Sir" (30), although she is unsure of his existence.[22] Bliss for Stacey means "no voices. Except yours, Stacey. Well, that's my shadow. It won't be switched off until I die. I'm stuck with it, and I get bloody sick of it, I can tell you" (158–9).

In *The Fire-Dwellers*, Laurence elaborates the fictional techniques that she developed in *A Jest of God*, manipulating narrative and structure skilfully to dramatize a crazily complex culture and the efforts of the individual to survive in a society that swamps her: "Narration, dreams, memories, inner running commentary – all had to be brief, even fragmented, to convey the jangled quality of Stacey's life" (GG 86). She adopts a postmodernist typography to convey Stacey's fragmented inner and outer worlds[23]: Stacey's inner monologue introduced by a dash, her memories indented, her fantasies in italics, and news broadcasts in capitals in a multi-media method mirroring Expo 67.[24] While F.M. Watt opines, "This book contains flaws enough to sink half a dozen books by lesser novelists" (198), Sylvia Fraser, in her afterword, applauds Laurence's postmodernist methods: "Perhaps more than any other of Laurence's novels *The Fire-Dwellers* partakes of its time. Using sophisticated techniques which allowed her to pass easily from past to present, from reality to fantasy, from interior monologue to exterior observation, incorporating bits from television newscasts, clips from magazines and movies, Laurence recreated the kaleidoscopic sixties as experienced by Stacey MacAindra" (*FD* 284–5). Clara Thomas agrees: "*The Fire-Dwellers* is technically the most complex of the novels – a fast-shuttering multi-screen camera and soundtrack technique [for] 'orchestrating' the whirling kaleidoscopic facets of Stacey's mind and imagination" (*MW* 124).

Communication is a central theme here, emphasized by the fact that Stacey's youngest child, Jennifer Rachel, her "flower," does not speak: the breakthrough of the novel occurs when Jen turns to her mother and inquires, "Want tea, Mum?" (273). Stacey cannot communicate with any of her children: "I can't get through the sound barrier" (203), she complains, as she contemplates "[a]ll your locked rooms" (198).[25] Stacey's relationship with her eldest daughter, Katie, epitomizes the generation gap: a hangover from the jitterbugging generation of boogie-woogie, Stacey is "a stranger in the now world" (274) – the sixties counterculture of marijuana and flower power.

The major communication gap, however, occurs between Stacey and her husband, Mac, who has escaped from frenetic family life into an underground cave inside his skull (24): "whatever the game happens to be, it's a form of solitaire for Mac" (44). Their communication gap is sexual as well as verbal: "in bed he makes hate with her, his hands clenched around her collarbones and on her throat until she is able to bring herself to speak the release. *It doesn't hurt*" (150).

James King considers *The Fire-Dwellers* Laurence's "most overtly autobiographical fiction" (262) to date, reflecting the tensions of her married life in Vancouver in the sixties, as "Stacey is Margaret's version of herself as a mad Vancouver housewife" (325). Although Laurence claims "It's not autobiographical," she acknowledges that Stacey reflects herself, speaks in "my voice," and reflects her own "streak of spiritual masochism," the "black Celt" (King 256–7). Laurence's friends and fellow writers Jean Murray Cole and George Bowering both consider that *The Fire-Dwellers* reflects the Laurence's marriage at the time she was writing the novel.

Ostensibly, *The Fire-Dwellers* is told in the third person, as Stacey is not the official narrator of her experience that Rachel is in *A Jest of God*. But Laurence insists, in "Time and the Narrative Voice," that *The Fire-Dwellers* "is really a first-person narrative which happens to be written in the third person, for the narrative voice even here is essentially that of the main character" (156).[26] Stacey's salty vernacular, which Laurence calls "my own idiom" (TYS 22), does dominate the narrative, but her vivid undercurrent of imagery is just as poetic as Rachel's. *The Fire-Dwellers* is also as schizoid as *A Jest of God*, since Laurence creates a counterpoint of viewpoints, alternating first- and third-person narrative techniques, as Stacey contradicts each actual utterance with a tacit comment introduced by a subtle dash. "These lies will be the death of me" (34), she fears: "God forgive me a poor spinner" (119), for "My kingdom it extendeth from lie to shining lie" (177). Stacey is split like Rachel in character and experience: she exclaims, "Help, I'm schizophrenic" (106), because "What goes on inside isn't ever the same as what goes on outside" (34), and it is always a shock to be transported "[o]ut of the inner and into the outer" (161). Significantly, Stacey writes two letters home to her mother, the actual one and the imaginary one, as she wonders "what would happen if just for once I put down what was really happening?" (138).

Laurence symbolizes this schizoid existence by the mirror motif introduced early in the novel, where "Stacey sees mirrored her own self in the present flesh," next to her wedding photograph (8).[27] The real and unreal war in mirrors as on television, where newsreels of the war in Vietnam appear as unreal as Western serial violence: "The full-length mirror is on the bedroom door. Stacey sees images reflected there, distanced by the glass like humans on TV, less real than real and yet more sharply focused because isolated and limited by a frame" (7). But Stacey is in control of her perspectives, whereas Rachel is the victim of psychic forces beyond her control. An escape artist, Stacey left the manacles of Manawaka far behind, emerging from the mausoleum of the Cameron Funeral Home. Stacey recalls her fond farewells: "Good-bye to Stacey's sister, always so clever. (When I think you're still there, I can't bear it.) Goodbye, prairies" (12). Stacey's children force her to keep a hold on reality, unlike Rachel, who realizes, "They think they are making a shelter for their children, but actually it is the children who are making a shelter for them" (*JG* 28).

Counterpointing inner and outer realities is only the beginning in this novel, however. In *The Fire-Dwellers*, Laurence combines this technique used in *A Jest of God* with another method employed in *The Stone Angel*. The past is ever-present for Laurence's characters, and Stacey, whom Laurence calls "Hagar's spiritual grand-daughter" (TYS 22), counterpoints past and present in a series of memories indicated by indentation (11). Reminiscence becomes self-therapy, as Stacey lays the ghosts of her past to rest, recognizing that her heritage from her parents' past will be her legacy for her children's future.

Laurence considers the form of *The Fire-Dwellers* wider than *A Jest of God*, as it includes "third-person narration as well as Stacey's idiomatic inner running commentary and her somewhat less idiomatic fantasies, dreams, memories" (TYS 22). Paralleling Stacey's memories of the past are her fantasies of the future – daydreams and nightmares that Laurence presents in italicized paragraphs counterpointed with the actual occurrences. Many are science fiction fantasies, but none is more far-fetched or poignant than this one: "*Out there in unknown houses are people who live without lies, and who touch each other. One day she will discover them, pierce through to them. Then everything will be all right, and she will live in the light of the morning*" (85).

The catalyst for overcoming Stacey's identity crisis and communication gap is the same as Rachel's – a summer romance. At the depths of her despair, upset by Mac's suspicion that she has had sex with his best friend Buckle Fennick, Stacey heads, as always when in need of spiritual sustenance, straight for the sea. Luke Venturi, an Italian dressed in an Indian sweater with Haida totems of eagle wings and bear masks (162), materializes beside her, fearing that she intends to drown herself. A cool counterculture type, sometime fisherman and science fiction writer,[28] he invites her into his borrowed A-frame filled with fishnets, where he dispenses, if not tea and sympathy, then "coffee and

sex" (206). Every housewife's fantasy figure, he listens and loves –
with no strings attached – assuring Stacey that "You're not alone"
(165), that real mothers do cry, that *everything really is all right*. For-
tified by fantasy come to life, Stacey can go home again to cope with
her realities, because Laurence believes that "You have to go home
again" (*D* 324).

"A BIRD IN A GILDED CAGE": SYMBOLIC PATTERNS IN *A JEST OF GOD*

Both sister novels are rich in symbolism, employing titles, epigraphs,
songs, names, and settings as clues to their themes. Each opens with a
nursery rhyme. Rachel's rhyme reflects her duality:

> *The wind blows low, the wind blows high*
> *The snow comes falling from the sky,*
> *Rachel Cameron says she'll die*
> *For the want of the golden city.*
> *She is handsome, she is pretty,*
> *She is the queen of the golden city.* (7)

Poignant in its multiple implications, the song suggests discrepancies
between Rachel's repressive reality and her liberated ideal. The symbol of a golden city, echoed in the hymn "Jerusalem the Golden" (48),
signifies Rachel's goal, but she fears the winds of fate that will waft
her thither. Inserting her name, *Rachel Cameron*, into the song emphasizes her Cameron ancestry, as well as her biblical namesake, mourning her lost children. But Rachel is not ready to be a mother, for she
is still an infant, as Calla's epithet *child* (52) emphasizes. Hearing her
children (8) sing the same song that she sang in the same schoolyard
twenty-seven years ago reinforces the impression that Rachel is entombed in a perpetual childhood in the Cameron Funeral Home.

Settings are symbolic in all the Manawaka novels, and Rachel's existence above the mortuary where her father reigned as king of the
dead emphasizes her living death, although the town denies the facts
of death: "No one in Manawaka ever dies, at least not on this side of
the tracks. We are a gathering of immortals. We pass on, through Calla's
divine gates of topaz and azure, perhaps, but we do not die. Death is

rude, unmannerly, not to be spoken to in the street" (19–20). Rachel is a zombie, resembling a ghost in her white raincoat. No wonder one suitor, a travelling salesman in embalming fluid, like an Egyptian pharaoh's mortician, admired her for her "good bones" (23).

Both sister novels employ identical time settings, beginning with the approach of summer and concluding with the onset of fall. Laurence makes rich use of seasonal and landscape symbolism, as well as imagery of flora and fauna. Calla, named for the lily, but brash as a sunflower (15–16), initiates the motifs of spring and rebirth by proffering Rachel "a hyacinth, bulbously in bud and just about to give birth to the blue-purple blossom" (15). April is the cruelest month for Rachel, recalling her humiliation at being ridiculed as a "peeping Thomasina" (85), outcast from life's feast by the young lovers when she crouched to smell the crocuses on the hill beyond the cemetery: "*I wandered lonely as a cloud* – like some anachronistic survival of Romantic pantheism, collecting wildflowers ... to press between the pages of the *Encyclopaedia Britannica*" (86). Rachel's sense of self-irony here and elsewhere suggests a fundamental sanity underlying her neuroses.

Characters are also symbolized by birds and animals, emblems of the threat they represent to the paranoid Rachel. Willard Siddley, the sadistic school principal, appears to Rachel as a reptile (14); her mother, May, named for spring, looks like "a butterfly released from winter" (46); and Nick slithers out of his flannels "like a snake shrugging off its last year's skin" (97) – like the slippery figure he turns out to be. Rachel's self-images are the most telling: she views herself as "a lean greyhound" (46), "a giraffe woman" (81), or as "gaunt bird[s]" (121) – an awkward "ostrich" (183), a "crane" (121), or "a tame goose trying to fly" (136), for she has yet to try her wings.

A Jest of God, almost as full of birds as *A Bird in the House*, is also inhabited by angels, birds of a different feather. Calla whistles "*She's Only a Bird in a Gilded Cage*" (53), suggesting that Rachel's situation is symbolized by Calla's canary's gilt cage. The canary is clearly a symbol for Rachel: Calla calls him Jacob, name of the biblical Rachel's husband: "So-named because he climbs the ladder all the time. He won't sing. No ear for music. All he does is march up and down that blasted ladder ... Maybe the angel at the top can't be seen by me" (143). Like Jacob, Rachel has not yet found her voice; the question will be: can she see the angel at the top of her ladder? She does imagine angels, but they are the "Angel of Death" (100) or the "angel-maker[s]" (170) of abortionists, until she tells "a joke about an angel who traded his harp for an upright organ" (132).

The most important animal in *A Jest of God* is Jonah's whale, which provides the epithet to the novel in this stanza from Carl Sandburg's "Losers":

> *If I should pass the tomb of Jonah*
> *I would stop there and sit for awhile;*
> *Because I was swallowed one time deep in the dark*
> *And came out alive after all.* (np)

Resurrection from what Laurence calls "the tomb-like atmosphere of her extended childhood" (TYS 21) is essential for Rachel. The winds of tempest that God sent to engulf Jonah are also overwhelming Rachel. Stretched out in her bathtub, with its "claw feet taloned and grasping like a griffin's" (143), she considers that her "flesh does have a drowned look" (145), as she recalls *The Tempest* and *Moby Dick*. Jonah cried, "The waters compassed me about, even to the soul" (2:5), and Rachel also fears she has "drowned" (145). Like Jonah, Rachel will be rescued from the belly of the whale, but not until she has suffered a sea change.

Laurence echoes the biblical Jonah in the name of Hector Jonas, the proprietor of the mortuary downstairs. Rachel enters the whale's belly when she descends the forbidden steps of her early nightmare down to the land of the dead (25). The courage required to confront her fear of death, "the skull beneath the skin" (128), gives her the nerve to express herself: for the first time in her narrative, her inner and outer voices unite when she thinks silently, and then speaks overtly to Hector, "Let me come in" (125). The Japonica Funeral Chapel is a comically grotesque Hades, resembling a cartoon version of "Ye Olde Dungeon" (124), presided over by a "comic prophet, dwarf seer" (131), who, like King Hades himself, leads Rachel, a Persephone figure, "like a bride up the aisle" (132) of his chapel of death in a parody ritual resurrection.[29]

Rachel has always been haunted by the ghost of her dead father, and, to penetrate his mystery, she must quest him in his own kingdom. But she searches in vain among the green glass bottles for clues to his secret. Desperate, she turns to Hector Jonas to solve the mystery of her missing father. His reply, "he had the kind of life he wanted most" (131), prompts Rachel's recognition: "*The life he wanted most. If my father had wanted otherwise, it would have been otherwise. Not necessarily better, but at least different. Did he ever try to alter it? Did I, with mine?*" (131). She realizes she must be the author of her own life. Accepting the fact of death, she can now face the facts of life.

But Rachel has another lesson to learn. Softened by Hector's sympathy, Rachel weeps – an outburst as significant as her first orgasm with Nick or Hagar's first true tears – when Hector serenades her with this saccharine song that echoes her "*golden city*" rhyme (7):

There is a happy land
Far far away –
Where saints and angels stand
Bright, bright as day – (133)

Touched by her newfound vulnerability, Hector – named incongruously for the Trojan warrior – shares his own sore point (or Achilles heel) with Rachel: "At the crucial moment, my wife laughs. She says … I look funny" (134). Hector's confession prompts Rachel to see another human being from inside for the first time. Before, "Hector's eyes are lynx eyes, cat's eyes, the green slanted cat's eyes of glass marbles" (130), echoing her nightmare (25). But now, "I look into his face then, and for an instant see him living there behind his eyes" (134). Encouraged by this communion, Rachel aborts her compulsion to apologize and replaces it with appreciation (134). Reaching the turning point in her development, Rachel climbs the stairs out of Hades back to life.[30]

But she has not yet emerged from the belly of the whale. A putative pregnancy provides the crucible in which Rachel is ground: "There are three worlds and I'm in the middle one, and this seems now to be a weak area between millstones" (100). Torn between her private desire for birth and the public need for abortion, Rachel agonizes: "*What will become of me,*" and "It can't be borne" (166). Suicidal, she settles down with lethal legacies from both parents – a bottle of her father's whiskey and fourteen of her mother's sleeping pills – one for each of Rachel's years as a spinster schoolteacher in Manawaka and Jacob's years of labour for his Rachel. Realizing, "*They will all go on in some how, all of them, but I will be dead as stone and it will be too late then to change my mind"* (176–7), she tosses the pills onto the mortuary lawn, where they belong.

In the belly of the whale, she falls on her knees and prays to God, the "last resort": *"Help me"* (177) – like Jonah, who "prayed unto the Lord his God out of the fish's belly ... out of the belly of hell cried I, and thou heardest my voice" (Jonah 2:1–2). But Rachel does not hear any reply: "If You have spoken, I am not aware of having heard. If You have a voice, it is not comprehensible to me. No omens. No burning bush, no pillar of sand by day or pillar of flame by night" (177). She finally realizes, "There isn't anyone, I'm on my own. I never knew before what that would be like. It means no one. Just that. Just – myself" (171). Rachel rejects death for the sake of the embryo she believes is "lodged" within her bonehouse (179). Realizing, "I could bear a living creature" (169), she elects life for herself and her offspring: "Look – it's my child, mine. And so I will have it. I will have it because I want it and because I cannot do anything else" (177). As a result of choosing to bear a child, with the trials that involves for a single woman, Rachel develops into an independent adult. She even liberates herself from her chains of guilt when her mother plays her trump card, a weak heart: "My mother's tricky heart will just have to take its own chances" (183).

Here comes the punch line, the jest of God of the title: Rachel is not gestating life but death. She imagines that Doctor Raven's waiting room is "death's immigration office and Doctor Raven some deputy angel allotted to the job of the initial sorting out of sheep and goats, the happy sheep permitted to colonize Heaven, the wayward goats sent to trample their cloven hoofprints all over Hell's acres. What visa and verdict will he give to me? I know the country I'm bound for, but I don't know its name unless it's limbo" (183). Doctor Raven, well named for a harbinger of death, sends her plummeting into purgatory when he discovers that she is incubating not an embryo but a tumour. "How can non-life be a growth?" (187), she questions. Overwhelmed, like Jonah, by the waters of grief, a new voice wells up from the depths of her spirit: "My speaking voice, and then only that other voice, wordless and terrible, the voice of some woman mourning for her children" (187) – the voice of Rachel. Surgery proves that "Doctor Raven was right, dead right" (189): the growth was a deadly, not a living one.

Stretched on a metal table like the one in Hector's mortuary, with her feet strapped in the stirrups to ride birth, Rachel delivers death.

This is the ultimate jest of God, for the decision that cost Rachel so much seems all for nothing. However, the tumour is not *malignant* but *benign* – like God Himself, for Rachel does give birth, not to an infant but to an adult self. She has also gained a child, for she realizes, "I am the mother now" (191, 203). God has the last laugh, but Rachel finally gets the joke. She has always been terrified of being foolish: "I'm not a fool" (52), she insisted; "I can't bear watching people make fools of themselves" (34). She said, "If I believed, I would have to detest God for the brutal joker He would be if He existed" (48). St Paul taught, "*If any man among you thinketh himself to be wise, let him become a fool, that he may be wise*" (141). Rachel has taken a long time to develop a spiritual sense of humour: embarrassed by her sexual awkwardness with Nick, she said, "All right, God – go ahead and laugh, and I'll laugh with you, but not quite yet for a while" (121). At last she gets the joke: "All that. And this at the end of it. I was always afraid that I might become a fool. Yet I could almost smile with some grotesque lightheadedness at that fool of a fear, that poor fear of fools, now that I really am one" (188). Having become a fool, she can be wise – wise enough to pity the Joker: "God's mercy on reluctant jesters. God's grace on fools. God's pity on God" (209).[31]

Like Jonah and Job, Rachel has survived suffering and learned joy, as she recalls Psalm 51:8: "Make me to hear joy and gladness, that the bones which Thou hast broken may rejoice" (208). The novel ends with embarkation, as Rachel sets out on the road of life with her "elderly child" (208), her infantilized mother.[32] Finally allowing the winds of fate to waft her, she sets off for her "golden city," en route to reunion with her sister Stacey in a new spirit of freedom and in an affirmative vision of the future: "Where I'm going, anything may happen … The wind will bear me, and I will drift and settle, drift and settle. Anything may happen, where I'm going" (208–9).

"BANK YOUR FIRES": SYMBOLIC PATTERNS
IN *THE FIRE-DWELLERS*

Stacey's journey parallels Rachel's artistically, for Laurence employs the title, epigraph, and opening nursery rhyme of the novel to symbolize

Stacey's development. The title, *The Fire-Dwellers*, introduces the central symbol of the purgatorial flames Stacey must endure before she can be saved.[33] Stacey's prototype, the Emperor Nero, who fiddled while Rome burned, underlines the main emblem of fire in this epigraph drawn from Carl Sandburg's "Losers":

> *If I pass the burial spot of Nero*
> *I shall say to the wind, "Well, well" –*
> *I who have fiddled in a world on fire,*
> *I who have done so many stunts not worth doing.* (np)

Nero, who burned Christians like candles, according to Laurence, highlights the fire motif. Like Nero, Stacey merely "fiddles," doing "stunts." The nursery rhyme that opens Stacey's narrative emphasizes the fire motif further, while applying it to Stacey's situation as wife and mother:

> *Ladybird, ladybird,*
> *Fly away home;*
> *Your house is on fire,*
> *Your children are gone.*

This insidious little rhyme is repeated at three significant points in the novel: at the beginning (7), at the turning point (209), and at the end (280), structuring the entire narrative. The significance of the rhyme is double-edged for Stacey, the original Ladybird (13), suggesting both her desire to escape from the trap of her four walls and her fear that Providence will punish her for her sins through her most vulnerable point, her children, hostages to fortune.

The theme of *Judgment* (270) is underlined by the motif of thunder and lightning, echoed comically in the name of Thor Thorlakson, the phoney god of thunder, and Valentine Tonnerre, French for thunder, who will free Stacey from her false god. "I seem to believe in a day of judgment" (241), says Stacey, the original sinner. Recalling the fire that burned Piquette Tonnerre with her children, she fears the same fate for her own offspring: "Piquette and her kids, and the snow and fire. Ian and Duncan in a burning house" (241). Fear of fire fuels her paranoid fantasies: "*The house is burning. Everything and everyone in it. Nothing can put out the flames. The house wasn't fire-resistant. One match was all it took*" (141). Her first fantasy involves a forest fire, where she must traverse a tree bridge across a bottomless void. But she can rescue only one of her children from the fire, while she hears the voices of the other three calling to her from the flames – *Stacey's choice* (30–1).[34]

Stacey's world is on fire both literally and figuratively, internally and externally. Fiery by nature, Stacey was always warned by her mother, "*you must learn to bank your fires*" (194). Surrounded by flaming red-haired MacAindras indoors and "the eternal flames of the neon forest fires" (154) outdoors, smothering her own flames proves difficult. Sexually and emotionally unsatisfied in her marriage, she recalls, "Better to marry than burn, St. Paul said, but he didn't say what to do if you married *and* burned" (193). Stacey is burned literally when she scorches her hand on the red-hot burner of her stove, branding her palm with two crescent lines – "My brand of stigmata. My western brand. The Double Crescent" (130) – recalling the crucified Christ.[35]

But it is not just Stacey's inner world that is burning; the whole outer world is in flames, as the television is constantly reminding the reader in newscasts rendered in capital letters: "EVEROPEN EYE ... MAN BURNING. HIS FACE CANNOT BE SEEN. HE LIES STILL, PERHAPS ALREADY DEAD. FLAMES LEAP AND QUIVER FROM HIS BLACKENED ROBE LIKE EXCITED CHILDREN OF HELL. VOICE: TODAY ANOTHER BUDDHIST MONK SET FIRE TO HIMSELF IN PROTEST AGAINST THE WAR IN (116)." "*Doom everywhere*" (58) is Stacey's impression, recalling "the fall of Rome" (117), when Nero fiddled. She watches transfixed as napalm spreads its stain across an infant's face (90) and listens appalled as a disembodied voice announces a Vietnamese village burned or American city aflame.

The torch of war is carried back into the past and forward into the future: Stacey recalls her father's Great War, with his tears over the boy caught between the legs by an exploding shell, as well as her husband's Second World War, with the mine blast which left him forever responsible for the life of Buckle Fennick. Forecasts of the holocaust trigger her fantasies, as she imagines escaping to the northern wilderness with her family. Her two lethal legacies from her undertaker father are, appropriately, "firewater" and firearms: she has saved his army revolver as a souvenir so that, in case of a cataclysm, she can dispatch the final thunderbolt that will free her offspring from suffering. Eventually, the purgatorial flames that persecute Stacey will become a refining fire from which she will emerge, if not purified, then at least tempered.

The antidote to fire is water: after trying to drown her sorrows in spirits, Stacey awakens with a hangover, thinking, "Help. Water. Water. I'm dying of thirst" (104), but her need for healing water is spiritual as well as physical. If Stacey's nightmares involve fire, her daydreams concern water. Stacey lives in the "jewel of the Pacific Northwest" (10), and the first time she escapes from her "Home Sweet Home" (104), she heads for the waterfront, where she admires the free-flying gulls. Birds are a symbol of the spirit in all Laurence's writing, and Stacey, living now on Bluejay Crescent, recalling her past persona whirling in the Flamingo Dance Hall, sees the seagulls as "prophets in bird form" (13) – although vultures, the "tomb birds" (270), also threaten. But fish, inhabitants of water, do not fare so well as waterbirds, if we think of Tess Fogler's goldfish, symbol of Nature red in tooth and claw. "Dog eat dog and fish eat fish" (92), Stacey thinks, when Tess recounts watching the big fish eat the little fish, revealing the depths of her sickness before her suicide attempt (191). Fish symbolism is sinister for Stacey, always a strong swimmer (161), who envisions herself as a mermaid (15). Significantly, Luke calls her "merwoman" (166) – appropriately, for Stacey's thoughts are free-floating, like seaweed underwater (34): *"Everything drifts. Everything is slowly swirling, philosophies tangled with the grocery lists, unreal-real anxieties like rose thorns waiting to tear the uncertain flesh, nonentities of thoughts floating like plankton, green and orange particles, seaweed – lots of that, dark purple and waving, sharks with fins like cutlasses, herself held underwater by her hair, snared around auburnrusted anchor chains"* (34).

Stacey's happiest memories are of lakes, as she recalls her first lovemaking with the airman from Montreal on the shores of Diamond Lake (71) and her Edenic honeymoon at Timber Lake, where she said to Mac, "I like everything about you," and he replied, "That's good, honey. I like everything about you too" (38). Regretting the loss of the loons from Diamond Lake, with their "voices of dead shamans, mourning the departed Indian gods" (159), she fantasizes about escaping with her family from the fiery cataclysm to a cool lake up north in Cariboo country.

Timber Lake features in her "death wish" (14) also, for it is there that she drowns her father's infamous revolver. Like Rachel, Stacey sometimes longs for oblivion. She sings an escapist song that echoes the saccharine hymn with which Hector serenades Rachel in his underworld:

There's a gold mine in the sky
  Faraway –
We will go there, you and I,
Some sweet day,
And we'll say hello to friends who said goodbye,
When we find that long lost gold mine in the sky.
    Faraway, faraw-a-ay – (129)

In the depths of her despair, Stacey is blinded by tears of sympathy for her father-in-law, Matthew, when he repeats Psalm 69:1, "*Save me, O God, for the waters are come in unto my soul*" (152). But Stacey does not drown; like Rachel, she suffers a sea change – a "change of heart" (221).

Stacey's lover Luke, a fisherman named for the Evangelist, seems to Stacey "like the rain in a dry year" (187), bringing salvation. Surnamed Venturi, suggesting adventure, Luke offers to fulfill her escapist fantasy by taking her north with him to Cariboo country. A fisher of souls, he invites her to blissful oblivion by crossing the Skeena River on a ferry driven by a Charon figure (208).[36] Confronted by choice, Stacey knows she can never abandon her children. Mocking her sense of responsibility, Luke repeats the Ladybird rhyme for the second time (209), as Stacey decides, "I have to go home" (209). She returns home to a reprieve: sensing disaster, and fearing that Ian has died for her sins, she is forgiven when Mac explains, "Stacey – it's not Ian ... It's Buckle" (211). But Stacey does not escape disaster so easily, and the motif of drowning is not yet finished, for her favourite, Duncan, is almost drowned at the seashore. Blinded by salt tears, she watches the seawater pump from his mouth until she hears him utter the infant wail of a newborn (267–8).[37]

As Sylvia Fraser concludes, "The attempted suicide of a neighbour, the death through bravado of her husband's best friend and the near-drowning of one of Stacey's sons creates the novel's triple climax [as] Stacey discovers the strength to rededicate herself more courageously to life" (286).

Finally, Mac confronts his ultimate fear, Stacey's suicide stunt, by asking her what she did with her father's revolver. Rejecting "*Pre-mourning*" (15) in favour of affirmation, she threw the gun into Timber Lake, drowning death, like Ethel Wilson's "Swamp Angel" – Excalibur in reverse.[38] Ultimately, Stacey and Mac are reconciled and truly make love for the first time in the narrative, for Stacey has realized that Mac is not really an Alien Other or "Agamemnon King of Men" (8), but a person, like herself, who needs support and sympathy as much as she does.

At the conclusion of *The Fire-Dwellers*, Stacey repeats the Ladybird rhyme for the third and last time, thinking, "Will the fires go on, inside and out? Until the moment when they go out for me, the end of the world" (280). Laurence writes, "In *A Jest of God* and *The Fire-Dwellers*, both Rachel and Stacey are in their very different ways threatened by the past and by the various inadequacies each feels in herself. In the end, and again in very different ways and out of their very different dilemmas, each finds within herself an ability to survive – not just to go on living, but to change and to move into new areas of life. Neither book is optimistic. Optimism in this world seems impossible to me. But in each novel there is some hope, and that is a different thing entirely" (*HS* 8). She does not promise perfect happiness, but Stacey has surfaced from despair and survived: as she falls asleep on the eve of another decade, she prays, "Give me another forty years, Lord, and I may mutate into a matriarch" (281) – "Hagar's spiritual grand-daughter" indeed.[39]

So both sister novels end with acceptance and affirmation, as Rachel and Stacey, having laid to rest the ghosts of the past and survived the present, are ready to embark on the future. Reconciled with the people they live with, but accepting their human limitations, they are ready for a change. At the end of *The Fire-Dwellers*, Stacey, who has recently given houseroom to Mac's aging father, receives a letter from Rachel announcing that she is moving to the coast with their elderly mother (276). Anticipating reunion, Stacey and Rachel realize that they can forgive each other for living. Sisters under the skin,[40] they may even learn to feel for each other the compassion that their creator has taught us to feel for both of them.

CHAPTER 10

"Death and Love": Romance and Reality in *A Bird in the House*

A Bird in the House, Laurence's 1970 collection of eight short stories set in Manawaka, is a Canadian female *Bildungsroman* chronicling the maturation of protagonist Vanessa MacLeod. *A Bird in the House* is also a metafictional *Künstlerroman*, like *The Diviners*, a fiction about fiction chronicling the development of an artist, because Vanessa becomes a novelist, like Morag Gunn and Margaret Laurence. As Isabel Huggan says in her afterword to the book, "*A Bird in the House* is a portrait of the artist as a young girl, a child in the process of becoming a writer" (*BH* 192). Narrated by Vanessa, as an adult remembering her childhood, *A Bird in the House* offers a dual perspective, ironizing the chasm between the child's fantasies and the mature writer's memories.[1] Laurence chronicles the creation of a writer by embedding Vanessa's own stories in the narrative, as her development is measured by the maturation of her fiction. The name Vanessa, Greek for both "butterfly" and "psyche," emphasizes the transformational element of the text, reinforced by the narrator's retrospections that conclude significant stories – "The Mask of the Bear," the title story "A Bird in the House," "The Loons," and the concluding story "Jericho's Brick Battlements" – thus underlining the development from the child's to the adult writer's perception of reality.

A *Bird in the House* is not merely metafiction, however; it is, in the author's own words, "semi-autobiographical fiction" (*HS* 8). As Laurence acknowledges in her essay titled "On 'The Loons,'" "The character of Vanessa is based on myself as a child, and the MacLeod family is based on my own childhood family" (805). Laurence's biographers affirm the autobiographical element of these stories: James King confirms that "Most of the stories which comprise *A Bird in the House* have an originating point in Margaret's own life history" (302), for "Many of the episodes in *A Bird in the House* can be traced to real-life events" (325). Lyall Powers concludes, "The collection is strongly autobiographical, a fictionalized depiction of the two immediate strands of Margaret's family: the Connors are based on the Simpsons, and the MacLeods on the Wemysses. Vanessa is thus Margaret's alter ego" (327). "Vanessa MacLeod, who was me as a young girl" (*SL* 320), as Laurence writes to Wiseman, is, according to Laurence's friend Budge Wilson, "the character most essentially Margaret of all her heroines" (13). Appropriately, Laurence dedicates *A Bird in the House* "*for my aunts and my children*," emphasizing her "autobiographical impulse."² As Clara Thomas observes in *The Manawaka World of Margaret Laurence*, these stories are "fictionalized autobiography" (96) in Laurence's words, "not in exactitude of detail but in truth of spirit" (97).

A *Bird in the House* is not only autobiographical metafiction but *meta-autobiography* because the stories that Vanessa MacLeod writes are the very same stories that Margaret Laurence wrote, as a comparison with her juvenilia can confirm. Both actual and fictional authors write a story about pioneers entitled "The Pillars of the Nation," and both write a tale about the fur trade set in nineteenth-century Quebec. The chronicle of Vanessa's development as an artist reflects Laurence's own creative growth. Laurence explains in "On 'The Loons'" that "The ways in which memories and 'created' events intertwine in [*A Bird in the House*] probably illustrate a few things about the nature of fiction" (805). This artistic alchemy is illuminated by exploring the meta-autobiographical aspects of *A Bird in the House* as exemplified by Vanessa's stories.

The short story is an ideal genre for conveying the relation between art and life. Laurence battled with her editor, Judith Jones of Knopf, to retain *A Bird in the House* in story form when Jones pressured her to rewrite it as a novel because short story collections did not sell well – as Laurence explains in *Dance on the Earth: A Memoir* (198). Her

"Revisions and Disagreements" responding to Jones's suggestions clarify her determination to maintain her dual narrative method, including her retrospective conclusions.[3] Clearly, she felt strongly that the short story form was appropriate for this text. As she writes in "Time and the Narrative Voice," "Each story is self-contained in the sense that it is definitely a short story and not a chapter from a novel, but the net effect is not unlike that of a novel. Structurally, however, these stories as a group are totally unlike a novel" (New 158). Another reason for her decision was the fact that all the stories except the last one, which was written to conclude the collection, had been published previously. Although *A Bird in the House* was not published until 1970, the earliest stories were published before her first Manawaka novel, *The Stone Angel*, in 1964. Published between 1963 and 1970, they thus coincide with the composition of her first three Manawaka novels. Therefore, as Jonathan Kertzer argues in *That House in Manawaka*, "These stories serve as doors, first into her larger fictional 'houses' (the novels) and then into her greater fictional 'world' of Manawaka" (13).

For Laurence, the story, with its lyric form, is the perfect vehicle for the theories of memory that she expounds in *The Diviners*, because Vanessa's vignettes, like Morag Gunn's *Memorybank Movies*, dramatize the spots of time that mark turning points in Vanessa's life. Each story in *A Bird in the House* recreates an epiphany, a negative epiphany as in James Joyce's *Dubliners*, as Vanessa becomes disenchanted or disillusioned – disabused of her childish faith in fair play in real life.

In "The Sound of the Singing," the first story in *A Bird in the House*, Vanessa, age ten, struggles to create "an old-fashioned lady" (20) out of a clothespeg, pipe cleaners, and crepe paper – inspired by the dresser doll adorned with a curly yellow coiffure and a hoop skirt of fluted apricot *crêpe de chine* among the treasures in Aunt Edna's bedroom, the gift of an old admirer (26) – but Vanessa becomes frustrated when the lady's skirt refuses to stick properly on the doll: "It had become, somehow, overwhelmingly important for me to finish it. I did not even play with dolls very much, but this one was the beginning of a collection I had planned. I could visualise them, each dressed elaborately in the costume of some historical period or some distant country, ladies in hoop skirts, gents in black top hats, Highlanders in kilts, hula girls with necklaces of paper flowers. But this one did not look at all as I had imagined she would. Her wooden face, on which I had already pencilled eyes and mouth, grinned stupidly at me, and I leered viciously back. *You'll be beautiful whether you like it or not*, I told her" (*BH* 22).[4] Laurence observes, "There is a lot of history in my fiction" (Fabre 208), and she portrays Vanessa here as a would-be historian, marshalling her marionettes to reflect myriad cultures in a manner that allows her to play God, to control the chaos of the past, rather than confront her own present – as Peggy Wemyss did in constructing and furnishing her dwarfs' house (*DE* 71).

Vanessa's Grandmother MacLeod aspires to be an old-fashioned lady, with her Irish linen and Birks' silver, in the next story, "To Set Our House in Order."[5] Vanessa's father, Ewen MacLeod, modelled on Laurence's father, Robert Wemyss, explains, just "like Grandfather MacLeod being interested in Greek plays," so "your grandmother was interested in being a lady" (55). Vanessa discovers in her father's own books – "*Seven-League Boots. Arabia Deserta. The Seven Pillars of Wisdom. Travels in Tibet. Count Lucknor the Sea Devil*" (56)[6] – that he aspired to be an explorer, not a doctor. Vanessa becomes an explorer of the heart, realizing that everyone cherishes a dream. But the challenge is bridging the chasm between dream and truth.

Both authors, actual and fictional, possess private places to dream, to let the theatre of the mind run rampant, and to let their unruly feelings spill over onto the orderly lines of a scribbler. As we have seen, Robert Wemyss built a life-size playhouse for his daughter Peggy "to brood upon life's injustices, to work off anger, or simply to think and dream" (64), as she explains in *Dance on the Earth*, and Laurence gives Vanessa a similar playhouse to escape to in *A Bird in the House*. Later, Laurence found that the loft over the garage for her Grandfather Simpson's McLaughlin-Buick provided privacy for writing: "I used to cheat on my violin practice and whip up to the loft, where I kept my five-cent scribblers in which I was writing a novel entitled 'The Pillars of the Nation'" (*DE* 67). Vanessa also escapes to the loft to write, hiding her scribblers in Grandfather Connor's old McLaughlin-Buick: she says, "I began to size up the inner situation, which was a relief from the outer. I already had half a five-cent scribbler full of the story I was writing" (*BH* 164–5). As Isabel Huggan observes, "Her scribblers are not meant to reflect reality, but to deflect it. Art is the method she has devised for escaping the dreary hardships of her depression childhood" (*BH* 195).

Laurence is a realist par excellence, employing verisimilitude as the vehicle for her vision. Her fiction is rich with myth and metaphor, but the surface action is convincingly realistic. But youth is romantic, and the progression from romance to realism chronicles the maturation process, as Myer H. Abrams defines those terms: "Realistic fiction is often opposed to romantic fiction. The *romance* is said to present life as we would have it be – more picturesque, fantastic, adventurous, or heroic than actuality; realism, on the other hand, is said to represent life as it really is" (174). Giovanna Capone applies this concept in her essay "Margaret Laurence on Order and the Artist": "In Margaret Laurence's *A Bird in the House* the distance between the real and the imaginary is the ordering theme of the cycle of stories, built as they are on the spaces between experience and its imaginative reconstruction. As the stories follow one another the confrontation of the narrator's reconstructions with her childhood vision of the world gradually becomes more explicit" (161). In "Time and the Narrative Voice," Laurence explains, "To Set Our House in Order" is "actually a story about the generations, about the pain and bewilderment of one's knowledge of other people, about the reality of other people, which is one way of realizing one's own reality, about the fluctuating and accidental quality of life (God really doesn't love Order), and, perhaps, more than anything, about the strangeness and mystery of the very concepts of *past, present and future*" (New 159). In *A Bird in the House* Laurence chronicles a progression from romanticism to realism in Vanessa that reflects her own maturation process.

Like Vanessa, Laurence as a child preferred reading romantic tales of heroism and adventure: "My favourites were adventure stories. I don't think it ever occurred to me that such adventures could never happen to me, a girl. I never pretended, even in fantasy, to be a boy. I saw myself as myself, doing deeds of high bravery on the high seas and the low moors. I was the female version of Alan Breck. Yet what a pity that the girls of my generation had so few women role models in fiction who were bold and daring in life and work" (*DE* 64–5). Margaret Laurence and Vanessa MacLeod share a love for Sir Arthur Conan Doyle's historical romance *The White Company* (*BH* 102; *DE* 64). In "Books That Mattered to Me," Laurence confesses that she admired both Stevenson's Alan Breck – "my ideal of bravery and adventure" – and Arthur Conan Doyle's boy hero, "the lad Alain, with whom I identified totally" (240).

Peggy Wemyss's writing was just as heroic as her reading: in *Dance on the Earth*, Laurence recalls writing about "voyages to exotic lands"

(61). Vanessa also prefers "stories of spectacular heroism in which I figured as central character" (14), just as the nameless narrator of Alice Munro's "Boys and Girls" composes stories about herself that present "opportunities for courage, boldness and self-sacrifice" (113). Easingwood is correct when he asserts, "The autobiographical impulse is there not only in the incidental detail of realistic presentation but even more decisively in the ... element of romance" (24). The creative development Laurence recreates in *A Bird in the House* reflects her real experience: Laurence's mother advised her to "Write what you know" when she wrote stories about "dukes and ladies" ("Geography") and Laurence portrays Vanessa learning the same lesson from *"Real Life"* (265), the original title of Munro's short story collection *Lives of Girls and Women*, published in 1971, one year after Laurence's *A Bird in the House*.

A REALIST'S PROGRESS

In *A Bird in the House* Laurence recreates a realist's progress. In "The Sound of the Singing," Vanessa is beginning to worry about reconciling romance with reality in her stories: I was planning in my head a story in which an infant was baptised by Total Immersion and swept away by the river which happened to be flooding. (Why would it be flooding? Well, probably the spring ice was just melting. Would they do baptisms at that time of year? The water would be awfully cold. Obviously, some details needed to be worked out here.) The child was dressed in a christening robe of white lace, and the last the mother saw of her was a scrap of white being swirled away towards the Deep Hole near the Wachakwa bend, where there were bloodsuckers" (*BH* 24–5). No doubt Vanessa visualizes herself heroically saving the infant from a fate worse than death. It is interesting to witness her inner debate as she questions the plausibility of her fictional adventures.

Vanessa draws her material from literature, not life, finding her inspiration in the Bible. In "The Sound of the Singing" she explains how she prepares for the catechism of her devout Grandmother Connor at Sunday dinner at the Brick House:

I rarely listened in Sunday school, finding it more entertaining to compose in my head stories of spectacular heroism in which

I figured as central character, so I never knew what the text had been. But I had read large portions of the Bible by myself, for I was constantly hard-up for reading material, so I had no trouble in providing myself with a verse each week before setting out for the Brick House. My lines were generally of a warlike nature, for I did not favour the meek stories and I had no use at all for the begats.

"*How are the mighty fallen in the midst of the battle*," I replied instantly. (*BH* 14–15)

Vanessa's biblical text refers to her battle with "The Great Bear" (63) himself, Grandfather Connor, reflecting Laurence's conflict with her patriarchal Grandfather Simpson. When Timothy Connor criticizes Vanessa's father, Ewen MacLeod, the town doctor, for missing Sunday dinner at the Brick House because he is attending ailing Henry Pearl, Vanessa leaps to his defence: "'It's not his fault,' I replied hotly. 'It's Mr. Pearl. He's dying with pneumonia. I'll bet you he's spitting up blood this very second'" (23). Vanessa's imagination goes to work immediately, turning fact into fiction: "Did people spit blood with pneumonia? All at once, I could not swallow, feeling as though that gushing crimson were constricting my own throat. Something like that would go well in the story I was currently making up. *Sick to death in the freezing log cabin, with only the beautiful half-breed lady* (no, *woman*) *to look after him, Old Jebb suddenly clutched his throat* – and so on" (23). As Capone observes, "Vanessa is a juvenile storyteller by vocation; and side by side with the life she is living, she lives the story she is currently making up, so that at times a word from reality evokes a literary atmosphere, a sentence, or a paragraph from a would-be story" (165) – not unlike the way Hagar is continually transported to the past by a casual word or occurrence in the present. Thus, Vanessa is living a double life – her actual existence and the refurbished version supplied by her imagination.

Old Jebb may be a figure from Vanessa's novel: in "The Sound of the Singing" she announces proudly, "'I'm writing a story ... *The Pillars of the Nation* ... It's about pioneers'" (29). When Aunt Edna replies, "'You mean – people like Grandfather?'" Vanessa reacts, "'My gosh ... Was he a pioneer?'" Edna responds, "'I'll tell the cockeyed world'" (29). The mature narrator explains: "That had been my epic on pioneer life. I had proceeded to the point in the story where the husband, coming back to the cabin one evening, discovered to his surprise that he was going to become a father. The way he ascertained this interesting fact was that he found his wife constructing a birch-bark cradle. Then came the discovery that Grandfather Connor had been a pioneer, and the story had lost its interest for me. If pioneers were like *that*, I had thought, my pen would be better employed elsewhere" (*BH* 68). Reality deflates romance. Vanessa is not really interested in writing about actual pioneers, but only in fabricating a glamorous fantasy. As Easingwood explains, "When reminded that her Grandfather Connor was a pioneer, Vanessa immediately abandons her juvenile attempt at writing a romance of pioneer life: the prospect of romance is spoiled by this confrontation with the known reality" (22). In *Dance on the Earth* Laurence gives a strikingly similar account of her own pioneer epic: "I had just completed my masterpiece, 'The Pillars of the Nation,' which filled two or three scribblers and was the story of pioneers. I believe it was in that story that the invented name Manawaka first appeared. The only part of the story I recall was a sensational scene in which the young pioneer wife delicately communicates to her husband that she is pregnant by the tactful device of allowing him to arrive home and witness her making a birch-bark cradle" (*DE* 73). "I guess if I'd stuck to birch-bark cradles in my fiction, the book-banning elements loose in Canada wouldn't have hit on me as a target" (73), Laurence remarks wryly, referring to the "Controversy" – the attack on her novels in Peterborough County in 1976 and again in 1985. As she recalls proudly, the "The Pillars of the Nation" received honourable mention, and her story, "The Case of the Blond Butcher," was published in the young people's section of the Saturday *Free Press*: "It was a murder story in which it turned out that no murder had been committed after all. (In those days I favoured happy endings. I still do – who wouldn't? But nowadays they're not always possible" (*DE* 73).

This is the lesson Vanessa has yet to learn, for she still likes love stories to have happy endings: "I was much occupied by the themes of love and death, although my experience of both had so far been gained principally from the Bible, which I read in the same way as I read Eaton's Catalogue or the collected works of Rudyard Kipling – because I had to read something, and the family's finances in the thirties did not permit the purchase of enough volumes of *Doctor Doolittle* or the *Oz* books to keep me going" (65).

Later, in "The Mask of the Bear,"[7] when Aunt Edna inquires, "'How's *The Pillars of the Nation* coming along?'" Vanessa's response is terse: "'I quit that one,' I replied laconically. 'I'm making up another – it's miles better. It's called *The Silver Sphinx*. I'll bet you can't guess what it's about'" (68). Edna's reaction is gratifyingly obtuse: "'The desert? Buried treasure? Murder mystery?'" Vanessa shakes her head and pronounces only one word: "'Love.'" Edna responds with straight-faced surprise: "'Good Glory. ... That sounds fascinating. Where do you get your ideas, Vanessa?'" Vanessa responds mysteriously, "'Oh, here and there. ... You know'" (69). With no real knowledge of love, Vanessa turns to the next best thing to Eaton's Catalogue – the Bible, storehouse of stories: "For the love scenes, I gained useful material from The Song of Solomon. *Let him kiss me with the kisses of his mouth, for thy love is better than wine*, or *By night on my bed I sought him whom my soul loveth; I sought him but I found him not.* My interpretation was somewhat vague, and I was not helped to any appreciable extent by the explanatory bits in small print at the beginning of each chapter – *The church's love unto Christ. The church's fight and victory in temptation,* et cetera ... To me, the woman in The Song was some barbaric queen, beautiful and terrible, and I could imagine her, wearing a long robe of leopard skin and one or two heavy gold bracelets, pacing an alabaster courtyard and keening her unrequited love" (*BH* 66). Laurence mentions in her memoir reading selections from the Song of Solomon in her *Pocket Book of Verse* in high school and wondering at "the accompanying comment on that great love poem found in my grandmother's Bible: 'Christ's marriage to the church'" (*DE* 77). Vanessa's creation is inspired by Solomon's Song, but she romanticizes it in a comically exotic pastiche:

The heroine in my story (which took place in ancient Egypt – my ignorance of this era did not trouble me) was very like the woman in The Song of Solomon, except that mine had long wavy auburn hair, and when her beloved left her, the only thing she could bring herself to eat was an avocado, which seemed to me considerably more stylish and exotic than apples in lieu of love. Her young man was a gifted carver, who had been sent out into the desert by the cruel pharaoh (pharaohs were always cruel – of this I was positive) in order to carve a giant sphinx for the royal tomb. Should I have her die while he was away? Or would it be better if he perished out in the desert? Which of them did I like the least? With the characters whom I liked best, things always turned out right in the end. (*BH* 66)

Like Grandfather Connor, who complains, "It's not fair" (39), Vanessa has a strong sense of fairness, using fiction to mete out justice, like the Old Testament God, rather than to reflect reality.

As Vanessa matures, she turns from literature to life for the inspiration for her fictions. She confesses, "I was a professional listener" (18), a prerequisite for professional writers, perhaps. She eavesdrops on conversations downstairs from her secret "listening post" upstairs via an air register like the one that visitors to the Margaret Laurence Home in Neepawa can observe. "If you put your ear to the iron grille, it was almost like a radio" (58), Vanessa explains. Intrigued by Edna's romance with glamorous Jimmy Lorimer, Vanessa decides to "slip upstairs to my old post, the deserted stove-pipe hole. [But] I could no longer eavesdrop with a clear conscience" (83–4): "Although I spent so much of my life listening to conversations which I was not meant to overhear, all at once I felt, for the first time, sickened by what I was doing. I left my listening post and tiptoed into Aunt Edna's room. I wondered if someday I would be the one who was doing the talking, while another child would be doing the listening. This gave me an unpleasantly eerie feeling. I tried on Aunt Edna's lipstick and rouge, but my heart was not in it" (*BH* 77). Later, when she overhears her aunt crying in her room, her view of true love is drastically revised, as reality explodes romance, teaching Vanessa a valuable but painful lesson about real life: "Like some terrified poltergeist, I flitted back to the spare room and whipped into bed. I wanted only to forget that I had heard anything, but I knew I would not forget. There arose in my mind, mysteriously, the picture of a barbaric queen, someone who had lived a long time ago. I could not reconcile this image with the known face, nor could I disconnect it. I thought of my aunt, her sturdy laughter, the way she tore into her housework, her hands and feet which she always disparagingly joked about, believing them to be clumsy. I thought of the story in the scribbler at home. I wanted to get home quickly, so

I could destroy it" (*BH* 78). Vanessa finally realizes that in real life lovers do not always live happily ever after. This epiphany is under-lined dramatically by her apocalyptic vision of northern lights, which transform the yard of the Brick House into "a white desert [as] the pale gashing streaks of light pointed up the caverns and the hollowed places where the wind had sculptured the snow" (*BH* 77).

"REST BEYOND THE RIVER"

Vanessa likes to write about death as well as love: "the death scenes had an undeniable appeal, a sombre splendour, with (as it said in Ec-clesiastes) the mourners going about the streets and all the daughters of music brought low. *Both death and love seemed regrettably far from Manawaka*" (66, italics mine). These are famous last words indeed. When Agnes Connor dies in "The Mask of the Bear," and Vanessa glimpses the grotesque grief of the man behind the mask of the bear, she learns to distinguish reality from romance – the lesson in life that is at the heart of the maturation and creative process. Vanessa reflects, "I had not known at all that a death would be like this, not only one's own pain, but the almost unbearable knowledge of that other pain which could not be reached or lessened" (80). Christian Riegel writes in "'Rest Beyond the River': Mourning in *A Bird in the House*," "the experience of observing grief in others allows her a first-hand experi-ence of how people react to death – an experience that ultimately af-fects the way she, too, grieves" (72).

Vanessa, "protected from the bizarre cruelty of such rituals" (188) by her youth, does not attend her Grandmother Connor's funeral. In-stead, she plans to stage her own memorial service: "I wanted now to hold my own funeral service for my grandmother, in the presence only of the canary. I went to the bookcase where she kept her Bible, and looked up Ecclesiastes. I intended to read the part about the mourn-ers going about the streets, and the silver cord loosed and the golden bowl broken, and the dust returning to the earth as it was and the spirit unto God who gave it. But I got stuck on the first few lines, be-cause it seemed to me, frighteningly, that they were being spoken in my grandmother's mild voice – *Remember now thy Creator in the days of thy youth, while the evil days come not* – "(*BH* 82). Vanessa real-izes that true art reflects real life, rather than an escape from reality.

After her father dies in the title, and pivotal, story, "A Bird in the House," a fictionalization of the death of Laurence's own father, Vanessa recognizes the facts of death: "*Rest beyond the river. I knew now what that meant. It meant Nothing. It meant only silence, forever*" (105).[8] Laurence explains the autobiographical source of this: "On January 13, 1935, our father Robert Wemyss died of pneumonia. I have written about this in a story called 'A Bird in the House.' The story is fiction, but in that particular story, fiction follows facts pretty closely" (*DE* 55). Laurence excised the last sentence of the story from her typescript – "I understood at last what the bird in the house had really been" – which was to follow the description of Vanessa's burning of the 1919 letter and photograph of the French girl and her final published statement, "I grieved for my father as if he had just died now" (65).[9] This omission is unfortunate, however, for this sentence throws new light on the title of the story, suggesting that it refers not simply to death – as in Noreen's prophesy, "A bird in the house means a death in the house" (98) – but to freedom. In Laurence's "Revisions and Disagreements," she explains, "In a way, she *does* grieve as though her father had just died now, because she is for the first time seeing him as an individual, not just as her father. And it's too late for her to let him know she understands" (np). As Laurence explains in "Time and the Narrative Voice," "in the story Vanessa has the sudden, painful knowledge of his reality and his intricacy as a person, bearing with him the mental baggage of a lifetime, as all people do, and as she will have to do. The events of the story will become (and have become to the older Vanessa) part of her mental baggage, part of her own spiritual fabric" (New 159).

But in "The Loons," the story after "A Bird in the House," Vanessa reduces Piquette Tonnerre to a romantic stereotype.[10] Vanessa's vision of Indians is inspired by literature like Longfellow's *Hiawatha*. She asserts, "I was a devoted reader of Pauline Johnson at this age, and sometimes would orate aloud and in an exalted voice, *West Wind, blow from your prairie nest; Blow from the mountains, blow from the west*" (112). Piquette piques Vanessa's interest when "I realised that the Tonnerre family, whom I had always heard called half-breeds, were actually Indians, or as near as made no difference" (112). Vanessa mythologizes the Métis girl: "my new awarness that Piquette sprang from the people of Big Bear and Poundmaker, of Tecumseh, of the Iroquois who had eaten Father Brebeuf's heart – all this gave her an instant attraction in my eyes" (112). Vanessa also romanticizes Piquette: "It seemed to me that Piquette must be in some way a daughter of the forest, a kind of junior prophetess of the wilds, who might impart to me, if I took the right approach, some of the secrets which she undoubtedly knew – where the whippoorwill made her nest, how the coyote reared her young, or whatever it was that it said in Hiawatha" (*BH* 112).

When Vanessa tries to interest Piquette in the loons, to learn "forest lore" (113), Piquette's rebuff deflates Vanessa's romantic conception: "as an Indian, Piquette was a dead loss" (114). Years later, when Vanessa meets Piquette in the Regal café, and Piquette's blank mask slips to reveal a desperate need to belong to a social order she rejected, Vanessa says, "I saw her" (117). Later still, when she learns of Piquette's death in the fire at the Tonnerre shack, Vanessa realizes Piquette "might have been the only one, after all, who had heard the crying of the loons" (120). The adult narrator recreates both Piquette's true poignance and her own childish misconception. In her essay "On 'The Loons,'" Laurence writes, "The loons seemed to symbolize in some way the despair, the uprootedness, the loss of the land that many Indians and Métis must feel" (805–6). In "Time and the Narrative Voice," she explains, "The loons, recurring in the story both in their presence and in their absence, are connected to an ancestral past that belongs to Piquette, and the older Vanessa can see the irony of the only way in which Piquette's people are recognized by the community in the changing of the name Diamond Lake to the more tourist appealing Lake Wapakata" (160). So Laurence doubly ironizes the racism inherent in Manawaka's view of Aboriginals.

Vanessa learns an important lesson about reality and fantasy from her cousin Chris Connor, who, in the story "Horses of the Night," comes to live in the Brick House to attend high school.[11] The character of Chris is based on Laurence's cousin, Lorne Simpson, or Bud, addressed in her poem, "For Lorne" (*DE* 257–62), which exhibits interesting parallels with "Horses of the Night." Chris is a dreamer who escapes harsh realities by creating romantic fictions for himself to inhabit. He explains, "I got this theory, see, that anybody can do anything at all, anything, if they really set their minds to it. But you have to … focus on it with your whole mental powers, and not let it slip away by forgetting to hold it in your mind. If you hold it in your mind, like, then it's real, see?" (131). He copes with Grandfather Connor's temper by blithely ignoring it, whereas Vanessa fights. He regales ten-year-old Vanessa with enchanting tales of his Criss-Cross Ranch at Shallow Creek, beyond Galloping Mountain, where he keeps his riding horses Duchess and Firefly. She imagines "the house fashioned of living trees, the lake like a sea where monsters had dwelt, the grass that shone like green wavering light while the horses flew in the splendour of their pride" (135). When Vanessa visits Chris three years later, after her father's death, she is shocked by the reality of the fly-blown farmhouse and the work horses, Trooper and Floss: "I guess I had known for some years now, without realising it, that the pair had only ever existed in some other dimension" (*BH* 136). Thus, Chris provides Vanessa a negative example of the artificiality, and danger, of fantasy.

During the war, Chris, a *traveller* (133), is hospitalized after he suffers a mental breakdown.[12] He writes to Vanessa, "they could force his body to march and even to kill, but what they didn't know was that he'd fooled them. He didn't live inside it any more" (143). Vanessa realizes this was "only the final heartbreaking extension of that way he'd always had of distancing himself from the absolute unbearability of battle" (143), a way "to make the necessary dream perpetual" (144).

Vanessa holds a private memorial service for Chris, just as she did for Grandmother Connor, with the miniature saddle he fashioned for her: "I put the saddle away once more, gently and ruthlessly, back into the cardboard box" (144), she recalls, as if burying it in a coffin. The word *gently* reflects her affection for Chris, while *ruthlessly* suggests her rejection of the escape fantasy symbolized by the saddle. Whereas Chris uses fiction to escape from reality, Vanessa learns to employ fiction to understand real life. As Bruce Stovel observes in "Coherence in *A Bird in the House*," "Unlike the private world of Vanessa's cousin Chris, the imaginary world in Laurence's book is one that many people can walk into and inhabit" (95). In "Revisions and Disagreements" on *A Bird in the House*, Laurence states, "Chris's dilemma impinged on V's life." Like Marlow with Kurtz in Conrad's novella *Heart of Darkness*, Vanessa is allowed to look over the edge and then draw back, as Chris demonstrates the dangers involved in romanticizing reality.

In the next story, "The Half-Husky,"[13] when paper-boy Harvey Shinwell torments Vanessa's puppy Nanuk, Vanessa fantasizes about revenge, but realizes that her fantasies are not realistic: "Whenever I tried to work out a plan of counter-attack, my rage would spin me into fantasy – Harvey, fallen into the deepest part of the Wachakwa River, unable to swim, and Nanuk, capable of rescue but waiting for a signal from me. Would I speak or not? Sometimes I let Harvey drown. Sometimes at the last minute I spared him – this was more satisfactory than his death, as it enabled me to feel great-hearted while at the same time enjoying a continuing revenge in the form of Harvey's gibbering remorse. But none of this was much use except momentarily, and when the flamboyant theatre of my mind grew empty again, I still did not know what to do, in reality" (*BH* 151–2). Vanessa is maturing to the point where she is no longer able to escape from reality into fantasy: "I no longer wove intricate dreams in which I either condemned Harvey or magnanimously spared him. What I felt now was not complicated at all. I wanted to injure him in any way available" (154). When she visits Harvey Shinwell's grim home on the wrong side of the tracks and sees his aunt hit him across the face with a spoon, she realizes that he himself is a victim of the cycle of abuse. Laurence employs the stolen telescope to symbolize vision for Vanessa. So, like Nanuk, "[Harvey] wasn't safe to go free," although his abusive aunt is free to walk the streets, and "this was probably not fair, either" (160).[14] Unlike Grandfather Connor, Vanessa learns early that life is unfair.

ESCAPE ARTIST

In the final story, "Jericho's Brick Battlements," the only story written specifically for *A Bird in the House*, Vanessa, now twelve at the outset, and a would-be escape artist, like many adolescents and most Laurence heroines, is writing a tale of escape.[15] Laurence says, "I used to write up in my loft, leaving the little door open for light and filling scribblers with stories, one of which I recall took place in a nineteenth-century inn in Quebec, a place and time about which I could scarcely have known less" (*DE* 68), reinforcing the meta-autobiographical parallel. Vanessa explains:

> The tale was set in Quebec in the early days of the fur trade. The heroine's name was Marie. It had to be a tossup between Marie and Antoinette, owing to a somewhat limited choice on my part, and I had finally rejected Antoinette as being too fancy.

Orphaned young, Marie was forced to work at the Inn of the Grey Cat. *La Chat? Le Chat?* And what was Grey? They didn't teach French until high school in Manawaka, and I wasn't there yet. But never mind. These were trivial details. The main thing was that Marie overheard the stealthy conversation of two handsome although shabbily dressed *voyageurs*, who later would turn out to be the great *coureurs-de-bois*, Radisson and Groseilliers. The problem was now plain. How to get Marie out of her unpromising life at the inn and onto the ship which would carry her to France? And once in France, then what? Neither Radisson nor Groseilliers would marry her, I was pretty sure of that. They were both too busy with changing back and forth from the side of the French to the side of the English, and besides, they were too old for her. (165)

Vanessa is beginning to become a realist who is no longer satisfied by mere fantasies of escape: "I lay on the seat of the MacLaughlin-Buick feeling disenchantment begin to set in. Marie would not get out of the grey stone inn. She would stay there all her life. The only thing that would ever happen to her was that she would get older. Probably the *voyageurs* weren't Radisson and Groseilliers at all. Or if they were, they wouldn't give her a second glance. I felt I could not bear it. I no longer wanted to finish the story. What was the use, if she couldn't get out except by ruses which clearly wouldn't happen in real life?" (*BH* 165). Just as desperate as Marie (or Margaret) to escape, Vanessa is nevertheless becoming a "moral realist," as Rosalie Murphy Baum observes in "Artist and Woman: Young Lives in Laurence and Munro": "Vanessa's progress as a writer, from a very early age, reflects her increasing grasp of 'real' life, her attempts to face reality" (201–2).

Teenage Vanessa is "frantic to get away from Manawaka and from the Brick House" (186). From the outset, the Brick House is portrayed as a prison, a "crusader's embattled fortress in a heathen wilderness" (*BH* 11). But, like the ladybird, Vanessa is "unaware that she possessed wings and could have flown up" (*BH* 60). Patricia Morley says *A Bird in the House* is Vanessa's *spiritual odyssey*: "its themes are bondage, flight, and freedom" (42). Laurence affirms, in a letter to Alan Maclean, her Macmillan editor, that *A Bird in the House* is about "captivity and freedom," and, in a sample blurb sent to her publisher, she explains,

"A BIRD IN THE HOUSE explores aspects of Vanessa's need to free herself," as Richard A. Davies records in his essay, "'Half War/Half Peace': Margaret Laurence and the Publishing of *A Bird in the House*" (341, 343).[16]

Claustrophobia increases as Vanessa matures, cresting in the concluding story, whose title, "Jericho's Brick Battlements," suggests a walled fortress. Indeed, Vanessa's mother, Beth, claims that defying Timothy Connor is just "batting your head against a brick wall" (163). Jericho also suggests Joshua, and Vanessa is the young warrior who defies the stronghold: "I shouted at him, as though if I sounded all my trumpets loudly enough, his walls would quake and crumble" (184). Vanessa must learn that freedom is achieved not by shouting but by singing, not by war but art. In the words of Keith Richards, "You can build a wall to stop people, but eventually, the music will cross that wall. That's the beautiful thing about music – there's no defense against it. I mean, look at Joshua and fucking Jericho – made mincemeat of that joint. A few trumpets, you know?" (Palmer 87). This is the lesson that Vanessa must learn – that language, like music, can liberate.

Vanessa, like Laurence, does eventually escape – to university in Winnipeg – liberated ironically by the sale of the MacLeod silver and Limoges china and her grandfather's old "bonds" (187). But, even though she escapes Manawaka, "I did not feel nearly as free as I had expected to feel" (187). Ultimately, she realizes that escape does not mean freedom. Freedom is achieved by acceptance, not negation. For Vanessa, like Laurence, freedom is realized not by running away from reality but by writing about it. In "A Place to Stand On," Laurence says, "my own writing has followed the same pattern – the attempt to assimilate the past, partly in order to be freed from it" (*HS* 6). Even though James Joyce rarely returned to Ireland after the death of his mother, he wrote about Dublin obsessively from his Continental exile, for art sets one free. Similarly, Vanessa, like Laurence, frees herself from the stifling aspects of her past by exorcising it in her creative fiction.

Vanessa returns to Manawaka when her grandfather finally dies. His funeral, her first, is a revelation when the minister claims, "Timothy Connor had been one of Manawaka's pioneers" (188). Bored all her life by his repeated accounts of his epic journey, Vanessa finally realizes its true significance. Ironically, the funeral eulogy, by recounting his life story, makes him real to Vanessa. In her "Revisions and Disagreements" on *A Bird in the House*, Laurence emphasizes Vanessa's epiphany: "The pioneer bit now means something different to V [*sic*] than it did when she heard it from the old man, and was bored. Now she sees what it really meant."

After the funeral, Vanessa holds her own memorial service for her grandfather, as she did for her grandmother and for her cousin Chris. She visits the stable-garage and his coffin-like chariot, the MacLaughlin-Buick, observing, "Rust grew on it like patches of lichen on a gravestone" (189). She recalls a "memory of a memory" of her childhood vision of her hero: "I remembered myself remembering driving in it with him, in the ancient days when he seemed as large and admirable as God" (190). She recalls "gazing with love and glory at my giant grandfather as he drove his valiant chariot through all the streets of this world" (166). She is surprised by his death: "Perhaps I had really imagined that he was immortal. Perhaps he even was immortal, in ways which it would take me half a lifetime to comprehend" (189). She acknowledges, "I had feared and fought the old man, yet he proclaimed himself in my veins" (191).

Margaret Laurence experienced the same epiphany Vanessa MacLeod does. In "A Place to Stand On," the first in her collection of travel essays *Heart of a Stranger* (1976), she explains:

> The final exploration of this aspect of my background came when I wrote – over the past six or seven years – *A Bird in the House*, a number of short stories set in Manawaka and based upon my childhood and my childhood family, the only semi-autobiographical fiction I have ever written. I did not realize until I had finished the final story in the series how much all these stories are dominated by the figure of my maternal grandfather, who came of Irish Protestant stock. Perhaps it was through writing these stories that I finally came to see my grandfather not only as the repressive authoritarian figure from my childhood, but also as a boy who had to leave school in Ontario when he was about twelve, after his father's death, and who as a young man went to Manitoba by sternwheeler and walked the fifty miles from Winnipeg to Portage la Prairie, where he settled for some years before moving to Neepawa. He was a very hard man

in many ways, but he had had a very hard life. I don't think I knew any of this, really knew it, until I had finished those stories. I don't think I ever knew, either, until that moment how much I owed to him. One sentence, near the end of the final story, may show what I mean. "I had feared and fought the old man, yet he proclaimed himself in my veins." (8)

Ironically, Laurence employs a quotation from her fiction to illustrate her actual feelings. Clara Thomas writes, in *The Manawaka World of Margaret Laurence*, "For Margaret Laurence, the writing of these stories was a journey back in time and memory, to exorcize the intimidating ghost of her grandfather and to sublimate her youthful bitterness towards him by the processes of art, until all bitterness burned away and the old man became part of her and Canada's past ..." (100–1).

Carol Shields explains Vanessa's method of dealing with patriarchal Grandfather Connor in "Leaving the Brick House Behind: Margaret Laurence and the Loop of Memory" (77): "[Vanessa's] chief tactic is the employment of her imagination, the same imagination that will enable her to leave the Brick House and become a writer. She invents, for instance, elaborate scenes of confrontation and insult which are never played out; she scribbles into her notebooks melodramas of villainy and punishment; she recognizes, and vanquishes, those qualities in herself that hunger for power; and she transcends, through the loop of memory, her early image, recognizing in her fear of her grandfather a root of solid love."

Although Laurence recreated the death of her father, grandmother, and grandfather in fictional form, she never fictionalized the death of her mother or stepmother, even though Judith Jones urged her to do so. Laurence's response, in her "Revisions and Disagreements" is illuminating: "Re: story about Beth – I don't feel this is necessary. Beth's relationship with Vanessa comes out in every story, I think, & Beth's manner of coping with life after Ewen's death comes out in the latter stories. I think the basic closeness of the relationship between V & her mother comes out without any underlining of it. Beth's relationship with the whole family is a continuing one, & she comes gradually more & more to resemble her own mother, Grandmother Connor, but I don't think she needs a story of her own – She is *there* in all the stories. In a sense, that is the whole point about Beth."

Twenty years later, after the death of her mother, Vanessa revisits Manawaka for the last time, visiting the family graves to grieve. But she says, "I did not go to look at Grandfather Connor's grave. There was no need. It was not his monument" (191). Instead, she visits the Brick House, called a "massive monument" to Timothy Connor on the first page of *A Bird in the House* (11). In *That House in Manawaka* Jon Kertzer demonstrates that the Brick House is Connor's monument. But I suggest that Vanessa's narrative is his real memorial, just as Laurence's Canadian stories constitute John Simpson's true monument. Perhaps Vanessa does compose her pioneer story, "The Pillars of the Nation," after all, but its title is *A Bird in the House* – just as Del Jordan completes Uncle Craig's history of Wawanash County in Alice Munro's collection *Lives of Girls and Women* (1971), but in her own idiom. The narrators, like their creators, have learned to free themselves for the future through fiction. As Buss states in *Mother and Daughter Relationships in the Manawaka Works of Margaret Laurence*, "Vanessa writes to free herself, to tell the story of the maternal world existing unrealized and often unnoticed inside the patriarchal structure. In telling these stories Vanessa defines her own womanhood by describing its shaping influences" (63). And, in "Cages and Escapes in Margaret Laurence's *A Bird in the House*," Arnold Davidson concludes, "Beyond the narrator who delimits her life's story, is the fictionalist who frees it. If in one sense the author is the exhibitor of cages, the proponent of the human condition, with all its limitation, then she is also the master of escapes. For Laurence, the last escape is art, the achievement of an extra dimension. The young Vanessa is an aspiring writer who composes imitation conventional romances. As an adult, she is a promising writer who explores the partly fictitious reality of her past" (100). Kertzer claims Vanessa "wants to perfect the power of imaginative recall until it can roam freely through the past and forge an over-arching vision, which is sympathetic, creative and human" (34). In *A Bird in the House* Margaret Laurence recreates in the character of Vanessa MacLeod the development of an artist who learns about life through the painful experiences of love and death and who progresses from romance to realism, freeing herself from the past through writing.

CHAPTER 11

"(W)Rites of Passage":
A Portrait of the Writer in *The Diviners*

Writes of Passage is the original title Laurence gave to the penultimate section of *The Diviners* in her typescript of the novel. Ultimately, however, she eliminated the initial letter, at the request of her editors, transforming *Writes* to *Rites*. But writing casts a long shadow over the rituals of passage in this novel, for Morag Gunn is a novelist, like Laurence. Like Laurence, she is writing her fifth and final novel. And, like Laurence, the novel she is writing is *The Diviners*.

In "Margaret Laurence: The Shape of the Writer's Shadow," Aritha van Herk says, "Throughout *The Diviners*, Laurence uses Morag Gunn to address and to deconstruct the terrible shadow cast by writing, the shadow of living with writing, writing as a living, the communion of the writing act" (138). *The Diviners* is indeed full of shadows. Laurence called the novel a "spiritual autobiography" in *Dance on the Earth: A Memoir* (6). Morag is a spiritual sister or shadow self, a mirror image reflecting her creator. The Scots moniker *Morag* suggests *Margaret*, and Morag even resembles Margaret in appearance, with her straight black hair and heavy glasses, suggesting a wise owl.[1]

The Diviners is a *künstlerroman*, chronicling the development of an artist, like *A Portrait of the Artist as a Young Man* (1916) by James Joyce. *The Diviners* might be titled *A Portrait of the Artist as a Middle-Aged Mother*, for mothering her babies and her books, her two types of offspring, is as important to Morag in *The Diviners* as it is to Margaret in *Dance on the Earth*, which she terms "a book about my mothers and about myself as a mother and writer" (*DE* 8). Laurence calls herself a "Method writer" (TNV 127), because she identifies so closely with her heroines. Morag reflects, "They'd been real to her, the people in the books. Breathing inside her head" (67). "Possession or self-hypnosis" (429) is her definition. In *The Diviners* such identification is understandable, because Morag Gunn reflects Margaret Laurence so nearly. As van Herk asserts, "Of all Laurence's work, it might be considered the text that shadows Laurence the most, that seems to intercept the writer and her life, her dread and desire, her living profession and its issue" (136).² In *River of Now and Then: Margaret Laurence's* The Diviners, Susan Warwick says, "The reader's recognition of *The Diviners* as both Morag's text and Laurence's text suggests that it may be read as both a fictionalized rendering of Morag's life and of Laurence's" (45).³

The Diviners is metafiction, a fiction about fiction, as numerous commentators have observed.⁴ By dramatizing Morag's reality as a writer, Laurence gives the reader insight into her own creative processes. Readers are fascinated by the artistic alchemy by which the artist transforms life into fiction, and nowhere is this metamorphosis clearer than in the metafictional *künstlerroman*.

The Diviners, the last of the five Manawaka novels, represents the culmination of all the trends – increasingly explicit feminism and increasingly experimental postmodernism – we have noted throughout the Manawaka cycle. Thus, it furthers Laurence's emphasis on self-empowerment for women, especially the female artist, intensifies her use of metafictionality and meta-autobiography employed in *A Bird in the House*, and extends her use of innovative narrative strategies employed in *The Fire-Dwellers* – combining the autobiographical quality of the former with the postmodernist features of the latter. As James King observes, "*The Diviners* – also a book about the growth and development of a writer – is a sequel to *A Bird in the House*, but one whose stylistic experimentations ... owe much to *The Fire-Dwellers*" (325). In manuscript, *The Diviners* was an even more radically metafictional and meta-autobiographical text, however, but Laurence's editors persuaded her to eliminate over one hundred passages. Thus, the typescript constitutes a shadow text, haunting the published novel. Exploring this shadow text by examining Laurence's own visions and revisions throughout the editorial process can reveal the artist's creative processes.[5]

"A LOOSE, BAGGY MONSTER": THE EDITING OF *THE DIVINERS*

The Diviners was accepted in 1973 by all three of Laurence's publishers: Macmillan in London, Knopf in New York, and McClelland and Stewart in Toronto. They all worked from photocopies of the same typescript, typed from Laurence's original manuscript by her daughter, Jocelyn. The original draft, at nearly seven hundred pages, fulfilled Henry James's definition of the novel as a loose, baggy monster. The second typescript totalled 578 pages, however, and Laurence intended to reduce it by another hundred pages. Perhaps that is partly why Laurence claimed that "writing *The Diviners* was one of the most difficult and exhausting things I've ever done" (*DE* 201).

The Canadian and English publishers agreed to allow Knopf editor Judith Jones to be the sole editor for *The Diviners*, and they relayed all suggestions for revisions to her. Laurence addressed their requests for revisions in her notes[6] titled "Alterations made in *The Diviners* on the basis of criticism from Knopf, McClelland and Stewart, and Macmillan." Caroline Hobhouse of Macmillan confined herself to what she called "nitpicks": for example, she noted that the poem Morag's Sunday school teacher misquotes is not by G.K. Chesterton, but by Hilaire Belloc. Jack McClelland's reactions were more searching: in a 12 June 1973 letter, he called the manuscript ambitious and Laurence a great writer, but expressed distaste for the "infactuality" section and for the headings "memory bank movie," "inner film," and especially "writes of passage."[7] But he approved the plan that Laurence work solely with Jones and offered to share plant costs with Knopf.

On 4 June 1973, after meeting with Allan Maclean and Hobhouse of Macmillan in London, Jones met with Laurence at Elm Cottage in Penn, Buckinghamshire, where Laurence wrote most of her Manawaka novels, for a six-hour session on revising *The Diviners*.[8] Laurence termed it "probably the best session of my entire life with an editor/friend." In a June letter, in which she called it "a marvellous book," Jones itemized

107 requests for excisions. These excisions were duly implemented by Laurence, who crossed out the paragraph or page with a bold diagonal line drawn in black marker. Laurence responded with a list titled "Points of Possible Disagreement with Judith. Explanation of What I've Done or Not Done" to clarify her artistic intentions.

Despite some disagreements, Laurence implemented most of Jones's requests for excisions. Jones had been Laurence's editor for several years, and Laurence had great respect for her ability. In a 5 June 1973 letter to *Boss* Jack McClelland of *McStew*, she called Jones "one of the really great editors of this world, with whom I work in real intensity and harmony and sometimes in battle." They disagreed once, when Laurence resisted Jones's urging to restructure the stories of *A Bird in the House* as a novel (*DE* 198). Laurence headed her list of alterations to *The Diviners* with this note: "Approx. 100 pp. cut out." Jones wrote to Jack McClelland on 28 August 1973: "You will see there has been some major surgery performed – all to the good, I'm convinced ... And we have agreed, thank heaven, that WRITES OF PASSAGE will be RITES OF PASSAGE."[9]

The requests for excisions focused on two primary areas: the metafictional framework and the embedded *künstlerroman*. Laurence titled the opening section of the novel *River of Now and Then*, suggesting the two levels of narrative she outlined in her preparatory notes at York University – "Now – done in Past tense. Then – done in Present tense" – in order to convey the simultaneity of past and present. Laurence addressed these two levels in her list of alterations: "MORAG AS WRITER – both in Present and Past sequences, this has been cut a lot."[10]

"WORDSMITH": THE METAFICTIONAL FRAMEWORK

Laurence frames *The Diviners* with images of Morag, the writer, seated at her kitchen table in front of the window overlooking the river, trying to write, in the Now of the novel.[11] These images dominate the frame sections – the first section, "River of Now and Then," and the final of the five sections, "The Diviners." But they also provide a frame of reference for introducing the central sections: "Halls of Sion" begins, "Morag sat at the table in the kitchen, with a notebook in front of her and a ballpoint pen in her hand. Not writing" (185). Such images are self-reflexive, reflecting Laurence writing *The Diviners* in The Shack (*HS* 147), her cabin on the Otonabee River. Robert Kroetsch writes, in "Sitting Down To Write: A Discourse in Morning," "Morag Gunn sits down at her kitchen table to a typewriter. The kitchen table is one of the marks of her own self-construction – part of what we might call her signature ... Perhaps the kitchen table is not only a mark of Morag Gunn's signature; it is also a mark of Margaret Laurence's signature" (131).

But Jones directs Laurence to omit many of Morag's reflections on writing, noting, "too much in here about *this* novel and its problems," although Laurence responds, "Morag constantly relates fiction to life." The first passage Jones cuts out is a paragraph on the opening page revealing that Morag has been suffering for two years from a painful case of writer's block. Jones has Laurence omit several passages where Morag agonizes about being unable to write. Knowing that Morag is shut out of her wellspring of creativity makes sense of her neuroses throughout the entire narrative.

Pique's sudden overnight departure for Manawaka is the catalyst that shocks Morag out of her literary paralysis. The note comparing herself to Ophelia that Pique inserts in Morag's typewriter provides the inspiration *and* the beginning for Morag's novel on the opening page of *The Diviners*. As Kroetsch says, "Pique's note on the first page of the novel becomes the first page of the novel" (132). The shock of her daughter's departure for her mother's hometown impels Morag to review her collection of photographs, which, in turn, provide the rationale for her retrospective narrative.[12] Putting the photographs in order suggests putting her life in order in preparation for death – as Laurence did in writing *The Diviners*, a rich tapestry interweaving strands of her life and art. As Laurence says, "Morag consciously sets out to write down her memories, to get her life into some kind of perspective, to see what happened to her. One might call it 'an examined life'" (Sullivan 76).

Jones directs Laurence to omit several passages where Morag broods about mutability and mortality, contemplating the Grim Reaper. The Cassandra of McConnell's Landing, Morag, like Stacey in *The Fire-Dwellers*, prophesies gloom and doom. Like Stacey, Morag contemplates her middle-aged self in the mirror, reflecting on age and death, indulging in "*Pre-Mourning*" (*FD* 15). Jones directs, "Cut introspection re imagined death." Laurence argues, "The Black Celt side of her is *there*, for life, but she has to come to terms (in a Jungian sense) with the *shadow* [my italics] in herself." Although these reflective passages are related to her creative block, since Morag writes to live and lives to write, Laurence cuts them out, despite her protests, as Jones directs.

Morag's meditations on mortality suggest *The Diviners* may be as much a *vollendungsroman*,[13] to employ Constance Rooke's term, meaning a novel of completion or winding up, as *The Stone Angel*, for Morag bids farewell to creativity and passes the creative torch to her daughter, Pique, who combines her parents' Scots and Métis heritage and their gifts of words and music in songs. Like Royland, the "Old Man of the River" (113) – "Old Man River. The Shaman. Diviner" (308) – Morag loses her gift for divining. And like Laurence, she prophesies *The Diviners* will be her last novel. On 3 February 1973, Laurence wrote to Al Purdy, "this is the end of a 12-year involvement with Manawaka and its inhabitants ... I don't know where to go now – this is why I've always said this would likely be my last novel" (*FL* 270). Mourning becomes Morag, and Margaret, but the excision of Morag's meditations on mortality undermines the meta-autobiographical element.

In the metafictional framework of *The Diviners*, Laurence recreates the reality of a writer, both internal and external. The externals include Morag's correspondence with agent Milward Crispin, her telephone conversations with ruthlessly honest editor Constance (who may reflect Jones), and her conversations with aspiring writers. Jones has Laurence omit this verisimilar vehicle. In the typescript, Crispin tells Morag he has sent "Piper Gunn and the Bitch Duchess" to every journal on the continent: one editor would consider it if she cut it by two-thirds and changed the title to "The Ghostly Ranting Pipes of McBain" in Laurence's own satire on the publishing process. Morag writes critical articles for subsistence during her creative block, but Laurence states in her list of revisions, "articles cut entirely." Avoiding writing the articles involves compulsive cleaning to ward off the internal chaos, and the third passage cut from the typescript shows Morag getting out her photographs as an evasion technique. Ironically, this ploy initiates the narrative of the novel.

Morag *reads* herself into the *Snapshots* the way a critic reads meaning into a text, interpreting her unseen presence hidden behind the body of her dead mother, where she is "buried alive, the first burial" (15), prophesying the final burial that Morag broods about, and also suggesting the tomb-to-womb comic life cycle that the novel celebrates. Two of the six *Snapshots* are excised and then reinstated in the typescript. These *shadows* (15) from her past haunt Morag's present.

In a sudden compulsive action, Morag burns her photographs of these people from her past – Christie and Prin, Brooke and Ella – all except Pique's father, who was superstitious about having his picture taken. Appalled, she fears that she has destroyed her past, but realizes that she carries her past like unclaimed baggage forever circling the carousel in her skull. Similarly, Laurence realizes, "I would carry the land [the prairies] and town [Neepawa] all my life within my skull" (*HS* 172). But Jones objects: "the burning of the photographs hard to believe." Perhaps Jones did not realize what a latter-day Hedda Gabler Laurence was, for she incinerated many a manuscript. Ironically, burning the pictures initiates Morag's narrative by providing a motive for memory. She must *re-member* her past, now that the tangible evidence has gone up in smoke. The six "Snapshots" in "River of Now and Then" recall the traumatic turning point in her life, the death of her parents. "The Nuisance Grounds" recreates her past life. In a passage excised from the novel, Morag reflects on memory, realizing how we fabricate our past. Although Laurence omits the passage, she states in her notes, "People fictionalize their lives, not only in 'fiction' but also in memories." Morag refers twice to her "invented memories" (17, 18), just as Vanessa MacLeod recalls "the memory of a memory" (190) in *A Bird in the House*. Indeed, the fictionalizing quality of memory is one of Laurence's major subtexts in *The Diviners*: she writes, "*A popular misconception is that we can't change the past – everyone is constantly changing their own past, recalling it, revising it*" (70).

"MORAG'S FIRST TALE": THE EMBEDDED KÜNSTLERROMAN

In her *Künstlerroman*, Laurence uses three methods to dramatize Morag's creative development. First, she employs a tripartite educational model of reading, critiquing, and writing. Moreover, she includes mentors – Christie Logan, Miss Melrose, and Brooke Skelton – who teach Morag to read and write. Most importantly, she embeds Morag's fictions in the narrative to illustrate her literary development. These embedded fictions form Jones's primary target. Excising Morag's fictions may be the easiest way of cutting the text, but it may not be the best way. Granted that *The Diviners* was drowning in detail, the question is, did Laurence's editors miss her metafictional aim?

Morag recalls herself as a child creating characters even before she is able to read and write – "Peony. Rosa Picardy. Cowboy Joke. Blue-Sky Mother. Barnstable Father. Old Forty-Nine" (19) – characters taken from songs such as "'Cowboy Jack' and 'The Wreck of the Old Forty-Nine'" (20). Morag, hiding beneath the "angels, dark angels" (19) of the sweeping spruce boughs, creates her *"spruce-house family"* (20) to people the darkness after the death of her parents. Creativity is an antidote to death for Morag, and for Margaret, who also created a character named "Blue Sky" after her mother's death and imagined a "'funny' house" with a fictional family (*DE* 40). Morag wonders, "*What kind of a character am I?*" (21), for she creates shadow selves in the personae of Peony and Rosa, alter egos prefiguring her fictional heroines, Lilac, Mira, and Fiona. In the embedded *Künstlerroman* she answers this question, recreating her creative development.

Christie Logan is Morag's first mentor, who teaches her the power of myth. Morag, an orphan, is a *nuisance*, and so it is logical that she is *collected* by the *Scavenger*, who tends the *Nuisance Grounds*, as Manawaka terms its garbage dump – the graveyard where the townsfolk consign their bottles of spirits and aborted babies – the refuse that they refuse to acknowledge. Christie, a Celtic Christ, or scapegoat figure, is a saver, or *saviour*, as Michel Fabre observes, and Morag is one of *"Christie's salvage operations"* (26). Manawaka views Morag as *white trash*, but Christie's view is "Bad Riddance to Good Rubbish" (51). Christie has "the gift of the garbage-telling" (85): "By their garbage shall ye know them" (48), he preaches. Christie provides Morag with a room of her own where she can rewrite reality, as he teaches her how to transform garbage into gold.

Christie gives Morag not just a home but a history. When Morag discovers in *The Clans and Tartans of Scotland* that "The chieftainship of Clan Gunn is undetermined at the present time, and no arms have been matriculated" (58), Christie creates a myth for her in his Tales of Piper Gunn, the legendary figure who led the dispossessed

Scottish crofters from Sutherland to the Red River Valley: "Piper Gunn, he was a great tall man, a man with the voice of drums and the heart of a child and the gall of a thousand and the strength of conviction" (59). Because Jones notes, "There are too many Piper stories here told successively," Laurence responds, "I have cut out the bizarre and funny ones, as not having the right tone and also not being necessary." Morag tells Christie on his deathbed, "you've been my father to me" (420), because he gave her an ancestral mythology.

Christie gives Morag not just a history but a *herstory* (*DE* 4), a term Laurence uses in *Dance on the Earth*, by creating a namesake, a matriarch or Madonna figure, in Piper Gunn's wife: "Now Piper Gunn had a woman, and a strapping strong woman she was, with the courage of a falcon and the beauty of a deer and the warmth of a home and the faith of saints, and you may know her name. Her name, it was Morag" (60). Laurence portrays Morag weaving her own fictions around her namesake in "Morag's First Tale of Piper Gunn's Woman," who has *"the power and the second sight and the good eye and the strength of conviction"* (61). Morag also weaves Christie into her saga as Clowny Macpherson, an apt pseudonym for Christie, that archetypal jester or wise fool, who wears a loony mask to protect his true self from scorn. In the typescript, Morag gives Clowny an axe named for Bonnie Prince Charlie, incorporating history and myth.[14] Laurence argues, "Morag's early story about Clowny Macpherson ... this has to remain, because it is her way of dealing with Christie at that point, trying to make him (although she does not realize it) into a kind of acceptable figure in her mythology, the scrawny funny guy who at the same time is a great axeman and chops down the trees for making houses, at the time of Piper Gunn." Ironically, Morag realizes Christie by fictionalizing, or mythologizing him, just as Margaret did by transforming John Simpson into Timothy Connor in *A Bird in the House* (*HS* 8). The mature Morag also reflects Christie's influence when she declares, "The myths are my reality" (415).[15]

Christie also gives Morag her factual history by weaving stories of her father, Colin Gunn, into his tales of Piper Gunn. The typescript shows Morag composing a story about her father as a war hero saving his mate's life in a bloody battle and being decorated with a medal for courage. Jones directs Laurence to "Cut Morag's tale of Gunner Gunn."

Laurence responds, "Morag's childhood stories of Piper Gunn's wife and the chariot (influence Ossian) and Clowny Macpherson (a reimagining of Christie) and her father Colin are, I think, necessary," yet she cuts them anyway. This story is interesting because it shows Morag incorporating fact and fiction. She says subsequently, "I like the thought of history and fiction interweaving" (341), a major subtext of *The Diviners*, in which Laurence questions the authority of history as it is traditionally taught, suggesting that it is just another kind of narrative, or story, for "history" and "story" derive from the same root. "What is a true story? Is there any such thing?" (159), Morag asks herself. She considers her profession: "Wordsmith. Liar, more likely. Weaving fabrications. Yet, with typical ambiguity, convinced that fiction was more true than fact. Or that fact was in fact fiction" (33).

Jules Tonnerre reinforces Christie's model of the oral tradition of folklore and myth later in his "Tale of Rider Tonnerre" celebrating the *Chevalier*, "Prince of the Braves," leader of the Métis, or *Bois-brûlés*, who had a rifle called *La Petite*[16] and a magical horse named *Roi du Lac* that arose from a lake in a dream, like King Arthur's sword *Excalibur* in Malory's legendary *Morte d'Arthur*. Jules appears to Morag as a *Shadow* on her first, secret visit to the Nuisance Grounds, for he, too, is a scavenger who shares Christie's gift of turning garbage into gold. Jules *saves* Morag sexually and helps make her a writer by liberating her true *voice* from "someplace beyond language" (153). Although voice is a central concern for Laurence right from her first published book, Jones directs, "Cut story. Summary good." Laurence responds, "I've cut a little, but left them pretty much as they were, with a few later references to them by Morag." The conjunction of Jules's and Christie's tales is important, however, as it demonstrates to Morag the deficiencies of history as taught in school.

School continues Morag's training as a writer by introducing her to the print culture. Morag anticipates the first day of school: "when she goes home today she will know how to read" (40). But Eva "Weakguts" Winkler, the alter ego who commits the acts that Morag fears doing, teaches Morag the importance of retention. Morag learns to contain her emotions, like her precious bodily fluids, spilling them onto the orderly lines of a scribbler: "She still does not know how to read. Some school this turned out to be. But has learned one thing for sure. Hang onto your shit and never let them know you are ascared" (42).

When Morag is introduced to print culture in school, Christie's critique of the canon is concise: "What in hell is this crap? *I wandered lonely as a cloud.* This Wordsworth, now, he was a pansy, girl, or no, maybe a daffodil? Clouds don't wander lonely, for the good christ's sake. Any man daft enough to write a line like that, he wanted his head looked at, if you ask me. Look here, I'll show you a poem, now, then" (72). And he reads her a poem about the Celtic warrior Cuchullin by the Gaelic poet Ossian[17] from two of his favourite tomes, introducing her to the oral tradition that was so important for Laurence's own literary training.

Morag's attempt to follow Ossian into poetry proves abortive, for the Sunday school teacher, Mrs McKee, is not impressed with Morag's verse version of "The Wise Men." When she reads aloud a poem by Hilaire Belloc – "He made Him small fowl out of clay, / And blessed them till they flew away" (92) – Morag is so deflated that she burns her poem. So Mrs McKee is a failed mentor, although she teaches Morag that poetry is not her métier – a lesson Laurence also learned.

Morag's true mentor is Miss Melrose, her high school teacher modelled on Mildred Musgrove, perhaps, who taught Laurence English at Neepawa Collegiate (*DE* 77).[18] Miss Melrose gives Morag literary models, like Wordsworth, but more important, she encourages her to write stories. Musgrove encouraged Laurence to write and publish poems like "Pagan Point" and stories such as "Goodwill Towards Men" in Viscount Collegiate's *Annals of the Black and Gold*, which Laurence edited.[19] Melrose helps Morag realize writing will be her life's work: "Now it is as though a strong hand has been laid on her shoulders. Strong and friendly. But merciless" (136). In her memoir, Laurence recalls a similar epiphany when she realized at fourteen, "I have to be a writer" (*DE* 74). A writer must be a lover of language, and Morag is as much a "Wordsmith" (268) as Laurence: "Words words words. Words haunt her" (219), as Morag, a modern, female Hamlet, reflects.

A writer must be a *seer*, a *see-er*. Perceiving Morag's myopia, Miss Melrose urges her to get glasses, a symbol of vision for Laurence. Although they make Morag resemble "a tall skinny owl whose only redeeming feature is a thirty-six-inch bust" (137), she can now *see*. So elated is she at being able to see leaves on trees that she composes a story that she says "will never see the light of day. 'Wild Roses'" (138). Little did Laurence know how right Morag was, for Jones asks her to omit the story and replace it with this summary: "Sentimental in places? The young teacher not marrying the guy because she couldn't bear to live on a farm – would that really happen? Maybe all that about the wild roses is overdone?" (138). Perhaps Jones was right, for the story *is* sentimental and the style adolescent. But that was Laurence's point – to demonstrate Morag's crude idiom and literary immaturity. Morag's fictions dramatize her development, as does the developing idiom of Stephen Dedalus from childish lisp to sophomoric pedantry in *A Portrait of the Artist as a Young Man*. Laurence omits most of Morag's stories as Jones directs, merely noting, "I have left in one or two of her very early stories because I think these are necessary, and they are also very short."

Laurence reflects her own literary training in another manner by including Morag's experience as a journalist. Morag reports for the *Manawaka Banner*, reflecting the *Neepawa Banner*, where Laurence worked before she ultimately graduated to the *Winnipeg Citizen*. Morag's experience in journalism proves abortive, however, when "a genuine news story" (173) – the death of Piquette Tonnerre and her babies in a fire – makes her realize that she cannot profit from another's pain.[20] Although fiction, not fact, is Morag's métier, reporting influences her writing, as it has for so many authors, by teaching her the importance of *infactuality*, meaning fact-based, a term she coins in the typescript of *The Diviners*. Although journalism proves not to be Morag's métier any more than it was Margaret's, she promises Christie, "I'll – write" (189). And she does, though not to him.

"Halls of Sion" portrays Morag, desperate to escape her hometown, like young Peggy Wemyss, "swifting into life" (190) in Winnipeg. At the university, she is influenced by the poetry of Donne and Milton, which is taught to her by Professor Brooke Skelton in a seventeenth-century course like the one that Malcolm Ross taught at United College in 1946 in which Peggy Wemyss was a student.[21]

Brooke is the mentor who teaches Morag the English canon and critiques her compositions, censoring her lack of historical contextualization. But Jones directs, "Condense all these literary essays. Enough to give a sense of what attracted Brooke." Laurence responds, "the Milton and Donne bits have been cut, and the whole university scene, literature-wise, has been put into one scene which carries on the narrative and includes Brooke's first attraction to Morag." Laurence omits this interesting footnote to Morag's literary development – both Morag's essays and her marginalia on *Paradise Lost* that prophesy problems that will plague the Skelton marriage.

Morag writes "Fields of Green and Gold" about Al McBain, who is "a young farmer during the drought, who nearly gives way to despair, but who finally determines to stay alive and to stay with the land" (197). In the typescript, he is in the barn about to hang himself, when his young daughter interrupts him, and he changes his mind. When the story is published in the college paper *Veritas*, meaning truth, under her real name, Morag is upset: "Why did she submit it under her own name. Imagine writing *Morag Gunn* in cold blue ink" (204). Laurence recalls publishing poems in the *Manitoban* under a pseudonym and regrets that it took her so long to find her own voice (*DE* 5). Similarly, Morag thinks, "*I do not know the sound of my own voice*" (277). Discovering her voice as a woman writer is the process Laurence recreates in *The Diviners*. But Morag's, or Margaret's, voice is silenced in this story, because Jones directs, "Summarize story – its ideas rather than plot." Laurence replaces the story with a skeleton plot outline that lacks the life of Morag's sentimental, adolescent style. Morag's reflections on her character's resemblance to herself seem suggestive, however, as she realizes, "The child *isn't* her. Can the story child really exist separately? Can it be both her and not her?" (197) – reflecting the way Morag resembles Margaret. Even though the story is omitted, it proves pivotal in Morag's personal life, for it catalyzes her friendship with Ella Gerson, modelled on Adele Wiseman, and it instigates her relationship with Brooke, who finds the story "promising" (206) – so promising that he initiates a romance with the girl. A Pygmalion figure, Brooke wants to mould this girl with the "mysterious nonexistent past" (212) in his image. He wants her to be a *tabula rasa*, a desire with which she complies at first, but she outgrows that fiction. Pygmalion's creation becomes a Frankenstein monster when Morag becomes a feminist.

Morag also composes "The Mountain," a tale of Austrian Count Breuckner who replicates his family's feudal system in Canada. Laurence published a similar story, "*Tal des Walde,*" in *Vox*, the United College journal, in which she employs a framework that prefigures her narrative methods in *The Diviners*. She excised the story on Jones's advice, only this brief summary remaining: "The story is about an Austrian nobleman who comes to this country complete with the peasants from his family's lost estate and who tries to create a replica of that feudal system here" (*D* 209). It is unfortunate that she excised this feudal fiction, for it prophesies Morag's relationship with Brooke, a Prospero figure who colonizes Morag and, ironically, judges the story to be "implausible" (209). Prospero is the central figure of Oliver Mannoni's *Prospero and Caliban: The Psychology of Colonization*, a text that greatly influenced Laurence. Laurence alludes to his theories of colonial interdependency when she says, "Brooke is a colonial man ... She's the colony" (Sullivan 74). She acknowledges, "To me, Prospero is a very sinister character" (Sullivan 67).

Marriage to Brooke means leaving Morag Gunn behind in Manawaka to become Mrs Skelton in Toronto when he is hired as Professor of English at the university. But marriage promotes her education, as Morag reads through Brooke's library. His condescending critiques of her creative compositions make her realize they are "trivial and superficial" (242). But she continues to write, progressing from stories to novels, as she searches for her own voice through ventriloquism via her heroines. Her defence of G.M. Hopkins' poetry in Brooke's honours seminar demonstrates that writing provides the *rite* of passage that gives her the *right* to express her own opinions.

Brooke is a hard man to *read*, but his nightmares in "Raj Mataj" about Minoo, his Hindu *Ayah* who initiated him sexually, reveal the "demons and webs" (*JG* 189) that help Morag to interpret his sexual games, as he demands, "Have you been a good girl?" (264).[22] Deprived of a baby by Brooke, who wants to keep Morag as his "little one" (276), his "idiot child" (281), Morag gives birth to her first protagonist, Lilac Stonehouse, who abandons her brutal father and her hometown and "lights out for the city. An old story" (244) – Morag's story, in part. Morag's heroine, Lilac Stonehouse (her surname reflecting the symbolism of *The Stone Angel*), and the novel, *Spear of Innocence*, with its Freudian implications, recalls Morag's own background, just as *The Diviners* reflects Margaret's. The dust jacket even features "a spear, proper, piercing a human heart, valentine" (282), reflecting the Logan crest, "A passion nail piercing a human heart, proper" (57).

Morag writes five novels in *The Diviners*: *Spear of Innocence, Prospero's Child, Jonah, Shadow of Eden,* and *The Diviners*, plus a collection of stories titled *Presences* which parallel Laurence's own creative production. Lyall Powers judges, "The difficulties and sacrifices in Morag's life as she creates her five books of fiction repeat those of Margaret's life as she created the five books of the Manawaka Saga" (*AH* 402). Most of Morag's embedded fictions are omitted from the novel at Jones's request, with brief summaries replacing several pages of plot. Laurence responds to Jones: "Plots of her novels have been cut entirely. Instead, I have tried to work into the central narrative some idea of what she is writing about, without breaking the narrative flow by telling plots. I've just included, in most cases, enough to (hopefully) give some idea of what her material is; how it connects and also doesn't connect with her own life; and enough comments from her, and also a few bits of reviews of her books, to give credence to the fact that she *is* a writer." Morag's embedded novels act as mirrors to reflect her literary development and, by extension, Laurence's artistic alchemy, as she portrays Morag transforming life into fiction. Laurence argues, "Each novel is a subtle distortion of Morag's life or expression of it, but in masked terms until the last novel (Diviners) [which could also be said of Laurence's novel]. I think just a glimpse of each novel (character *and* theme) is necessary, plus some reference to the ways it *relates* and also *does not* relate to Morag." Laurence embeds summaries of Morag's novels in *Memorybank Movies,* while omitting the actual stories, as Jones directs. The way Morag's heroines reflect her own situation suggests how Morag mirrors Margaret, making *The Diviners* resemble a hall of mirrors. King claims, "Like a mirror reflecting other mirrors, *The Diviners* reflects multiple images of the creator creating" (326), and that is precisely what makes this novel so fascinating.

In *Spear of Innocence*, Laurence portrays a writer's reality, recreating the creative process – from the "half-lunatic sense of possession" (280), through the editorial criticism, which seems like "the Revealed Word" (280), and painful process of revision, to the reviews – but Morag's marginal responses to the reviews are omitted from the manuscript. While the novel itself is excised from the text, the summary suggests that Lilac Stonehouse may be Morag's shadow self, reflecting her inner reality, as well as facets of other people in a composite character, combining Fan Brady's vulnerability, Eva Winkler's abortion, and Morag's own escapist impulse.

Spear of Innocence proves to be Morag's *Open Sesame*, for she escapes from her prison in the Skeltons' Crestwood Ivory Tower, where she dramatizes herself as Rapunzel, by writing – her *(w)rites* of passage. Fictions become frictions when she realizes she is living a lie, painting on a smile for Brooke when she would rather join Lilac in the seedy nightclub, Crowe's Cave (245). Morag, who experiences a "half-lunatic sense of possession, of being possessed" (280), stops writing hours before Brooke gets home so that she can emerge from her fictional character, her shadow self, and get back inside her own skin – as Laurence records doing in her memoir. This first novel proves pivotal when Morag realizes she has outgrown Brooke and his condescending critiques. When she rebels, she does so in Christie's idiosyncratic idiom, his "loony oratory, salt-beefed with oaths" (276) – swearing "by judas priest and all the sodden saints in fucking Beulah Land" (277) – for she has yet to find her own voice, just as Laurence claims in her memoir (6).[23]

When *Spear of Innocence* is published, Morag is empowered to abandon Brooke, her Prospero. An Ariel figure, she is aided in her escape by Jules,[24] a Caliban perhaps, the *shaman* (294) who performs the "magic" (294) (rough magic?) of liberating her by impregnating her, for a mother can not be a "Child," Brooke's nickname for Morag. In the manuscript, Morag wonders whether she left with Jules just to get the plot for a new novel. Publishing *Spear of Innocence* under the name Gunn, not Skelton, signals to Brooke Morag's new independence. In a similar fashion, *The Stone Angel* empowered Laurence to separate from Jack and embark on independence by moving to England with her children and the manuscript of her first Manawaka novel (*DE* 158). Parallels between Morag's and Margaret's manuscripts and the relationship between actual and fictional authors and their protagonists suggest that the original text of *Spear of Innocence* would illuminate Laurence's creative process further, but the excised pages have been destroyed.

Morag's second novel reflects her own marriage explicitly. She describes it in a letter to Ella that replaces the fiction Jones excised from the text: "It's called *Prospero's Child*, she being the young woman who marries His Excellency, the Governor of some island in some ocean very far south, and who virtually worships him and then who has to go to the opposite extreme and reject nearly everything about him, at least for a time, in order to become her own person. It's as much the story of H.E." (353). "H.E." reflects Brooke Skelton, but this skeleton outline does not clarify the artistic alchemy of transforming life into fiction that could illuminate Laurence's own creative processes.[25] Morag notes, "It's done in semi-allegorical form, and also it has certain parallels with *The Tempest*" (352) – parallels *The Diviners* shares, as Gayle Greene notes,[26] although the parallels of Mira's marriage with Morag's and, by extension, with Margaret's, may be even more intriguing. Laurence notes, "Morag admits parallels with Shakespeare and with her own life." Morag reflects on these parallels in a suggestive passage of the typescript that Jones directs Laurence to omit.

Morag's next publication is a collection of short stories entitled *Presences*, which may reflect *A Bird in the House*. But *Presences* fails to illuminate Laurence's own creativity, for the only references left in the text are the facts that Morag hates the title and that Mr Sampson, proprietor of Agonistes Bookshop (383), proudly displays it in the window (384).

Morag's third novel, *Jonah*, is also excised and replaced with a skeleton summary. But the brief outline of Coral, "who is so uncertainly freed by Jonah's ultimate death" (390), and her widower father, Jonah, a fisherman who "inhabits Morag's head, and talks in his own voice" (390), reflects Morag's relationship with Christie, whose tales of Piper Gunn Morag is repeating to Pique. *Jonah* also recalls *A Jest of God*, which employs a verse about the tomb of Jonah from Carl Sandburg's poem *Losers* for its epigraph.

"Rites of Passage," the penultimate part of *The Diviners*, could indeed have been titled "Writes of Passage," for Morag lives by her pen, and her confidence grows with each additional publication: "*Jonah* has been taken by a book club, *Spear of Innocence* and *Prospero's Child* are coming out in paperback, and a film option has been taken on *Spear*" (437). Morag has arrived as a writer just as clearly as Laurence, who won the 1966 Governor General's Award for *A Jest of God*, which was optioned by Paul Newman and Joanne Woodward and made into the 1968 film *Rachel, Rachel*. Morag's success, like Margaret's, has been achieved "by right" (153), by write.

Morag's fourth novel is titled *Shadow of Eden*, recalling her marginalia on Milton's *Paradise Lost*, "Exit from Eden," which was omitted from the published text. The ten-page narrative in the typescript is replaced by Morag's account in a letter to Ella that clarifies her historical sources: "Odd – the tales Christie used to tell of Piper Gunn and the Sutherlanders, and now this book deals with the same period. The novel follows them on the sea journey to Hudson Bay, through that winter at Churchill and then on the long walk to York Factory in the spring ... The man who led them on that march, and on the trip by water to Red River, was young Archie Macdonald, but in my mind the piper who played them on will always be that giant of a man, Piper Gunn, who probably never lived in so-called real life but who lives forever. Christie knew things about inner truths that I am only just beginning to understand" (443). Laurence notes, "A letter to Ella contains all I am going to use re the novel and all I am going to use of Infactuality, in a few pages." *Shadow of Eden* is all that is left of the part of *The Diviners* called "Infactuality" that recounts the history of the Highland Clearances that Laurence researched. Perhaps the editors were right to excise the historical material, but Morag's novel is a major loss, because Laurence's notes reveal that *Shadow of Eden* recounts the experience of Fiona MacLeod, who emigrates with the Sutherlanders to the Red River Valley. Her husband, the piper, perishes on the voyage, and she arrives in the new land, perceived as a "Dark Eden," a widow with an infant – a single mother like Morag and like Laurence herself at the time of writing *The Diviners. Shadow of Eden* reflects Christie's Tales of Piper Gunn, as well as the biography of Archibald Macdonald that Laurence's friend Jean Murray Cole was writing while Laurence was researching *The Diviners.*[27] *Shadow of Eden* takes Morag over three years to write, just as *The Diviners* did Laurence. It reflects *The Diviners* and is mirrored in "The dispossessed" (402), a portrait of a Scots woman, in which "the flesh mirrors the spirit's pain" (402), set against burning crofts, painted by Morag's Scots lover Dan McRaith – his very name suggesting a ghost. *The Diviners* is indeed like a hall of mirrors, and *Shadow of Eden* may be the missing reflection.

Morag's last novel is not named, although the fifth and final part of *The Diviners* is titled "The Diviners." At the end of the narrative, Laurence writes, "Morag returned to the house, to write the remaining private and fictional words, and to set down her title" (477). As Lyall Powers concludes, "Morag wrote her last novel, telling Margaret's story, *The Diviners*" (403). She *sets down* her title in the dual sense of inscribing it and passing the torch to the younger generation embodied in Pique, who combines the words and music, Celtic and Métis myths, to celebrate her dual heritage in the song that concludes *The Diviners*.[28] Like Royland, whose gift of divining is gone, Morag becomes the Prospero figure who breaks her wand and frees her spirit, Ariel, when she says to her daughter, "Go with God" (475), as Pique heads west, continuing the migratory cycle symbolized by birds. "The inheritors ... the gift, or portion of grace, or whatever it was, was finally withdrawn, to be given to someone else" (477), Morag reflects. Although she gives Pique the Tonnerre hunting knife that severed the thread of her father's life, she withholds the plaid pin until she is "gathered to [her] ancestors" (474). Thus, Laurence reunites the two emblems that link her first Manawaka novel, *The Stone Angel*, with her last, *The Diviners*, knitting the entire cycle together.

We may assume that the title Morag sets down would be *The Diviners*. And we would be right, for in both her notes and manuscript, Laurence concludes with a final page inscribing the words, "THE DIVINERS, an unpublished novel by Morag Gunn," surrounded by a black border like an obituary notice. This separate closing page is also an opening title page, creating a Möbius strip effect as it brings the novel back to its origin in a cyclical motion.[29] But Jones objected: "Cut plot – too closely related to the problems of this novel ... same applies to title."[30] So we will never know how Morag's final fiction related to Laurence's last novel. Silence has the last word in *The Diviners*: "*Look ahead into the past, and back into the future, until the silence*" (477).

What, then, has been gained and lost in the editorial process? The excision of over one hundred passages achieved comparative concision and rescued the novel from becoming an unwieldy monster, but at what cost? The summaries replacing Morag's stories have none of the vitality of the word made flesh in fiction. Morag's literary development in the maturation of her idiom is lost. The connections between Morag's life and fiction, which might reflect parallels between Laurence's life and art, are lost. Such reflections could illuminate Laurence's artistic alchemy, clarifying the way she transformed life into art. These missing links are revealed by the typescript of the novel, however, which consequently constitutes a shadow text, haunting *The Diviners*.

Despite these excisions, however, *The Diviners* remains Laurence's most metafictional and meta-autobiographical novel. It also continues the progression of her feminism, as she portrays the developing self-empowerment of women. "Morag comes closer to what might be termed the god within" (Miner 18), Laurence affirms: "Morag in *The Diviners*, ... more than any of the others, is able to assimilate her past and to accept herself as a strong and independent woman, able to love and to create" (IT 258–9). Perhaps this is partly why *The Diviners* was labelled blasphemous by fundamentalists in Laurence's home county of Peterborough in 1985. Laurence actually attempted to write a novel, to be titled *Dance on the Earth*, which was inspired by this "Controversy," as it was labelled, and which was intended to conclude the Manawaka cycle. But Laurence may have been too distressed by the attack to complete the novel. Laurence writes to Gabrielle Roy 23 March 1976, "I cannot help feeling hurt at having my work [*The Diviners*] so vastly misunderstood ... In fact, at its deepest level, it is a novel about God's grace" (*VLS* 175).

CHAPTER 12

"Dance on the Earth": Laurence's Unfinished Novel

"Margaret, are you grieving ...?"
~ "Spring and Fall: *to a young child*" by Gerard Manley Hopkins

"To every thing there is a season, and a time to every purpose
under the heaven: A time to be born, and a time to die ... a time to
mourn and a time to dance ..."
~ *Ecclesiastes* 3: 1–4.

Laurence predicted that *The Diviners*, the final of her five Manawaka novels, would be her last. And it was, just as the novel that Morag Gunn is writing in *The Diviners* is predicted to be her last. But *The Diviners* was not the last novel Laurence tried to write; it was merely the final novel she succeeded in finishing. As she writes in the Forewords to her memoir, "I have tried over the past years to write another novel. In fact, I have tried many times. I have not succeeded. It has finally become clear to me that the novel I thought I wanted to write was simply not there to be written. I prophesied this at the end of *The Diviners*, but I didn't know how much it would hurt" (*DE* 6–7). These attempts are confirmed in recent biographies by James King and Lyall Powers and in recent editions of Laurence's letters by John Lennox, Ruth Panofsky, Paul Socken, and J.A. Wainwright.

What was the novel that she tried so hard to compose? And why was she unable to complete it? These questions have haunted readers ever since her *Dance on the Earth: A Memoir* was published posthumously in 1989. Not until a decade later was it possible to answer these questions because Laurence's holograph notes and drafts for this novel were not available until 1997 when they formed an accession of material in the Margaret Laurence Archives at McMaster University. Nevertheless, this fascinating addition to Laurence's oeuvre has been virtually ignored to date.[1]

Surprisingly, the title of her unfinished novel is "Dance on the Earth" – the same as her memoir. Clearly Laurence first attempted to compose *Dance on the Earth* as a novel. Only after she failed to write the fiction did she compose *Dance on the Earth* as an autobiographical work of non-fiction.[2]

The notes and drafts for the unfinished novel confirm Laurence's assertion that she tried hard to compose *Dance on the Earth* as a fiction. The 1997 accession includes ten pages titled "Dance on the Earth," dated 20 February 1983, in a blue notebook; twelve pages of "Mairi's Novel," dated 1982, handwritten on loose leaf; sixty-eight pages of handwriting on loose leaf of "Mairi's early life in Canada – age 10 to 12"; thirty-five pages of handwriting on loose leaf, plus nineteen pages of notes titled "Allie's Milton Classes" and dated 3 August 1982; fourteen pages of handwriting on loose leaf titled "Closing the Cottage," dated 3 August 1982, in a dark green notebook; and a yellow notebook, undated, containing a detailed chronology. All are written in sprawling handwriting on foolscap or in lined scribblers – "the only extant pieces of fiction in Margaret Laurence's handwriting," as King points out (393). In the section titled "Portion of Grace," subtitled "Memoirs," covering 1926–45, Laurence says the notebooks were begun in 1978 and abandoned in 1979 and the next notebooks resumed in 1984. She cautions, "these are unedited and unrevised and may not be published."[3]

But the fictional and non-fictional versions share several parallels, as one might suspect. They share more than a title, for the novel, like the memoir, is dedicated: "For Jocelyn and David [her children], with faith, hope, and love." Because it is a fiction, however, Laurence adds the customary caution: "All the characters and towns in this novel are purely imaginary. Only the landscapes are real." For the epigraph to her novel, she intended to use the first verse of Sydney Carter's modern hymn, "Lord of the Dance," which is featured in the Forewords to her memoir, *Dance on the Earth*, introducing the celebratory spiritual element so central to both fictional and non-fictional versions.

Laurence also intended to feature in her novel her own poem, "Old Women's Song," which frames *Dance on the Earth*, concluding her Forewords (18–19) and introducing her Afterwords (225–8). Her novel "Dance on the Earth" was to feature old women dancing too, as we will see.

A list titled "Dance on the Earth – Plans for Opening" specifies the epigraphs that she planned for her novel: "'Lord of the Dance,' first verse; 'Mary kept all these things, and pondered them in her heart,' Luke 2:19; Bailey's poem?; [plus]Acknowledgements to Canada Council; [and] Dedication." She also hoped to use for the cover of her novel a photograph of the sculpture "Crucified Woman" by Almuth Lutkenhaus, a stylized female nude with arms outstretched in cruciform that Laurence describes in her memoir as "dancing, on the earth" (*DE* 17). The sculpture may have inspired her poem "Old Women's Song" as well as the title for both her unfinished novel and published memoir.

Laurence's plans for the novel make it clear that the fiction version of "Dance on the Earth" was to parallel the memoir in being a feminist work celebrating a matrilinear line of descent: just as the memoir is structured as a tribute to her three mothers, so her novel was to record three generations of Marys: the narrator's mother, Mairi Macduff, now eighty-two; her daughter, Mary Chorniuk, dead at four; and her granddaughter, Mary Chorniuk, now age four and the potential audience for Allie's narrative. Just as she counters the term "wisemen" with the coinage "wisewomen" in her memoir, so Laurence counters the term "shaman" with the word "shawomen" in her draft novel, including in her notes a list of "shawomen" or "storytellers."[4]

Just as this feminist aspect is integrally related to the spiritual element of Laurence's memoir, where she emphasizes the importance of "the female principle as being part of the Holy Spirit" (14), so her choice of the name Mary for the matrilineal line of her novel is no coincidence, because her notes make it clear that she intended her novel "Dance on the Earth" to make a religious statement. For example, she lists epithets for Mary, the mother of God, such as Mystical Rose, Tower of Ivory, House of Gold, Queen of Angels, and Refuge of Sinners, and quotes prayers to the Virgin, such as "Mary mother of God, be a mother to me" from Prayers for Confession. We have already noted the epigraph that she planned for her "Dance on the Earth" novel: "But Mary kept all these things, and pondered them in her heart" from the Gospel according to Saint Luke. Perhaps Mary, as "the one constant ... representative of our sex" (*DE* 14), and a relic of pre-Christian matriarchal religions, was related to the feminist spirituality that Laurence explored in her last years in Lakefield. Her notes for the novel include a catalogue of Christian denominations – "Scots Presbyterian, Anglican, United, Roman Catholic, Pentecostal" – like other Manawaka novels, notably *A Jest of God* and *The Diviners*, in which her heroines visit churches of different denominations.

A final link between fictional and non-fictional versions is the autobiographical element of both. While the published *Dance on the Earth* is labelled a memoir, not an autobiography, it does include many facts of Laurence's own life in the course of paying tribute to her three mothers. Similarly, the novel was clearly intended to be fictionalized autobiography, for it reflects the "Controversy": that is, the attack on Laurence's work by fundamentalists that so deeply disturbed Laurence's last years.

"Dance on the Earth," the novel, has even more in common with *The Diviners*, however, than it does with *Dance on the Earth*, the memoir – not surprisingly, since it was clearly intended to form the finale of the Manawaka cycle. Like *The Diviners*, the fictional "Dance on the Earth" features two time-lines, past and present, as in other Manawaka novels – beginning with Hagar Currie Shipley, who is "rampant with memory" in *The Stone Angel* (5), and ending with Morag Gunn, whose "Memorybank Movies" replay her real and her "invented memories" (17). It also features two geographical centres: like Morag Gunn in *The Diviners*, and Margaret Laurence herself, the heroine of "Dance on the Earth" has divided her life between western and eastern Canada: she remembers her past as a child in Manitoba while living her present life in Ontario. Laurence also planned to include the Old Country, both Britain and the Ukraine, and her notes include quotes from *The Clans and Tartans of Scotland* – a work featured in *The Diviners*. Aritha van Herk celebrates the scope of the last published Manawaka novel in "Margaret Laurence: The Shape of the Writer's Shadow": "*The Diviners* casts a prophesying shadow of national Canada that is brilliantly inclusive, culturally, psychically, and spatially: from Manitoba to Toronto to Vancouver, to England and Scotland and then back to Ontario; from small-town to city to rural setting; from orphan and wife to mother and writer; from aboriginal to settler in their conjunction" (140).

But "Dance on the Earth," the novel, was to be even more ambitious than *The Diviners*. It is so far-reaching in its historical and geographical scope that it must have been intended to conclude the cycle,
spanning, as it does, over a century of Canadian history. Laurence's
preparatory notes include a list of place names – including Manawaka,
South Wachakwa, Freehold, and Galloping Mountain – that link the
fiction to her other Manawaka novels. Her list of her protagonist's
schoolmates includes Vanessa MacLeod, narrator of *A Bird in the
House*; Stacey Cameron, heroine of *The Fire-Dwellers*, and Morag Gunn,
protagonist of *The Diviners* – true to Laurence's method in the Manawaka cycle of giving the star of one novel a cameo role in another character's narrative. Her notes also mention the deaths of Henry Pearl in
South Wachakwa, of Agnes Connor in Manawaka, and of Ewen Mac-
Leod from pneumonia. They also mention that Peter Chorniuk, ances-
tor of characters in "Dance on the Earth," delivered wood to John
Simpson of *A Bird in the House*, with his dog Natasha, whose pup,
Nanuk, Vanessa MacLeod persuades her grandfather to let her keep
in the story "The Half Husky." They note that Theresa Chorniuk marries Nestor Kazlik of Manawaka, becoming the mother of Nick Kazlik, Rachel Cameron's lover in *A Jest of God*. They also mention a
Métis woman named Marie Sansregret from Galloping Mountain, who
married Lazarus Tonnerre, making her the mother of Jules Tonnerre
and the grandmother of Pique Gunn Tonnerre of *The Diviners*; they
note that Marie kept house for Bram Shipley, making her the "half-
breed girl" (*SA* 166) mentioned in *The Stone Angel*. All these connections suggest that the novel "Dance on the Earth" was intended to
wind up all the threads of the Manawaka cycle, making it Laurence's
grand finale, her farewell to fiction.

Laurence planned this final Manawaka fiction carefully, and her co-
pious notes reveal a highly schematic structure that was clearly intended to make certain specific points. She constructed the novel in
terms of a series of intertwining oppositions: two cultural heritages,
two time-lines, two geographical centres, two types of histories, both
personal and political, and two narrative voices. An examination of
these intertwined oppositions will clarify the points Laurence intended
to make.

First, there are two families that intermarry, one British, one Ukrainian – oil and water, as Rachel Cameron says in *A Jest of God* – two

of the primary ethnic strains of both Neepawa and Manawaka. The British line, combining English and Scots strains, includes the Mac-Duff and Pryce families; the Ukrainian line features the Chorniuks and Melanchuks; and the two heritages unite in the principal characters: the narrator, Allie Pryce Chorniuk, and her sister-in-law, Stella Melanchuk Chorniuk. Laurence's notes include genealogies for both lines of descent, beginning with the emigration from the Ukraine of Wasyl and Olga Chorniuk in 1893 and of Antin and Wanda Melanchuk in 1898.

For her major character, Mairi MacDuff, she includes notes on the Clan MacDuff from Fifeshire, which enjoyed the privilege of crowning the Scottish king, leading the Scots army, and seeking sanctuary at the cross of MacDuff in Fifeshire. She notes the origin of the name MacDuff in *dhuibh*, the Scots word for black (Dan McRaith calls Morag Gunn "Morag Dhu. Black Morag" [400] in *The Diviners*) as well as the origin of her family name Wemyss in the word "*weem*," meaning an ancient Pict cave, suggesting Laurence's own personal involvement in Manitoba's multicultural heritage.

Second, there are two time-lines that Laurence notes are "to alternate in each chapter," as in other Manawaka novels, beginning with Hagar Currie Shipley's retrospections in *The Stone Angel* and concluding with Morag Gunn's memories in *The Diviners*,[5] where the "River of Now and Then" symbolizes the dual time-line. Even her Cameron sisters, Rachel and Stacey, play back and forth between present and past in *A Jest of God* and *The Fire-Dwellers*, and Vanessa MacLeod's retrospections that conclude key stories in *A Bird in the House* give her narrative depth. The time-lines in the unfinished novel are even more ambitious than in the other Manawaka novels, covering an entire century: the historical framework begins in 1885 with the Northwest Rebellion and the earliest emigrations from Galicia in 1891 and follows the principal events of the century right up to the 1980's, including the First and Second World Wars so central to the Manawaka cycle. Both the first and the last of the Manawaka novels, *The Stone Angel* and *The Diviners*, span a long period through flashbacks and historical references, but this unfinished novel was to bring that history into the actual story line through the generations represented by her characters.

Third, there are two geographical centres in Manitoba and Ontario – again as in *The Diviners* and in Laurence's own life: Manawaka, Wachakwa, Freehold, and Galloping Mountain in Manitoba; and Jordan's Lake, Jordan's River, and Jordan's Landing in Ontario, echoing "McConnell's Landing," where Morag Gunn lives in *The Diviners*, and Lakefield, Ontario, where Laurence herself lived in her last years. Founded by a Colonel Jordan, "a feudal lord of the manor," who brought immigrants, victims of the potato famine, from Ireland in 1845,[6] the settlement turned out not to be the utopian community he envisioned: "So much for the arrogant Eden of Jordan's dreams," the narrator, Allie, comments. The notes make it clear that Jordan's Landing is to be an Ontario microcosm paralleling Manawaka: they list the primary institutions and personages of the town, including the newspaper, the *Jordan's Landing Times* edited by Ben Falles, the local television station directed by Hailey McKay, the Royal Bank, Dominion Supermarket, Carson's Pharmacy, Tooper's Variety, and Farrell's Hardware. Churches, as always in Laurence's novels, are featured prominently, with the Reverend James Hopkins of the United Church providing a contrast to Jake Flood of the Tabernacle of the Risen and Reborn. The town doctors, Rosie Redington and Timon McGinnis, are mentioned, along with Allie's next-door neighbours, Grant and Molly Newcombe. Most important are Allie's fellow teachers at Jordan's Landing District High School: Principal Colin Garnett, English teachers Bertha Crawford, Terence Dooley, and Julia Scribner, and gym teacher Kelly Drakeson. She also details the students in Allie's grade thirteen class, some of whom are children of the town's principal citizens, while others represent the town's ethnic groups: "Charlotte Garnett, Jerry Tapperton, Marigold Smith (Ojibway), Lynne Abrahams, Marshall Slugger McGinnis, and Debbie and Donno Flood" [*sic*]. And, of course, Allie and her sister-in-law Stella, a nurse, like two of Laurence's aunts, at Saint Michael's Mount Hospital, represent two popular professions for women of their generation in Canada. The two sisters inhabit an old red brick house on Bluedale Avenue – "an unreal sanctuary from the anonymity, the indifference of cities" – reminiscent of Manawaka's Brick House and Laurence's Lakefield home.

Fourth, there are two types of histories, personal and political, because the history of each family is interwoven with major socio-cultural upheavals, beginning with the waves of immigration from Britain after the Irish potato famine in 1845 and from Galicia (which was to become the Ukraine in 1919, following the Russian Revolution) beginning in 1891. She notes the following connections: the Northwest Rebellion takes place in 1885, the same year Peter Chorniuk is born in the Ukraine; World War I ends in 1918, and Mairi MacDuff marries Albert Pryce; Winnipeg has a General Strike in which the RCMP attack strikers at Winnipeg's Labour Temple in 1919, the same year both Mairi MacDuff Pryce and Rose Melanchuk Chorniuk give birth to sons and Marie Sansregret marries Lazarus Tonnerre at Galloping Mountain; the Stock Market Crash occurs in 1929, ushering in the Depression and the drought and the deaths of Louisa and Colin Gunn of polio in South Wachakwa; many Canadians enlist in the Lincoln Brigade in the Spanish Civil War in 1936, the year Bram Shipley dies in Manawaka and John Shipley and Arlene Simmons are also killed on the trestle bridge; Hitler invades Poland in 1939, the year Ewen MacLeod dies of pneumonia in Manawaka; Canada declares the War Measures Act in 1940, the same year that Allie Pryce goes to Winnipeg for teacher training; Japan bombs Pearl Harbour in 1941, the year Allie marries Steve Chorniuk; a Royal Air Force camp is set up near Manawaka in 1943, and Mary Chorniuk is born to Allie and Steve; the United States bombs Hiroshima and Nagasaki in 1945, the year Mary Chorniuk drowns. Such correspondences are no coincidence: clearly Laurence wished to emphasize the connections between the political and the personal realms, as she does in her presentation of the Tonnerre family in her Manawaka novels, especially *The Diviners*. The cataclysmic concluding events – the death of the daughter and bombing of Japanese cities – an event that had a profound impact on the young Margaret Laurence (*DE* 99) – are clearly intended to emphasize that correspondence. Thus, "Dance on the Earth," the novel was to be an even more explicitly political text than *The Diviners*.

Laurence had intended to write a novel about Winnipeg's Old Left, as James King points out in his chapter on "Lost Histories, 1977–85," and Laurence's notes for her novel "Dance on the Earth" make it clear that the Chorniuk family was to be deeply involved in Winnipeg's labour unions, including the federal agents' seizure of Ukrainian Labour Temples on 6 June 1940. Her notes list major events of the Communist Party history in Winnipeg – a movement she was involved in when she worked as a reporter for the *Westerner* (*DE* 107), a Communist paper – such as the internment of Ukrainian Communists when the Communist Party was declared illegal in 1940. "Dance on the Earth" was clearly to include a sweeping, and critical, portrait of Canadian history. King concludes: "This assortment of holograph material ...

demonstrates her intent to deal with the themes of other, abandoned novels: the origins and nature of fundamentalism and the historical significance of the Old Left in Winnipeg. In this novel, Margaret would also have been concerned with the Ukrainian immigration to Canada and the central importance of that group in the history of Manitoba; she intended to comment as well on the Scots migration and thus speak – directly and forcefully – of Canada as a blend of various ethnic groups" (393).

Fifth, Laurence's notes make it clear that there were to be two narrative voices representing the two generations: octogenarian Mairi MacDuff's history of her emigration from Britain in the early years of this century as recounted to her daughter, sixty-year-old retired English teacher Allie Pryce Chorniuk, and Allie's narrative of her own history recorded on tape for her four-year-old granddaughter, Mairi Chorniuk, to hear when she is a grown woman. Allie begins her narrative, "This story is for you, Mairi." Other sections of narrative are to be divided, the notes state, between Allie and her sister-in-law Stella Melanchuk Chorniuk, who records her mother, Rose Melanchuk Chorniuk's reminiscences, representing the intertwining of the novel's two cultural heritages. Thus, the narrative form of this mother-and-daughter novel would represent not only Canada's complex cultural heritage, but also the matrilinear legacy that Laurence celebrates in her memoir. While all the published Manawaka novels address the mother-daughter dynamic (as Helen Buss's monograph, *Mother and Daughter Relationships in the Manawaka Works of Margaret Laurence*, emphasizes), her unfinished novel would have highlighted that maternal-filial relationship even more centrally.[7]

The question is, why was Laurence so determined to write this novel? Besides her desire to write a text celebrating a matrilinear heritage and feminist spirituality, an answer may lie in the censorship controversy that engulfed Laurence in her own county of Peterborough in 1976 and again in 1985. "In 1976, to my total horror and surprise," she writes in her memoir, "*The Diviners* was attacked as being pornographic, blasphemous" (*DE* 214).[8] A letter to the editor in the *Peterborough Examiner* read, "We know that Margaret Laurence's aim in life is to destroy the home and the family" (216). Laurence records, "My books were attacked again in 1985 ... not only was *The Diviners* vilified but also *A Jest of God* and, for the first time, *The Stone*

Angel, which was called demeaning to human nature" (*DE* 215). She believed that the fundamentalist Christians who attacked her books were not preaching Christian love but "hatred, authoritarianism and a suppression of humankind's thoughts, queries, and aspirations" (216). The Peterborough Committee for Citizens on Decency petitioned to ban the book from the Grade 13 curriculum, and the Reverend Sam Buick opened his Dublin Street Pentecostal Church in Peterborough so people could sign the petition in 1976; Gabrielle Roy wrote to Laurence on 27 March 1976, the Controversy "places you in the company of Flaubert, Lawrence, and several others among the greatest" (Socken 10). Material on "the Controversy" was collected and sold to the York University Archives, and the proceeds used to fund a celebration of Margaret's sixtieth birthday on 18 July 1986. She suggested drinking a toast: "To the people who want to ban Margaret Laurence's books, without whom this party would not have been possible" (*DE* 217).

It was logical that Laurence, who was so wounded by the Fundamentalist Christian attack on her books in her own county of Peterborough, would try to write about this literary assassination. It was also logical that Laurence, who always tried to view her characters from within, and who portrayed her protagonists as trying to see even their enemies from behind their eyes, would attempt to write a novel portraying such prejudiced people. And she did in her novel "Dance on the Earth." In January 1979, she wrote to Hugh MacLennan, "I would like some day to deal with some of this in a novel, but although I've been thinking of it for over a year, it's too close: I can't do it yet. Maybe it will not ever be given to me to explore that region. I can only wait and try to understand, as a novelist, the very people whom I am battling in my role as citizen" (*VLS* 117). She wrote to Adele Wiseman, on 20 January 1979, reflecting, "I want to do something, sometime, with the evangelist thing, but I wonder if at this point in my life it would come out sounding like a desire for revenge" (*SL* 353). "Dance on the Earth" was to be that evangelist novel.

The occasion for the novel and catalyst for Allie Pryce Chorniuk's narrative is just as devastating as the morning that Morag Gunn comes downstairs at the outset of *The Diviners* to find the note from her daughter Pique stuck in her typewriter announcing that she is going west, alone – a note that, ironically, by sending Morag to look for her family photographs, launches the retrospective that inspires her narrative, as Robert Kroetsch explains in "Sitting Down to Write: A Discourse of Morning." Allie's catalyst in "Dance on the Earth" is an attack by fundamentalists in Jordan's Landing led by the Reverend Jake Flood, preacher of The Tabernacle of the Risen and Reborn, modelled on the real-life Reverend Sam Buick of Peterborough's Pentecostal Church.

Allie teaches English in grade 13: "grade 13 unlucky?" she asks. John Milton's *Paradise Lost* is on the curriculum, and Allie teaches it with great enthusiasm for Milton's epic poem of the cosmic war between the forces of good and evil. Laurence's plans for the novel include twenty-four pages of notes and quotes from Milton's poem, which she studied with Malcolm Ross at United College, now the University of Winnipeg, in the 1940s. Her notes emphasize the doctrines of free will and original sin, the concepts of grace and God's elect, and, of course, Milton's view of women – a topic Morag Gunn questions in her seventeenth-century poetry course with Professor Brooke Skelton in *The Diviners*, where she objects to the line "He for God only; she for God in him" (208). Laurence lists similar quotations in her plans for the novel: "God is thy law, thou mine" and "Noble Adam. False Eve." She quotes from David Daiches' commentary on Milton and from her grandfather's copy of Taine's *History of English Literature* (1871), inscribed "John Wemyss, Glasgow College, 1880."

In teaching *Paradise Lost*, Allie questions the doctrine of original sin in such passages as "Some have I chosen of peculiar grace / Elect above the rest; so is my will," the justice of the Fall in lines like "I made him just and right, / Sufficient to have stood, though free to fall," and the patriarchal nature of Adam, who "smiled with superior love." She emphasizes Satan's "heroic energy," as well as "the seductive power of evil," arguing that Satan is the true hero of *Paradise Lost*: "Blake said that Milton was of the Devil's party without knowing it." She notes, "Milton was in sympathy with the great rebel of heaven," adding, "I tend towards the so-called Satanist school of literary thought."

Unluckily, the Reverend Flood's twin son and daughter, Debbie and Donno, are in Allie's class and, when Allie suggests that Milton portrays Satan sympathetically, they accuse her of blasphemy and conclude that she is a Satanist. The son leaves the room, saved by the bell, "as though pursued by all too imaginable demons," to report her heresy to his father. They also disapprove of Allie for questioning Milton's views of women because they think women should be submissive and inferior: "The Fall *was* woman's fault." They interpret her views, reflecting Laurence's own, on the female principle in the Holy Spirit as blasphemous. "And they approve the Elect (as long as it is them!)."

Jake Flood has his own television talk show titled, ironically, "Paradise Path," which he uses to promulgate his propaganda. An innocent incident fuels the flames of bigotry. In a passage entitled "Closing the Cottage," Allie and Stella dance together beside the lake, observed by Flood's spies: "That day, Allie and Stella danced. Two old women, *dancing on the earth* [my italics]. That was the day they prepared to close the cottage for the winter. Fall was quiet here at Jordan's Lake. Spring forward, Fall back. What was the earth if not a metaphor for resurrection? This was their refuge. Here they could be children, fools, wisewomen. Here each could be a shawoman, foremother, Sha-womb-an. As it once was, perhaps, in the dawn of all the tribes. They danced. Two women of the elders, dancing memory, dancing the dance of time, dancing because there were times when they chose to dance." Outraged, the Pentecostals accuse the two women of everything from lesbianism to communism. Eventually the entire community of Jordan's Landing becomes involved in the controversy. The attack escalates over the winter, until the School Board is obliged to request Allie's retirement. This recalls Robert Buchanan, head of Lakefield Collegiate's English Department, who opposed the book-banning by school trustees led by James Telford, called "Philistines" by Laurence (King 341). The parallels between Allie's anguish when attacked by the Pentecostals and Margaret Laurence's own anxiety over her literary assassination by fundamentalists are striking: Laurence was accused of communism and lesbianism as well, and her reactions also evolved from hurt to humour.

So Allie, at sixty, is mourning the premature end of her career as a teacher: "She had believed in Education as the golden key. What a laugh!" Free at last, and "sick of being a good example to the young," Allie goes west to Manawaka to visit her mother, Mairi, now eighty-two. Laurence went west for the last time in 1983 to visit her brother, Robert, who was dying of pancreatic cancer, like their mother, Margaret Simpson Wemyss – a trip commemorated in her poem "Via Rail and Via Memory," which mourns her past in her "heartland" in the Afterwords to *Dance on the Earth* (275). In her draft novel, Easter brings redemption of a sort: in a section titled "Portion of Grace," the two sisters, deeply wounded by the attacks, as Laurence herself was, comfort themselves by considering "women in the past" and "the female principle" so central to her published memoir.

In Manawaka, Allie's mother, Mairi, who has lost none of her wits, regales her with the story of her life. And it is this story that Allie records in the present narrative for her granddaughter, Mairi, to hear when she is a grown woman: "Mairi, this is for you, my only grandchild." Laurence writes: "Allie thought of the Marys. That first Mairi, her mother, and the second Mary, always four, and the new Mairi. Stella thought of Rose, still alive and so old now ... Baba Chorniuk. The last names are always the fathers' names. For her grand-daughter, Allie would have liked to set down the line of descent through the mothers."[9] Mother Mairi's history is at the heart of the novel "Dance on the Earth." Now an octogenarian and suffering from glaucoma, Mairi has not lost her sense of humour: "Thank God I can still laugh," she crows. A Scot, like Christie Logan, she shares elements of Christie's idiom: "They call us 'senior citizens,' the bloody idiots," she fulminates. "Just plain 'old' is good enough for me." She calls her daughter "Kiddo" and declares, when Allie comes to visit her out west, "Well, I'm blessed" – like Christie, who responds, when Morag says to him on his deathbed, "you've been my father to me," "Well – I'm blessed" (D 420). The parent figure here is not the father, however, but the mother, reflecting Laurence's increasing emphasis on the matrilinear line.

Mairi MacDuff hails from the Gorbals, the slums of Glasgow. Unsure whether she can remember her mother ("I get pictures in my head sometimes," she reflects) and uncertain whether her mother abandoned her or died of influenza, Mairi has only her name for her heritage and its secret spelling – MAIRI – for her mother, a "Lowland Scots teacher of common sense," taught her "the mysteries of reading and writing" before she disappeared. "Fragments of memories rise up, talismans, pieces of incomprehensible but powerful magic. The long lost histories of her people can never be reclaimed – there are no traceable records. This will haunt her all her life, that lost history," Laurence records, recalling Morag's parental "shadows" in The Diviners (27). Like nineteenth-century novelists, such as Charlotte Brontë and Charles Dickens, in novels like Jane Eyre and David Copperfield, Laurence understood the value of the orphan-figure in fiction as a barometer of social conscience:

so Mairi MacDuff reveals the sins of her society as vividly as Morag
Gunn reflects the errors of her own era. A twelve-page holograph
foolscap draft, dated 1982, entitled "Mairi" records the skeleton history of "Mairi MacDuff of the Lowland Scots," from her birth around
1900. A sixty-eight-page draft dated 1982 and titled "Mairi's early life
in Canada – age 10 to 12," fleshes out the skeleton.

A "street sparrow," Mairi is swept up by a do-gooder, transferred
to a London orphanage, and then transported to Canada at age ten as
a "Barnardo Child" – an orphan brought from Britain to Canada to
provide farm labour.[10] Her only relic, besides the hymnbook and Bible
in her box, is the photograph taken of the children as they disembarked
at Point Lévis, Quebec, a grainy newspaper photograph in which Mairi
cannot even distinguish her childhood self. Her best friend on this
"travesty of an ark," Rhoda, a blonde Cockney waif whose prostitute
mother died when she was a baby, is adopted by a rich lady because
she resembles her own dead daughter. Rhoda has no memories of her
mother, but has "invented, created a mother," like Morag Gunn in *The
Diviners* (20). Later, Rhoda will name her own daughter Mairi. Scots
Mairi McDuff, in contrast to the fair Rhoda, looks Indian, with her
black hair, dark slanted eyes and hawkish features – again, like Morag
Gunn and also like Margaret Laurence, who was known as "the Squaw"
in Neepawa.

Adopted by a family named Hogg, aptly, as it turns out, who have
farmed at Tanwood, north of Toronto, on the edge of the Laurentian
Shield, since 1850, Mairi cries at night in her room in the attic (her
first room of her own) – again like Morag. Mairi likes singing the
hymns at church, where the minister preaches hellfire for sinners like
Mairi. Sam Hogg beats her black and blue in the barn for blasphemy
when he overhears her swear, calling her "Blasphemer. Whore of Baby-
lon," while his teenage sons Jim and George spy. Laurence's notes read:
"Barn – boys – attempted rape – Sam – M's periods – prayers. God?
Him?" Mairi remembers only the beating and something worse – a
rape? one wonders – and then "the gap in memory." She wishes only
to "bury those years." She runs away from the Hogg farm at age twelve
in 1914 on the eve of the First World War. Two good ladies give her
room and board in the town in exchange for domestic work. Like Pique
Gunn Tonnerre, Mairi, now "Mary," moves west to Manitoba, where
she works as a domestic servant.

There, she marries Albert Lansdowne-Pryce, a remittance man who emigrated to Canada from England in 1910. They have two children: Alleyn, who dies, and Alys, who becomes the Allie who narrates the novel. After they lose their farm in the Depression of the Thirties, they move to South Wachakwa, where Mary works as a cleaning lady in the CNR station, while Bert, depressed, writes poetry until his death in 1953 at age fifty-eight. The variations on themes of the Manawaka novels, especially *The Stone Angel* and *The Diviners*, suggest how well "Dance on the Earth" would fit in.

Mairi MacDuff's history underlines the issues of Canadian cultural complexity and matrilinear heritage that Laurence wished to emphasize in this draft novel. Mairi's narrative, recorded by her daughter for her great-granddaughter, provides the necessary layering of multiple cultural heritages, ancestral histories, geographical centres, and narrative voices that enriched *The Diviners* and that would have rendered her novel "Dance on the Earth" a fitting conclusion to her Canadian fiction.

Perhaps inspired by her visit to her mother, Allie begins to write a journal, like Laurence herself, in which she recalls "that damn prairie town she'd hated so much. Hated because she was always a stranger there, an outsider, doing housework for her room and board. The oppression of the war."[11] Daughter of a cleaning lady and depressed poet in South Wachakwa, Allie attends high school with Vanessa MacLeod, Stacey Cameron, and Morag Gunn in Manawaka. After graduation, Allie goes to Winnipeg – like Morag, Vanessa and Laurence herself – to train as a teacher. There she marries Steve Chorniuk in 1942, and they have two children: Mairi, who dies at age four, and Stefan. After Steve dies at fifty in 1962, Allie moves east to Jordan's Landing in Ontario with her teenage son, Stefan – again like Morag and Laurence – to join her sister-in-law Stella in the old house on Bluedale Avenue and to teach English literature in Jordan's Landing Secondary School.

Clearly, "Dance on the Earth," if completed, would have been an intriguing Canadian novel and would have complemented the other Manawaka novels well. It is unfortunate indeed that Laurence was unable to complete it. The question remains, why was she unable to finish this final novel when she was so determined to do so, as evidenced by her numerous notes and drafts?

Laurence had predicted that *The Diviners* "will be the last Manawaka fiction, as all the threads are tied in this novel" (*VLS* 97), and

"I've always said this would likely be my last novel" (*SL* 270). She was right: the gift was withdrawn; *The Diviners* was destined to be her last completed novel. In fact, after completing *The Diviners*, Laurence sold her cabin on the Otonabee River because she thought that it had served its purpose and that it was too bound up with *The Diviners* (*VLS* 189). Powers concludes, "It was clear to those closest to Margaret that *The Diviners* indeed marked the end of the Manawaka Saga ... and very likely the end of her career as a novelist" (*AH* 433). In her memoir Laurence explains, "I've never been able to force a novel. I have always had the sense of something being given to me. You can't ... force into being something that isn't there. Amazingly, the gift was given to me once again" (199). That "gift of grace" (214) produced *The Diviners*. She wrote to Purdy on 15 February 1977, "If another true real novel comes along, and it may, then that will be a gift, a bonus" (*SL* 341). But that bonus did not materialize. A female Prospero figure, Morag Gunn broke her wand metaphorically when she passed the torch, in the form of Jules's knife, to her daughter Pique, who combines her mother's gift for words with her father's gift for music in "Pique's Song" (489–90), which concludes *The Diviners* (373). Laurence wrote to Adele Wiseman, on 20 September 1981, "There is always the fear that perhaps the gift really *has* departed. If so, (and I don't say it *is* so) Morag never knew the half of how painful that would be" (King 352).[12]

Laurence's correspondence with fellow writers confirms her struggle. She writes to Frank Paci, 5 September 1981, "After thinking about a novel for about 3 years, I've finally got going . . (after 5 false starts) . . rather depressing. It sure doesn't get any easier. I'm making slow progress, but I'm not about to give up" (*VLS* 149). On 3 March 1980 she writes to Gabrielle Roy, "My writing goes so slowly and so badly, of late. I have three times made a false start on a novel, and so far have torn up about 50 pp of handwriting" (*VLS* 186). Again, she confesses to Adele Wiseman, on 20 September 1981, "I hate everything I've written so far in this damn so-called novel. The problems are still there, namely that the forum [*sic*] is formulas and the writing is garbage" (quoted in King 352).

The personal factors that made Laurence feel so passionately about writing this novel may also have been the very reasons why the narrative was too painful for her to complete. Perhaps she was unable to get inside the heads of people as closed-minded as Jake Flood (or Sam Buick). She wrote to Ernest Buckler on 24 November 1976, "as a fiction writer I have to try to understand their point of view, I mean really to try to make that leap of the imagination to get inside (to some extent) the minds and hearts of people like the Rev. Sam Buick of the Dublin Street Pentecostal Church" (VLS 40). But she tells Wiseman on 20 January 1979, "a danger at this point would [be] that I would lean over backwards to be fair to the pentecostals, thus softsoaping their very real dangers" (SL 353).[13]

Perhaps she was too close to her subject in both time and place, for her usual method was to write about a place, Africa or Canada, when she was far removed geographically and temporally. Perhaps she had simply written herself out in her Manawaka cycle: she confesses to Wiseman in 1979, "I *cannot go* back into Manawaka country, because that would be pushing it. The five books out of that territory were all necessary and demanded to be written, and together they form some kind of whole. But this time, I think I latched onto that background not because I really wanted to write out of it again, but as a kind of *refuge*, which isn't the right reason" (SL 353).

Perhaps the task she had set herself was too ambitious, with too many narrative strands – even more than *The Diviners*. As her narrator, Allie, confesses in desperation, "I don't know how to divide up these memories so they'll have some kind of form, Mairi."[14] Allie's later address to her granddaughter, Mairi, may reflect Laurence's own struggle to write this novel: "I've tried so often to put all this down, & couldn't. I've started time & again, in notebooks, scrawling with a pen, or on a typewriter. Useless. Words wouldn't come." Perhaps Laurence was not well enough, as King's account suggests, to meet such a challenge. Probably all these factors contributed to forcing her to bid farewell to fiction. In a 20 January 1979 letter to Wiseman, she explains why she is giving up on "Dance on the Earth," the novel, in favour of the memoir that was to become *Dance on the Earth*: "Snags (real, not imagined) with novel. I am going to have to set it aside temporarily and work on memoirs ... I will put away the notes etc for the novel and let it simmer on the back burner, and will go on with the memoirs" (SL 353–4). She adds, "Some guiding spirit has always prevented me, thank God, from writing a mock-up" (SL 353). *Dance on the Earth: A Memoir* was to give her the opportunity to celebrate the matrilinear heritage and feminist spirituality that she had planned to explore in her unfinished novel.

The question remains, however, why was Laurence so determined to write a text entitled "Dance on the Earth" in fictional *or* non-fictional form? Laurence clearly had a message for her inheritors, and it was not to mourn but to *dance on the earth*, to celebrate life. "Closing the Cottage" is the title of the draft of a scene in which Allie and Stella dance beside Jordan's Lake – two aging sisters in the autumn of the year – in a section that was intended to conclude the novel: "That day, Allie and Stella danced. Two old women, *dancing on the earth*, dancing their lives, dancing grief and blessings. Dancing hope. Bleakworld, wanworld, deathworld. Perhaps. But still, they danced. Somewhere, sometimes, perhaps they will still be dancing. For themselves and for the children, willing the dance to go on, and the willing dance will go on. [my italics]" This scene, with its echoes of the memoir, even to the use of the title trope, "dancing on the earth," is clearly intended to celebrate closure. The chapter, titled "Portion of Grace," subtitled "Memoir," and set at Easter, closes with the sentence, "The child dances." Laurence came to see the dance as the ultimate celebration of life and planned to close her novel, just as she concludes her memoir, with the image of dance as a celebration of the continuity of life: "May the dance go on" (*DE* 222).

PART FOUR

Endings
"Full Circle"

CHAPTER 13

Snow Angels and Monarch Butterflies: Laurence's Children's Fiction

Margaret Laurence is so famous for her Manawaka cycle of adult fiction that most people are not aware that she also published four books for children: *Jason's Quest* in 1970, *Six Darn Cows* and *The Olden Days Coat* in 1979, and *The Christmas Birthday Story* in 1980. In fact, Laurence frequently expressed interest in children's literature. In her 1981 essay, "Books That Mattered to Me," she recalls that, as a child, she received books – by Stevenson, Conan Doyle, Twain, Kipling, and L.M. Montgomery – for Christmas (239–41). In "Upon a Midnight Clear," from *Heart of a Stranger*, she records that she and her children still give each other children's books for Christmas, "because we've always liked good children's books" (*HS* 155). In *Dance on the Earth: A Memoir*, she recalls her early love of L.M. Montgomery and many other authors of books for young adults (64). In a 1975 interview with Beatrice Lever, Laurence emphasizes the need for more "good children's novels" (32), and in her 23 March 1976 letter to Gabrielle Roy she exclaims, "There is such a desperate need in this country for good children's books" (*VLS* 175). She writes to Roy on 1 December 1979, of her own books, "these kids' books are a kind of gift. A sort of grace given" (Socken 73).

Strangely, her four children's books have been virtually ignored by critics. The fact that three of her four children's books have been out of print for many years is no doubt a factor in this neglect. The only essays devoted to them are diametrically opposed. In "Mother of Manawaka: Margaret Laurence as Author of Children's Stories," published in 1981, immediately after the publication of Laurence's last three children's books, D.R. Letson claims Laurence's children's work is fiction that "all our children should read or have read to them. Not only is it artful and entertaining literature, but it is also instructive" (17). Two decades later, Janet Lunn begins her 2001 essay, "To Find Refreshment in Writing Children's Books: A Note on Margaret Laurence's Writing for Children," with this condemnation: "Margaret Laurence wrote four books for children. The only thing that is interesting about them is that she wrote them at all. They might be called a footnote to her adult fiction and criticism, but they are not really even that. They are irrelevant, not only to Laurence's larger body of work, but to the larger body of literature for children in Canada" (145). Not only is Laurence's children's fiction relevant to her adult fiction, as I hope to demonstrate here, but it also makes a significant contribution to Canadian children's literature. This chapter's exploration of her children's books will aim to validate Letson's commendation and counter Lunn's condemnation.

Quite apart from the delight that Laurence's children's fiction affords readers of all ages, these children's texts, most of them written at the end of her career, can illuminate her adult novels by reflecting their themes and symbols, especially the quest for community in her adult fiction – the quest often focusing on something that is lost and then found. As Morley observes, "The search for inner freedom, Laurence's primary theme, implies a quest structure" (42). The development of her children's fiction also reflects the developing feminism of her Manawaka fiction, as she progresses from a patriarchal model to a matrilinear mode in these books for children. Laurence constructs her memoir in a matrilinear sequence that pays tribute to her three mothers, as well as to herself as mother to her two children and her many books. We have witnessed a similar development in her adult fiction from the male protagonists of her African novel *This Side Jordan* to the gallery of powerful female protagonists in her Canadian fiction. To demonstrate Laurence's progression from a patriarchal model to a matrilinear mode in her children's fiction, I will consider her four children's texts in approximately chronological order of composition, tracing a growth in emphasis on gender equality and matrilinear heritage. Since Laurence's children's books are not well known and are largely out of print, I will outline the plots briefly in order to provide a context for the commentary.

"HERE BE DRAGONS": *JASON'S QUEST*

Jason's Quest, her first published children's book, illustrated by Swedish artist Staffan Torell, was published by Macmillan in 1970, the year she published her "semi-autobiographical fiction" (*HS* 8) *A Bird in the House*. *Jason's Quest* could also be called semi-autobiographical, for it grew out of her own family community during the decade when she lived in Elm Cottage in the village of Penn, Buckinghamshire, England, where she wrote her Manawaka books. Written to entertain her children, Jocelyn and David, in the sixties, this "animal fantasy" (*DE* 188) was inspired by the underground colony of moles at Elmcot. One morning the family found their lawn dimpled by molehills, and that was the genesis of *Jason's Quest*. Laurence said, "the whole of *Jason's Quest* was given to me just like that – a great and glorious gift," as Clara Thomas reports in "Saving Laughter" (46).[1]

Jason's Quest is a delightful parody of classical models of heroism – all male models, of course. Jason, the young mole hero, named for the Greek hero who rescued the Golden Fleece, sets out on a quest for a cure for the ailing ancient city of Molanium – recalling Sophocles' *Oedipus Rex*, where the tragedy is initiated by Oedipus's quest to cure the illness that Tiresias warns plagues Thebes. Jason has always been tempted to visit the dangerous land of *Thither*, the world above the ground, and finally he sets off on his great adventure: "Jason felt extremely happy. Nothing was settled, nothing was yet discovered, but it was good simply to be going somewhere, to be on the road to who-knows-what" (29) – recalling Margaret's excitement at the opening of *The Prophet's Camel Bell* – "There you go, rejoicing, as so you should, for anything may happen" (9) – and Rachel's anticipation at the conclusion of *A Jest of God*: "Where I'm going, anything may happen" (208–9).

Upon his departure Jason is showered with gifts: his mother, Calpurnia, who fusses over him in a manner that Hagar cannot muster when her son Marvin goes off to the Great War in *The Stone Angel*, gives him a needle and thread, the thread suggesting Theseus and the Minotaur's labyrinth. His sisters, Grace, Beauty, and Faith, who stay home, give him a handkerchief that can be used as a flag; and the Venerable Mole (a parody of the Anglo-Saxon historian, the Venerable Bede) gives him his blessing and presents him with the "Cap of Deeper Thinking" – recalling the cleverness of Odysseus, who is advised by Athena, goddess of wisdom, whenever he finds himself in danger. Similarly, in a crisis, Jason feels a tingling in the Cap of Deeper Thinking that inspires a fortunate premonition that seems intuitive, recalling Laurence's own "famous Celtic second sight" (*DE* ix), as her daughter puts it in her preface to *Dance on the Earth*. Later, Jason is presented with a magic umbrella: when he turns the knobs labelled *Onward* and *Upward* (182),[2] he sails safely over the heads of his assailants – presaging ET in Stephen Spielberg's 1982 film.

In this delightful animal fantasy, Jason is joined by an owl named Oliver and two cats named Calico and Topaz, modelled on the Laurence family's own felines (*DE* 174).[3] The traditional male model of heroism prevails, as timid Jason is named Captain of the expedition, and Oliver Owl is dubbed "Chief of Signals," while the female cats are mere beasts of burden who bear Jason and Oliver on their backs: "When the two cats heard about the quest, they readily agreed to join it and to act as steeds for the other two" (20). Calico and Topaz seem to be before and after stereotypes of femininity. Flirty Topaz, her name recalling Chaucer's foolish knight, is a parody of femininity, concerned with bows and furbelows, but, when it comes to the crunch, this little cookie does not crumble. Topaz is the poet of the group who composes their motto, "*Bash on, bash on in majesty, And thwart the fouling churls –* " (54), in a parody of the triumphal Easter hymn, "Ride on, ride on in majesty."[4] Laurence also parodies Dumas' three musketeers' motto, as the quartet's rallying cry is "*Four for One and One for Four. / Together till the Journey's o'er*" (55). Calico is an older and wiser cat, whose role is peacekeeper. Laurence gives Calico's address as "*Calico, Elm Cottage, Penn, Buckinghamshire, England*" (42), Laurence's own home address.

Together, the four set off on a quest that recalls *The Wizard of Oz*, for Oliver seeks wisdom for which owls are renowned, just as the Cowardly Lion seeks courage, which seems his natural right. James King notes, "As in many quest stories, the hero learns that the real discoveries are internal ones" (253); Laurence writes in *Jason's Quest*, "Wisdom has to be learned from life itself" (155). Only the cats have no noble motive for the trip, merely a frivolous wanderlust. Laurence's editor at Macmillan writes in her notes on the typescript, "The Quest seems to have been forgotten in an adventure. Perhaps in the beginning of their trip a brief mention by the cats of their quest to right wrong and also some mention by Jason of his purpose. Otherwise readers will feel that the 'Quest' was only a device to get a group together." Laurence agrees: "True, Calico and Topaz had a right to their part in the quest for noble deeds."[5] And so, "The quest had begun" (29). Jason explains each animal's quest to Winstanley, the traveller they meet along the way, who turns out to be a wicked thief: "Jason told him how the four of them had met, and why they were going on a quest, each for his own purposes; Oliver to look for wisdom, the cats to perform noble deeds, himself to find a cure for the mysterious illness that was causing the downfall of Molanium" (34). As Letson rightly observes, "the quest becomes a search for wisdom and self-esteem" (18) – recalling Hagar Currie Shipley, who journeys to the seacoast in search of wisdom and truth in *The Stone Angel*.

Jason's Quest could be subtitled "Animal Farm Goes to Town" or "Mole in the City," because Laurence's animal allegory is modelled on another literary tradition – the picaresque novel. Timid Jason is an unlikely *picaro*, but the adventures that befall him recall the trials of Odysseus, Don Quixote, Tom Jones, and other fictional wanderers. His quest is beset by perils: "*Here be dragons*" (32), his map warns. In London, Jason meets many challenges, and he must learn to overcome his self-doubt to triumph over his ordeals. "I will try" (21) is his motto. He succeeds, beginning with the "heroic rescue" (104) of Oliver the owl from a cage in "Nicolette," a Bond Street boutique.

Jason's heroism in these perilous adventures is rewarded not only with a cure for his tribe, but also with a new love in the form of the charming mole actress Perdita, meaning "lost girl," echoing Shakespeare's romance, *A Winter's Tale*. No sooner is Perdita found, however, than she is lost, true to her namesake, when she is captured by the vicious gang of Blades, young mice hoodlums, led by their lieutenant Jacko and their governor, "G.R." But this is a comedy, and Jason discovers and rescues his Perdita from the lair of the Great Rat. The Purple Petunias of the Petunia Patch, Perdita's nightclub, present each of the quartet with a gift to commemorate their quest: to Jason they give the "Drums of the Night" and the "Trumpets of the Day" (179), recalling the talking drums of Laurence's African texts, such as "The Drummer of All the World" in *The Tomorrow-Tamer and Other Stories* and *Long Drums and Cannons: Nigerian Dramatists and Novelists*.

Jason leads Perdita to Molanium in triumph. Perdita, the beautiful dancer, star of the London Mousedrome, is the classic trophy mole wife. But she is also wise: she discovers the cure to the illness that plagues Molanium. The song "*Molanium The Mighty, With Twenty Tunnels Blest*" (23), proclaims the motto, "*Festina Lente! Hasten slowly!*" (188–9), emblematizing the social paralysis that afflicts Molanium. Molanium is still living in the Roman Britain that Laurence parodies so wittily in her portrait of Londinium. Moving to England in 1962, Laurence toured the Tower of London and other historical sites with her two children and sent home comical accounts of ancient traditions that appeared archaic to a young Canadian woman. Jason realizes, "Molanium has been dying of BOREDOM! … Everything had to change and grow … But Molanium had been afraid to change" (154–5). He explains to the Elders, "You see, we've been living too much in the past … Everything just the same for hundreds of years. Monotony. Everyone sort of lost heart, without realizing it. Sirs, elders and mole-folk, that was the invisible sickness – boredom" (186–7). People must adapt to change or petrify. As a sign of their ability to adapt, the mole colony names Jason Mayor of Moleville, where he introduces numerous progressive changes, such as reforming the Mole Council to include Youngers as well as Elders and instituting a scientific research institute called "M.I.S., Moles In Space" (190) decades before Jim Henson's "Pigs In Space." Perdita composes a new motto to suit the new progressive spirit: "*Take A Care, Then Do and Dare*" (189). Although *Jason's Quest* begins with a male protagonist and two male expedition leaders, Jason accepts the two felines as equals, and his bride, Perdita, helps reform Molanium. Laurence, who rebelled against the restrictions of her small-town home in the Canadian prairies and first experienced traditional Britain in postwar London with Jack in 1950, celebrates change and the freedom that both her African protagonists and her Manawaka heroines seek.[6]

Reviews of *Jason's Quest* were very mixed. Clara Thomas exudes praise in "Bashing On": "This book is a *tour de force*, built on the quest theme, its every detail embroidered with joyful imaginings ... When Margaret Laurence's inventive powers and pervasive humour are turned towards such fantasy, the result is a proliferation of details of ridiculous delight ... Underneath all this sun-shower of invention, the mythic quest, of course, goes on – good battling evil" (89). But Diana Goldsborough judges, in the 20 June 1970 *Toronto Daily Star*, "the story is a tedious disappointment ... Never has a children's book seemed so long" (59). Laurence recalls in her memoir that Sheila Egoff, in *The Republic of Childhood*, her book about Canadian children's literature, calls *Jason's Quest* "the most disappointing book in all of Canadian children's writing" (*DE* 189).[7] Janet Lunn concludes her unenthusiastic review of *Jason's Quest* in the 27 June 1970 *Globe and Mail*, thus: "somehow it's a great relief to everyone when the adventure's over" (17). Lunn's view has not changed, as she judges in her 2001 essay, "The fantasy is neither original nor particularly imaginative" (147). An anonymous reviewer for *Publisher's Weekly* 197, no. 22 for 1 June 1970, disagrees, however, calling *Jason's Quest* a "fantasy which in its unpretentious way is a triumph ... because its author is a triumphant writer" (66). I agree with this last assessment, and I disagree, again, with Lunn: Laurence's animal fantasy is both imaginative and entertaining in its playing with traditional children's literature motifs and its parodying of stultified conventions. As Lyall Powers states in *Alien Heart*, "[*Jason's Quest*] is an engaging fable, full of fun and adventure and fascinating characters" (*AH* 289).[8]

Laurence's children's books, while entertaining, focus on themes that reflect the concerns of her adult fiction, as *Jason's Quest* exemplifies. Laurence calls *Jason's Quest* "a frivolous retelling of the 'heroic monomyth': Departure – Initiation – Return" (King 253). Clara Thomas puts it well: "Writing [*Jason's Quest*] Margaret Laurence was at play, but still it contains the themes that were central to all her work: the unexpected finding of courage, one's rightful attitude to the ancestors, and the perilous effects of their over-influence, the unexpected blessings vouchsafed to 'strangers in a strange land,' and the inescapable pressure on every individual to change and grow" ("Saving Laughter" [46]). The mythic quality of Laurence's adult work is reflected in her children's fiction, although the good and evil forces of her children's books are external, while the moral conflicts of her adult fiction are primarily internal, as protagonists like Hagar, Rachel, and Morag battle their inner, psychological demons. James King judges, "In the tragic-comic world of her first children's book, not only are heroes and villains easily distinguishable from each other, but also goodness confronts and vanquishes evil" (253). His allegorical interpretation recalls Clara Thomas's view of "this joyfully inventive tale" as a "confrontation between the forces of darkness and light."⁹

"LO AND BEHOLD": *THE CHRISTMAS BIRTHDAY STORY*

The Christmas Birthday Story is an example of a gift that is lost and found. "As so often in my writing life, this book was a kind of gift" (*DE* 219), Laurence writes, for when she left Vancouver (and her husband Jack) in 1962, she recalls, "I lost the only copy I had." Years later, in Lakefield, she met a woman who still had a copy of Laurence's Nativity story and sent it to her: "the story finally came back after having been lost for so long" (*DE* 220).¹⁰

    The Christmas Birthday Story, the last children's book that Laurence published, indeed the very last book she published before her death in 1987 – published in Canada by McClelland and Stewart and in the United States by Knopf in 1980 with illustrations by Helen Lucas – was actually written in 1960 and was, thus, the first juvenile fiction that Laurence composed.¹¹ Although it was the first children's book she wrote, the fact that it was lost for almost two decades gave her the opportunity to revise it in preparation for its publication in 1980, and thus it falls between *Jason's Quest* and her last two children's books. It too was inspired by a real-life situation: when the Laurence family was living in Vancouver – between their return to Canada after seven years in Africa upon the death of her mother in 1957 and Margaret's departure with her children in 1962 for a decade in England – they attended the Unitarian Church. She was horrified when the Sunday school teachers suggested that the children not be told the Nativity story in Sunday school because angels are not real. Because she did not want her children denied their Christian heritage or the Nativity narrative that offers such basic truths, as she explains in her memoir (*DE* 219), she offered to write a version of the Nativity that would be acceptably realistic and ecumenical.

    Laurence's version of the Nativity is remarkable for its realism: there is no Annunciation, no angel, and no suggestion of the supernatural.¹² She explains in her memoir, *Dance on the Earth*, "I had thought the story ought to be understood by young children. I had not, therefore, written of the divinity of Jesus or the Virgin Birth or any of those thorny theological matters, which I as an adult have found difficult, and sometimes quite impossible, to believe in, and which I felt would confuse young children totally" (220). Laurence's Mary and Joseph are true-to-life, down-to-earth people: Joseph is a hard-working carpenter, and his wife, Mary, is going to have a baby. Laurence writes, "Joseph and Mary were happy because soon they were going to have a baby. They didn't mind at all whether it turned out to be a boy or a girl. Either kind would be fine with them. They just hoped their baby would be strong and healthy." Her emphasis on gender equality was labelled blasphemous by some readers. Laurence comments, "Those few and, as it turned out, controversial sentences express much of my own life view and my faith, with its need to recognize both the female and male principles in the Holy Spirit" (*DE* 221). In her foreword to her memoir, she laments the fact that "the Christian ritual is male-oriented" (*DE* 14) and says that she prefers to think of "the female principle as being part of the Holy Spirit," to think of "God the Father and the Mother" (*DE* 14). She laments her former fear of writing about the miracle of birth. In a sense her version of the Nativity validates childbirth for all women, as she writes in her typescript, "Mary borned her baby that same night" – her coinage "borned" emphasizing the value of birth and maternity.

Laurence actually composed a "Note to Parents" dated 1978 that she suggested should be a "rip-out page so book will belong to kid," in which she explains that she wanted "to re-tell the story in such a way that children of our own times might relate their known world to that world of long ago. I have tried to tell the story very simply, in terms that small children could understand readily at this point in their lives, and to emphasize above all the birth of the beloved child into a loving family, and the connection of the holy child with all children, all people and all of earth's creatures."[13] She also notes that Helen Lucas wanted her illustrations to be in black and white so that children could add the colours, "and in this way it could be each child's own book." In her memoir she recalls that Fredelle Maynard, author of *Raisins and Almonds*, an autobiographical account of a Jewish girl's childhood in prairie towns, said it was "the only retelling of the Christian Nativity story that she would wish to give to a Jewish child. I felt honoured and grateful" (*DE* 220).

She based her retelling on elements from the two Gospels in which the Nativity is described, Matthew and Luke, taking from Matthew the star and the three wise men, with their gifts of gold, frankincense, and myrrh, and from Luke the trip to Bethlehem and the child's birth in the manger. Nature dominates her narrative: the manger is realistic and comfortable, with a lowing cow and a ewe baaing to its lamb.[14] All her children's books – including *Jason's Quest, Six Darn Cows*, and *The Olden Days Coat* – feature animals that exhibit some sympathy with human beings. Laurence adds to the traditional tale a folkloric, fairytale quality. The three wise men sound like the three bears: the first is tall with a gold crown, the second is middle-sized with a silver crown, and the third is short with a gold-and-silver crown. Laurence, influenced by her sojourn in Somaliland, rhapsodizes about the camels that play such a crucial role in desert life – a detail not usually found in versions of the nativity.

Drawn by the golden star, the three kings come to Bethlehem to the stable and see the newborn child lying in the manger. Impressed by the child, they offer gifts that turn out to be very practical, as well as emblematic: gold and frankincense and myrrh. Laurence takes pains to demystify the nativity narrative for children. She employs vernacular vocabulary, allowing herself only one "Lo and behold" to introduce the birth of the baby. She dramatizes the tale, employing dialogue, as the first two kings prophesy, like the fairies in the Sleeping Beauty story, admirable but realistic human qualities for the infant, qualities he inherits from both his father and his mother, while the third king prophesies that he will be "a wise teacher and a friend to all people" (np).

In her memoir Laurence writes, "The story has been told thousands of times over two thousand years, according to the perceptions and historical era of the teller. I retold it in a way that I myself could understand it and believe in it. Jesus is spoken of as a beloved child, born into a loving family, a child who grew up to be a wise teacher, and a friend to all people. That is really how I think of our Lord" (*DE* 220–1). By portraying the Holy Family as a real human family, Laurence not only brings the Nativity story down to earth but, in turn, sanctifies the concept of the family. As Letson comments, "*The Christmas Birthday Story* is a celebration of love and family. There is no complicating theology, just a stress on the love of parents and the humanity of the Christ child who, in a sense, is an everychild ... There is no sexual bias within the family of man" (21). So Laurence's Nativity story reflects her emphasis, in her adult fiction, on gender equality.

"GOING HOME": SIX DARN COWS

Laurence's children's book *Six Darn Cows* (1979) was written for James Lorimer's reader series, *Kids of Canada*, to which Margaret Atwood contributed *Anna's Pet* (1980), a story about a pet tadpole that turns into a frog. Despite a severely restricted vocabulary,[15] Laurence emphasizes the family community again, but includes more gender equality than she can in the Nativity story.

Six Darn Cows is structured in six parts or miniature chapters that summarize the quest motif: "Everyone Helps," "The Gate," "Looking," "The Dark Woods," "Going Home," and "Home." These headings could stand for the sections of Laurence's first Manawaka novel, *The Stone Angel*, in which Hagar escapes first from her husband, Bram Shipley's farm near Manawaka, and later from her son's city house, wanders in the wilderness in her purgatorial period at Shadow Point and is finally escorted, a Persephone figure, from the seashore up the hillside stairs and home by her son. The headings recall Laurence's previously noted interpretation of *Jason's Quest* as "a frivolous retelling of the 'heroic monomyth': Departure – Initiation – Return" (King 253).

Set on the Bean family farm, the very name suggesting growth, the story tells of the quest of two young children, Jen and Tod Bean, perhaps modelled on Laurence's children, for six missing cows, reflecting the motif of Jason's quest. The brother and sister – their genders indistinguishable in Ann Blades' simple but vivid illustrations with their bold primary colours – share responsibility for accidentally leaving the gate open and allowing the cows to escape. This motif recalls Alice Munro's story "Boys and Girls" from her first collection, *Dance of the Happy Shades* (1968): in this story, the nameless girl deliberately opens the gate, allowing Flora, the female work horse that has been consigned to the glue factory, to escape; when the time comes to shoot the beast, her little brother joins the men and participates in the killing in a coming-of-age ritual, while the sister is relegated to the house with her mother because "She's only a girl" (127). Laurence emphasizes the equality of Jen and Tod Bean as they share the responsibility for the loss of the six cows. Hot and dusty on this summer day, they want to go swimming in the river, but remember the maxim, "On a farm, everyone helps." Tod had said, "Those darn cows. I wish they'd just get lost."[16] So, when the cows really do get lost, the kids feel guilty for wishing it.

The kids' quest for the cows begins. Even though it is getting late and they are tired, they know they must find those cows. The Bean family is not well off, and they need the cows for milk that generates their income. The dangers are real: the cows can fall in the river and drown, or they can wander out onto the highway and get run down by a truck. There is nothing for it but to follow the cows into the woods. But the woods look "dark and spooky" even in the daytime, and now it is getting dark. The woods are dangerous: they have "bushes with sharp thorns," and Jen remembers that a neighbour saw a wolf in the woods. Zip, the farm dog, accompanies the kids into the woods.

When Zip growls, they think he's seen a wolf, but when they hear soft wings and a bird call, they realize it is only an owl, recalling Oliver of *Jason's Quest*. Birds are always emblematic in Laurence's fiction, especially in *A Bird in the House*, and *Six Darn Cows* is no different, for the owl leads the Bean kids straight to the lost cows wandering in the woods. Zip helps them to herd the cows out of the woods and onto the road for home. One cow heads to the marsh with deep mud that could drown a cow – recalling the horses that Laurence's father witnessed drowning in the mud of the Flanders trenches – a fact that she reflects in her story "Horses of the Night" (*BH* 141). Jen runs "quick as a rabbit" and catches the cow just in time, pulling its ear to turn it into the road.

Not only does *Six Darn Cows* reflect the emphasis on the quest motif and themes of community and responsibility from Laurence's adult fiction, but it also reflects Laurence's use of a moralized landscape: that is, employing features of the terrain to symbolize elements of the story's themes. For example, the woods recall Hagar's purgatorial period at Shadow Point, as she, in turn, reflects the wandering in the wilderness of her biblical namesake; the river that is enticing and dangerous recalls "The river [that] flowed both ways" (11) in *The Diviners*; the farm recalls the pioneers of the Manawaka novels, especially the Shipley farm of *The Stone Angel*; and the road and the open gate reflect the journey of life and the importance of going home. The *Kids of Canada: Teacher's Guidebook* (1981) includes questions and topics for discussion on each section of Laurence's text, including a board game complete with a map of the terrain, titled "Finding the Cows."[17]

Despite the simplicity of the narrative, Laurence's emphasis on feminism and enlightenment prevails, for she instills the story with a matriarchal note. As the kids walk along the dark road, they see a light flickering in the darkness: it is their Mum, Meg Bean – "Meg" being a short form for "Margaret" – with a flashlight to lead them home. Rather than berating them, however, Meg commends their courage, calling them "brave kids." Thus, Laurence highlights the mother figure.

The story ends with everyone "safely home" – the cows in the barn and the kids in the house – reflecting the traditional pattern – home/away/home – of children's fiction.[18] This pattern is also found in Laurence's adult fiction, for she believes, to quote T.S. Eliot's *Little Gidding*, "the end of all our exploring / Will be to arrive where we started /And know the place for the first time" (222). The kids' Dad, Dan Bean, is also home from his part-time job fixing TVs in town to supplement his income as a farmer, and they all sit down to dinner together. Their dad says, "I'm proud of you ... You did well," recalling Mr Ramsay's comment to his son James as they reach the lighthouse at the end of Virginia Woolf's *To the Lighthouse*: "Well done" (306). Dan sings a song to celebrate their fortune in their family – like the songs that conclude *The Diviners* (481–90).[19] Laurence ends *Six Darn Cows* on an affirmative note: "Jen and Tod felt happy. And the next day it was still summer," echoing the last sentence of Maurice Sendak's 1963 children's book *Where the Wild Things Are*: "and it was still hot" (np).

"A FAMILY HEIRLOOM": *THE OLDEN DAYS COAT*

Laurence's best-loved children's book, *The Olden Days Coat*, reflects her Manawaka fiction and her own life more clearly than any of her other children's books – no doubt because it was a story that did not involve a limited vocabulary or a familiar narrative to restrict her imagination. Neil Besner judges in "Canadian Children's Regional Literature: Fictions First," *The Olden Days Coat* is "typical of Laurence's fiction" in the "recurring explorations, evocations, and invocations of time, memory, and the work of the imagination," for all her fictions "invoke the imagination and its powers to teach, transform, instruct, and delight" (20–1). Sheila Egoff writes in *The New Republic of Children*, "A slight and gentle story, beautifully written, is Margaret Laurence's *The Olden Days Coat* (1979). It is the most successful of her four books for children, chiefly because it is closest to her adult books, linking, as it does, the present with the past by bridging generations … it is a family-history fantasy narrating the experience of ten-year-old Sal, who travels back into her grandmother's childhood" (252). Lyall Powers concludes, "*The Olden Days Coat* appears to be a kind of coda to *The Diviners* and perhaps to the whole Manawaka saga. The handsome little fantasy (or myth) is concerned with the present-ness of the past and the continuity of both past and present into the future and also with the importance of ancestors" (*AH* 415). Because it was the last children's book she composed, it reflects the growing feminism evident in her adult fiction, as we see it echoed in the matri-linear lineage and emblem of the story. Focusing on the gift of a family heirloom, *The Olden Days Coat* is also Laurence's gift to her friends and their families, a celebration of the community of writers she called her "tribe," as the ten-year-old heroine, Sal, is named for the daughter of Laurence's friend Jean Murray Cole, and the book is dedicated "for my friend Tamara Stone who is ten this year," the daughter of Laurence's friend Adele Wiseman.[20]

Like *The Christmas Birthday Story*, *The Olden Days Coat* is set at Christmas. Christmas is an important season for most Christian families, and Laurence remembers the family traditions that she continued at Elmcot in the essay "Upon a Midnight Clear" in her collection of travel essays, *Heart of a Stranger* (1976), where she celebrates "the sense of God's grace, and the sense of our own family and the sense of human community" (156). *The Olden Days Coat* opens on a typical Canadian Christmas scene: "The snow outside Gran's house was fine and powdery, and it shone in the late afternoon sun as though there were a million miniature Christmas lights within it." Sal considers "lying down in the fresh snow and sweeping her arms to and fro to make a snow angel" – like "the angel with spread wings" (*SA* 81) the widow Hagar, the stone angel, imagines making – but she thinks better of it because "the snow looked so good as it was, with not even a footprint in it," and so she decides to leave it untouched. But Sal is to find something better than a snow angel. Maybe angels are real after all, because Sal is to discover a flesh-and-blood angel in the snow.

Sal is feeling "depressed, miserable, and sad" because this is the first Christmas of all the ten Christmases of her life that she will not be spending in her own home with her special Christmas tree decorations – the silver bells, the Santa Claus, and the gold and blue glass peacock. Sal's grandparents had always spent Christmas at Sal's house in town, and "Sal didn't want things to change." But things do change, as Jason learned: Sal's Grandad has died, and her Gran wants to spend this one Christmas in her own house where she and Grandad lived so long. Perhaps this may be her Gran's last Christmas. Just as she does in her Manawaka novels, Laurence shows Sal beginning to understand that other people have feelings like her own.

Bored, and ashamed of it, Sal goes outside to play. Since the village streets are deserted on Christmas day, she wanders into the shed behind the house, opens the trunk, and pulls out the old photograph albums. Leafing through the family portraits – like Morag Gunn in "River of Now and Then," the opening section of *The Diviners* – Sal comes across photos of her Gran as a young girl standing on the steps of the brick house. Surprised by the old-fashioned style of Gran's frilly dress and high-buttoned boots, Sal is reassured by her Gran's own eyes and smile beaming back at her.[21] Sal chortles at the styles of bygone days and then wonders whether her jeans and T-shirt will look strange to some other kid in the future. In a sudden epiphany, Sal contemplates the phenomenon of selfhood and the changes wrought by time: "What a strange thing Time was. It went on and on, and people came into it and then went out again, like Grandad. There was a time when she, Sal, had not even existed, and now here she was, and would grow up and maybe have children of her own. Maybe someday she would even have a grand-daughter. It was as hard for Sal to think of herself being old like Gran as it was to think of Gran having once been ten years old" (np). Vanessa MacLeod contemplates identity and mutability, birth and death, in a similar manner when her brother is born alive after her sister died at birth in the story "To Set Our House in Order": "I thought of the dead baby, my sister, who might easily have been I … I thought of my brother who had been born alive after all and now had been given his life's name" (*BH* 60–1). Time is the theme of Laurence's last novel, *The Diviners*, as seen in her subtitle, *The River of Now and Then*.

Sal's epiphany of identity is about to be tested. Under the photograph albums lies an old navy coat with a red sash, an olden day's coat, a Red River coat named for the Selkirk settlers' colony of Assiniboia in the Red River Valley of Manitoba in the early nineteenth century. When Sal puts it on, she becomes a time traveller who is transported back to the olden days of the village when her Gran was a girl. Sal's trance reminds us of the trances entered into by the Somali storytellers that Laurence celebrates in *A Tree for Poverty*, and it also gives us insight into the way Laurence found herself possessed by her characters, like Hagar Currie, the olden days heroine of *The Stone Angel* (*DE* 156). Time-travel fantasy is a conventional trope in children's fiction, of course, dating back to Edith Nesbit's novels at the turn of the twentieth century.[22] Although such fantasy motifs do not enter into the realist mode of Laurence's adult fiction, except in the secret fantasies of characters like Stacey MacAindra, her sense of history is omnipresent.

Sal opens her eyes on a village that resembles the pictures from her grandmother's girlhood more than the village of today. In fact, the village sounds like Manawaka in Hagar's day. Sal recognizes the village from the church, but her Gran's house is nowhere to be seen. Lost in the past, Sal longs to get back to the future long before the film of that name, recalling the line at the end of *The Diviners*: "*Look ahead into the past, and back into the future, until the silence*" (477).

As Sal wanders down a country road, searching for her family, a swan-shaped sleigh painted bright crimson with gold swirls, drawn by two horses jingling with bells, draws up beside her.[23] The driver, a girl about Sal's age, greets her with a broad grin and warm brown eyes. When she introduces herself as Sarah of New Grange Farm and asks the young stranger about her family, Sal is confused because she knows she must not tell a lie, but realizes that she cannot tell the truth. Sal is saved from her moral dilemma when she catches sight of a flash of blue and distracts the driver, who explains that the bird is a blue jay and that jays often follow her to take bread from her hands. She explains that she is allowed to take out the cutter alone because "Papa knows I'm as good as my brothers with the horses." Sal is impressed: "A girl who could tame birds and drive a team of horses." Sal is delighted when Sarah offers to take her for a ride in the sleigh.

Sarah explains that she has just visited her friend's house to show off her Early Present, and Sal says that her family has the same tradition of opening one present on Christmas Eve. Sarah shows Sal the gift – a beautiful box carved by her father with a monarch butterfly painted by her mother and an inscription on the underside: "*To Sarah, from her loving parents.*"[24] Sarah says, "I shall cherish it always. I'll hand it on ... to my children and their children." This Christmas gift recalls the desk Margaret's father, Robert Wemyss, built for her on the Christmas before she turned ten, the last Christmas of her father's life – a loss she describes in her memoir *Dance on the Earth* (55). Sal knows it is a monarch butterfly because her father had told her on a visit to the village last spring that monarchs are called that because they were "the kings and queens of all the butterflies."[25]

When Sarah invites Sal home to visit her family at New Grange Farm, Sal panics because she knows she cannot go, but cannot explain why, either. Again, Sal is saved when a shower of icicles, sharp swords of frozen water, falls from a tree branch, startling the horses, who plunge forward, sending the precious box flying into the snow as Sarah reaches for the reins. When Sarah finally draws Brownie and Star to a halt, Sal offers to search for the box. Sure that she will never find the small box in the deep snow, Sal is drawn to it by a blue jay searching in the snow – just as the owl leads the Bean kids to the cows. Such animal guides are common to children's literature. As she hands it to Sarah, Sal forms a desperate plan. The olden days coat transported her into the past, and so the Red River coat must take her back to the future. As Sarah drives the sled away, Sal slips out of the coat and tosses it into the back of the sleigh, where it will travel to New Grange Farm: "It would travel through history until –."[26]

Everything goes black, and Sal opens her eyes to find herself sitting on the floor of the shed with the photograph albums spread out around her. In the bottom of the trunk, she sees a navy blue coat with a hood and red sash. Just as she is about to try it on, her father's voice booms into the shed, waking her from her reverie and inviting her to open her early present.

Entering the house, she sees that her parents have decorated the Christmas tree with the peacock and the silver bells and the small Santa, her own decorations from home. When her Gran, with her snow-white hair, her hands gnarled like tree branches, but her smile and brown eyes as warm as ever, asks Sal which present she wants to open, Sal surprises herself by saying Gran's. When Sal unwraps the gift, she sees a carved wooden box painted with a monarch butterfly. "'I've been saving it,' Gran said. 'Your Grandad and I didn't have a daughter, but your Dad and Mother gave us a very fine grand-daughter. I've kept this to give you the year you were ten. My father carved it and my mother painted it, and they gave it to me the year I was ten.'" Sal sees the inscription, "*To Sarah, from her loving parents,*" and realizes she has been named for her grandmother because Sal is short for Sarah. She blurts out, "Gran, it's beautiful. I'll always cherish it." The words echo in her head, but she cannot remember who said them. She only knows that she will remember this Christmas all her life. Gran calls the box "a family heirloom" and explains that she almost lost it in the snow the very day she was given it. When Sal asks how she found it, Gran smiles a faraway, but very close, smile and says, "I never could quite remember, afterwards." As Letson observes, in *The Olden Days Coat*, "Laurence provides a Christmas story which provides a lesson in love and rebirth" (20). The family heirloom recalls the plaid pin Hagar gave her son John, who traded it for the Tonnerres' hunting knife, in *The Stone Angel*, Laurence's first Manawaka novel – two emblems that are reunited by Pique Gunn Tonnerre, who inherits both from her parents, Morag Gunn and Jules Tonnerre, in the last Manawaka novel, *The Diviners*, knitting the Manawaka cycle together.

Thus, *The Olden Days Coat*, more than any of her children's books, reflects the emphasis on the matrilinear heritage that we find both in Laurence's memoir, *Dance on the Earth*, in which she celebrates all her mothers and their legacy, and in her Manawaka novels, in which Rachel and her sister Stacey accept their aging mother in *A Jest of God* and *The Fire-Dwellers,* and Morag and her daughter Pique are finally reconciled in *The Diviners*. All four of her children's fictions reflect the emphasis on the importance of community in her adult fiction, as well as the focus on an emblem, a gift that is lost and then found, in her Manawaka cycle.

CHAPTER 14

Lady of the Dance: Choreographing a Life in *Dance on the Earth: A Memoir*

Dance on the Earth: A Memoir, Laurence's final text, published posthumously in 1989, reflects her Manawaka fiction in significant ways. First, it reflects the growing interest in women, especially mothers, observed in *The Stone Angel*, *The Fire-Dwellers*, and *The Diviners* in particular. Second, it reflects the artistry of her fiction in her deliberate structuring of the narrative and in her use of the dance trope to connect the sections of the text. Third, although it purports to be autobiographical, *Dance on the Earth* reveals the art of the novelist in Laurence's tendency to fictionalize memory.

Laurence titled her memoir *Dance on the Earth* for good reason. Perhaps foreseeing biographies following her death, she chose to choreograph her own life, offering her own version. She rejected the linearity of conventional autobiography in favour of the memoir form that allowed her to "dance around" private issues that she did not wish to publicize, while expanding on public issues that interested her. She explains this preference in her Forewords to *Dance on the Earth: A Memoir*: "I didn't want to write the entire story of my life, for numerous reasons, one of them being that it *is* mine and from the start I recognized that there were areas I wasn't prepared even to try to set down. I wanted to write more about my feelings about mothers and about my own life views. I realized finally that this could only be done by coming as close as I could bear to my own life, but in such a way that I could also deal with broader themes that interested and absorbed me.[1] Her daughter, Jocelyn Laurence, elaborates on this method in her preface to *Dance on the Earth*: "She conceived of a new structure, one in which she could not only incorporate the facts of her own life but also touch upon the lives of her three mothers, as she called them – her biological mother, her aunt, who became her stepmother, and her mother-in-law. This new approach allowed her momentary digressions, too, into the issues that most concerned her: nuclear disarmament, pollution and the environment, pro-choice abortion legislation" (xi). As Helen Buss notes, in "Writing and Reading Autobiographically," Laurence chose "a style that allowed her to speak of her own growth as a female writer while making the digressions into the larger communal and global issues that were so much a part of Laurence's public commitment" (89). In her introduction to *Prairie Fire*'s 1997 "Life Writing" issue, Buss explains, "autobiography offers a different contract with the reader, a guarantee that the writer is taking the risk of offering a revelation of some part of her/his own personal life" (6). Laurence, a private person, was not willing to offer that contract or to guarantee revelations. Memoirs suggest a more selective reminiscence: Donald J. Winslow states in *Life-Writing*, "*Memoir* differs from autobiography in being ordinarily less formally organized and in centering more upon social and historical background, less upon private life ..." (26).[2] In "Reading Margaret Laurence's Life Writing: Toward a Postcolonial Feminist Subjectivity for a White Female Critic," Buss argues that memoir offers a different kind of contract than autobiography between reader and writer: "memoirs' discourse seeks a contract with the reader in which the reader is actively involved in the construction of the subjectivity of the text. The advantage of the memoir form lies in its ability to break the barriers between the public and the private, to undo the truth/fiction dichotomy of literary generic classification ... by a process of writing on the boundaries between fiction and autobiography. Another advantage is found in the ability of the form to make the political personal and the personal theoretical" (53).[3] These advantages of the memoir form suited Laurence's purposes in *Dance on the Earth*.

As a relatively young woman of thirty-six, Laurence recalls in her memoir, she joked about writing her autobiography, suggesting she might call it *A Broken Reed* (163). But, after the suicide of Sylvia Plath in 1963, she realized, "I was definitely not a broken reed" (163). Nor did she write her autobiography then. Perhaps foreseeing, with her "Celtic second sight" (xii), the imminence of her premature death, she did attempt a conventional autobiography in 1984. But, after completing hundreds of handwritten pages and only reaching the age of eighteen, she claims she was bored by the project: "I knew what was going to happen next. There was none of the mysterious excitement that one feels in writing a novel" (7).[4] Autobiography was too much "a life sentence of sentences" (TYS 23), in her words. Moreover, how does a writer impose closure on her own life, even in a literary representation? As Jocelyn Laurence acknowledges in her preface to *Dance on the Earth*, an autobiography was "altogether too bounded, with a beginning and a middle and presumably an end. It had nasty implications of mortality. I realized I hadn't wanted her to write her life story because I couldn't allow myself to believe that her life would ever be over" (xi–xii). Writing an autobiography may constitute an acknowledgment of the imminence of death – an act of "Pre-mourning" (*FD* 15).

There is nothing mournful about the title of Laurence's memoir, however. The dance trope is no mere rhetorical flourish or arabesque; rather, it provides the major metaphor of the memoir, winding through the text as an emblem of life – as the river that flows both ways provides the undercurrent that runs through *The Diviners*. A few reviewers have noted the centrality of the dance trope to her memoir: Greta M. Coger, for example, observes in her review essay, "Dance, Nurture, Write": "Laurence's title, *Dance on the Earth*, sums up her central idea both literally and metaphorically." But none of these critics has followed the dance trope of Laurence's title to its logical conclusion.

Laurence cared passionately about the titles of her books, as she emphasizes in her *Heart of a Stranger* essay, "Living Dangerously ... by Mail," where she records defending her chosen titles. Clara Thomas recalls in her review of *Dance on the Earth*, "On the day that she found her title in 'Lord of the Dance,' a hymn she particularly loved, she was especially joyful" (88). Laurence quotes Sydney Carter's modern hymn in her Forewords to *Dance on the Earth*:

I danced in the morning when the world was begun,
And I danced in the moon and the stars and the sun
And I came down from heaven and I danced on the earth –
At Bethlehem I had my birth.
> Dance then wherever you may be;
> I am the Lord of the Dance, said he,
> I'll lead you all, wherever you may be,
> I will lead you all in the Dance, said he. (16–17)

As Joan Givner states, in "Thinking Back Through Our Mothers: Reading the Autobiography of Margaret Laurence," she "assumes the central role and positions herself as lord of the dance" (89). *Lady* of the Dance, Laurence leads us all in the dance in her memoir, as she employs the dance trope of her title to provide the major metaphor for her text. As Laurence notes in a statement in her typescript that was omitted from the published version of *Dance on the Earth*, "'Dance' here is a figure of speech, a symbol, and yet an actuality as well" (17).

Laurence presents herself as a literal and figurative dancer in *Dance on the Earth*: "Dancing, both as metaphor and as actuality, has always been part of my own life. When I was a young woman I loved to go dancing" (17), she records. She reflects that youthful enjoyment of dancing in Stacey Cameron MacAindra, heroine of *The Fire-Dwellers* (1969), who recalls nostalgically in middle age, "I used to love dancing. I used to be a good dancer" (*FD* 100).

During the war, Margaret danced with her first love, Derek Armstrong, the English airman. She affirms that "dancing with someone who also loved to dance was not just a sexual experience; it almost went beyond the sexual. The uncertainties of war meant we danced with a heightened tribal sense of being together. Dancing became a passionate affirmation of life and the desire to go on living" (87). Similarly, "Stacey Cameron, under the green-purple neon starlight of the Wapakata Dancehall, danced with the airman from Montreal" (*FD* 71) as a prelude to lovemaking. So dance, in Laurence's life and in her art, is a metaphor for mating, but also a symbol of the joy of living.[5]

As a married woman in Africa, Margaret enjoyed dancing the Highlife with her husband, Jack: "One of my greatest pleasures when my husband and I lived in Ghana was to dance in one of the African nightclubs in Accra, to West African high-life music with its counterpoint rhythms of the drums. I was pretty good at it, too. When young African men asked me to dance, I was honoured – they didn't ask just anyone" (17). Laurence reflects this excitement in her African novel *This Side Jordan* (1961), which opens at the Weekend in Wyoming nightclub, as the band is "playing the Fire Highlife, playing it with a beat urgent as love" (*SJ* 1), connecting dancing with loving.

Laurence recalls, "When my children were little, I used to dance with them sometimes and that was pure joy, as their small bodies whirled and spun and occasionally tripped and righted themselves, laughing, and the dance went on" (17). Ultimately, however, Margaret danced alone: "Later, during some of the most difficult times of my life ... , I often used to dance to my favourite music – 'Zorba's Dance,' African high life, some of the jazz or boogie from the forties. I danced alone in my study when the kids were asleep, dancing pain, worry, loneliness. And the dancing helped" (17). Similarly, Stacey, on the brink of middle age, becomes a solitary dancer as well as a secret drinker. Like Stacey, who says, "from now on, the dancing goes on only in the head" (276), Margaret's dancing also became metaphorical: "I don't dance any more ... I know there are many ways of dancing other than the literal ones. The other ways, of friendships, of work, of stubborn hoping in a terrifying world, I pray to be able to go on with until my own dance ends and I leave the earth" (17). Affirming that one's "dance is lifelong" (18), she continues her "life dance" (17) in her memoir, until she foresees the end of her "dance of life" (222) on the final page of her text.

We can consider Laurence as choreographer of her memoir by exploring her dance metaphor. First, as composer of her life story, Laurence constructs her dance of life essentially as a solo. Readers who were hoping to learn salient secrets of her marriage and divorce were disappointed because *Dance on the Earth* is no confessional. Many reviewers lamented the lacunae in this text, but Laurence declined to intrude on the privacy of her former husband and his second wife, Esther. Instead, she blames the separation on that "holy terror" (*SA* 304) Hagar, for Jack disliked *The Stone Angel*: "Strange reason for breaking up a marriage: a novel" (158), she acknowledges. Margaret's memoir is not a *pas de deux*, then, or even a supported *adagio*, although she acknowledges Jack's financial support, which freed her for writing fiction: "I should add, with gratitude, that in the early years of my children's lives, I didn't have to earn a living" (135). Appropriately, she dedicates her Somali memoir, *The Prophet's Camel Bell*, to her husband, even though they were then separated.

Nor does she construct her life story as a *pas de trois* for, although a love triangle was at the heart of their separation, she neglects to mention her catalytic love affair with Barbadian novelist George Lamming. In his controversial 1997 biography of Laurence, James King reveals that she "embarked on an affair with Lamming" and suggests that "a love affair with a black man was a way of making a rebellious – if covert – statement in opposition to prevailing norms" (168–9). But, as Alexandra Pett notes, "in the myth of the Canadian woman writer which she creates, sexual relationships outside marriage have no place" (214). The Laurence marriage was coming to an end, and Lamming's departure for London was a catalyst in its final demise, as Margaret "decided to follow Lamming to London, where she hoped to rekindle their brief affair" (King 170). King says that her "search for Lamming [in London pubs] took on the appearance of a quest for some sort of romantic hero to rescue her" (179). He records their eventual encounter in October 1963 at a party at the home of Mordecai Richler, whence a distraught Laurence had to be led away in tears (191). No hint of this relationship is mentioned in Laurence's memoir.

Laurence also declines to make her memoir a *pas de quatre*, for she explains that her children's lives are their own, and so she includes only their "birth stories" (135) as part of her own life story: "I had, in thinking of this memoir, a lot of doubt on the matter of writing about my children. I have always refused to talk about them in interviews. Their lives belong to themselves, not to me, much less to the media. I finally decided, however, that their births are an integral part of my story as well as theirs, and that I was justified in writing about them as children solely in terms of our situation when I was writing each of my books" (135). She does, in fact, include some material about her children's lives, apart from their birth stories, in her memoir, but these are merely amusing anecdotes. For example, when the family moved to England, although she claims the children adjusted easily, David was confused when his definition of "BC" as "British Columbia," instead of "Before Christ," was called incorrect (161). Even in the journal that she kept during the last year of her life, right up to the hour of her death, she records only amusing anecdotes about her children: for example, at the wedding of Margaret's Macmillan editor,

Alan Maclean, to William Empson's daughter Robyn, when she pointed out that the man sitting beside them was Prime Minister of England, David exclaimed, "You're kidding!"[6]

Important events involving her children occurred during the family's time in England, however. Again, King records painful episodes in Laurence's maternal life, when she left her children to take up the post of writer-in-residence at Massey College at the University of Toronto in 1969 and at the University of Western Ontario and Trent University in 1973–74, leaving them at Elm Cottage in the care of a Canadian couple named Ian and Sandy Cameron. Most touching is the scene after the meeting with Lamming in London, when ten-year-old Jocelyn comforted six-year-old David as their mother sobbed herself to sleep (King 191). Most traumatic was Margaret's suicide attempt after her divorce in 1969 when she locked herself in the bathroom, yelling that she was going to kill herself, and then slept for two days after taking an overdose of tranquillizers (King 275). She excluded all these incidents from *Dance on the Earth* as being too personal.

Laurence choreographs her dance of life with a supporting cast composed not of her immediate family, as in the Freudian family romance, then, but a *corps de ballet* of old crones, beginning with Hagar. In *Dance on the Earth* she explains how she left her husband for Hagar: "I had to go with the old lady" (158). Embarking for England by airplane with her children, she lightened her overweight luggage by dispatching her only copy of *The Stone Angel*, along with David's Meccano set and old tennis shoes, to London by surface mail. She recalls that it took three months to arrive: "During those months I was in agony every single day, imagining it gone forever. This was the novel for which I had separated from my husband and embarked on who knew what, uprooting and dragging along my two children, and I almost seemed to be trying to lose it. Guilt and fear can do strange things to the mind and the body. I questioned my right to write, even though I knew I had to do it" (159). She concludes her Forewords with "Old Women's Song," her poem about the dance of her chorus of old crones, the wisewomen or shawomen, our foremothers: it begins, "I see old women dancing / dancing on the earth," and concludes, "I am one among them / dancing on the earth" (18–19).[7]

Let us let Laurence lead us in the dance, as we follow the dance trope of her title as it weaves through her memoir. Laurence's favourite dance song, "Zorba's dance" (17), from the film based on Kazantza-kis's novel *Zorba the Greek*, is a circle dance traditionally performed by men, but in *Dance on the Earth* the circle dance is performed by her *corps de ballet* of old crones as they link arms through the ages, symbolizing continuity: "foremothers with them joining / all of their hands" (19).

Rejecting the linear march of autobiography, Laurence chooses the circle dance of matriarchy. The child is mother of the woman, for the body of the mother is the literal link between the past and the future. The locus of history is "herstory" (4). She begins her memoir with a celebration of birth as an emblem of continuity, with memory as the umbilical cord of history: "[Motherhood] is the very core of our being" (4), she affirms; "I hear old women singing / singing children's birth" (18), echoes her chorus of old crones. Maternity is central to Laurence's fiction: not only are all her Manawaka heroines mothers – even Rachel Cameron gives birth to a "benign" tumour and becomes the mother of her "elderly child" in *A Jest of God* (170, 208)[8] – but all her fiction focuses on the connection between past and present. Like Hagar Ship-ley, Laurence is "rampant with memory" (*SA* 4) in *Dance on the Earth*, for a memoir is a record of memories, although she tends to fictional-ize her memories. Lyall Powers refers, in *Alien Heart*, to "Margaret Laurence's creative memory" (24): "Again, Margaret Laurence's adult and artistically creative memory has adjusted temporal and spatial de-tails to accommodate her unconscious psychological needs" (23). As Morag suggests in *The Diviners* (17–18), memory invents the past, fab-ricating history just as an artist creates a myth.[9]

Centring her memoir on the matrix of maternity, she constructs her text not as autobiography, but as a tribute to four mothers: her bio-logical mother, Verna Simpson Wemyss; her stepmother, Margaret Simpson Wemyss; her mother-in-law, Elsie Fry Laurence; and herself, Margaret Wemyss Laurence, as a mother to her two children, Jocelyn and David, and to her books, her two kinds of offspring: "This is a book about my mothers and about myself as a mother and writer" (8). In fact, Powers reports that "she [in]tended to call the nascent memoirs 'Four Mothers' (sometimes 'Three Mothers')" (459). Timothy Findley states, in "A Vivid Life," his review of *Dance on the Earth*, "This mem-oir is a book about ... being a mother – and having a mother" (9). As Virginia Woolf writes in *A Room of One's Own*, "we think back through our mothers if we are women" (83).

Laurence presents each of her foremothers as a dancer, literally or figuratively, employing dance as the symbol of their several arts: "All of them were talented artists in their various ways – music, teaching, writing" (10). For example, she reflects, "I never saw my maternal grandmother [Jane Bailey Simpson, the model for Vanessa MacLeod's Grandmother Connor in *A Bird in the House*] dance, although I think she must have, both ballroom dancing and square dancing with a fiddler and a caller in country schoolhouses. In her quilts and hooked rugs she also danced some of her perseverance, her gentleness, her hard work, her pain, her life" (18). Feeling guilt for the "barbarity of youth" (13) she exhibited in rejecting the Wild Rose quilt her grandmother made for her as a child, she had her friend Alice Williams make a Wild Geese quilt for her son and a flowered quilt for her daughter, continuing the family tradition. Williams made a loon quilt for Margaret, but since she knew she was dying, she said she would only borrow it. Dance is the umbilical cord connecting the memory of generations of women in Laurence's memoir. She laments: "I never saw any of my mothers dance, although I feel sure that they did, and that my own young mother perhaps even danced with me when I was a very young child. My mothers must have danced the dances of their youth: the waltz, the Charleston, the two-step … I never saw my mothers actually dancing, but they all danced in the other ways, the ways that are different from the dance observed as dance"(18).

She concludes the portrait of each of her three mothers with her dance metaphor as a celebration of continuity, as her "dance of life" weaves through the memoir, linking the generations together, just as the circle dance links the dancers: "foremothers with them joining / all of their hands" (19). Of her biological mother, Verna Simpson Wemyss, a gifted musician and pianist who died from an acute kidney infection at age thirty-four, two days after her daughter Peggy's fourth birthday, she says, "I mourn that young mother of mine still, and always will. Yet she passed on marvels to me. Humour. Music, although my music has been made with words. She danced on the earth, in her way, in the time that was given to her. Danced laughter, danced youth, danced love, danced hope in a child. She passed her dance on to me" (42). She concludes her portrait of her stepmother and aunt, Margaret Simpson Wemyss, with this invocation: "May your spirit still dance on the earth, in stillness and in the lives of your inheritors. I will always miss you, but I will always celebrate you" (121). She ends her portrait of her mother-in-law, Elsie Fry Laurence, whose legacy "pro-claim[s] itself in the dance of life that goes on in us, your children, your grand-children, your great-grand-children," with the invocation, "Dance on, Elsie, dance on, and you will live on, in all of us" (132). Not only does she portray the life and art of her foremothers as a dance but she also mourns their deaths through the dance trope, for this is "a time to mourn *and* a time to dance," as she rehearses her mothers' deaths in preparation for her own. She concludes her Forewords with her dance trope: "I had three mothers. I have countless foremothers. I never saw my mothers dancing. But now I know their dance" (19). And she teaches their dance to her readers in *Dance on the Earth*.

She extends her metaphor of the maternal dance from humanity to spirituality by celebrating the statue of "Crucified Woman" by Cana-dian sculptor Almuth Lutkenhaus. It depicts a female figure suspended in air, arms outstretched in cruciform. Laurence observes, "'Crucified Woman' is almost dancing, on the earth, the life dance of pain and love" (17). Thus, the dance of life is not only a dance of joy and cel-ebration, but also a dance of pain and suffering.[10] It is a time to dance *and* a time to mourn, for "mourning has no season" (226): "I see old women dancing, / dancing in their grief" (226). In *The Fire-Dwellers*, Stacey urges herself to "Dance hope, girl, dance hurt" (125), and the old crones sing, "I see young women dancing / dancing through the fire" (227), for the "life dance of pain and love" implies that love can be painful "for the sorrow dancer" (226) and that nurturing involves suffering. Extending her dance trope to "Crucified Woman," a female Saviour figure, suggests that Laurence is acknowledging the mourning involved in maternity. She writes, "To me, she represents the anguish of the ages, the repression, the injustice, the pain that has been inflicted upon women, both physically and emotionally" (16). On the other hand, she affirms, "'Crucified Woman' also speaks to me of the com-fort and help I have known from my mothers and the unconditional love I feel for my own children" (16). Laurence wished to use the sculp-ture for the cover of her memoir: she wrote to the sculptor, "My sense of myself, and my 3 mothers, is that of women dancing pain, dancing joy, dancing humankind's dilemma ... and in a deeply religious sense, your sculpture says all that to me" (*AH* 461). Thus, her dance metaphor can act as a metaphor for her meaning in the memoir, allowing her to imply ideas that she hesitates to articulate explicitly. Her positioning herself as *Lady* of the Dance may imply an identification of herself as a female Christ figure, a concept that Stacey suggests in her stigmata (*FD* 38, 101). Dr Lois Wilson, a Moderator of the United Church of Canada and Laurence's friend, recalls in her reminiscence, "Faith and the Vocation of the Author," that Laurence "was involved in a great stir over the mounting of Canadian sculptor Lutkenhaus-Lackey's *Crucified Woman* in the Bloor Street United Church during Easter Week, 1979: in that sculpture [now at Emmanuel College] Margaret saw a recognition by the Christian community of the terrible agonies suffered by women as victims" (152). Laurence wrote, "The sculptor, through showing Woman in the form of the Cross, is, I believe, attempting to portray women's pain, throughout history. To me it is a profound statement of faith and affirmation" (Dyke 43).[11]

Calling herself a Christian, albeit an unorthodox, and certainly a feminist, Christian (13), with fervent faith in the Social Gospel, Laurence laments the patriarchal character of Christianity with its masculine Trinity of God the Father, Son, and Holy Spirit. Believing that "women are an integral part of the Holy Spirit" (13), that "the female principle [is] part of the Holy Spirit" (13), and that the Holy Spirit incorporates "the female principle in faith, in art, in all of life" (15), she views the Holy Family, composed of "God the Father *and* the Mother [my italics]" (14) nurturing their child, as a model for the human family.[12] She illustrates this idea in *The Christmas Birthday Story* (1980), her revision of the nativity, which begins thus: "This story is about a newborn baby and his mother and father" (np). After reciting "Lord of the Dance," she adds, "Women, as well as men, in all ages and in all places, have danced on the earth, danced the life dance, danced joy, danced grief, danced despair, and danced hope" (17). She urges, "dance on, old women / dance in holy praise" (226–8). Of her own life, she exults, "I was out there dancing on the earth" (108), for Laurence advocates not the dance of death but the "dance of life" (222). Even while planning her funeral service with her old friend Lois Wilson, whom she had asked to lead the memorial service, Laurence declared, "Life is for rejoicing – for dancing ... And I've danced. I've danced" (Wilson 161).

But Laurence's memoir *is* a dance of death, a mourning text in which she laments and celebrates a life that she, like Hagar, realizes is ending. It is a time to mourn as well as a time to dance: "I hear old women mourning / mourning children's death" (19). Stacey rejected "*Premourning*" (*FD* 15), but Laurence's last Manawaka heroine, Morag Gunn, reflects on her image in the mirror, mourning her lost youth and pre-mourning her impending death in sections that Laurence omitted in response to requests from her Knopf editor, Judith Jones. Just as *The Stone Angel* is a novel of winding up, so *Dance on the Earth* may represent the urge to eternize a life that was soon to terminate. Pett claims Laurence "prefigures and comes to terms with her own imminent death" (205) here. Like Hagar, Laurence's final action was to review her life, like the drowning woman whose life flashes before her eyes. Laurence concludes *Dance on the Earth* with these words: "I know now, as I did not know when I wrote the first draft of these memoirs, that my own dance of life has not much longer to last. It will continue in my children, and perhaps for a while in my books. It has been varied, sometimes anguished, always interesting. I rejoice in having been given it" (222). Laurence ended her own life three months after she completed her memoir, on Epiphany Sunday, 5 January 1987.[13]

Laurence's death was the closing step in her dance of life. Coger writes, "She danced her dance and died content" (*ARCS* 268). While no one who has read Laurence's final journal, in which she wrote right up to the very hour of her death, could believe that she was content to die, she does make it clear to her family and friends that she embraces death as a welcome release from the suffering and humiliation involved for herself and her family in her terminal illness: "Please, my near & dear ones, forgive me & understand. I hope this potion works. My spirit is already in another country, & my body has become a damned nuisance. I have been so fortunate" (King 388). At the end of 1986, she wrote, "I want to die" (*AH* 470). She said, "I don't want to be Hagar" (King 382). At the beginning of December, she confided in her journal, "Unlike Hagar, I do not want to 'rage, rage against the dying of the light.' I want to 'go gently into that good night'" (*AH* 471).[14]

Ultimately, however, Laurence's memoir is not so much a dance of death as it is a dance of life in which she celebrates the positive aspects of her time on the earth while dancing around the black holes of her existence. Some critics consider Laurence whitewashed her life: Pett comments, "Many readers of her memoir have found Laurence's perspective of her life disappointing, even dishonest, in its concealment of what was really at issue and in its seemingly intended silencing of readers' questions" (203). Colin Nicholson complains that *Dance on the Earth* "glides rather too quickly away from areas of potential difficulty … I was left wanting more" (182–3). James King judges, Laurence "carefully crafted what she would reveal about herself [in *Dance on the Earth*]. The result is much more apologia than autobiography. In it she tells of some of the circumstances that formed her, but it is self-consciously fictional in that she relates her life history very much in the manner of a novelist telling her readers exactly what she wants them to know – and no more. The result is deliberately evasive" (xviii). He concludes, "*Dance on the Earth* remains a shadowy book, one in which the complexities of the autobiographer's existence are scarcely hinted at. Readers who, before they read it, may have been puzzled by the circumstances of the famous writer's life, remained so" (xix). As Laurence wrote to Harold Horwood on 31 December 1978, "I do not intend to spill every bean, I hardly need say" (*VLS* 101). Powers acknowledges, "Margaret's perceptions do not always tally factually with what available evidence indicates occurred" (461). Ultimately, as Pett concludes, "*Dance on the Earth* raises more questions than it answers" (204). Certainly, Laurence deftly sidesteps negative elements of her life, including the addictions to alcohol and nicotine that are implicit in *The Fire-Dwellers* and explicit in King's biography. As Pett notes, "she omits those negative self-images which balance the need for self-fulfillment" (211). Laurence perpetuated the myth of the Canadian literary matriarch, a myth exploded by King's biography.

Laurence was more concerned with public causes than with private confessions in *Dance on the Earth*, which Pett calls "a politicization of the personal" (213). Buss notes that, in the memoir form, "Laurence discovered a mode suitable to her own subject position as a feminist writer who sincerely believed she had moral agency in the world" (*PF* 188). Buss explains, "the autobiographer offers a portion of the vulnerability of the personal self in a gesture of public testimony in order to facilitate some communal therapeutic purpose, to effect some change, some healing, some new way of being in the world" (*PF* 6). If that is so, what is the change Laurence wishes to effect in her memoir? We can explore the way she employs her dance trope to convey her message in *Dance on the Earth*.

Laurence's memoir is a dance on the *earth*, advocating conservation, nuclear disarmament, and ecology, all the causes she supported through Project Ploughshares, the Greenpeace Movement, and CARAL, or pro-choice abortion legislation, causes she addresses in the text of her memoir and also in her Afterwords, in articles that Jocelyn says her mother chose for their relevance to her memoir (xiv): "A Constant Hope: Women in the Now and Future High Tech Age" (229), "A Fable – For the Whaling Fleets" (291), and her foreword to *Canada and the Nuclear Arms Race* (287). Laurence frames her memoir with a protest against war and a promise of the value of human life: she opens her Forewords by saying, "I have heard it said that war is for men what motherhood is for women" (3), and begins her Afterwords by singing, "I hear old women singing / life's holy worth" (227).

In titling her memoir *Dance on the Earth*, Laurence offers not only a description of her own life but also an injunction to us for ours, for the *Dance* of her title operates both as a noun and as an imperative verb: "dance on, old women" (19, 228). In "Celebrations," Clara Thomas defines Laurence's memoir as "the testament of her own life directed as a legacy" (126). In her memoir Laurence leaves a legacy of hope to her "inheritors" (*D* 477) – just as Morag passes the torch to her daughter, Pique Gunn Tonnerre, who combines her mother's words with her father's music in "Pique's Song," which ends *The Diviners* (489–90). Laurence bequeaths her legacy to Manitoba graduands in 1986, the last year of her life: "You are among my inheritors. I give you my deepest blessings, my hope and my faith."[15] In her "Message to the Inheritors" at York University in 1980, she addresses the graduands as "my generation's inheritors" and bequeaths them her heritage of "faith, hope and love" (283),[16] the same legacy that she leaves to her children in her memoir.

Her last words are a legacy: "May the dance go on" (222); and then she shows us how to dance. Laurence's Afterwords to *Dance on the Earth* point us in the direction to take *afterwards*. They may constitute a kind of afterbirth. Appropriately, they begin with "Old Women's Song" (225–8), which concludes her Forewords, framing her text and forming a circular Möbius strip, suggesting the continuity of the circle dance. She concludes her essay on "A Constant Hope" for women with the motto of the plaid pin that connects *The Stone Angel* with *The Diviners*, linking the Manawaka cycle together: "To women in the future, I have to say: "*My Hope Is Constant In Thee*" (238).

She structures her memoir as a tribute to continuity, ending with a list of fifty-two photographs (297–8) – from her Great-grandmother Wemyss, through her three mothers, to her two children – which dance through the memoir like the crones in the circle dance, linking generations together – "the continuum of ancestors, those who dance on the earth" (270), as Coger puts it. This closing list returns us to the maternal lineage that is at the heart of her memoir: "I write this book for my mothers and for my children. I write as a child and as a mother" (10), Laurence says. She dedicates the memoir to her children: "*For Jocelyn and David with faith, hope, and love.* " Her two children frame the work, for Jocelyn opens the text with her preface, and David closes the book with his photograph of his mother. Laurence appears to be a Janus-faced figure "*Look[ing] ahead into the past, and back to the future until the silence*" (D 477). But "The rest is not silence" (Kirkwood 30), for the memoir celebrates the continuity of community. As Paul Denham concludes, "Her dance on earth is done, but the dance goes on" (34).

Laurence employs her dance metaphor as a celebration of sorority, of female community. In her Forewords, she recalls, "Twice, not so long ago, my daughter and I danced, a stately dance, not the exuberant rhythms of my past or her present, a graceful easy dance, at a slight distance from each other, hands touching lightly, a dance with no name" (18). Such a celebration of community is a far cry from Stacey and her daughter Katie's solitary dances in *The Fire-Dwellers* (127). Coger notes, "Mothers pass on love and nurture to their daughters as each dances her life on earth" (260). Buss observes, the "sense of a dialogic mother/daughter utterance is very strong in the Laurence memoir" (*PF* 188). In her Afterwords, Laurence celebrates sisterhood in personal poems, such as "For My Daughter" (250), "For Adele Wiseman Stone" (245), and, finally, "For My Sisters" (293), which celebrates her female friends, whose talk is a river "Flowing both ways," linking past and future:

> You are my sister-sojourner here
> As all my mothers were
> And in memory remain. (296)[17]

So Laurence does not present her life dance as a virtuoso performance that upstages other women; rather, she invites the reader, like her daughter and sisters, to join her in the unending dance of life.

The structure of *Dance on the Earth* is a tribute to community, for, in her acknowledgments, Laurence thanks her daughter Jocelyn for editing the book, her son David for the photograph of her, and her friend Joan Johnston for typing the manuscript. Even the composition of the text constitutes a monument to a community of women. Margaret completed a draft of her memoir just before her sixtieth birthday on 18 July 1986. A month later, on 26 August, Jocelyn's thirty-fourth birthday, she was diagnosed with terminal lung cancer and refused treatment. With characteristic consideration, she postponed informing Jocelyn because she did not want to spoil her birthday (10).[18] Following surgery, she attempted to revise her handwritten manuscript on the typewriter as usual – this time sitting up in her hospital bed with tubes coming out of the incision in her chest – but she was too sick. She wrote to Wiseman on 12 November 1986, "the spirit is willing but the flesh is weak" (*SL* 406). Her amanuensis Joan Johnston suggested Margaret dictate her memoirs onto tapes so Joan could type up the draft for Margaret to revise. Jocelyn recalls that soon she was dictating "like a mad businesswoman" (xiii). The taping and typing worked: Margaret began dictating her memoirs on 11 September, and Joan finished typing them by 6 October.[19] Laurence was racing with death.

She planned to go over the draft with Jocelyn in January, but she ended her life in the new year, leaving Jocelyn to edit the typescript – a painful task because *Dance on the Earth* is the book "most literally written in her voice" (xiv). Thus, although Laurence had choreographed her life as a solo, her untimely death meant that her dance had to be edited by her daughter. Jocelyn notes, "My role was simply to smooth out some portions and eliminate any repetitions that inevitably arise from the spoken rather than the written word" (xiv). As editor, however, she exercised her privilege to excise material that she considered too private for publication: in the interests of economy and privacy, she eliminated 377 passages, from sentences to paragraphs, including her mother's discussions of marriage and maternity, as well as passages extolling Alice Walker's *In Search of Our Mothers' Gardens*, a text that influenced Laurence as she was composing *Dance on the Earth*. Thus, the daughter intensified the process of exclusion that the mother initiated.

The lacunae in *Dance on the Earth* have led readers to wonder whether Laurence's memoir is fact or fiction. "Traditionally, autobiography is considered a lesser art than fiction by those who make and break literary canons" (*PF* 5), as Buss observes. But Laurence affirms, "Life is always more important than Art" (166). In a review of *Dance on the Earth*, Timothy Findley distinguishes between biography and autobiography: "In biography, there is no pattern: there is only progress. Whereas in *auto*biography, a pattern can be superimposed on that progress to provide a story line" (10). Art orders experience, and Laurence employs her metaphor of dance in her memoir to impose a pattern on the kaleidoscopic chaos of the quotidian. But the frontiers between fiction and non-fiction blur, especially for a novelist who maintains that composing an autobiography, as noted earlier, has "none of the mysterious excitement that one feels in writing a novel" (7).

As we know, Laurence originally intended to compose *Dance on the Earth* as a novel. Only when all attempts to write "Dance on the Earth" as fiction failed did Laurence compose her last dance as an autobiographical work of non-fiction.[20] "The memoirs idea is a godsend," she wrote to her literary sister, Adele Wiseman, in 1979 (*SL* 354). Inevitably, the unfinished novel influenced the memoir, however, for the fictional and non-fictional versions of *Dance on the Earth* have more in common than just their titles, as we have seen.[21] Although the memoir purports to be fact, in fact, it is choreographed so artistically that Laurence can dance around the pitfalls of her life – maintaining her privacy while publicizing her message. As William Butler Yeats asks rhetorically in "Among School Children": "How can we tell the dancer from the dance?"

"The Mystery at the Core of Life": Closure in the Texts, Career, and Life of Margaret Laurence

It seems appropriate to conclude this study of Laurence's oeuvre with a consideration of her use of closure, for closure clarifies the pattern of a text and, hence, the author's statement, as Frank Kermode argues in *The Sense of an Ending* (1966). As Marianna Torgovnick declares, in her *Closure in the Novel* (1984), "Endings, closures reveal the essences of novels with particular clarity" (7). Barbara Herrnstein Smith explains in *Poetic Closure* (1968), closure provides "a point from which all the preceding elements may be viewed comprehensively and their relations grasped as part of a significant design" (34). Aristotle insisted in his *Poetics* that a work should have a beginning, a middle, and an end, and he defined the ending as "that which has nothing following it" (65). But Virginia Woolf suggested in her essay "Mr. Bennett and Mrs. Brown" that, in the interests of realism, fiction should eschew the logic of beginnings, middles, and ends. Recent women writers are intent on "writing beyond the ending" (5), in the words of Rachel Blau Du Plessis. Laurence, in her fiction, employs open endings that affirm the possibility of a future.

Closure usually represents a resolution of a dilemma, and this is true for all Laurence's fiction. Her Manawaka protagonists are paralyzed by a problem in the present: Rachel is imprisoned in a prolonged adolescence by her possessive mother and her own neuroses, Stacey is trapped by the four walls of her home with four children and an uncommunicative husband, Vanessa feels jailed by childhood and her authoritarian grandfather, Morag is suffering from an acute case of writer's block, and Hagar is, of course, dying. Ultimately, they survive with a little help from their friends – a friend like Rachel Cameron's colleague Calla Mackie, a lover like Stacey MacAindra's Luke Venturi, a family member like Hagar Shipley's son Marvin, or even a patron saint like Morag Gunn's "Saint Catherine" or a celestial confidant like Stacey's "God, Sir" (*FD* 30)[1] – so they can overcome the problems of the present and proceed into the future.

Even Hagar survives in the spirit, if not the flesh, for, Laurence affirms, survival is essential. By survival, however, she does not merely mean existing but, rather, "to survive with some dignity" (TYS 21). She insists that the "theme of survival" (*HS* 8) is central to her Manawaka cycle: "The quest for physical and spiritual freedom, the quest for relationships of equality and communication – these themes run through my fiction and are connected with the theme of survival, not mere physical survival, but a survival of the spirit, with human dignity and the ability to give and receive love" (IT 258). She relates these themes to her five heroines:

> It will be obvious that these themes relate to Hagar, in *The Stone Angel*, who finally even in extreme old age can find something of that inner freedom; to Rachel in *A Jest of God*, who will remain nervous and neurotic to some extent but who does succeed in freeing herself from her mother's tyranny and from her own self-doubt and self-hatred; to Stacey in *The Fire-Dwellers*, who comes to terms with her life and recognizes herself as a survivor; to Vanessa in *A Bird in the House*, who escapes from the authoritarian regime of her grandfather and who is ultimately able to be released from her hatred and fear of the old man; and finally, to Morag in *The Diviners*, who, more than any of the others, is able to assimilate her past and to accept herself as a strong and independent woman, able to love and to create. (IT 258–9)

She observes, "My viewpoint generally comes down on the side of impulse or inner direction. Morag comes closer to what might be termed the god within" (Miner 18). She concludes this point by explaining the religious thrust of these themes: "The themes of freedom and survival relate both to the social/external world and to the spiritual/inner one, and they are themes which I see as both political and religious. If freedom is, in part, the ability to act out of one's own self-definition, with some confidence and with compassion, uncompelled by fear or by the authority of others, it is also a celebration of life and of the mystery at life's core. In their varying ways, all these characters experience a form of grace" (IT 259).

In order to survive with dignity, Laurence's heroines must make peace with the past in order to free themselves for the future. They may have to lay to rest the ghosts of the past – as Rachel must the ghost of her mortician father, Niall Cameron, the king of the dead (*JG* 25) – before they can come to life. Sometimes they have to repent past sins – as Hagar does, with the help of her father-confessor figure, Murray Ferney Lees, in atoning for her guilt in the death of her son John – before they can pass on to the afterlife. They may have to accept the present, as Stacey finally does, before they can embark on the future. They may have to pass on the torch to the future generation, as Morag does with Pique, before they pass on.

Laurence resolves her heroines' dilemmas not by a dramatic rescue, a *deus ex machina* descending out of the blue to make everything "all right," as Stacey would say, but through the character's finding the inner strength to shoulder her burdens and carry on. In *The Fire-Dwellers*, for example, nothing really changes – a status quo that is dramatized by the fact that the closing scene is identical to the opening one, complete with the same books, his and hers, still unread: "Two books are on the bedside table – *The Golden Bough* and *Investments and You*, Hers and His, both unread" (278). The development, on the contrary, is internal. Stacey who, feeling overwhelmed, quoted Psalm 69, "*Save me, O God, for the waters are come in unto my soul*" (152), finds the strength not only to support her husband and four children emotionally, but also to take on her ailing father-in-law Matthew and to welcome her mother May and her sister Rachel. Robert Chalmers writes in "The Women of Margaret Laurence," "Like all of Laurence's women, Stacey is a true survivor: she weathers her mother, her husband's periodic disaffections, the near drowning of her son, even a love affair which brings her perilously close to destroying what she hopes to protect" (211). Laurence writes to John Metcalf on 28 March 1972, "Whatever strength one finds, ultimately, must come from inside oneself, and in a literal sense, no one can save anyone else, although you can reach out to touch others" (quoted in King 302).

Laurence ends her Manawaka novels with a sense of affirmation dramatized by embarkation – like James Joyce, who concluded his semi-autobiographical *Bildungsroman*, *A Portrait of the Artist as a Young Man*, with the flight of Stephen Dedalus (275–6). *A Jest of God* is perhaps the most blatant example of embarkation, as Rachel plans to board a bus with her mother, her elderly child, in tow, to travel to the coast and a new life, where "anything may happen" (208). Hagar, in *The Stone Angel*, has finally freed herself from the chains of pride by two generous acts of love, and her narrative ends with her speaking the breathless words, "And then – " (308), concluding with an anticipatory dash, as she embarks on the unknown afterlife. Even Stacey, who is trapped by family obligations, is, in fact, embarking on a new decade of her life with renewed confidence in her own strength: "Give me another forty years, Lord, and I may mutate into a matriarch" (*FD* 281). Laurence called herself a matriarch and was labelled "Matriarch of Manawaka" by Valerie Miner. Morag looks to the future as she bequeaths her family legacy to her daughter, Pique, her inheritor: "*Look ahead into the past, and back into the future, until the silence*" (477). In *Dance on the Earth: A Memoir*, Laurence also passes on her legacy to her inheritors before passing on.

Laurence concludes her fiction not with optimism but with hope for the future. In her African fiction, she concludes on a hopeful note. In her first novel, *This Side Jordan*, Nathaniel Amegbe exhorts his newborn son to "Cross Jordan, Joshua" (282). But "the promised land of one's own inner freedom" (TYS 21) is still remote, Laurence acknowledges, and the difficulties of such a quest have been clearly dramatized in the course of the narrative. Her short story collection, *The Tomorrow-Tamer*, also ends on a hopeful note, as Mammii Ama becomes an earth mother figure: "Like a royal palm she stood, rooted in magnificence, spreading her arms like fronds, to shelter the generations" (244). But Laurence ironizes this image, undercutting the idealism with realism, for Mammii Ama's dream of "Free-dom" has been deflated: she had boasted to the skeletal white woman that "Market woman all dey come queen mammy" (237), that all will ride the bus "free" (238), but she is quickly disabused of her dream. Of her African fictions, Laurence says, "They are not entirely hopeful books ... but they do reflect the predominantly optimistic outlook of many Africans and many western liberals in the late 1950s and early 1960s" (TYS 18).

In her Manawaka fiction, Laurence dramatizes hope, rather than facile optimism. She states, "There is this feeling in all my books not of optimism – because you'd have to be a fool to be optimistic in this world – but of hope" (Twigg 271).[2] She acknowledges in her "Statement of Faith": "Ours is a terrifying world. Injustice, suffering and fear are everywhere to be found. It is difficult to maintain hope in such a world, and yet I believe there is hope ... We must not give way to despair. We must have faith. We must hope. We must try to love, to proclaim humanity and the only spirit indwelling in life" (SF 56, 60). In a 1980 dialogue sermon with Dr Wilson, Laurence insists, "All my work is informed by hope. I don't think any of it is optimistic. One would have to have a very simplistic or narrow view of life to be optimistic in a world such as ours. Hope is different. Hope is something I couldn't live without. And given god's grace, somehow one feels the planet and its creatures will survive. I think of optimism as saying, 'Everything's fine.' Only a fool would say that everything's fine" (Wilson 155). She asserts, "I think each of the novels – especially The Diviners – ends on a profound sense of hope" (Miner 20).

Laurence acknowledges the "Black Celt" (DE 26) in herself, like "Morag Dhu. Black Morag" (400), as Daniel McRaith labels the heroine of The Diviners: "The Black Celt gives you a feeling of ambiguity, a knowledge that life in many ways is somber. You have to recognize this inner darkness so that you're not too threatened by it" (Miner 20). But Laurence refuses to allow this shadow self to triumph. Although – like Stacey McAindra, who sees "gloom and doom" in the "world on fire" in which this ladybird dwells – Laurence acknowledges social evil, she refuses to allow it to quench her fire or quell her hope. She explains, "The death of hope is the death of the will and perhaps of the spirit" (DE 98). She affirms, "I feel that life and the world can be pretty gloomy and that people can certainly be hard and cruel to each other but I am convinced that gloom is not doom. There is hope and in most people there is a faith, a belief in the possibility of change that will come out" (Fabre 194).

Hope is Laurence's legacy. She dedicates her final work, *Dance on the Earth: A Memoir*, to her children: "For Jocelyn and David, with faith, hope, and love" (np). She concludes her 1985 essay, "A Constant Hope: Women in the Now and Future High Tech Age," by recalling, "In my novel, *The Diviners*, the protagonist, Morag, receives a symbol of her ancestors, a symbol that also points to the future, a Scots plaid pin with the motto: 'My Hope Is Constant In Thee.'" She concludes, "To women in the future, I have to say: *My Hope Is Constant In Thee*" (*DE* 238).[3]

In her 1980 "Message to the Inheritors," she leaves a legacy of hope to her inheritors: "You, my generation's inheritors, inherit a deeply troubled world. We are certainly not passing on a secure heritage to you. But I hope we *are* passing on to you, even in the midst of a terrifying world, some sense of hope, some sense that these lifelong struggles are worthwhile because life itself is worthwhile, and is given to each of us for a short time – to protect, to honour, and to celebrate ... It is my hope for you that you will sustain hope within yourselves" (*DE* 283).

Closure is a crucial concept, not only for Laurence's novels, but also for her writing career. She attempted repeatedly to write another novel to be titled *Dance on the Earth*, despite her conviction, when she completed *The Diviners*, that that novel would be her last. She believed that writing was a "gift" and that her novels were "given" to her to write.[4] But, once given, the gift could be taken away and given to another. Just as Royland loses his gift for divining in *The Diviners*, so Laurence, like Morag, lost her gift for writing. Just as Royland breaks his wand, so Margaret, like Morag, drowns her book. But Laurence did not despair. She turned her formidable passion and powers to causes in which she fervently believed: "nuclear disarmament, pollution and the environment, pro-choice abortion legislation" (*DE* xi). She involved herself in peace movements such as Operation Dismantle and Project Ploughshares, in conservationist organizations, and in feminist organizations such as CARAL. She penned numerous essays, some of which she selected before her death for the "Afterwords" to *Dance on the Earth: A Memoir*, including "The Greater Evil" about censorship and her foreword to *Canada and the Nuclear Arms Race*.

First and foremost of her causes was ecology or conservation of the earth: she concludes her "Prayer for Passover and Easter" with the affirmation, "We are one / People in our only home / Earth" (*DE* 264).[5] Laurence sees "holiness in life itself, in trees and rivers and the earth and all creatures" (*DE* 14). We can see this view of nature – reminiscent of Wordsworth's deism, as expressed in his *Prelude* and "Tintern Abbey," or Hopkins' theory of inscape and instress, as expressed in *The Wreck of the Deutschland* and in his sonnets "The Windhover" and "God's Grandeur" – reflected in her fiction, notably in the current of water symbolism that runs through *The Diviners*. In "My Final Hour" Laurence affirms, "Earth is my home" (188), and she laments its pollution in her memoir: "Water killed. Earth killed" (*DE* 39). In *The Diviners*, she writes, "Morag had once believed that nothing could be worse than killing a person. Now she perceived river-slaying as something worse" (*D* 12). In *Dance on the Earth*, Laurence asserts, "I continue to believe, all evidence to the contrary, that it is not too late to save our only home, the planet earth, and that it is not too late, even at this very late date, to learn to live on and with the earth, in harmony with all creatures. Part of that belief is social belief, part of it is religious faith" (*DE* 98). She enjoins us all, in both her unfinished novel and her memoir, to "dance on the earth."

Laurence writes that, in our Edenic innocence, we believed "the generations of mankind and of all creatures are like the leaves on a tree; they fall, but a new generation arises, and the earth endures forever" (*DE* 279). All that is changed since "our species has the technological power to destroy all life on earth and possibly our earth itself" (*DE* 279). She warns, "The individual is the leaf on the tree. The leaves fall but the tree endures. New leaves are born ... Now the tree itself is threatened" ("Artist" 62). For a writer with such reverence for Nature, nuclear armaments are anathema. For a writer who was first shocked into political consciousness by Dieppe in 1942 and the bombing of Hiroshima and Nagasaki in 1945, nuclear arms pose a major threat: "I believe that the question of disarmament is the most pressing practical, moral, spiritual issue of our times" ("Hour" 189), she insists. She begins her foreword to Ernie Regehr's *Canada and the Nuclear Arms Race* with this eloquent passage about "Canada's complicity in the nuclear arms race" (*DE* 288), as exemplified by the testing of the cruise missile over Alberta skies:

Our lives and the lives of all generations as yet unborn are being threatened, as never before, by the increasing possibility of nuclear war. I believe that the question of disarmament is the most pressing practical, moral and spiritual issue of our times. If we value our own lives and the lives of our children and all children everywhere, if we honour both the past and the future, then we must do everything in our power to work non-violently for peace. These beliefs are not only an integral part of my social and moral stance but of my religious faith as well. Human society now possesses the terrible ability to destroy all life on earth, and our planet itself. Can anyone who has ever marvelled at the miracle of creation fail to feel concerned and indeed anguished, every single day, at this thought? (*DE* 287)

Laurence also espouses the cause of feminism or "self-liberation" (*DE* 6). All her work is implicitly feminist, especially her Canadian fiction, but in her later years her feminism becomes explicit – notably in her last published work, *Dance on the Earth: A Memoir*, where she regrets "the downgrading of women in every field" (*DE* 4), including, or especially, women's writing. She discusses "feminists, of whom I count myself one" (*DE* 4) explicitly in "A Constant Hope: Women in the Now and Future High Tech Age": "It is to be hoped that the financial situation of women writers, and women in general, will improve in the future" (*DE* 235). She advocates "human values of love, tolerance, individual worth, compassion, responsibility" (*DE* 233) to counteract the potency of the machine; she hopes "the human values of caring and compassion and conscience will prevail" (*DE* 238). She urges women to "take a very active part in informing themselves and in proclaiming their right … because I think the voices of women are needed in every area" (*DE* 231, 236). Her legacy to women, ultimately, then, is hope.

Laurence writes frequently, especially in her later years, of "the mystery at the core of life." By this, she seems to intend God or the Holy Spirit, and she believes that the purpose of art and her responsibility as an artist is to express that mystery: in "The Artist, Then, Now and Always," she affirms, "Art … is an act of faith, an acknowledgement of the profound mystery at the core of life … All art is a product of the human imagination. It is, deeply, an honouring of the past, a perception of the present in one way or another, and a looking towards the future. Whatever the medium of any particular artist, art is a reaching out, an attempt to communicate those things which most concern us seriously in our sojourn here on earth" (62). She adds, "my responsibility seems to me to be to write as truthfully as I can, about human individuals and their dilemmas, to honour them as living, suffering, and sometimes joyful people. My responsibility also must extend into my life as a citizen of my own land and ultimately of the world" (62).

Laurence sees fiction as her way of fulfilling her responsibility to the past and to the future: "Fiction, in the political sense, both binds us to and frees us from our ancestors; it acknowledges our dilemmas; it mourns and rages at our inhumanity to one another; and sometimes it expresses our faith in growth and change, and honours our children and our trust in them" (IT 252):

> The novelist attempts ... to communicate to the reader ... the pain and struggle, the joy and anguish of characters who – although they are fictional – are felt by the writers to be as real as anyone we know. The writer's life view, the way in which people and their dilemmas and their society are seen, permeate any work of fiction. Fiction, for me at least, then becomes a matter of the individual characters moving within a history, which includes past, present, and future, and the emergence through these characters of beliefs which cannot be didactic but which in the most profound way are both religious and political. (IT 252–3)

She affirms, "it is no coincidence, I believe, that two of the major threads running throughout all my work have been, in some form or another, religious and socio-political themes" (DE 99).

Laurence says, "Religion is a frequent theme in the novels. I don't have a traditional religion, but I believe that there's a mystery at the core of life" (Miner 18). Religion is implicit in all her writing, and, in her memoir, Dance on the Earth, and in her later essays, she acknowledges herself explicitly as a Christian: "I am a Christian, or at least aspire to be, although perhaps not an orthodox one" (DE 13). In her essay "Upon a Midnight Clear," she says, "My background and heritage are strongly Christian" (HS 151). In her 1980 dialogue with Lois

Wilson, Laurence says, "I think also that many writers who would not consider themselves religious people in fact have a great deal of faith even though they may not define it in Christian terminology. And I long ago realized this about myself. The act of writing itself expresses some kind of faith and some kind of hope, and the very fact that the novelist is concerned deeply with the human individual and the preciousness, the value of the individual in itself is a kind of religious faith" (153).[6] In "Books That Mattered to Me," she affirms, "To me, the act of writing is itself an act of faith" (247). In "Open Letter to the Mother of Joe Bass" in *Heart of a Stranger*, Laurence writes, "I have spent fifteen years of my life writing novels and other things. I have had, if any faith at all, a faith in the word. *In the beginning was the Word, and the Word was with God, and the word was God*" (159). In "A Statement of Faith," she declares, "I want to proclaim my belief in the social gospel, as a Christian, a woman, a writer, a mother, and a member of humanity, a sharer in a life that I believe in some way to be informed by the holy spirit" (188–9).

Hers is a feminist Christianity, however: she desires recognition of "the female principle as part of the Holy Spirit ... the recognition of the female principle in faith, in art, in all of life" (*DE* 14–15). She laments the fact that "Women have been intentionally excluded from so many of the rituals and practices and words of Christianity, and ... of the other monotheisms" (*DE* 14–15). Speaking of her "foremothers," she asserts, "These women are an integral part of the Holy Spirit" (*DE* 15, 13), for she prefers to think of the Holy Spirit as "God the father and the mother" (*DE* 14). She explains her feminist Christianity to Wilson: "I have a feeling that there has to be more recognition of the kind of female principle in god ... we cannot really define the informing spirit of the universe because that is the mystery at the core of life. Whatever the spirit is and however we receive it into our lives, there must be a kind of male and female principle involved; there must be the father and the mother. I think many ... feel the need to incorporate that sense of both the motherhood and the fatherhood in the Holy Spirit" (154). In her memoir she says she views "Crucified Woman" by Canadian sculptor Almuth Lutkenhaus as a symbol of the female principle in the Holy Spirit (*DE* 15).

To conclude this consideration of closure in Laurence's writings and in her career as a writer, we can also consider the question of closure in her life. In *The Life of Margaret Laurence*, James King claims that Laurence "commit[ted] suicide" (386), but the journal that she kept during the last year of her life suggests "self-administered euthanasia" might be a more accurate definition of the death of the terminally ill Laurence. Indeed, she refers there to death as "self-deliverance" (King 386). Laurence knew that she was dying, and the cancer that riddled her lungs and kidneys made her very sick. In addition, she fell and broke her leg and so was bedridden and helpless, a burden to her friends and family. Her final journal entry, written while she awaited death, states, "Please, my near & dear ones, forgive me & understand. I hope this potion works. My spirit is already in another country, & my body has become a damn nuisance. I have been so fortunate" (King 388). In her dialogue sermon with Wilson she said, "[Death is] as natural an event as birth. The two are the beginning and the end of life … My sense of what happens in that kind of transformation is something I can't define, any more than I can define God. Because it's a mystery" (155).[7] Lois Wilson said she views the death of Margaret Laurence as "an affirmative action." The fact that she planned her death on Epiphany Sunday surely has affirmative implications. The Feast of the Epiphany, or "Twelfth Night," celebrates the manifestation of Christ to the Magi – a fact that James Joyce makes use of in his autobiographical *Stephen Hero* and in "The Dead." Thus, her choice of the day of her death may represent her return to the church of her childhood.

Laurence's last texts reinforce this sense of death as embarkation, or, indeed, as a return to an earlier state, for they describe a circular pattern, as we have seen. *The Diviners* ends with Morag returning to the house "to write the remaining private and fictional words, and to set down her title" (477), suggesting a Möbius strip. While embarkation as closure may be characteristic of modernist texts, such as Joyce's *Portrait of the Artist as a Young Man* or Lawrence's *Sons and Lovers*, the Möbius strip is more characteristic of postmodernist texts, such as Doris Lessing's *The Golden Notebook* (1962), which ends as it begins, or Ian McEwan's novel *Atonement* (2001), which employs an enclosing narrative frame. Such circularity is appropriate for metafictional texts, especially *Künstlerromane* like *The Diviners* or *A Bird in the House*, where Grandfather Connor's true "monument" (191) is Vanessa's stories. Even *The Fire-Dwellers* concludes exactly as it began. *Heart of a Stranger* describes a circular journey, and *Dance on the Earth* describes the umbilical cord linking the generations of mothers and daughters in a continuous cycle. Thus, the endless text moves beyond beginnings and endings to suggest continuity, recalling the Oroboris, the image of the snake with its tail in its mouth, symbolizing the eternal cycle.

Ultimately, Laurence hopes her work will leave a legacy of life on earth to future generations. She reveres life and believes we must safeguard the future for our children. She believes we must cherish all children for, as she affirms in "My Final Hour," "*all* children are our children" (191). She writes, "My guess would be that what we have to understand maybe is that all of us – if the human race survives – are going to be ancestors some day" (*HS* 224). She ends "Books That Mattered to Me" thus: "the books, whether fiction, non-fiction, or poetry, that have mattered the most to me throughout my adult life have been those that have a sense of our past and a belief that life itself is immeasurably valuable, to be worked for, hoped for, understood and proclaimed in whatever ways we are given to do" ("Books" 249). Clearly, Laurence's books have done that. As Noelle Boughton writes in *A Gift of Grace: A Spiritual Biography*, "Margaret Laurence's life and work were a gift of grace, and we, her inheritors, are still being blessed by them" (6).

Notes

CHAPTER ONE

1 See Charles Steele's *Taking Stock: The Calgary Conference on the Canadian Novel* for a complete account. Steele labelled the top one hundred list "List A" and the top ten list "List B."

2 See "CanLit Combat" by Nicholas Pashley, *The University of Toronto Magazine* (Winter 1999).

3 Unless otherwise indicated, all references to Morley will be to her revised edition of this text.

4 Jack Laurence told me in a 1994 interview that these African stories are his own personal favourites among his former wife's works.

5 This essay was originally published in 1970, just two years after the publication of *Long Drums and Cannons*.

6 These are the writers Laurence critiques in *Long Drums and Cannons*.

7 Laurence's original, unpublished introduction to *Long Drums and Cannons* is in the McMaster University Archives.

8 Laurence's unpublished, undated talk "Geography – Outer or Inner?" is in the Laurence archives, 1980–001, box 22, file 155, in the Scott Library at York University. Headed "Humanities Society" with "(& U of T Creative Writing Class)" pencilled beneath, it was likely presented during the 1969–70 academic year when Laurence was writer-in-residence at Massey College, University of Toronto. In that essay Laurence explains, "Later on, in Africa, I was writing much more out of actual experience for at least I was describing what was immediately around me, and the physical

descriptions of Africa are certainly authentic. Perhaps the characters were authentic to some extent as well, but of this I could never be even halfway certain" (np). In her 1969 essay, "Gadgetry or Growing," she writes, "I had decided I could never get deeply enough inside the minds of African people – or, at least, I'd gone as far as I personally could as a non-African – and had a very strong desire to go back and write about people from my own background, people whose idiom I knew and whose concepts were familiar to me" (82).

9 In *Dance on the Earth: A Memoir*, Laurence records that she put aside *The Stone Angel* in order to edit her Somali diaries for *The Prophet's Camel Bell* (157). In fact, *The Prophet's Camel Bell*, *This Side Jordan*, and *The Stone Angel* were all published by Knopf on the same day in June 1964.

10 In "Ten Years' Sentences," Laurence identifies the theme of her African writing as freedom, but finds that, with the writing of *The Stone Angel*, it has changed to survival: "With *The Stone Angel*, without my recognizing it at the time, the theme had changed to that of survival ..." (21). In "A Place to Stand On," Laurence writes, "The theme of survival ... runs through two of my novels other than *The Stone Angel* (in which it is, of course, the dominant theme)" (*HS* 8).

11 Gayle Greene discusses these parallels in her essay "Margaret Laurence's *Diviners* and Shakespeare's *Tempest*: The Uses of the Past" in *Women's Revisions of Shakespeare*.

12 The typescript of *The Diviners* is in box 3, files 3–13 of the McMaster University Archives.

13 This letter is in the University of British Columbia Ethel Wilson Archives.

14 Edward Steichen assembled an exhibition of photography – *The Family of Man*, at the Museum of Modern Art in New York in 1955 – that proved immensely popular. The book, *The Family of Man* (1955), based on this exhibit, brought his photographs to a wider audience.

15 James King says, "Most of the stories which comprise *A Bird in the House* have an originating point in Margaret's own life history" (302). Helen Buss examines the "identity theme" in her essay "Margaret Laurence and the Autobiographical Impulse." Peter Easingwood explores it further in his essay, "Semi-autobiographical Fiction and Revisionary Realism in *A Bird in the House*."

CHAPTER TWO

1 Issues of *Annals of the Black and Gold* in which Laurence published poems and stories are stored in the Margaret Laurence Home in Neepawa. I wish to thank Florence Campbell Henderson and her friendly staff for assisting me in photocopying these items. *Vox* is archived at the University of Winnipeg, and the *Manitoban* is archived in the University

of Manitoba Library. I wish to thank Dr Lois Freeman Wilson for sharing her copies of *Vox* with me and Barbara Kelcey and the University of Manitoba library staff for their assistance in photocopying Laurence's juvenilia.

2 All references to Coger in this chapter will be to her interviews in the *Margaret Laurence Review*. I wish to thank Greta M. Coger for sending me copies of her interviews.

3 Interestingly, Laurence refers to this story (which, unfortunately, does not survive) in her memoir by its fictional title, "Pillars of the Nation," rather than its actual title, "Land of Our Fathers" – an intriguing instance of fiction replacing fact for Laurence (*DE* 67).

4 Christl Verduyn discusses this name in "Cavewomen Div(in)ing for Pearls: Margaret Laurence and Marian Engel" (24–5).

5 Mildred Musgrove, whom I met at a Margaret Laurence conference at the University of Brandon in 1988, remarked to me that Laurence demonstrated talent as a writer in high-school English.

6 Elaine Ostry, in her review "In the Flush of Youth: Offerings from the Juvenilia Press," writes, "Laurence's stories – such as 'Tal des Walde' ... reveal her interest in the cultures that make up Western Canada. Juvenilia can thus serve to illustrate a writer's development" (159).

7 Laurence is identified as assistant editor of *Vox* in September 1946, in the last issue of her final year, by the name "Peggy Laurence," although she and Jack Laurence did not marry until 1947.

8 A typescript of this poem donated by Mildred Musgrove to the Margaret Laurence Home in Neepawa has the handwritten annotations "JMW" and "About 1942," suggesting that it may be the earliest surviving poem by Laurence.

9 The phrase "embryo words," which provides the title for this chapter and for the first volume of juvenilia, is from Laurence's early poem, "*Bread hath he ...,*" reprinted in *Embryo Words*, 17.

10 Laurence's typescript of "North Main Car" is in Accession 5, box 1, file 18 of the Margaret Laurence Collection in the Archives and Special Collections in the Scott Library at York University in Toronto. It was first published in *Colors of Speech* and was subsequently published in in *Prairie Fire* in 2000.

CHAPTER THREE

1 The typescript of *Heart of a Stranger* is in box 4, files 1–2, of the Margaret Laurence Archives in the Special Collections of the Mills Memorial Library at McMaster University. Sections excised from this typescript are referred to in my discussion as "unpublished" passages. I wish to thank the Laurence Estate for permission to examine and copy these materials and Librarian Carl Spadoni and the staff of the Mills Memorial Library at McMaster University for their assistance.

2 Although Woodcock mentions *Heart of a Stranger* in "Many Solitudes: The Travel Writings of Margaret Laurence," his primary focus is on her Somali travel journal, *The Prophet's Camel Bell.*

3 All references in this chapter, unless otherwise stated, will be to *Heart of a Stranger* and will be given in the text.

4 Appenzell focuses on "this recurrent relevance to the novels that is the principal interest uniting what on the surface seems a very miscellaneous grab-bag of journalistic and semi-journalistic pieces" (277), but he does not perceive their relevance to Laurence's life journey. His article, which focuses on all Laurence's published essays, including those collected in *Heart of a Stranger*, in terms of their connections with her fiction, was published in 1983, however, years before *Dance on the Earth: A Memoir*, James King's *The Life of Margaret Laurence*, or Lyall Powers' *Alien Heart: The Life and Work of Margaret Laurence* (2003) clarified the pattern of her life journey.

5 Laurence's original title for *Heart of a Stranger* was "Road from the Isles." A cancelled statement from her typescript suggests her title was at one point "A Statement of Faith," the title of an essay that was omitted from the collection. After debate with her publisher, Laurence realized that she had found the perfect title for the volume in *Heart of a Stranger*, and Jack McClelland concurred. Laurence writes to Gabrielle Roy on 23 March 1976, "I've just completed work on a collection of essays and articles, written over the years, and I think McClelland & Stewart will publish it in the fall. A good many of them are travel articles. Not deathless prose, but fairly interesting, I hope. Jack McClelland and I are having our usual amiable battle over the title ... he doesn't like my title, and I refuse to allow him to choose one, naturally. I have called it after one of the articles .. 'Where the World Began,' which refers to my world beginning in a small prairie town" [*sic*] (Socken 7).

6 "Half War, Half Peace," which corresponds, in part, with Laurence's essay "Living Dangerously ... by Mail," is in the Margaret Laurence Archives in the Scott Library at York University.

7 This essay, which Laurence presented to the Institute of Commonwealth Studies in London in 1969, the year after she published *Long Drums and Cannons*, forms, in effect, an afterword to that study. The essay, located in the Margaret Laurence Archives in the Scott Library at York University, was published for the first time in the 2001 edition of *Long Drums and Cannons*. Since the format of the typescript of this essay suggests that it was intended for publication in *Heart of a Stranger*, it was also included as an appendix to the 2003 edition.

8 Laurence explains, "I think that what helped me understand the plight of the Highland tribesmen was my study of tribal cultures in Africa,

which is kind of ironic, to think it was Africa that helped me to understand in a sense my own people. But of course the Highland Scots who fought at Culloden in 1746, that was the last tribal battle of Europe" (Sullivan 70). James King comments, "All her life, Margaret empathized with outsiders, persons who in some ways had been deprived of their birthrights. In Africa, she had identified with the Somalis and the Ghanaians. During the writing of *The Diviners*, she transferred those associations to the Métis, her use of that group offering her a way to Canadianize some of the themes of her early work" (304–5).

9 Laurence's manuscript of *A Bird in the House*, with revisions and deletions, is in the Margaret Laurence archives, box 2, files 3–13, at the Mills Memorial Library at McMaster University.

10 The "we" here refers to Margaret and Jack Laurence: their twelve-day tour of Greece in June 1964 was an attempted reconciliation.

11 Laurence recalls this legend in *The Fire-Dwellers*, when Stacey takes a course on "Ancient Greek Drama" (33). Stacey even thinks of her husband Mac as "Agamemnon, king of men" (8).

12 Laurence says, "I really knew that I didn't want to go on writing about Africa, because otherwise my writing would become that of a tourist. I had written everything I could out of that particular experience, and I very much wanted to return home in a kind of spiritual way" (Sullivan 68).

13 Ironically, a similar situation occurred when Laurence's study of Nigerian literature, *Long Drums and Cannons: Nigerian Dramatists and Novelists, 1952–1966*, was published after the Nigerian civil war had broken out, an event that undermined the relevance of her study, as she explains in her 1969 essay, "Tribalism As Us Versus Them."

14 Lyall Powers reports, "At the Easter break in 1965, Margaret took Jocelyn and David up into the Highlands of Scotland, to Jemimaville, about forty-five kilometers from Inverness on the Moray Firth, for a week with the Scots writer Jane Duncan" (247). He adds that her essay "In Pursuit of My Past on the Road from the Isles" resulted from this visit.

15 This essay was also published in *Maclean's* in October 1968. She omitted this sentence from the typescript of her introduction to the essay in *Heart of a Stranger*: "Perhaps we both, Canadians and Americans, must try to develop the sense of the tribe as *Us In Relation To Them* in which both groups' identity is respected and truly recognized by the other." She also omitted the following sentences from the typescript of the essay: "I am a Canadian nationalist in the sense that I believe profoundly that my place, my people, my land, matter. And I believe that it is our selves, Canadians, who should control our industries and our natural resources" (220).

16 In *The Fire-Dwellers*, published in 1969, the protagonist, Stacey MacAindra, views a newspaper photograph in which a Vietnamese mother tries to remove napalm from her child's face (90).

17 "Dance on the Earth," Laurence's unfinished final novel, is in files 1–6 of the 1997 accession of the Laurence archives in the Scott Library at McMaster.

18 Laurence says, "I still have a strong sense of that ancestry, but in terms of the ancestors that are knowable, my roots are in that town. And of course this comes in very strongly with Morag's experience in *The Diviners* because the same thing happens to her, although her people had come from the Highlands" (Sullivan 70).

CHAPTER FOUR

1 Unless otherwise specified, all references to Xiques will be to her introduction to *A Tree for Poverty*. References to her *Canadian Literature* essay will be indentified by *CL*.

2 Unless otherwise specified, all references to Sparrow will be to *Into Africa with Margaret Laurence*. Her essay collected in Coger's edition will be identified by *NP*.

3 Unless otherwise specified, all references to Laurence will be to *A Tree for Poverty*.

4 Laurence writes to Wiseman on 2 May 1951, "I've been mainly collecting information about Somaliland. I've also been trying to learn Somali ... a hideous task, since it must be the hardest language in existence. So far, Hersi, our interpreter, who is teaching me, and Abdi, our driver, and Mohamed, can understand what I say in Somali" (*SL* 51).

5 Laurence usually employs the spelling *gabei*, but occasionally uses the spelling *gabay*.

6 Her complete translation of Salaan Arrabey's *gabei* "To a Faithless Friend," in which each section ends with the statement, "Exceeding is the evil in such a man," is in the Laurence Archives at York University. Her literal translation, which had never before been published, and her poetic rendering, which was published in *The Somali Journal*, are printed in full in the appendix to the 2003 edition of Laurence's *Heart of a Stranger*.

CHAPTER FIVE

1 Unless otherwise stated, all references will be to Margaret Laurence, *Long Drums and Cannons: Nigerian Dramatists and Novelists, 1952–1966*, edited by Nora Foster Stovel, 2001.

2 Laurence's African library is in the Mills Memorial Library at McMaster University.

3 Laurence's typescript of *Long Drums and Cannons* is in box 2, file 1 of the Laurence Archives in the Mills Memorial Library at McMaster.

4 Laurence's original introduction to *Long Drums and Cannons* is also in the Laurence Archives in the Mills Memorial Library at McMaster University. This introduction, which was not published in the original 1968 edition, is quoted in my introduction to the 2001 edition.

5 The full epigraph is: "I have visited the prodigal ... / in palm grove, / long drums and cannons: / the spirit in the ascent" – the last four lines from Part IV, "Lustra," poem ii, of "Heavensgate" (31) by Christopher Okigbo.

6 These are the words that Achebe quotes with special commendation in *Morning Yet on Creation Day*. He comments, "The Canadian novelist and critic, Margaret Laurence, saw this happening already in the way many African writers are interpreting their world" (18). He continues, "And in the epilogue to the book, she makes the same point even more strongly: 'No writer of any quality has viewed the old Africa in an idealized way, but they have tried to regain what is rightfully theirs – a past composed of real and vulnerable people, their ancestors, not the figments of missionary and colonialist imaginations'" (18).

CHAPTER SIX

1 *The Prophet's Camel Bell* (11, my emphasis). Unless otherwise indicated, all references in this chapter will be to this text. *The Prophet's Camel Bell* was published by Knopf as *New Wind in a Dry Land* on 15 June 1964, the same day Knopf published *This Side Jordan* and *The Tomorrow-Tamer and Other Stories* in an unprecedented publishing maneouvre.

2 G.D. Killam's 1976 introduction to *This Side Jordan*, ix–x. All references to Killam in this chapter will be to this preface.

3 Laurence writes to Wiseman on 17 August 1963, "It had a lovely review on the BBC Somali service – written by the guy who took the pictures, some bias might have crept in!" (*SL* 165), and, on 20 September 1963, "The Somaliland book, as I anticipated, has had very few reviews. A few good ones in the Telegraph, Guardian, etc. But damn few" (*SL* 168).

4 Laurence's letter, written from Elm Cottage and dated 23 January 1964, is in the Ethel Wilson archives at the University of British Columbia.

5 Some of the photographs included in *The Prophet's Camel Bell* were taken by Laurence and others by the former information officer for the Somaliland Protectorate. Ironically, although Laurence deplores the image of Africa as a blank continent, the map she includes in the frontispiece of the text seems to endorse that view.

6 Laurence recalls, "I wrote the first draft of *This Side Jordan* when we were living in Ghana, or what was to become Ghana, and then I finished it when we came back to B.C." (Sullivan 61).

7 Laurence writes in her précis of *This Side Jordan*, "Johnnie, out of a desire to hurt as well as a long-hidden curiosity, violates a young African girl, only to discover at last, through her, their common humanity." "This Side Jordan," Laurence's précis, "SJ,"is at McMaster.

8 To be fair, I should add that this review concludes with faint praise: "The novel is well written and gives a convincing picture of Accra and the Ghanaian background" (New 102).

9 Kwame Nkrumah (1909–72) became the first prime minister of Ghana on 6 March 1957 when the Gold Coast became the first sub-Saharan African nation to win independence. A 1960 plebiscite made Ghana a republic and elected Nkrumah as president (Appiah 487).

10 Dobbs may well be the writer to whom Laurence refers in *Dance on the Earth*, where she credits a reviewer who objected to the birth scene in *This Side Jordan* with inspiring her "self-liberation in the area of writing" because "after that I never hesitated to write about birth, and I never did so again except from the viewpoint of the mother" (*DE* 6).

11 W.J. Keith notes that this story is not included in standard Laurence bibliographies and has not been discussed by critics, in spite of its significance. He observes that "one of its chief claims to interest, indeed, lies in the fact that it is set in Somaliland and thus provides an interesting link between the non-fiction material later written up in *The Prophet's Camel Bell* and the African stories that grew out of her Gold Coast (Ghana) experiences" (203). "Uncertain Flowering" was published by *Story: The Magazine of the Short Story in Book Form* 4 (1953): 9–34. Laurence writes to Wiseman on 6 May 1960, "I want to do about 12 stories set in West Africa. I've got 7 done" (*SL*115).

12 "The Rain Child" was first published by Macmillan in *Winter's Tales* 8 (1962): 105–42. Asha/Ayesha recalls Rider Haggard's Ayesha, pronounced Assha, in *She* (1887) – Carl Jung's example of the *anima* (*The Oxford Companion to English Literature* 426) – and *Aissa Saved* (1932) by Joyce Cary.

13 "The Drummer of All the World" was published in *The Queen's Quarterly* 63 (Winter 1956): 487–504. The editor was Malcolm Ross, Laurence's teacher at United College, and later editor-in-chief of the New Canadian Library. Laurence refers to this story as her first published story (*DE* 157), although the first story she published was "Uncertain Flowering."

14 "The Perfume Sea" was published in *Winter's Tales* 6 (1960): 83–120. "The Exiles," an abridged version, appeared in the *Saturday Evening Post*, 3 June 1961, 28–9 (*SL* 127n).

15 "The Merchant of Heaven" was published in *Prism International* 1, no. 1 (September 1959): 52–74.

16 "The Tomorrow-Tamer" was published in *Prism International*, 3, no. 1

(Fall 1961): 36–54. Laurence reveals the origins of this story in her "Author's Commentary": "The Tomorrow-Tamer began in my mind when I was living in Ghana, where my husband was an engineer working on a new harbour there. One weekend we went to see a bridge which was being constructed across the Volta River. ... I talked with a bridgeworker. ... The next week I heard that he had been killed – he'd fallen from the top of the bridge" (71). She adds, "I began to think of what it would be like, for a village in West Africa, to have a bridge flung across their river, a river which was sacred and which had an indwelling spirit" (72).

17 "The Spell of the Distant Drum," an abridgement of "The Voices of Adamo," was first published in the *Saturday Evening Post* on 5 May 1962, 24–5 (*SL* 130n).

18 "Godman's Master" was first published in *Prism International* 1, no. 3 (Spring 1960): 46–64. On 6 May 1960, Laurence writes to Wiseman, "I had another story in 'Prism,' entitled 'Godman's Master,' a story about a dwarf who was being used as an oracle by a fetish priest and who was freed by a young pharmacist, who then found that he could not get rid of the grateful and also helpless dwarf" (*SL* 115).

19 "A Gourdful of Glory" was published in *Tamarack Review* 17 (Autumn 1960): 5–20.

20 "Mask of Beaten Gold" was published in *Tamarack Review* 26 (Winter 1963): 3–21. In her "Letter to Bob Sorfleet," Laurence explains: "'Mask of Beaten Gold' has an odd history. When I was compiling my West African stories for the collection *The Tomorrow-Tamer*, I think that 'Mask ...' must have been with *Tamarack Review*, which ultimately published it. I can't think how it was that I didn't have another copy. In any event, unbelievable though this sounds, I forgot about it and hence it is not included in the collection!" She adds, "I'm not sorry, really – it was, I believe, the last story I wrote out of West Africa, when we were back in Canada and living in Vancouver, and it now seems to me to be a bit attenuated and strained" (52).

21 Donez Xiques states, in *Margaret Laurence: The Making of a Writer*, "Her abilities as a writer were challenged and rewarded during her years in Africa, which required of her both an immersion in a culture remarkably different from that of Canada, as well as a kind of detachment that involved both taking up and working from viewpoints not her own" (311).

CHAPTER SEVEN

1 Joan Coldwell states in *The Oxford Companion to Canadian Literature*, 2nd ed. (1997), "Laurence's greatest achievement lies in the four Canadian novels dominated by the town of Manawaka" (634).

2 Unless otherwise stated, all parenthetical references will be to *Heart of a Stranger*. This passage is read aloud as background narration to *First Lady of Manawka* to excellent effect.

3 Laurence explained the location of her first Manawaka novel, *The Stone Angel*, to Alfred Knopf in this way: "Manawaka is meant to be located somewhere in southern Manitoba, like the town of Neepawa, where I grew up" (King 189).

4 Fraiberg's 1959 study appeared when Laurence was raising young children. The book was popular through the sixties and early seventies when Laurence was composing her Manawaka Cycle and *Heart of a Stranger* essays, including "A Place to Stand On."

5 A former mayor of Neepawa, and a contemporary of Margaret Laurence, recalls that Peggy Wemyss and her friends used to repair to the Riverside Cemetery for privacy.

6 Interestingly, this publication names the mayor of Neepawa, 1926–27, as a "Mr. Stonhouse" [*sic*], a surname that Laurence adapts for Hagar's Aunt Dolly Stonehouse in *The Stone Angel*.

7 Laurence includes various denominations in her Manawaka fiction. For a fuller discussion of this topic, see my article, "Temples and Tabernacles: Churches in the Fictional Microcosms of Robertson Davies, Margaret Laurence and Alice Munro."

8 Laurence confesses to the temptation to "devilize" (10) her Grandfather Simpson in *Dance on the Earth: A Memoir*.

CHAPTER EIGHT

1 This conference was convened at the University of Calgary in 1982. Laurence topped "List A," heading the best 100 books, and she book-ended "List B," framing the top ten Canadian novels, with *The Stone Angel* as number one and *The Diviners* as number ten. See Charles Steele's *Taking Stock: The Calgary Conference on the Canadian Novel* (150).

2 Laurence's 5 September 1961 letter is quoted by Adele Wiseman in her afterword to the NCL edition of *The Stone Angel*. Unless otherwise stated, all references in this chapter will be to this edition of *The Stone Angel*, and all letters quoted will be taken from the afterword.

   In a 29 June 1963 letter to Jack McClelland, Laurence writes, "Personally, I think she is a hell of an old lady! Of course, I may be prejudiced. Anyway, for better or worse, the voice in which she speaks is all her own, and I think now that I can't ever again be content to write in anything except this idiom, which is of course mine" (King 184).

3 In "A Feminist Reading of 'The Stone Angel,'" Constance Rooke states, "If Hagar is Everywoman, she is apparently a woman on trial for her crimes against men" (27).

4 Laurence explains, "With The Stone Angel, [*sic*] which was about a woman in her nineties, I experienced the terrific pleasure of writing in my own idiom, or rather the idiom of my grandparents. Phrases kept coming back – phrases I thought I'd forgotten – my grandparents' way of expressing things" ("Geography" 2).

5 Several critics, beginning with William New and Sandra Djwa, have pursued this biblical parallel. New parallels *The Stone Angel* with Paul's discussion of Hagar in Galatians 4:22–27 in his introduction to the 1968 NCL edition (viii), and Djwa says the novel "moves through the Genesis account of Abram (Bram) and Hagar into the New Testament allegory of the covenant of grace as opposed to the covenant of the law" (47). Patricia Koster debates "Hagar's identification of herself as Egyptian" (41) in "Hagar 'The Egyptian': Allusions and Illusions in 'The Stone Angel.'"

6 Hagar has been compared to King Lear by S.E. Read, who states, in "The Maze of Life: The Work of Margaret Laurence," that "Hagar is a Lear-like figure" (51); by John Baxter, in "The Stone Angel: Shakespearian Bearings" in *The Compass: A Provincial Review* 1 (1977): 3–19; and by G.D. Killam, who writes, in "Notes on Symbolism in The Stone Angel" [*sic*], "Associations between the two texts proliferate and adumbrate their meaning" (94).

7 Laurence explains, "I'd say it was spiritual pride, using it in the Christian sense of the seven deadly sins, [and] social pride, keeping a sense of one's dignity" (Fabre 194).

8 Tennessee Williams employed these lines as epigraph for his play *Cat on a Hot Tin Roof* in 1954, a decade before *The Stone Angel*, to suggest Big Daddy's rage for life in the face of death. At one point Laurence suggested "Rage Against the Dying" as the title for her novel.

9 Laurence says, "I never knew anyone like Hagar. I had to start my Canadian work with the generation that shaped me. My grandfather Simpson was the only person of that age I ever knew. ... I thought I knew him all too well at times. I didn't appreciate him very much when I was young. But I think A Stone Angel and A Bird in the House [*sic*] helped me to come to terms with him" (Miner 19). She says, "I do not want to be an authoritarian figure as he was, but I recognize that, like Hagar, there is a good deal of the matriarch in me" (Cameron 99). Cameron comments, "She hated her grandfather, a stern old autocrat much like a male Hagar Shipley, but in writing the Vanessa McLeod [*sic*] stories in A Bird in The House [*sic*] she grasped that she was in some ways frighteningly like him" (Cameron 4). John Simpson lived, albeit in his dotage, to the ripe old age of 96, dying in 1953, a few years before his daughter Margaret Wemyss, who put up with his autocratic temperament all her life (*DE* 109).

10 The typescript of the novel at McMaster shows that, in fact, Laurence

emended that first sentence more than once. Walter Swayze claims, in "Margaret Laurence: Novelist-as-Poet," that the opening of *The Stone Angel* reads like poetry (5).

11 Clara Thomas writes, "The stone angel – the novel's over-arching, dominating symbol and, rapidly, our symbol for Hagar herself – is woven into a culture pattern that is entirely authentic, Protestant, nineteenth-century, and English Canadian" ("Novels" 156).

12 Natives of Laurence's hometown consider that Laurence modeled her stone angel on the Davidson memorial in Neepawa's Riverside Cemetery, but Laurence insisted that her angel was inspired by Genoa's Staglieno cemetery, "where marble angels loomed like spirits of vengeance" (*PCB* 6), in the view of the author, who visited Genoa en route to Africa in 1950.

13 Etruscan sarcophagi portray a tomb's inhabitant reclining on a couch, sitting up with a look of pleased surprise and stretching out a hand on whose palm lies an egg, symbol of rebirth.

14 George Woodcock states, "Hagar shares the obstinate, arrogant disposition of Jason Currie and even his attitudes to life. Pride is the besetting sin of both of them" (51). Diana Brydon states, in "Silence, Voice and the Mirror: Margaret Laurence and Women," "Refusing the self-censorship that is the traditional role assigned to women, [Hagar] speaks without thinking, just like a man. She proudly models herself on her father ... Although she tries, she can never be his inheritor, his replica; she can only be his property" (191). These masculine traits that Hagar emulates result in her garrison mentality. Constance Rooke claims, in "Fear of the Open Heart," "'The mistrust of pity, the contempt for weakness, the fear of the open heart' is very precisely Hagar's problem in *The Stone Angel*" (261).

15 Laurence notes, "much of the rather rigid Scots Presbyterian quality was instilled in her in childhood" (Fabre 195). Hagar's pride resulted from "both her upbringing and something she had inherited from her father, who was an authoritarian, proud, stiff-necked man. And even though she detested her father there was a great deal of his character in her" (Fabre 194). The Currie plaid pin and the Tonnerre hunting knife reunite in *The Diviners* (472–4).

16 Evelyn Hinz calls this relationship a modern version of Freud's "Electra Complex" (18).

17 As Thomas notes, "The word 'pharaoh' carries overtones of pride of power, enslavement, death-obsession, and incestuous sexuality" ("Novels" 156).

18 This motto from the Song of Solomon 2:4 suggests the combination of spiritual and sensual love. The motto is blazoned above the office of the Neepawa newspaper, titled *The Banner*, where Laurence worked during the summer when she was in high school.

19 The name Dolly Stonehouse is interesting, suggesting both a doll and a prison house. One G.V. Stonhouse [*sic*] served as mayor of Neepawa, 1926–27.

20 George Woodcock writes, "To this passion for the earth and its emanations in sensation and memory, Hagar adds the choler of her appropriate humour" ("Elements" 57).

21 Birk Sproxton pursues this point in his essay, "The Figure of the Unknown Soldier: Home and War in *The Fire-Dwellers*."

22 Hinz emphasizes the religious roots of *The Stone Angel*, noting the Christian connotations of Jason Currie's initials (18) and the portrayal of Hagar as the "Sorrowful Mother" (22).

23 As Constance Rooke states, "Writing is always an act directed against death" (32).

24 Laurence writes, "A first-person narrative can be limiting, of course, but in this case it provided an opportunity to reveal to the reader more of Hagar than she knew about herself, as her judgments about everything are so plainly and strongly biased" (GG 82).

25 Laurence explains, "Hagar's memories are chronological … I chose to have the time past recreated chronologically … [with] each of her long memory sequences triggered off by some occurrence in her present story" (Fabre 205). She admits, "The flashback method is, I think, a little overworked in it, and I am not at all sure that flashbacks ought to be in chronological order" (TYS 20), and "I feel now that the novel is probably too orderly" (GG 83).

26 I discuss these parallels between Laurence's *Stone Angel* and D.H. Lawrence's *Sons and Lovers* more fully in my article, "Lawrencean Legacy: D.H. Lawrence's *Sons and Lovers* and Margaret Laurence's *Stone Angel*." Hagar deprives John of a father at the age when Margaret Laurence lost her own father and at the age of her own children when she separated from their father, as she observes in her memoir, *Dance on the Earth*.

27 She also quotes the lines, "Old Meg was brave as Margaret Queen / And tall as Amazon" (163) – lines that doubtless amused the author, whose Christian name was Margaret. Joan Coldwell pursues the parallels between Hagar and Keats's Meg in "Hagar as Meg Merrilies, The Homeless Gipsy."

28 Eleanor Johnston pursues the parallels between Hagar and Coleridge's "Ancient Mariner" in "The Quest of *The Diviners*."

29 Laurence says, "That old cannery [in Point Roberts, south of Vancouver] was the actual model for the one in the book" (Cameron 3). "Shadow Point" may be based on "Grey Point" outside Vancouver. Clara Thomas discusses the sacramental symbolism in this scene.

30 Atwood summarizes Hagar's guilt: "when Hagar discovers his love affair

and tortures him with her disapproval and moral rigidity, he gets himself killed in an accident" (*Survival* 136).

31 Margaret Laurence's ashes are buried beneath a stone in Neepawa's Riverside Cemetery that reads "Wemyss" on one side and "Laurence" on the other, like the Currie-Shipley stone.

32 Laurence frequently quotes the first line of the "Old Hundredth" in Convocation addresses. She concludes her "Statement of Faith" thus: "If we have been given any commandment, as I believe we have, then surely it must mean that we pray and work and speak out for peace, and for human and caring justice for all people that on earth do dwell" (60). Laurence requested "All people that on earth do dwell" and "Unto the hills" for her memorial service.

33 Christian Riegel discusses "Hagar's Work of Mourning" in *Writing Grief: Margaret Laurence and the Work of Mourning*, 21–44.

34 Laurence's stepmother, Marg, gave Margaret her biological mother Verna's engagement ring when she and Jack became engaged.

35 Laurence alludes to Genesis 32:26, in which Jacob wrestles with the angel and says, "I will not let thee go, except thou bless me."

36 Laurence explains, "Hagar does only begin to become free when she releases her willful control over her dead family and her living son and daughter-in-law" (Fabre 195). She says, "Hagar does do those two free acts. She gives the bedpan to the young girl and tells Marvin that she loves him" (Miner 19). Earlier, Hagar identifies herself to Lees in relation to Marvin: "Marvin Shipley, my son. I'm Hagar Shipley" (221).

37 Laurence defined the theme of her work as "survival," but later, in "A Place to Stand On," she refined the theme of survival as "not just physical survival but the preservation of some human dignity and in the end some human warmth and ability to reach out and touch others" (*HS* 8). In 1971, Laurence said, "The theme of [*The Stone Angel*] is freedom" (Cameron 98), but in 1981 she defined it as "survival of the spirit with some ability to give and receive love. ... there is the sense of a possibility of a kind of redemption" (Fabre 193).

38 Laurence explains the apparent paradox: "This, even as she dies, is an example of a kind of spiritual pride. At the same time water also suggests a sense of redemption in her life ... She is still in character" (Fabre 202). Woodcock writes, "We are not told, but perhaps we can surmise that her snatching of the cup of water in her last moment is a symbol of her release from the agony of memory into the greater peace beyond life" (7). Barbara Pell concludes, "[Hagar] is finally redeemed through sacrificial love accompanied by Christian images of baptism, redemption, and grace, as the stone angel becomes real. In her final experience of love, joy, and freedom, she holds in her hands, perhaps, the cup of salvation" (34).

CHAPTER NINE

1 Margaret Laurence's cousin, Catherine Simpson Milne, believed Laurence exploited her situation. She had been a spinster schoolteacher living with her hypochondriac mother, Bertha, above the mortuary in Neepawa, following the death in 1935 of her father, mortician Stuart Simpson, Margaret's uncle, before she moved with her mother to British Columbia, where she later married (King 211).

2 G.D. Killam writes in his introduction to the 1966 NCL edition of *The Fire-Dwellers*, "the principal characters in the Canadian novels ... live in almost total isolation from the world around them, unable to give expression to their most profound desires and concerns" (np).

3 Laurence, after destroying many drafts, gave up writing *The Fire-Dwellers* in 1963 and began writing *A Jest of God*, later returning to Stacey's story in 1965. Laurence writes to Adele Wiseman on 31 December 1964, "I don't remember when I first met her but I think it must have been about six years ago. Now I know so much about her that the whole thing seems impossible" (*SL* 191).

4 "Only connect," the epigraph to E.M. Forster's novel *Howard's End*, could serve as the epigraph to most of Laurence's novels also. In *Mother and Daughter Relationships in the Manawaka Works of Margaret Laurence*, Helen Buss writes, "these two women are sisters because they are two sides of the same problem. Rachel is woman yearning for a feminine definition of her instinctive, emotional self in a context that allows for a religion of ecstasy. Stacey is woman desperate for a social context in which she can raise her children inside articulated feminine-maternal values" (53).

5 *A Jest of God* (7). Further references will be to this edition and will be cited in the text.

6 *The Fire-Dwellers* (7). Further references will be to this edition and will be cited in the text. The typescript of *The Fire-Dwellers* at McMaster shows that Laurence intended the ladybird rhyme to form a second epigraph to the novel, following the quotation from Sandburg's "Losers."

7 The final stanza of Sandburg's "Losers" suggests his version of "good losers," or tragic heroes:

> I could ask people to throw ashes on their heads
> In the name of that sergeant at Belleau Woods
> Walking into the drumfires, calling his men,
> "Come on, you ... Do you want to live forever?" (87)

8 Although there are numerous articles on each of these novels, Coral Ann

Howells is one of the first critics to explore their connections in "Weaving Fabrications: Women's Narratives in *A Jest of God* and *The Fire-Dwellers*," in which she examines "the breathing space" (93) that Laurence's fictional forms allow her female narrators. My essay, originally written for the Margaret Laurence memorial conference at the University of Brandon in 1988, predates all other comparisons.

9 Patricia Morley responds to Robert Harlow: "Harlow misses the multiple voices of Rachel, who thinks and voices a very complex self … The first-person point of view subsumes the many voices of Rachel, while the larger fictional form contains an ironic, implicit commentary through event, image, juxtaposition, and the reactions of the other characters" (90).

10 George Bowering says, "The form of the novel, first person and present tense, works as Rachel's opening-out does, to get naked" (211). Laurence writes, in a 31 December 1964 letter to Wiseman, "I know the character is there … but the problem of method continues to bug me" (*SL* 190). In "Gadgetry and Growing: Form and Voice in the Novel," Laurence says of *A Jest of God*: "I tried again and again to begin the novel in the third person, and it simply would not write itself that way … the character of Rachel would not reveal herself. So finally I gave up and stopped struggling. I began to write the novel as I really must have very intensely wanted to write it – in the first person, through Rachel's eyes. I knew that this meant the focus of the book was narrow – but so was Rachel's life" (84–5). Laurence says in a 17 August 1965 letter to Wiseman, "I can't help the way it turned out. I didn't know it would end like that, but it did" (*SL* 201). She calls the novel a "tour-de-force" (*SL* 201) and Rachel an "anachronism" (*SL* 202). Laurence wrote to Wiseman on 6 September 1965, "The parallel … is with Rachel (and the woman's name is Rachel) who for so long mourned for her children because they were not" (*SL* 204).

11 The title of the film, *Rachel, Rachel*, echoes the game of Blind Man's Bluff, where the seeker calls out, "Rachel, Rachel," and the hider responds, "Jacob, Jacob," recalling the biblical couple. Originally, the film was to be titled *Now I Lay Me Down*, and Laurence was relieved about the change of title, although Panther had already printed paperbacks with the original title (King 259).

12 In his interview with Laurence, Robert Kroetsch, in response to her remark, "one in a sense, divides oneself," mentions "the *döppelganger* thing" (46), which he says applies to both of them.

13 Mathew Martin in "Dramas of Desire in Margaret Laurence's *A Jest of God, The Fire-Dwellers,* and *The Diviners*," applies a Freudian Oedipal reading to Laurence's three Manawaka novels. This essay, a revised version of his term paper in my 1994 graduate seminar on Margaret Laurence, pursues my theory that the subtext of Rachel's arrested

development is her obsession with her father, whose death has curtailed her sexual development, as her sexuality has died with him. Until she seeks him in his kingdom of death, she cannot lay his ghost to rest and come to life.

14 In "The Eulalias of Spinsters and Undertakers," Aritha van Herk unites Rachel's religious glossalalia with her orgasmic eulalia: "*A Jest of God* undertakes to unearth Rachel's eulalia, long-buried: her glossalalia that cries out to God/father/lover/mortician for hearing" (134).

15 See Genesis 29-30 and Jeremiah 31. In a 6 September 1965 letter to Adele Wiseman, Laurence clarifies the intentionality of the biblical reference: "The parallel ... is with Rachel ... who for so long mourned for her children because they were not" (*SL* 204). These issues are developed further in my reader's guide, *Rachel's Children: Margaret Laurence's* A Jest of God.

16 The typescript of *A Jest of God* shows Laurence excised several passages, including Rachel's thoughts when the congregation of the Tabernacle sings a hymn – "The heavenly child in stature grows, / And, growing, learns to die; / And still his early training shows / His coming agony" – that makes her wonder how James Doherty may be scarred by Willard Siddley's beating.

17 In "Margaret Laurence's Dark Lovers: Sexual Metaphor and the Movement Toward Individualization, Hierogamy and Mythic Narrative in Four Manawaka Books," Buss writes: "Throughout the Manawaka novels of Margaret Laurence, a series of 'dark' lovers, men who come from socially disapproved or emotionally disadvantaged backgrounds, manifest a profound influence in the lives of Laurence's heroines. Bram Shipley, Nick Kazlik, Buckle Fennick, Luke Venturi and Jules Tonnerre present a developing motif of what Jungians would call 'the Shadow-Brute' or 'the animus' or what Rachel Cameron calls the 'Shadow Prince.' In every case they touch some unconscious element in the heroine, and the sexual experiences the women share with these lovers are the agency of this 'touching'" (98).

18 Elizabeth Waterston, in "Double Is Trouble: Twins in *A Jest of God*," explores Laurence's use of "the twin-motif" in the novel, claiming that "Nick is Rachel's double" (83).

19 Stacey makes a similar remark to Mac about Buckle Fennick's death: "You're not God. You couldn't save him" (240). Laurence remarks in her interview with Donald Cameron that, as a novelist, you must "realize that you are *not* God" (104).

20 Jill Franks comments, "Although Rachel and Stacey do not engage in specifically feminist activity ... they do exhibit a budding feminist consciousness that is easy to overlook when a 1990s reader focuses on their enmeshment in patriarchal domestic arrangements and mindsets"

(99–100). Christl Verduyn observes, "*The Fire-Dwellers* contains a sub-text illustrating three themes which dominate contemporary feminist critical thinking: language, body and identity" (128).

21 Laurence complains, in her interview with Graeme Gibson, "some of my work, particularly *The Fire-Dwellers*, received some real put-downs from a number of male reviewers. They didn't even say it was a bad novel; it was just that, if anybody like Stacey existed, they just would rather not know" (200).

22 In "The Narratee as Confessor in Margaret Laurence's *The Fire-Dwellers*," Brenda Beckman-Long addresses "Laurence's use of the confessional genre in a polyphonic novel to explore female subjectivity and to construct a narrative of self-transformation" (113). She argues that "*The Fire-Dwellers* is structured by a series of narratees, including God, Stacey herself, and several character-narratees, who serve as confessors to move the female protagonist from isolation to engagement and self-perception" (114–15). Lois Wilson notes in her essay "Faith and the Vocation of the Author" that Laurence often said, "Thank you, God, sir or madam" (154).

23 On a page accompanying her typescript of *The Fire-Dwellers* at McMaster, Laurence specifies the form of the novel: "Narrative Third Person – typed straight; Stacey's Thoughts – typed straight with hyphen; Fantasies and dreams – Italics; paragraphed to begin; Conversation – No quote marks; Radio & TV – capital letters, no paragraphing; Stacey's memories – 14 spaced indented. Her speech typed plain, others' speech in italics. Songs, hymns etc – Placed mid-page, italics."

24 Laurence attended Expo 67, and it influenced her in writing *The Fire-Dwellers*. Laurence even considered writing the novel in parallel columns, depicting Stacey's interior and exterior life.

25 Lyall Powers claims "Communication, its importance and its difficulty, is perhaps the main theme of *A Jest of God*" (*AH* 249). Laurence told Donald Cameron, "I feel that human beings ought to be able, *ought* to be able to communicate and touch each other far more than they do, and this human loneliness and isolation, which obviously occurs everywhere, seems to me to be part of man's tragedy" (105). See C.M. McLay's "Every Man Is an Island: Isolation in *A Jest of God*."

26 Laurence defends the dual narrative method of *The Fire-Dwellers*: "I did not want to write a novel entirely in the first person, but I did not want to write one entirely in the third person, either. The inner and outer aspects of Stacey's life were so much at variance that it was essential to have her inner commentary in order to point up the frequent contrasts between what she was thinking and what she was saying" (GG 86).

27 As Diana Brydon says of Laurence's Manawaka heroines, in "Silence, Voice and the Mirror: Margaret Laurence and Women," "each of these

women has her own special relationship with the mirror which underlines visually the dichotomy between role and real definitions of the self" (187). She adds, "For all Laurence women, the relationship with the mirror is an ambivalent one. Their reflection in the mirror confirms their reality while reminding them that the image in the mirror fails to match their ideal selves. The mirror provides confirmation of selfhood and scope for self-flagellation" (198).

28 In a typewritten page accompanying the typescript of *The Fire-Dwellers* at McMaster, headed "Revisions: Summary of what has been changed," dated "July 68," Laurence writes about "Luke's science fiction story": "I have cut this part drastically, reducing Luke's story from seven pages to one page and adding a little which may reveal slightly more of Luke than the SF plot did."

29 In *Mother and Daughter Relationships in the Manawaka Works of Margaret Laurence*, Helen Buss relates Rachel's affair with Nick Kazlik to the Demeter-Kore myth: "It is not accidental that much of the imagery that surrounds their affair reminds us of the Demeter-Kore myth; May – even her name is symbolic of the earth goddess – and Rachel live above the land of death, reached by a staircase of flowers (p. 145); Nick's Slavic appearance (p. 78) makes him seem to her a menacing figure, almost an abductor; they first make love near the graveyard where once Rachel picked the spring Crocuses, like Kore in her spring field" (43).

30 Lyall Powers comments, "The colloquy with Hector Jonas is actually a microscopic expression of the myth of death and rebirth as it informs much of the structure of the whole novel, a pattern of departure (or descent) initiation and return (or resurrection). Just as Rachel has descended the stairs to Hector's realm, so at the end of the colloquy she ascends the stairs to enter – however slowly – into a new life of liberation, self-reliance, and responsible maturity" (*AH* 256).

31 Laurence explains this phrase in her final journal found in box 7 of the Laurence Archives at McMaster University's Mills Memorial Library: humans have God to pity them, but God has only himself. George Bowering concludes "That Fool of a Fear" eloquently: "God's jests are not just vocal – the word is made flesh, i.e. the eternal present. It is in understanding this that Margaret Laurence chose wisely to write in the present tense, to present the fool made wise by folly" (225).

32 Margaret Atwood concludes her Afterword to the 1988 edition of *A Jest of God* thus: "What Rachel can offer us now as readers is something we still need to know: how to acknowledge our own human and necessary limitations, our own foolishness. How to say both No, and Yes" (215).

33 A latter-day Hedda Gabler, Laurence says of her problems with *The Fire-Dwellers*, "I even once burned, dramatically, nearly a hundred pages of a second draft, and then sat down at my typewriter and wrote a deeply

gloomy letter to a friend, which began, "I am a firebug" (GG 87). In a 20 January 1979 letter to Adele Wiseman, Laurence writes, "Once I burned 100 pp of manuscript when I got off to a false start with The Fire-Dwellers. I then realized I had to write A Jest of God first [*sic*]" (*SL* 354). In "Gadgetry or Growing," Laurence identifies two "interlocking themes" in *The Fire-Dwellers*: "the sense of anguish and fear which Stacey feels in bringing up her kids in a world on fire and also the question of a middle-aged woman having to accept middle age and learn how to cope with the essential fact of life, which is that the process of life is irreversible" (87).

34 The reference is to William Styron's 1979 novel *Sophie's Choice*. These points are developed further in my reader's guide, *Stacey's Choice: Margaret Laurence's* The Fire-Dwellers.

35 Alan Bevan discusses the "fire-hell symbol hunt" in his introduction to *The Fire-Dwellers* (xi): "The pervading image of fire, in many forms, is usually related to Stacey's state of mind" (xi).

36 Nancy Bailey, in "Identity in *The Fire-Dwellers*," gives a Jungian interpretation of Luke as "the internal self of the protagonist, as the animus" (116). Sharon Nancekevill, in "*The Fire-Dwellers*: Circles of Fire," employs the cosmogonic cycle of Joseph Campbell's *The Hero with a Thousand Faces* to trace Stacey's progress through this monomythic journey to self-knowledge: separation, initiation, and return. She concludes, "the heroine's quest leads to rediscovery of her inherent strength and recognition of her ability to cope with a world on fire by placing herself and that world in proper perspective" (170). Laurence refers to this myth in alluding to *Jason's Quest* as "a frivolous retelling of the 'heroic monomyth: Departure – Initiation – Return" (King 253). Lyall Powers, in "Stacey Cameron MacAindra: The Fire *This* Time," comments, "Luke manages, by coincidence and a kind of magic, to contribute to her *anagnorisis*: he leads her to confront herself and the nature of her fears and thus to her self-acceptance" (31).

37 In her memoir, Laurence recalls a similar incident when her husband, Jack Laurence, rescued her and their infant daughter, Jocelyn, on the shore of the Gold Coast (*DE* 143–4).

38 For a fuller discussion of these parallels, see my article, "Female Excalibur as Literary Legacy: Ethel Wilson's *Swamp Angel* and Margaret Laurence's *The Fire-Dwellers*."

39 Debra Dudek, in "Poetic Redress: Her Body, Her House in *The Fire-Dwellers*," concludes that Stacey "redresses her self in a poetics of dance and a multiplicity of voice" (188): "Though Stacey writes herself as heroine, she 'ends' her story in suspension between death and dancing" (187). Mitzi Hamovitch, in "The Subversive Voice in *The Fire-Dwellers*," concludes, "Laurence's protagonist in *The Fire-Dwellers* is an early instance

of a feminine subversive voice asserting itself in a patriarchal society" (*NP* 176).

40 Rudyard Kipling's 1896 poem "The Ladies" employs the refrain, "For the Colonel's Lady an' Judy O'Grady / Are sisters under their skins!" (410).

CHAPTER TEN

1 As Laurence writes in "Time and the Narrative Voice," "The narrative voice had to be that of an older Vanessa, but at the same time the narration had to be done in such a way that the ten-year-old would be conveyed. The narrative voice, therefore, had to speak as though from two points in time, simultaneously" (New 158–9).

2 Helen Buss examines the "identity theme" in "Margaret Laurence and the Autobiographical Impulse." Peter Easingwood explores it further in his essay, "Semi-autobiographical Fiction and Revisionary Realism in *A Bird in the House*." Lyall Powers says, "Margaret Laurence frequently admitted that *A Bird in the House* is quite heavily autobiographical" (15).

3 Laurence's responses to her Knopf editor Judith Jones are in "Revisions and Disagreements," box 2, file 2 of the Laurence Archives in the Special Collections at McMaster University. Jones wanted Laurence to revise the stories as chapters of a novel. She disliked the "overlapping of the stories" that Laurence repeatedly defends. James King discusses their disagreement on pages 268–70.

4 Unless otherwise stated, all references in this chapter will be to the 1970 published text of *A Bird in the House*. "The Sound of the Singing" was originally published in 1963 in *Winter's Tale* 9. In the revised version of the story in *A Bird in the House*, Laurence rewrote the first paragraph, excised a paragraph about Grandfather Connor, and added a suggestive sentence – "And what's more, for all you're always saying Vanessa takes after Ewen, you know who she really takes after" (41) – a sentence that may inspire Vanessa's decision to follow her Uncle Dan at the end of the story. Laurence also changed the name of Vanessa's father from Henry to Ewen and the family name Gunn (which she uses in *The Diviners*) to MacLeod when she revised the manuscript.

5 "To Set Our House in Order" was first published in *Argosy* in 1963 and the *Ladies' Home Journal* 81, no. 2, in March 1964 – with the subtitle, "A world of mystery was opening up, and I was afraid it might be too much for me" – and collected in *Modern Canadian Stories* in 1967. The title of this story, drawn from the Old Testament, where the prophet Isaiah reports Jehovah has warned, "Set thine house in order: for thou shalt die, and not live" (Isaiah 38:1), suggests impending death.

6 These travel books are modelled on the books that Robert Wemyss had in his study, just as the grandfather's ability to read texts in ancient Greek is

based on Laurence's Grandfather Wemyss. Powers says Laurence added "some 500 words to 'To Set Our House in Order' to strengthen the depiction of Vanessa's father ..." (328). As Laurence explains in "Time and the Narrative Voice," "her father passes on to her some actual sense of her grandparents – the adamant Grandmother MacLeod, whose need it has been to appear a lady in her own image of herself; the dead Grandfather MacLeod, who momentarily lives for his granddaughter when she sees for the first time the loneliness of a man who could read the Greek tragedies in their original language and who never knew anyone in the small prairie town with whom he could communicate" (New 159).

7   "The Mask of the Bear" was first published in *Chatelaine* in June 1964 and in *Winter's Tales* 11 in 1966. In her notes on revisions, Laurence writes, regarding the ending of this story, "I think this ending *must* stay, unless the titles are not used – otherwise, the title, Mask of the Bear, does not mean anything. I also think that this ending *belongs* & does not anticipate any other story – the ambiguity which is felt towards Grandfather by Vanessa *must*, I think, be apparent throughout."

8   "A Bird in the House" was first published in the *Atlantic Advocate* and *Winter's Tales from Canada*. In her "Revisions and Disagreements," Laurence notes, "re: ending of A Bird in the House – I think this ending should remain, as it pinpoints what Ewen meant, those years before, when he spoke to Vanessa about being away from the town during the war – she did not know, then, what he meant, & now she sees it, years after his death. It *has* to be like this" (np).

9   Laurence's typescript of *A Bird in the House* is in box 2, files 3–13 of the Laurence Archives in the Mills Memorial Library at McMaster University.

10 "The Loons" was first published in the *Atlantic Advocate* 56, no. 7 in March 1966 and broadcast by the Canadian Broadcasting Corporation in May 1963. The original title of this story was "The Crying of the Loons," a phrase that is repeated in the final words of the story. Tracy Ware explores the implication of this concluding sentence, suggesting that Laurence associates Piquette as a Métis with the disappearance of the loons: "Piquette is inscribed in a tragic fate in which she has no agency ... There are, then, two types of confusion in 'The Loons': the Métis are confused with the Indians; and both are confused with the loons" (79). See also Herbert Zirker's "Metaphoric Mapping in Margaret Laurence's Narrative." In her essay "On 'The Loons,'" Laurence writes, "The loons seemed to symbolize in some way the despair, the uprootedness, the loss of the land that many Indians and Métis must feel" (805–6). In "Time and the Narrative Voice," she explains, "The loons, recurring in the story both in their presence and in their absence, are connected to an ancestral past that belongs to Piquette, and the older Vanessa can see the irony of

the only way in which Piquette's people are recognized by the community in the changing of the name Diamond Lake to the more tourist appealing Lake Wapakata" (160). She excised the following interesting sentence from her typescript following the sentence, "She had been forced to seek the things she so bitterly rejected" (117): "Both the rejection and the deliberate seeking – on her part or on anyone's – seemed warped. How had she failed so deeply – and how had we?" Laurence's response to Jones's request for excision is highly ironic, given the numerous texts in which "The Loons" has been anthologized: "The Loons – ?? – I think this story should remain, although I *know* it isn't the strongest story in the collection [*sic*]."

11 "Horses of the Night" was published in *Chatelaine* in July 1967 and *Winter's Tales 15* in 1969. In "Revisions and Disagreements" Laurence argues passionately with Jones about the form of the story: "Horses of the Night – the story opens with Vanessa age 6, & then we proceed until she is about 18. But I *do* feel strongly that to put this story into a different form, with the younger Vanessa in flashback, would simply be to ruin it. It takes the thread of *Chris* through all the ages at which Chris's dilemma impinged on V's life, & I do not believe it can be done in any other way. This story was re-written many times. I do NOT think I can alter it basically now."

12 Christopher means, literally, Christ-bearer, and St Christopher is the patron saint of travellers. The title of this story is from an aubade by Horace – "*Lente, lente, currite noctis equi*" (Oh gallop slowly, you horses of the night) – a line quoted by Faustus in his final soliloquy at the end of Christopher Marlowe's play, *The Tragical History of Doctor Faustus*.

13 "The Half-Husky" was first published by *Argosy* and broadcast by the Canadian Broadcasting Corporation in 1967 under the title "Nanuk." Its title in the French translation was *Le Bâtard*.

14 The fact that Ada Shinwell recognizes Timothy Connor – added to Terence's tale about his father's carrying on with "some girl in Winnipeg" (84) and his views on "going to bed with an angel" (85), the term his father employed for his dead wife Agnes (83) – suggests that Ada Shinwell may be a prostitute whom Timothy has frequented in the past.

15 "Jericho's Brick Battlements" is the only story that was not previously published, suggesting that Laurence wrote it specifically for *A Bird in the House*. Originally titled "A Time of Waiting," it was published in *Chatelaine* in February 1970, the same year that the collection was published, under that title. In her "Revisions and Disagreements" Laurence notes, "I agree the opening of this story repeats previous material. I have therefore deleted a good deal of the first paragraph ... I do not think it is necessary to put these scenes into flashback unless the whole structure of the book

is to be changed, which is what I feel I cannot do." Laurence revisited Neepawa in 1969 before composing the final story, "Jericho's Brick Battlements." She wrote to Wiseman that, otherwise, she would not have been able to write the story.

16 Laurence's letter to Alan Maclean and the sample blurb that she sent to her publishers are found in Accession 1, box 12, file 8 of York University's Laurence Archives.

CHAPTER ELEVEN

1 Morag, looking at her reflection in the mirror, sees "Dark brown eyes, somewhat concealed (*good*) by heavy-framed glasses. Long, dead-straight hair, once black as tar, now quite evenly grey" (*D* 36). All references in this chapter, unless otherwise stated, will be to *The Diviners*.

2 Laurence writes to Wiseman on 25 January 1974, "a character like Morag, just as with Stacey and Rachel, is both me and not me ... but not me in the external sense *at all*. She is *herself*, of course" (*SL* 341). In a 1 January 1972 letter to Wiseman, Laurence acknowledges, "I don't seem to have done such a good camouflage job this time [in *The Diviners*]. They've all been there before, but better painted" (*SL* 320). Laurence writes to Wiseman on 13 January 1972, "the main character, Morag, is not me but alas is a writer about my age and certainly talks in one of my voices" (*SL* 319). Laurence writes in a 14 November 1972 letter to Harold Horwood, "[Morag] is a middle-aged female writer (not me, but related in many ways, of course)" (*VLS* 96).

3 James King judges, "Morag Gunn is the Margaret Laurence figure in *The Diviners*" (305), and "*The Diviners* is a *Bildungsroman*, a novel about the coming into being of a writer; it is also a book about the deprivations endured by Morag and her battle to find her spiritual center and her writing voice" (398). In "Genre and Gender: Autobiography and Self-Representation in *The Diviners*," Beckman-Long calls *The Diviners* "fictionalized autobiography" (103): "*The Diviners*, although it is cast in a third-person form, enters the domain of autobiography [for] Laurence creates, by blending the genres of realist fiction and autobiography, a gendered confession that claims the discursive authority of a patriarchal cultural practice to interpret the female subject" (108).

4 Ildiko de Papp Carrington concludes her "'Tales in the Telling': *The Diviners* as Fiction about Fiction" by stating, "Laurence dramatizes in detail the creative processes by which 'facts' become fictionalized [... as Morag] "confronts the multiple versions of herself in the mirror of her mind and speaks in her changing voices" (168).

5 The typescript of *The Diviners* in box 3, files 1–3, at McMaster University has been consulted with the permission of Laurence's heirs and the

assistance of librarians Charlotte Stewart-Murphy, Carl Spadoni, and staff. Laurence placed an embargo on reproducing excised, but legible, sections of the manuscript. Aritha van Herk writes, in "Margaret Laurence: The Shape of the Writer's Shadow," "Throughout *The Diviners*, the use of italics, itself shadow print, acts as a shadow text to the primary narrative … An act of faith, to write Canada in Canada, to write a woman writing, for these are all shadows of shadows, vulnerable souls that must be preserved from accident" (138–40).

6 Quotations from Laurence's unpaginated preparatory notes for *The Diviners* and her responses to Jones's requests for revisions, all collected in the York University Archives, are prefaced here by my phrase "Laurence notes" and included here with the permission of Laurence's literary executors.

7 Jack McClelland's correspondence is quoted with the permission of Jack McClelland. It is found in the McClelland archives at McMaster University.

8 Judith Jones remarked in a June 1998 interview with Nora Foster Stovel in her New York Knopf office that Laurence was "not very well" in 1973 – suggesting that Laurence was drinking heavily.

9 Jones told James King that, when she read the typescript of *The Diviners*, "she was convinced of two things: it bore the mark of genius and it was an utter mess" (King 313).

10 In "'Christie's Real Country. Where I Was Born': Story-Telling, Loss and Subjectivity in *The Diviners*," Paul Hjartarson concludes that "our understanding of *The Diviners* develops out of our sense of the relation between the two narrative levels, between the NOW and the THEN" (63).

11 As Laurence writes to Gabrielle Roy about the Shack on 9 June 1976, "The river is the same as I described it in THE DIVINERS – I wrote most of the novel here and the river just seemed naturally to flow through the book" (Socken 18).

12 Lorraine York discusses Morag's photographs in *The Other Side of Dailiness: Photography in the Works of Alice Munro, Timothy Findley, Michael Ondaatje, and Margaret Laurence*.

13 Rooke employs this term in "Hagar's Old Age: *The Stone Angel* as *Vollendungsroman*."

14 Cluny Macpherson is the name of a character in Robert Louis Stevenson's *Kidnapped*, a novel that Laurence loved, as she confirms in *Dance on the Earth* and in "Books That Mattered to Me."

15 In "You Have To Go Home Again: Art and Life in *The Diviners*," in *World Literature Written in English* 20 (1981), J.A. Wainwright discusses Morag's investigation of "the relationship between her art and her life" (293) and "between fact and fiction in her life" (311).

16 While some of these details reflect Arthurian legend, others are drawn from legends of Gabriel Dumont, the subject of Laurence's essay, "Man of Our People" (*HS* 161–8).

17 Eighteenth-century British author James Macpherson claimed to have discovered original poetry by the Gaelic poet Ossian, but his study was, in fact, a fabrication. Whether or not Laurence knew this is uncertain, but this fact certainly renders Christie's claim highly ironic.

18 Mildred Musgrove told Nora Foster Stovel in 1988 that *The Diviners* reflected Laurence's experience at Viscount Collegiate and affirmed that she was the model for Miss Melrose.

19 Laurence's juvenilia have been published by the Juvenilia Press, edited by Nora Foster Stovel, in two volumes – *Embryo Words* (1997) and *Colors of Speech* (2000).

20 The tragic death of Piquette and her children is the subject of Laurence's story "The Loons" in *A Bird in the House*.

21 I wish to acknowledge the encouragement that the late Malcolm Ross, my mentor during my graduate work at Dalhousie University, has given me regarding my work on Margaret Laurence.

22 Laurence explains, "Brooke is a product, actually, of a very colonial world. He was born and grew up in India under the British Raj, so of course that kind of colonial attitude helped to formulate his whole concept of life, his whole attitude toward other people. And I think that possibly – again at a subconscious level – I was influenced by Mannoni, by reading *The Psychology of Colonialism*" (Sullivan 74).

23 This rebellion may reflect the argument Margaret had with Jack over the manuscript of *The Stone Angel*. Although Wiseman destroyed Laurence's letter, as requested, her 20 April 1962 reply to Laurence suggests the seriousness of this disagreement: "I know how much you've always dreaded Jack's disapproval, and what this rebellion must have cost you" (quoted in King 164–5).

24 Laurence explains, "my sense of Jules is that he is a tribal brother to Morag. They have both grown up in the same place. Both have been oppressed by their culture, Jules particularly of course, but Morag growing up as the foster child of Christie and Prin Logan has been discriminated against by the town too, so they do have that in common right from their early childhoods. The other thing that they have in common, which they don't really discover until some time later, is that they are both diviners. And, this we see, in a sense, foreshadowed, or we get a kind of adumbration of this, early in the book when Morag hears Christie's tales and begins to write herself, and when Skinner Tonnerre suggests to her that his people have tales too" (Sullivan 5).

25 The names Skelton and McRaith suggest "skeleton" and "wraith." Skelton is also the name of the Scottish Chaucerian poet (1460–1529) from whom we derive the term "Skeltonic verse."

26 In "Margaret Laurence's *Diviners* and Shakespeare's *Tempest*: The Uses of the Past," Gayle Greene explores "Laurence's adaptation of Shake-

speare" in *The Diviners'* "parallels with *The Tempest*," arguing that Laurence portrays Morag assuming "the powers of Prospero" (178).

27 Cole's book is *Exile in the Wilderness: The Biography of Chief Factor Archibald McDonald*. Cole told Laurence that the piper who led the Selkirk settlers was named Robert Gunn (*DE* 201).

28 Laurence composed "The Ballad of Jules Tonnerre" herself, and it was sung and recorded by Ian Cameron. Laurence wished to have the disc of songs marketed with the novel. I wish to thank Joan Johnston for giving me a copy of this disc. Laurence taped interviews with Toronto folksinger Duke Redbird during the early 1970s when she was writing *The Diviners*. Although she did not complete his biography, it did influence her novel. In "Margaret Laurence's 'Album' Songs," Wes Mantooth claims that Laurence's "musical interests coalesced in *The Diviners'* Album" (167).

29 This circular motion, or Möbius strip, is typical of postmodernist novels, such as Ian MacEwan's 2001 novel, *Atonement*.

30 Laurence notes, "have deleted THE DIVINERS – but 'to set down her title' – I hope this does have a double meaning – both Morag putting down the title of the book (her childhood etc. which she's been writing) and *setting down* in the sense of giving over her title as novelist to the kids. This really *good*, not despairing."

CHAPTER TWELVE

1 Laurence's notes and drafts for this unfinished novel are in the Margaret Laurence Fonds, box 6 of the William Ready Division of Archives and Research Collections, Mills Memorial Library, at McMaster University in Hamilton, Ontario. I wish to thank the Laurence Estate for permission to examine and quote from this restricted material. In his 1997 biography of Laurence, James King includes a brief summary of this material in "Appendix: Dance on the Earth (The Novel)," pages 393–8. The Laurence Estate gave these materials to James King for his 1997 biography, and they were subsequently deposited at McMaster, where other scholars were allowed to examine them.

2 For the purpose of clarity, I will distinguish the fiction and non-fiction versions by placing the title of the unfinished novel in quotation marks and the title of the published memoir in italics.

3 "Dance on the Earth" is located in file 6, "Mairi's Novel" in file 2, "Allie's Milton Classes" in file 3, "Closing the Cottage" in file 5, and the "Portion of Grace" section in file 1 in box 6 of the 1997 accession of the Laurence Archives at McMaster University.

4 James King observes, in "Appendix: Dance on the Earth (The Novel)," the "mother and daughter novel which Margaret had hoped to write … would also have highlighted women as shawomen, tribal magicians and

healers who have mystical communion with the spirit world" (393–4).

5 Laurence's note reads: "TO ALTERNATE – IN EACH CHAPTER. A. PRESENT – Present tense; third person; Allie's viewpoint; B. (Allie's) Journal for Mairi – (taped the past histories)."

6 Laurence pursues the theme of a feudal lord who brings his serfs from Europe to Manitoba in her early story "Tal des Walde," collected in Embryo Words: Margaret Laurence's Early Writings (36–42) – a tale that she recycles as Morag's story, "The Mountain," in The Diviners (209).

7 As King notes in "Lost Histories," his chapter on Laurence's unfinished novels, "After she abandoned work on three projects for novels, Margaret became determined on one centred on mothers and daughters" (367). He suggests that "Dance on the Earth" was to be that novel.

8 Laurence writes to Gabrielle Roy on 23 March 1976, "THE DIVINERS is coming under fire in my own community here, I am sorry to say. It was on the Grade 13 high-school course, and a parent complained that it was 'obscene' because it contains some so-called four-letter words and a few sex scenes – the first are essential to the narrative line and the revelation of character" (VLS 175).

9 Laurence emphasizes the fact that women have only "surnames" or "sirnames" (DE 9).

10 In the 1880s Dr Thomas J. Barnardo founded homes in Manitoba and Ontario for orphans brought from Britain to provide farm labour (Harrison, 16–17).

11 Laurence kept a journal during various periods of her life: for example, her African memoir, The Prophet's Camel Bell (1961), is based on her 1951–52 Somali diaries. She also kept a journal during the last year of her life: these eight notebooks are in box 7 in McMaster's Laurence Archives.

12 Powers recalls Laurence's answer to his question about why she had stopped writing at this point: "Oh, if I were to continue the Manawaka fiction it would be by picking up Pique's story; people would say I was writing about Jocelyn. I couldn't expose my daughter to that" (AH xvi). King concludes, "The novel Dance on the Earth, in its re-creation of the condition of orphanage and the cruel indictment of the fundamentalists, was simply not a book that could be completed because in large part the process of writing it would have been too painful" (398).

13 In her letter to Buckler, Laurence says, "There is no way I could write about an Elmer Gantry [the eponymous protagonist of Sinclair Lewis's 1927 novel]. My feeling must be closer to what Joyce Cary did ... in the CAPTIVE AND THE FREE ..." (VLS 40).

14 This section continues, "Form is to try to give a shape to things so they'll be understood."

CHAPTER THIRTEEN

1 Laurence called in the local mole-catcher to exterminate the pests (*DE* 189). Laurence describes Elmcot in her essay "Put Out One or Two More Flags" in *Heart of a Stranger*, 107–12.

2 Margaret Laurence and Adele Wiseman often ended their letters to each other with their college slogan, "*Corragio! Avanti!*," meaning "Courage! Forward!"

3 Laurence records, "I based the characters of Topaz and Calico in *Jason's Quest* on our cats. Calico was an outdoor cat, dignified, a true lady. Topaz was a frivolous and affectionate slob who preferred to remain indoors" (*DE* 174). She uses her pets' actual names in her animal fantasy.

4 Unless otherwise specified, all references in this section will be to this edition of *Jason's Quest*.

5 Laurence's notes on revisions to *Jason's Quest* are in box 2, file 11 in the McMaster University Laurence Archives. Her Macmillan editor has three typed pages of suggested revisions, most of which Laurence accedes to in several hand-written pages of inserts. But when the editor suggests Zanzibar is "inland," Laurence responds succinctly, "Zanzibar is an island off the East coast of Africa." The editor suggests substituting for British terminology terms that would be more comprehensible to American readers: for example, she changes "cuppa" to "cup of tea" (4). To the editor's query about the two London cats' diction, Laurence responds, "I think 'mon' & 'gel' seem, in the first case, Scots & in the second case, establishment 19th Century England. I think your difficulty may arise out of intonation, as West Indians do have the soft long 'a,' but I don't think it is necessary to try to get across accent (as apart from idiom) in fiction. I think it is as well left as it is" (6). Laurence writes to Adele Wiseman, on 11 December 1967, "The kids' book has been accepted by Macmillan, and I am quite ridiculously pleased about that. I have to do some revisions, but not too many at this point. I am longing to see what kind of illustrations they get" (*SL* 284).

6 After travelling to England with her husband in 1949, Laurence sent home to the Wiseman family in Winnipeg a ten-page single-spaced typed Christmas story titled "England by Me" and subtitled, "Engelonde bei mir . . . . . translated from the well-known work of the philosopher Schmalz, by J.M. and J.F. Laurence." It begins, "There are several really important things in England today. One of these is HISTORY, and another is SCENERY" (McMaster Manuscript). The Laurences toured the Tower of London and other historical sites, and Margaret's letter includes comical, illustrated accounts of ancient traditions that appeared archaic to the young Canadian woman.

7 Sheila Egoff writes, in *The New Republic of Children* (1975), "Not even Margaret Laurence could meet the rigorous demands of animal fantasy. In fact her widely acclaimed success as a novelist makes her one book of fantasy for children, *Jason's Quest* (1970), the most disappointing book in Canadian children's literature" (81). In *The New Republic of Children* (1990), Sheila Egoff and Judith Saltman say, "Margaret Laurence's *Jason's Quest* (1970) offer[s] only counterfeits of animals and parodies of humans; there is insight into neither. Margaret Laurence, for example, was satisfied with a simple transference of human externals to the animal world ... The result bears more resemblance to a cartoon than to a genuine fantasy" (265).

8 In her first letter to Gabrielle Roy on 15 February 1976 Laurence confides: "Since I finished THE DIVINERS, several years ago, I have virtually written nothing except some articles and a lot of book reviews. No real writing. I'd like to try to write a children's book. I'm a bit hesitant about beginning, but no doubt will do so. I am assured by Sheila Egoff, in her book about Canadian children's literature, THE REPUBLIC OF CHILDHOOD [*sic*] that animal fantasies are looked upon with scorn by the young of today. I suspect that she herself doesn't much like them – I'm not sure about children. Anyway, mine will be an animal fantasy because that is what I want to write. I have done one children's book – an animal fantasy, JASON'S QUEST, which Ms. Egoff calls 'the most disappointing book in all of Canadian children's fiction.' If one is going to fail, by all means let us do so grandly! However, one cannot in the end be guided by critics or even potential readers" (*VLS* 174).

9 *The Canadian Encyclopedia*, 2nd edition, s.v. "Margaret Laurence."

10 Laurence explains the history of the book to Malcolm Ross on 10 August 1980: "[written] when my kids were 4 and 7. I lost my only copy in 1962 when I moved to England with the kids, and only found it 3 years ago, when I discovered quite by accident that it was still being used in the Unitarian Church Sunday School in Vancouver. I got a copy, re-wrote it to some extent, and asked the Toronto artist Helen Lucas if she would do the pictures" (King 361). She writes to Gabrielle Roy about this happy event in her 2 July 1978 letter, repeating the news on 25 September 1980: "A very happy thing happened to me recently. The story goes back 18 years to the time we lived in Vancouver. At that time I attended the Unitarian church, and once when some parents objected (!) to the Christmas story being told to the Sunday school children because the angels hadn't really been flying around in the sky, I was very upset and said I would not want my own young children to be deprived of that most important part of their heritage. I therefore offered to write a version of the story for use with very small children. I did so, and the story was used in the Sunday

school. When I left Vancouver I mislaid the story and thought it was gone forever. Then, last winter I was having dinner at some friends' home, and one of the guests was a woman from Vancouver who was a Unitarian. She asked me if I remembered the story, and I said certainly I did, but I had lost my copy years ago. To my astonishment, she told me the story is still being used in the Unitarian Sunday school! She subsequently sent me a copy, so it returned to me after 18 years. I rewrote it very slightly ... But it seemed as though the story were meant to be brought out as a small book, as it returned to me in that unlikely way" (Socken 58–9).

11 Laurence's typescripts of *The Christmas Birthday Story* are in the York University Archives. The original single-spaced typescript, with the name "Philip Hewett, Unitarian Church, Van, circa 1960" written at the top of the first page, has a note at the end reading, "1960 – slightly revised 1978." The second typescript is double-spaced and incorporates some insertions hand-written on the first typescript. References to changes in the text will be to these typescripts. For example, Laurence omitted the first two sentences of her version: "Have you ever heard a story about the olden days? I will tell you one" (1). She omitted the sentences, "How do you think they traveled? I'll tell you" (1). She inserted the following paragraph: "When darkness came, Mary and Joseph lay down to rest in the quiet countryside, with only the trees and the sleeping birds around them. The donkey rested, too. When morning came, they went on." And she expanded the concluding sentence in the published version. The story was also published as "The Christmas Birthday Story: Retelling the gospels of St. Matthew and St. Luke for the very young – and the young at heart" in *The Globe and Mail* on 25 December 1980, p. 7, accompanied by Helen Lucas's illustrations. All references will be to the unpaginated book publication.

12 Laurence wrote to Jack McClelland on 9 August 1980, "the little book may be condemned by the same rednecks who condemned *The Diviners* as blasphemous, because Mary and Joseph don't care whether their baby turns out to be a girl or a boy. Actually, I hope that doesn't happen – what a hell of a way to sell books. I've had enough of being called nasty names" (King 361). Laurence's 4 November 1980 letter to McClelland proves her fears were founded: "Wow! Was that ever a stinker of a review in the *Globe* last Saturday! That same babe, Jacquie Hunt, whoever she is, did a review last year of THE OLDEN DAY'S COAT, and said substantially the same thing – text terrible, pics great" (King 362). Such negative reviews of her children's books discouraged her.

13 This unpublished typed "Note to Parents" with handwritten annotations is in the York University Archives.

14 Laurence inserted the animals' vocalizations into the typescript by hand.

The ewe seems to be reassuring the lamb that "Everthing is all right," recalling Stacey's mantra in *The Fire-Dwellers*.

15 Laurence writes to Roy on 1 December 1979, "About my other little book [*Six Darn Cows*], this one was intended for beginning readers of 5 & 6 years old. The record was made only for promotion – it isn't being sold. But the tune of the song is my tune – wow!" (Socken 73). She recalls in *Dance on the Earth* (217–18) the delight of composing the song that was then played on the banjo by Bob Bossin of Stringband for the record that was included with the book.

16 Unless otherwise stated, all references in this section will be to this unpaginated text.

17 The *Kids of Canada: Teacher's Guidebook* (1981) contains no publication information, but appears to be printed by an educational facility and not to be by Margaret Laurence herself.

18 See Nodelman, Perry, and Mavis Reimer, eds, *The Pleasures of Children's Literature*, 197.

19 James Lorimer suggested that Laurence record the song, and a record with the story and song was circulated for promotional purposes (*DE* 218). See note 15.

20 *The Olden Days Coat* was first published in *Weekend Magazine* on 20 December 1975, with illustrations by Jack Tremblay. Later, Laurence revised it, and it was published by McClelland and Stewart in 1980 with illustrations by Muriel Wood. It was filmed by Atlantis Films, with Megan Follows as Sal in 1981. The National Film Board made a documentary film, with Laurence reading parts of the story aloud. Unless otherwise stated, all references will be to the unpaginated 1980 McClelland and Stewart book publication.

21 Laurence omitted the following passage, which recalls the aged Hagar looking in the mirror: "Were the eyes the only thing about a person that didn't change? And yet the eyes of the girl in the photograph looked different, too. This girl hadn't yet known all about everything that would happen to her, everything that was still in the future. Maybe that's what made the difference."

22 Laurence writes to Roy about *The Olden Days Coat* in her 12 February 1979 letter: "My writing is beginning again, but slowly. Not, this time, fiction, but something else – I don't know yet how it will turn out. I have also a small book .. a children's story .. coming out this year .. not the Nativity story, which will come out next year, but rather like a children's science fiction story! At least it involves a kind of magic time-travel" (Socken 66). Laurence's use of the trope recalls Philippa Pearce's novel, *Tom's Midnight Garden*, in which a boy living with an old woman enters the garden of her childhood (now an ugly urban scene) and plays with her as a child.

23 Laurence recalls in her memoir how *The Olden Days Coat* was inspired by a ride in an antique cutter owned by Dr H.E. Gastle near Lakefield (*DE* 218). In her acknowledgments to *The Olden Days Coat* Laurence notes that his sleighs and horses provided the inspiration for her story. She writes to Gabrielle Roy, 9 November 1979, "I hope this book gives you some pleasure. The houses are all taken from Lakefield houses! I love the pictures" (Socken 70).

24 This inscription was inserted into the story by Laurence in longhand.

25 This sentence is also inserted into the story in longhand.

26 Laurence rewrote much of this section, as her annotated typescript demonstrates.

CHAPTER FOURTEEN

1 *Dance on the Earth: A Memoir*, 7. Unless otherwise stated, all references will be to this text. The 305-page typescript of *Dance on the Earth: A Memoir* is located in box 4, files 5–6, and in 10 files in box 6. The typescripts, dated 20 October 1986, that Jocelyn edited, are located in box 6, files 8–10. I wish to thank the Laurence Estate for permission to examine and copy this typescript and librarian Carl Spadoni and the staff of McMaster's Mills Memorial Library for their assistance. The cover note on the typescript states, "The material in this box is publishable, with editing (by Jocelyn). First draft begun September 1985 and completed July 1986. Second draft begun 29 August 1986 and completed 3 October 1986. Third draft completed & typed – 20 October 1986 – typing by Joan Johnston completed 7 October 1986. Final draft of publisher's editing is to be given by Jocelyn Laurence. No changes in her edited copy to be made without her approval," signed "Margaret Laurence 9 September 1986." She added, "Ack Joc & David & Joan & also Almuth Lutkenhaus-Lackey for permission to use photo of her 'Crucified Woman' sculpture for colour photo by David for the jacket."

2 Donald J. Winslow, in *Life-Writing*, defines memoir as "[a] record of events, not purporting to be a complete history, but treating of such matters as come within the personal knowledge or within the memory of the writer, or are obtained from particular sources of information. The incidents recorded may come from a person's own life or persons whom he knows or has known ..." (26).

3 Helen Buss notes, in *Mapping Our Selves: Canadian Women's Autobiography*, that Laurence's form offers "resistance to 'systems' of various kinds, political, intellectual, and cultural" (188). In her essay, "Reading Margaret Laurence's Life Writing: Toward a Postcolonial Feminist Subjectivity for a White Female Critic," Buss places *Dance on the Earth* in what Karen Kaplan, in "Resisting Autobiography: Out-Law Genres and

Transnational Feminist Subjects," labels the "outlaw genre" capable of producing "transnational feminist subjects" (115) and also in what Lee Quinby, in "The Subject of Memoirs: The Woman Warrior's Technology of Ideographic Selfhood," defines as a "new form of subjectivity [that] refuses the particular forms of selfhood, knowledge, and artistry that the systems of power of the modern era ... have made dominant" (298). Sidonie Smith argues, in *Subjectivity, Identity, and the Body: Women's Autobiographical Practices in the Twentieth Century*, that the emerging female autobiographer "testifies to the collapse of the myth of presence with its conviction of a unitary self. Having untied her relationship to the conventions of the autobiographical contract from the idea of an atomized, central self, she de-centers all centerers and effectively subverts the patriarchal order itself" (59).

4 The statements, "I hated the way in which I was proceeding from point A to point B to point C" and "I wanted to write about my mothers and myself," are omitted from page 4 of the typescript.

5 Greta Coger comments, "Those who know the prairies and Africa understand why Laurence chose 'dance' as perhaps the most appropriate word for expressing the whole of life" (262). Powers judges, "Margaret's final choice of title for her memoirs was the [unfinished] novel's *Dance on the Earth* – and surely with firm recognition of the significance of 'dance'" (*AH* 459).

6 Laurence's final journal, recorded in eight notebooks during 1986, the last year of her life, is in box 7 of the Margaret Laurence Archives in the Mills Memorial Library at McMaster University. James King summarizes it in *The Life of Margaret Laurence*, pages 378–88.

7 Laurence's typescript of "Old Women's Song," differing substantially from the published version, is at York University. It includes the following lines: "Foremothers ... I feel in my depths my connection / with you a long time ago ... and want to dance and mourn with you ..." Paul Denham, in his review of *Dance on the Earth* in *NeWest Review*, refers to "Old Women's Song" appropriately as "Old Women's Dance" (34).

8 Di Brandt, in *Wild Mother Dancing*, notes the "The Absent Mother's Amazing Comeback" (19) in Laurence's Manawaka fiction, especially *The Stone Angel* and *The Diviners*. We find the culmination of this trend in *Dance on the Earth: A Memoir*.

9 Recent female theorists of autobiography discuss some of the creative aspects of memory: in "Authorizing the Autobiographical," Shari Benstock says, "the workings of memory, crucial to the recollection implicit in life writing, are found to be suspect. They slip beyond the borders of the conscious world; they are traversed and transgressed by the unconscious" (1053); Sidonie Smith claims "memory is ultimately a story about, and thus a discourse on, original experience, so that recovering the past is

not a hypostasizing of fixed grounds and absolute origins but, rather, an interpretation of earlier experience that can never be divorced from the filtering of subsequent experience or articulated outside the structures of language and storytelling" (45).

10 Carolyn Heilbrun, in *Writing a Woman's Life*, criticizes the tendency of previous women's autobiographies to "find beauty even in pain and transform rage into spiritual acceptance" (12).

11 Doris Dyke, in *Crucified Woman* (1991), quotes "a nuanced interpretation" by Laurence: "She is not portraying Our Lord, per se, but rather expressing a deep feeling for the anguish and also the strength of women, and in my view, the sense that there is a female aspect of the Holy Spirit" (43).

12 Laurence's statements, "I conceive of the Holy Spirit as both Mother and Father ... as with Nyame, the holiest and highest in the Akan pantheon, among the Ashanti people of West Africa," in the typescript of *Dance on the Earth* are omitted from the published text.

13 The Feast of the Epiphany is 6 January. In 1987, the Epiphany would have been widely celebrated on 5 January, which was a Sunday.

14 Laurence had employed these lines from Dylan Thomas's poem addressed to his dying father, "Do Not Go Gentle into That Good Night," as the epigraph for *The Stone Angel*.

15 This convocation address exists in the form of Laurence's typescript at York University.

16 This address, entitled "Message to the Inheritors" in Laurence's typescript at York University, is titled "Convocation Address, York University, 1980" in its published form in *Dance on the Earth*.

17 Laurence's epigraph to this poem is from Psalm 39:12, which she quotes in *The Fire-Dwellers* and *The Diviners*: "Hear my prayer, O Lord, and give ear unto my cry; hold not thy peace at my tears, for I am a stranger with thee, and a sojourner, as all my fathers were" (293).

18 It is interesting to note the connections between birth and death in *Dance on the Earth*. In the typescript of "Old Women's Song," Laurence writes, "dancing the child's birth / the child's death."

19 Powers says Laurence's "Newsletter" of 10 January 1986 reports, "selected memoirs, dealing mainly with my three mothers, has begun" (*AH* 461). I wish to acknowledge Joan Johnston's assistance in providing me with helpful material and information regarding Laurence's memoir. In her final journal, Laurence writes about *Dance on the Earth: A Memoir*, "I believed it was important to love people, raise my beloved children, & *write books* ... This last one, into which I have poured faith and energy, seems now to have been worth little. I don't know why I prayed & prayed, unconscionably, for a few more days, to complete a *book* that isn't worth anything" (King 382).

20 Laurence wrote Harold Horwood on 31 December 1978, "I am writing again, thank God. But it is a strange thing I'm trying to do, and I'm experiencing the usual awful doubts. I realized last summer that I had not one book but two, simmering in my mind. A novel that isn't ready to be written, and . . I tell you more or less in confidence . . a kind of memoir, a kind of discursive story of my life, not perhaps as it actually happened but as perceived by me. I do not intend to spill every bean, I hardly need say. But there are lots of interesting stories I'd like to share, and some strong views as well. I don't know if I will want it published. We'll see. But it feels good to be working again" (*VLS* 101).

21 Powers states, "The accepted project, the memoirs, continued to be associated in Margaret's mind with the forsaken novel ... and the novel's emphasis on women, on the female line of descent, included the four mothers important in Allie's life ..." (*AH* 459).

CHAPTER FIFTEEN

1 As Dr Lois Wilson recalls of Laurence, in her essay "Faith and the Vocation of the Author," "One of her favourite sayings was, 'Thank you, God, sir or madam'" (154).

2 Laurence draws a similar distinction in "A Place to Stand On": "Optimism in this world seems impossible to me. But in each novel there is some hope, and that is a different thing entirely" (*HS* 8).

3 Laurence acknowledges in her interview with Beatrice Lever that there is "a strong sense of the Old Testament" in her work, stemming from "the stern quality of [her] ancestors," but she attests that there is also "the New Testament sense of hope" (Lever 19).

4 In *Typing: A Life in Twenty-Six Keys* (2000), Matt Cohen recalls interviewing Laurence: "Margaret Laurence explained to me that what she wrote was divinely ordered and inspired and that the voices she heard, while writing, were God's voice" (186).

5 Lois Wilson notes, in "Faith and the Vocation of the Author," that Easter and Passover coincided in 1985, the year that Laurence wrote this poem. Margaret's children, Jocelyn and David, gave Wilson the original copy of this poem after their mother's death (161–2).

6 Wilson states, in "Faith and the Vocation of the Author," "Margaret's faith *did* inform her worldview and therefore her vocation as an author" (157). Consequently, as she writes, "her novels are profoundly informed by a religious dimension" (159).

7 On 9 January 1985, Laurence wrote to her friend, writer Budge Wilson, "Death is so strange. I aspire to be a Christian, yet I cannot say I feel certain of a life-after-death ..." (King 371).

Works Cited

Abrahams, Cecil. "Margaret Laurence and the Ancestral Tradition." In Coger, *New Perspectives on Margaret Laurence*, 137–42.

Abrams, M.H. *A Glossary of Literary Terms*. 6th edition. New York: Harcourt, Brace, Jovanovich, 1993.

Abusharaf, Rogaia Mustafa. "Unmasking Tradition." *The Sciences* 38, 2 (1998): 22–7.

Achebe, Chinua. *Arrow of God*. London: Heinemann, 1964.

– *A Man of the People*. London: Heinemann, 1966.

– *Morning Yet On Creation Day*. London: Heinemann, 1975.

– *No Longer At Ease*. London: Heinemann, 1960.

– *Things Fall Apart*. London: Heinemann, 1966.

Amadi, Elechi. *The Concubine*. London: Heinemann, 1966.

Anonymous review of *Jason's Quest. Publisher's Weekly* 197, 22 (1 June 1970): 66.

Appenzell, Anthony. "In the Land of Egypt: Margaret Laurence as Essayist." In Woodcock, *A Place to Stand On*, 276–88.

Appiah, Kwame Anthony, and Henry Louis Gates, Jr. *The Dictionary of Global Culture*. New York: Vintage, 1999.

Aristotle. *Poetics*. Translated by S.H. Butcher. New York: Hill & Wang, 1961.

Arnason, David and Dennis Cooley. "Outcasting: A Conversation with Margaret Laurence about the World of Manawaka." *Border Crossings* 5, 4 (1986): 32–4.

Atwood, Margaret. "Afterword." *A Jest of God.* Toronto: McClelland and Stewart, 1988, 211–15.
– "Face to Face: Margaret Laurence as Seen by Margaret Atwood." *Maclean's,* 7 May 1974: 38–9, 43–4, 46.
– *Survival: A Thematic Guide to Canadian Literature.* Toronto: Anansi, 1972.

Bailey, Nancy. "Identity in *The Fire-Dwellers.*" In Nicholson, *Critical Approaches to the Fiction of Margaret Laurence,* 1990, 107–18.
– "Margaret Laurence, Carl Jung, and the Manawaka Women." *Studies in Canadian Literature* 2 (1977): 306–21.
– "Margaret Laurence and the Psychology of Re-Birth in *A Jest of God.*" *Journal of Popular Culture* 15, 3 (1981): 62–9.
Baum, Rosalie Murphy. "Artist and Woman: Young Lives in Laurence and Munro." *North Dakota Quarterly* 52 (1984): 196–211.
– "Self-Alienation of the Elderly in Margaret Laurence's Fiction." In Coger, *New Perspectives on Margaret Laurence,* 153–60.
– "'Unique and Irreplaceable': Margaret Laurence's Hagar." In *Old Testament Women in Western Literature.* Edited by Raymond Jean Frontain and Jan Wojcik. Conway, AR: University of Central Arkansas Press, 1991, 262–83.
Baxter, John. "The Stone Angel: Shakespearian Bearings." *The Compass: A Provincial Review* 1 (1977): 3–19.
Beckman-Long, Brenda. "Authorizing Her Text: Margaret Laurence's Shift to Third-Person Narration." *Studies in Canadian Literature/Études en littérature Canadienne* 24, 2 (1999): 64–78.
– "Genre and Gender: Autobiography and Self-Representation in *The Diviners.*" *English Studies in Canada* 30, 3 (September 2004): 89–110.
– "The Narratee as Confessor in Margaret Laurence's *The Fire-Dwellers.*" *Literature & Theology* 17, 2 (2003): 113–26.
– "*The Stone Angel* as a Feminine Confession Novel." In Riegel, *Challenging Territory,* 47–66.
Beeler, Karin E. "Ethnic Dominance and Difference: The Post-Colonial Condition in Margaret Laurence's *The Stone Angel, A Jest of God,* and *The Diviners.*" In *Cultural Identities in Canadian Literature / Identités culturelles dans la littérature canadienne.* Edited by Benedicte Mauguiere. New York: Peter Lang, 1998, 25–37.
Bell, Alice. "Hagar Shipley's Rage for Life: Narrative Technique in *The Stone Angel.*" In Coger, *New Perspectives on Margaret Laurence,* 51–62.
Benstock, Shari. "Authorizing the Autobiographical." In *Feminisms: An Anthology of Literary Theory and Criticism.* Edited by Robyn R. Warhol and Diane Price Herndl. New Brunswick, NJ: Rutgers University Press, 1993, 1040–7.

Besner, Neil. "Canadian Regional Children's Literature: Fictions First." *Canadian Children's Literature* 86 (1997): 17–26.

Bettelheim, Bruno. *The Uses of Enchantment: The Meaning and Importance of Fairy Tales.* New York: Knopf, 1976.

Bevan, Alan. "Introduction." *The Fire-Dwellers.* Toronto: McClelland and Stewart, 1969. viii–xiv. Reprinted in New, *Margaret Laurence*, 205–11.

Bible, King James Version. Cambridge: Cambridge University Press, 1950.

Blanton, Casey. *Travel Writing: The Self and the World.* New York: Twayne, 1997.

Blau Du Plessis, Rachel. *Writing Beyond the Ending: Narrative Strategies of Twentieth-Century Women Writers.* Bloomington: Indiana Univeristy Press, 1985.

Blewett, David. "The Unity of the Manawaka Cycle." *Journal of Canadian Studies* 13 (Fall 1978): 31–9.

Boughton, Noelle. *Margaret Laurence: A Gift of Grace: A Spiritual Biography.* Women Who Rock Series. Toronto: Women's Press, 2006.

Bowering, George. "That Fool of a Fear: Notes on *A Jest of God.*" *Canadian Literature* 50 (1971): 41–56. Reprinted in New, *Margaret Laurence*, 161–76. Reprinted in Woodcock, *A Place to Stand On*, 210–26.

Boxhill, Anthony. "Review of *Long Drums and Canons.*" *Fiddlehead* 80 (May–July 1969): 105–6.

Brandt, Di. *Wild Mother Dancing: Maternal Narrative in Canadian Literature.* Winnipeg: University of Manitoba Press, 1993.

Browne, Sir Thomas. *Religio Medici.* 1635. Cambridge: Cambridge University Press, 1955.

Brydon, Diana. "Silence, Voice and the Mirror: Margaret Laurence and Women." In Gunnars, *Crossing the River*, 183–206.

Burton, Richard. *First Footsteps Into East Africa or An Exploration of Harar.* London: Tyeston and Edwards, 1894. Reprint edited by Gordon Waterfield. London: Routledge & Kegan Paul, 1966.

Buss, Helen. "Canadian Women's Autobiography: Some Critical Directions." In Neuman and Kamboureli, *A Mazing Space*, 154–66.

– *Mapping Ourselves: Canadian Women's Autobiography in English.* Montreal & Kingston: McGill-Queen's University Press, 1993.

– "Margaret Laurence and the Autobiographical Impulse." In Gunnars, *Crossing the River*, 147–68.

– "Margaret Laurence's Dark Lovers: Sexual Metaphor, and the Movement toward Individualization, Hierogamy and Mythic Narrative in Four Manawaka Books." *Atlantis* 7, 2 (1986): 97–107.

– *Mother and Daughter Relationships in the Manawaka Works of Margaret Laurence.* Victoria, BC: University of Victoria Press, 1985.

– "Reading Margaret Laurence's Life Writing: Toward a Postcolonial Feminist

Subjectivity for a White Female Critic." In New, *Margaret Laurence: Critical Reflections*, 39–58.
– "Writing and Reading Autobiographically." Introduction to "Life Writing" Issue, *Prairie Fire* 1997, 189.

Cameron, Donald. "Margaret Laurence: The Black Celt Speaks of Freedom." In *Conversations with Canadian Novelists*. Toronto: Macmillan, 1973, 96–115.
Capone, Giovanna. "*A Bird in the House*: Margaret Laurence on Order and the Artist." In *Gaining Ground: European Critics on Canadian Literature*. Edited by Robert Kroetsch and Reingard M. Nischik. Edmonton: NeWest Press, 1988, 161–9.
Carrington, Ildiko de Papp. "'Tales in the Telling': *The Diviners* as Fiction about Fiction." *Essays on Canadian Writing* 9 (1977–78): 154–69.
Cary, Joyce. *Mister Johnson*. New York: Berkley Medallion Books, 1961.
Chew, Shirley. "'Some Truer Image': A Reading of *The Stone Angel*." In Nicholson, *Critical Approaches to the Fiction of Margaret Laurence*, 35–45.
Clark, John Pepper. *Ozidi: A Play*. London and Ibadan: Oxford University Press, 1966.
– *The Raft. Three Plays*. London and Ibadan: Oxford University Press, 1964.
Coger, Greta McCormick. "The Creation of Women Protagonists." In *International Literature in English: Essays on the Major Writers*. Edited by Robert L. Ross. New York: Garland, 1991, 293–301.
– "Margaret Laurence: Growing Up in Neepawa." *The Margaret Laurence Review*. Vols 2 & 3 (1992–93): 33–51.
– ed. *New Perspectives on Margaret Laurence: Poetic Narrative, Multiculturalism, and Feminism*. Westport, CT: Greenwood, 1996.
– "Review Essay: Dance, Nurture, Write: Margaret Laurence's Memoir." *American Review of Canadian Studies* (Summer 1992): 259–70.
– "War in the Manawaka Novels as Macrocosm, Fictionalized Biography, and Imaginative History." In *New Perspectives on Margaret Laurence*, 115–28.
Cohen, Matt. *Typing: A Life in Twenty-Six Keys*. Toronto: Vintage, Canada, 2000.
Coldwell, Joan. "Hagar as Meg Merrilies, the Homeless Gipsy." *Journal of Canadian Fiction* 27 (1980): 92–100.
– "Margaret Laurence." *The Oxford Companion to Canadian Literature*. Edited by William Toye. Toronto: Oxford Univeristy Press, 1983, 434–6.
– *The Oxford Companion to Canadian Literature*. 2nd ed. Edited by Eugene Benson and William Toye. Toronto: Oxford University Press, 1997. 633–35.
Cole, Jean Murray. *Exile in the Wilderness: The Biography of Chief Factor Archibald McDonald 1790–1853*. Don Mills, ON: Burns & MacEachern, 1979.

Collu, Gabrielle. "Writing About Others: The African Stories." In Riegel, *Challenging Territory*, 19–32.

Comeau, Paul. "Hagar in Hell: Margaret Laurence's Fallen Angel." *Canadian Literature* 128 (1991): 11–22.

– *Margaret Laurence's Epic Imagination*. Edmonton: University of Alberta Press, 2005.

Cooley, Dennis. "Antimacassared in the Wilderness: Art and Nature in *The Stone Angel*." *Mosaic: A Journal for the Comparative Study of Literature and Ideas* 11, 3 (1978): 29–46.

Cooper, Cheryl. "Images of Closure in *The Diviners*." In *The Canadian Novel: Here and Now*. Edited by John Moss. Toronto: New Canadian Library, 1978, 93–102.

Dale, James. "Valuable addition to the Mac library." *Hamilton Spectator*, 8 March 1969, 26.

Darling, Michael. "'Undecipherable Signs': Margaret Laurence's 'To Set Our House in Order.'" *Essays on Canadian Writing* 29 (1984 Summer): 192–203.

Davidson, Arnold E. "Cages and Escapes in Margaret Laurence's *A Bird in the House*." *University of Windsor Review* 16 (1981): 92–101.

Davidson, Cathy N. "Past and Perspective in Margaret Laurence's *The Stone Angel*." *The American Review of Canadian Studies* 8 (1978): 61–9.

Davies, Richard A. "'Half War/Half Peace': Margaret Laurence and the Publishing of *A Bird in the House*." *English Studies in Canada* 17 (1991): 337–46.

Denham, Paul. Review of *Dance on the Earth* by Margaret Laurence. *NeWest Review* 15, 4 (April 1990): 33–4.

Dirie, Waris, and Cathleen Miller. *Desert Flower*. New York: William Morrow, 1998.

Dixon, Michael. Review of Margaret Laurence's *Heart of a Stranger*. *University of Toronto Quarterly* 46 (1977): 477–9.

Djwa, Sandra. "False Gods and True Covenant: Thematic Continuity between Margaret Laurence and Sinclair Ross." *Journal of Canadian Fiction* 1, 4 (Fall 1972): 43–50.

Dobbes, Kildare. "Outside Africa." *Canadian Literature* 8 (1961): 62–3.

Donne, John. "The Sun Rising." *The Oxford Anthology of English Literature*, Vol. I. Edited by Frank Kermode and John Hollander. Toronto: Oxford University Press, 1973, 1025–6.

Dorkenoo, Efua. *Cutting the Rose: Female Genital Mutilation: The Practice and Its Prevention*. London: Minority Rights Group, 1994.

Dowson, V.H.W. "Reviews: *A Tree for Poverty*." *Somaliland Journal* 1:1, 52 (December 1954).

Dudek, Debra. "Poetic Redress: Her Body, Her House in *The Fire-Dwellers*." *Great Plains Quarterly* 19, 3 (1999): 181–90.

Duncan, Isla. "Interview with Alan Maclean." *Margaret Laurence Review* 9 (1999): 13–17.
Dyke, Doris. *Crucified Woman*. Toronto: United Church Publishing House, 1991.

Easingwood, Peter. "The Realism of Laurence's Semi-Autobiographical Fiction." In Nicholson, *Critical Approaches to the Fiction of Margaret Laurence*, 119–32.
– "Semi-Autobiographical Fiction and Revisionary Realism in *A Bird in the House*." In *Narrative Strategies in Canadian Literature: Feminism and Postcolonialism*. Edited by Coral Ann Howells and Lynette Hunter. Milton Keynes: Open University Press, 1991, 19–29.
Ekwensi, Cyprian. *Jagua Nana*. London: Hutchinson, 1961.
– *Iska*. London: Hutchinson, 1966.
Eliot, T.S. "Little Gidding." *T. S. Eliot. Collected Poems 1909–1962*. London: Faber, 1963, 214–23.
– *The Waste Land. Collected Poems 1909–1962*. London: Faber, 1963, 61–86.
Engel, Marion. "Margaret Laurence." *Chatelaine*, 4 May 1974, 25.
– "Steps to the Mythic: *The Diviners* and *A Bird in the House*." *Journal of Canadian Studies/Revue d'études canadiennes* 13 (1978): 72–4.

Fabre, Michel. "The Angel and the Living Water: Metaphorical Networks and Structural Opposition in *The Stone Angel*." In Coger, *New Perspectives on Margaret Laurence*, 17–28.
– "From *The Stone Angel* to *The Diviners*: An Interview with Margaret Laurence." In Woodcock, *A Place to Stand On*, 193–209.
– ed. The Stone Angel *by Margaret Laurence: A Collection of Critical Essays*. Paris: Association française d'études canadiennes, 1981.
– "Words and the World: *The Diviners* as an Exploration of the Book of Life." *Canadian Literature* 93 (1982): 60–78.
Fanon, Frantz. *Black Skin, White Masks*. Translated by Charles Lam Markmann. London: Grove, 1967. First published 1952.
Findley, Timothy. "Afterword." *The Diviners*. 491–4.
– "Margaret Laurence: A Remembrance." *Canadian Woman Studies/Les cahiers de la femme* 8, 3 (1987): 15–6.
– "A Vivid Life." *Books in Canada* 18 (August 1989): 9–10.
Flecker, James Elroy. "The Gates of Damascus." *The Collected Poems of James Elroy Flecker*. London: Marin Secker, 1923, 163–9.
Forster, E.M. –*Howards End*. Harmondsworth: Penguin, 1910. *A Passage to India*. New York: Harcourt, Brace & World, 1924.
Fraiberg, Selma H. *The Magic Years: Understanding and Handling the Problems of Early Childhood*. New York: Scribner's, 1959.

Franks, Jill. "Jesting Within: Voices of Irony and Parody as Expressions of Feminism." In Riegel, *Challenging Territory*, 99–118.
Fraser, Sylvia. "Afterword." *The Fire-Dwellers*. Toronto: McClelland and Stewart, 1988, 283–6.
Friedan, Betty. *The Feminine Mystique*. New York: Dell, 1963.
Frye, Northrop. "Literature and Myth." In *Relations of Literary Study: Essays on Interdisciplinary Contributions*. Edited by James Thorpe. New York: Modern Languages Association, 1967.

Geddes, Gary, ed. *The Art of Short Fiction: An International Anthology*. Toronto: Harper Collins, 1993.
Gibson, Graeme. "Margaret Laurence." *Eleven Canadian Novelists*. Toronto: Anansi, 1973, 185–208.
Githae-Mugo, Micere. *Visions of Africa: The Fiction of Chinua Achebe, Margaret Laurence, Elspeth Huxley and Ngugi Wa Thiong'o*. Nairobi: Kenya Literature Bureau, 1978.
Givner, Joan. "Thinking Back Through Our Mothers: Reading the Autobiography of Margaret Laurence." *Room of One's Own* 15 (December 1992): 82–94.
Godard, Barbara. "Caliban's Revolt: The Discourse of the (M)Other." In Nicholson, *Critical Approaches to The Fiction of Margaret Laurence*, 208–27.
– "*The Diviners* as Supplement: (M)Othering the Text." *Open Letter* Series 7, no. 7 (1990): 26–73.
Godfrey, Dave. "Piquefort's Column." Review of *Long Drums and Cannons*. *Canadian Forum* (Feb. 1969): 249.
Goldsborough, Diana. Review of *Jason's Quest*. *Toronto Daily Star* (20 June 1970): 59.
Grace, Sherrill. "Crossing Jordan: Time and Memory in the Fiction of Margaret Laurence." *World Literature Written in English* 16 (Nov. 1977): 328–39.
– "A Portrait of the Artist as Laurence Hero." *Journal of Canadian Studies* 13 (Fall 1978): 64–71.
Greene, Gayle. "Margaret Laurence's *The Diviners* and Shakespeare's *The Tempest*: The Uses of the Past." In *Women's Re-Visions of Shakespeare: On the Responses of Dickinson, Woolf, Rich, H.D., George Eliot, and Others*. Edited by Marianne Novy. Urbana: University of Illinois Press, 1990, 165–82.
– "Margaret Laurence's *The Diviners*: The Uses of the Past." In Nicholson, *Critical Approaches to the Fiction of Margaret Laurence*, 177–207.
Gross, Konrad. "Margaret Laurence's African Experience." In *Encounters and Explorations: Canadian writers and European Critics*. Edited by Frank K. Stanzel and Waldemar Zacharasiewics. Wurzburg: Konighausen, 1986, 73–81.

Gunnars, Kristjana, ed. *Crossing the River: Essays in Honour of Margaret Laurence.* Winnipeg: Turnstone, 1988.
– "Listening: Laurence's Women." In Staines, *Margaret Laurence*, 121–8.

Hamovitch, Mitzi. "The Subversive Voice in *The Fire-Dwellers*." In Coger, *New Perspectives on Margaret Laurence*, 173–7.
Harlow, Robert. "Lack of Distance." *Canadian Literature* 31 (1967): 71–2, 74–5. Reprinted in New, *Margaret Laurence*, 189–91.
Harrison, Phyllis, ed. *The Home Children.* Winnipeg: Watson & Dwyer, 1979.
Heilbrun, Carolyn. *Writing a Woman's Life.* New York: Norton, 1988.
Herrnstein Smith, Barbara. *Poetic Closure: A Study of How Poems End.* Chicago: University of Chicago Press, 1968.
Hicks, Esther K. *Infibulation: Female Mutilation in Islamic Northeastern Africa.* New Brunswick, NJ: Transaction Publishers, 1993.
Hind-Smith, Joan. *Three Voices: The Lives of Margaret Laurence, Gabrielle Roy, Frederick Philip Grove.* Toronto: Clarke, 1975.
Hinz, Evelyn J. "The Religious Roots of the Feminine Identity Issue: Margaret Laurence's *The Stone Angel* and Margaret Atwood's *Surfacing*." *Journal of Canadian Studies/Revue d'études canadiennes* 22 (1987): 17–31.
Hjartarson, Paul. "'Christie's Real Country. Where I Was Born': Story-Telling, Loss and Subjectivity in *The Diviners*." In Gunnars, *Crossing the River*, 43–64.
Howells, Coral Ann. "Margaret Laurence: *A Bird in the House, The Diviners*." *Private and Fictional Worlds: Canadian Women Novelists of the 1970s and 1980s.* London: Methuen, 1987, 33–52.
– "Weaving Fabrications: Women's Narratives in *A Jest of God* and *The Fire-Dwellers*." In Nicholson, *Critical Approaches to the Fiction of Margaret Laurence*, 93–106.
Huggan, Isabel. "Afterword." *A Bird in the House.* Toronto: McClelland and Stewart, 1989, 192–7.
Hughes, Kenneth James. "Politics and *A Jest of God*." *Journal of Canadian Studies* 13 (Fall 1978): 40–54.
Hunter, Lynette. "Consolation and Articulation in Margaret Laurence's *The Diviners*." In Nicholson, *Critical Approaches to the Fiction of Margaret Laurence*, 133–51.
Hutcheon, Linda. *The Canadian Postmodern: A Study of Contemporary English-Canadian Fiction.* Toronto: Oxford University Press, 1988.
Hutchinson, Helen. "Margaret Laurence." 66–79.

Johnston, Eleanor. "The Quest of *The Diviners*." *Mosaic* 11, 3 (Spring 1978): 107–17.

Joyce, James. *Dubliners*. Paris: B.W. Huebsch, 1916. Reprint. New York: Viking, 1961.

– *A Portrait of the Artist as a Young Man*. 1916. Reprint edited by Seamus Deane. New York: Penguin, 1992.

Kaplan, Caren. "Resisting Autobiography: Out-Law Genres and Transnational Feminist Subjects." In Smith and Watson, *De/Colonizing the Subject*, 115–38.

Keith, W.J. "Margaret Laurence's *The Diviners:* The Problems of Close Reading." *Journal of Canadian Studies/Revue d'études canadiennes* 23, 3 (1988): 102–16.

– "'Uncertain Flowering': An Overlooked Short Story by Margaret Laurence." *Canadian Literature* 112 (1987): 202–5.

Kermode, Frank. *The Sense of an Ending: Studies in the Theory of Fiction*. New York: Oxford University Press, 1967.

Kertzer, Jonathan. *Margaret Laurence and Her Works*. Toronto: ECW Press, 1987.

– "*The Stone Angel:* Time and Responsibility." *The Dalhousie Review* 54 (1974): 499–509.

– "*That House in Manawaka*": Margaret Laurence's A BIRD IN THE HOUSE. Toronto: ECW Press, 1992.

Kids of Canada: Teacher's Guidebook. Toronto: Lorimer, 1981.

Killam, G.D. "Foreword." *Long Drums and Cannons: Nigerian Dramatists and Novelists, 1952–1966*, vii–x.

– "Introduction." *A Jest of God*. Toronto: McClelland and Stewart, 1974. np.

– "Introduction." *This Side Jordan*. Toronto: McClelland and Stewart, 1976, ix–xviii.

– "Margaret Laurence's *Long Drums and Cannons*." *Canadian Woman Studies* 2, 3 (Fall, 1987): 33.

– "Notes on Symbolism in The Stone Angel" [*sic*]. *Études Canadiennes/ Canadian Studies* 11 (1981): 89–103.

– "On African Writing." *The Journal of Commonwealth Literature* 9 (1970): 109–13.

King, James. *The Life of Margaret Laurence*. Toronto: Knopf Canada, 1997.

Kipling, Rudyard. "The Ladies." *Collected Verse of Rudyard Kipling*. London: Hodder and Stoughton, 1912, 408–10.

Kirkwood, Hilda. "Last Words." *Canadian Forum* 69 (June 1990): 30.

Koster, Patricia. "Hagar 'The Egyptian': Allusions and Illusions in *The Stone Angel*." *Ariel* 16, 3 (1985): 41–52.

Kreisel, Henry. "The African Stories of Margaret Laurence." *Canadian Forum* 41 (Apr. 1961): 8–10. Reprinted in Woodcock, *A Place to Stand On*, 106–112.

Kroetsch, Robert. "A Conversation with Margaret Laurence." In *Creation*.

Edited by Robert Kroetsch. Toronto: New Canadian Library, 1970, 53–63. Reprinted in Woodcock, *A Place to Stand On*, 46–55.
– "Sitting Down To Write: A Discourse of Morning." In Staines, *Margaret Laurence*, 129–34.

Laing, R.D. *The Divided Self*. London: Tavistock, 1960.
Laurence, Margaret. "The Artist, Then, Now and Always." In *Trace: Prairie Writers on Writing*. Edited by Birk Sproxton. Winnipeg: Turnstone, 1986, 61–3.
– "Author's Commentary." Unpublished typescript. York University.
– *A Bird in the House*. Toronto: McClelland and Stewart, 1970.
– "A Bird in the House – Revisions and Disagreements." McMaster, box 2, file 1.
– "Books That Mattered to Me." In Verduyn, *Margaret Laurence*, 239–49.
– "The Case of the Blond Butcher, A Wanted Man." *The Winnipeg Free Press*, 18 & 25 January 1941.
– *Colors of Speech: Margaret Laurence's Early Writings*. Edited by Nora Foster Stovel. Edmonton: Juvenilia Press, 2000.
– *The Christmas Birthday Story*. Toronto: McClelland and Stewart, 1980.
– "A Constant Hope: Women in the Now and Future High Tech Age." *Dance on the Earth*, 229–38.
– "Convocation Address, York University, Toronto, June 1980." *Dance on the Earth*, 278–83.
– *Dance on the Earth: A Memoir*. Toronto: McClelland and Stewart, 1989.
– *The Diviners*. Toronto: McClelland and Stewart, 1974
– *Embryo Words: Margaret Laurence's Early Writings*. Edited by Nora Foster Stovel. Edmonton: Juvenilia Press, 1997.
– *The Fire-Dwellers*. Toronto: McClelland and Stewart, 1969.
– Foreword to *Canada and the Nuclear Arms Race*. Edited by Ernie Regehr. Toronto: Lorimer, 1983. Reprinted in *Dance on the Earth*, 287–90.
– "Gadgetry or Growing: Form and Voice in the Novel." *Journal of Canadian Fiction* 27 (1980): 54–62. Reprinted in Woodcock, *A Place to Stand On*, 80–9.
– "Geography – Outer or Inner?" Unpublished essay. York University.
– "The Greater Evil." *Dance on the Earth*, 265–74.
– "Half War, Half Peace." Unpublished essay. York University.
– *Heart of a Stranger*. Toronto: McClelland and Stewart, 1976. Edited by and introduced by Nora Foster Stovel. Edmonton: University of Alberta Press, 2003.
– "Ivory Tower or Grass Roots?: The Novelist as Socio-Political Being." In *A Political Art: Essays and Images in Honour of George Woodcock*. Edited by W.H. New. Vancouver: University of British Columbia Press, 1978, 15–25.

– *Jason's Quest*. Toronto: McClelland and Stewart, 1970.

– *A Jest of God*. Toronto: McClelland and Stewart, 1966.

– "Letter to Bob Sorfleet from Margaret Laurence." *Journal of Canadian Fiction* 27 (1980): 52–3.

– "Living Dangerously ... by Mail." In *Heart of a Stranger*, 141–6.

– *Long Drums and Cannons: Nigerian Dramatists and Novelists, 1952–1966*. London: Macmillan, 1968. Edited by Nora Foster Stovel. Edmonton: University of Alberta Press, 2001.

– "Mask of Beaten Gold." *Tamarack Review* 26 (Winter 1963): 3–21.

– "Message to the Inheritors." *Dance on the Earth*, 278–83.

– "My Final Hour." *Canadian Literature* 100 (Spring 1984): 187–97.

– *The Olden Days Coat*. Toronto: McClelland and Stewart, 1979.

– "Old Women's Song." *Dance on the Earth*, 225–8. York University Manuscript.

– "On 'The Loons.'" In *The Art of Short Fiction: An International Anthology*. Edited by Gary Geddes. Toronto: Harper Collins, 1993, 805–6.

– "A Place to Stand On." *Heart of a Stranger*, 5–10.

– "Prayer for Passover and Easter." *Dance on the Earth*, 263–4.

– *The Prophet's Camel Bell*. Toronto: McClelland and Stewart, 1963.

– *This Side Jordan*. Toronto: McClelland and Stewart, 1960.

– "This Side Jordan." Unpublished précis. York University Archives.

– *Six Darn Cows*. Toronto: Lorimer, 1979.

– "Sources." *Mosaic* 3 (Spring 1970): 80–4.

– "A Statement of Faith." In Woodcock, *A Place to Stand On*, 56–60.

– *The Stone Angel*. Toronto: McClelland and Stewart, 1964.

– "Ten Years' Sentences." *Canadian Literature* 41 (1969): 10–16. Reprinted in New, *Margaret Laurence*, 17–23.

– "Time and the Narrative Voice." In *The Narrative Voice*. Edited by John Metcalf. Reprinted in New, *Margaret Laurence*. Toronto: McGraw-Hill, 1971, 156–160.

– *The Tomorrow-Tamer and Other Stories*. Toronto: McClelland and Stewart, 1963.

– *A Tree for Poverty: Somali Poetry and Prose*. Nairobi: Eagle, 1954. Hamilton: McMaster University Press, 1970. Toronto: ECW Press, 1993.

– "Tribalism As Us Versus Them." *Long Drums and Cannons*, 2001, 223–32.

– "Uncertain Flowering." *Story: The Magazine of the Short Story in Book Form* 4 (1953): 9–34. McMaster University Laurence Archives.

– "Via Rail and Via Memory." *Dance on the Earth*, 275–7.

– "The Voices of Adamo." *The Tomorrow-Tamer and Other Stories*. Toronto: McClelland and Stewart, 1963, 205–24.

– "Where the World Began." *Heart of a Stranger*, 169–74.

Lawrence, D.H. *The Rainbow*. London: Duckworth, 1915. Harmondsworth: Penguin, 1981.

– *Sons and Lovers*. London: Duckworth, 1915. Harmondsworth: Penguin, 1981.

– *St. Mawr & The Man Who Died*. New York: Viking, Random House, 1953.

Lemieux, Angelica Maeser. "The Scots Presbyterian Legacy." In Riegel, *Challenging Territory*, 163–86.

Leney, Jane. "Prospero and Caliban in Laurence's African Fiction." *Journal of Canadian Fiction* 27 (1980): 63–80.

Lennox, John. "The Correspondence of Margaret Laurence and Al Purdy." *Recherches anglaises et nord americaines* 24 (1991): 91–101.

– "Manawaka and Deptford: Place and Voice." *Journal of Canadian Studies* 13 (1978): 23–30.

– ed. *Margaret Laurence-Al Purdy: A Friendship in Letters: Selected Correspondence*. Toronto: McClelland and Stewart, 1993.

– "The Spirit and the Letter: The Correspondence of Margaret Laurence." In Staines, *Margaret Laurence*, 7–22.

– and Ruth Panofsky, eds. *Selected Letters of Margaret Laurence and Adele Wiseman*. Toronto: University of Toronto Press, 1997.

Lessing, Doris. *The Golden Notebook*. London: Michael Joseph, 1962.

Letson, D.R. "Mother of Manawaka: Margaret Laurence as Author of Children's Stories." *Canadian Children's Literature* 21 (1981): 17–24.

Lever, Bernice. "Literature and Canadian Culture: An Interview with Margaret Laurence." *Alive* 41 (1975): 18–19.

Lindberg, Laurie. "Wordsworth and Woman: Morag Gunn's Triumph Through Language." In Coger, *New Perspectives on Margaret Laurence*, 187–201.

Lunn, Janet. "Boys, Seals, Wolves, Moles and a Girl with Big Feet." Review of *Jason's Quest*. *The Globe and Mail*, 27 June 1970, 17.

– "To Find Refreshment in Writing Children's Books: A Note on Margaret Laurence's Writing for Children." In Staines, *Margaret Laurence*, 145–50.

Mannoni, Olivier. *Prospero and Caliban: The Psychology of Colonization*. 1950. Translated by Pamela Powesland. New York: Praeger, 1964.

Mantooth, Wes. "Margaret Laurence's 'Album' Songs: Divining for Missing Links and Deeper Meanings." *Great Plains Quarterly* 19, 3 (1999): 167–79.

Marshall, Joyce. "Margaret Laurence: A Reminiscence." In Staines, *Margaret Laurence*, 163–8.

Martin, Mathew. "Dramas of Desire in Margaret Laurence's *A Jest of God, The Fire-Dwellers,* and *The Diviners*." *Studies in Canadian Literature* 19, 1 (1994): 58–71.

McClintock, Anne. *Imperial Leather: Race, Gender and Sexuality in the Colonial Contest*. New York: Routledge, 1995.

McEwan, Ian. *Atonement*. New York: Anchor Books, 2003.

McKenzie, A.F. *Neepawa, Land of Plenty*. Brandon: Leech, 1958.

McLay, C.M. "Every Man Is an Island: Isolation in *A Jest of God*." *Canadian Literature* 50 (1971): 57–68. Reprinted in New, *Margaret Laurence*, 177–88.

McLean, Ken. "Dividing *The Diviners*." In Coger, *New Perspectives on Margaret Laurence*, 97–111.

Mills, Sara. *Discourses of Difference: An Analysis of Women's Travel Writing and Colonialism*. London: Routledge, 1991.

Miner, Valerie. "The Matriarch of Manawaka." *Saturday Night* (May 1974): 17–20.

Monk, Patricia. "Shadow Continent: The Image of Africa in Three Canadian Writers." *ARIEL* 8, 4 (1977): 3–25.

Morley, Patricia. "Canada, Africa, Canada: Laurence's Unbroken Journey." *Journal of Canadian Fiction* 27 (1980): 81–91.

– "The Long Trek Home: Margaret Laurence's Stories." *Journal of Canadian Studies* 11, 4 (1976): 38–51. Reprinted in Verduyn, *Margaret Laurence*, 38–51.

– *Margaret Laurence: The Long Journey Home*. Rev. ed. Montreal & Kingston: McGill-Queen's University Press, 1991.

"Muddling into Maturity." Anonymous review of *This Side Jordan*. *The Times Literary Supplement* (November 1960), 705. Reprinted in New, *Critical Views on Canadian Writers*, 101–2.

Mugo, Micere. "Somali Literature in Translation." Review of *A Tree for Poverty: Somali Poetry and Prose* by Margaret Laurence. *Journal of Canadian Fiction* 1, 2 (1972): 86–7.

Munro, Alice. "Boys and Girls." *Dance of the Happy Shades*. Toronto: McGraw-Hill Ryerson, 1968, 111–27.

– *Lives of Girls and Women*. Toronto: McGraw-Hill Ryerson, 1971.

Na' Allah, Abdul-Rasheed. "Nigerian Literature Then and Now." In Stovel, *Long Drums and Cannons: Nigerian Dramatists and Novelists, 1952–1966*. Edmonton: University of Alberta Press, 2001, lv–lxiii.

Nancekevill, Sharon. "*The Fire-Dwellers*: Circles of Fire." *Literary Criterion* 19 (1984): 158–72.

Neuman, Shirley and Smaro Kamboureli eds. *A Mazing Space: Writing Canadian Women Writing*. Edmonton: Longspoon NeWest, 1986.

New, W.H. "Every Now and Then: Voice & Language in Laurence's *The Stone Angel*." *Canadian Literature* 93 (1982): 79–86.

– Introduction. *The Stone Angel*. New Canadian Library 59. Toronto: McClelland and Stewart, 1968. Reprinted in New, *Margaret Laurence*, 135–42.

– "Margaret Laurence and the City." In Staines, *Margaret Laurence*, 59–78.

– ed. *Margaret Laurence: The Writer and Her Critics*. Toronto: McGraw-Hill Ryerson, 1977.

– "The Other and I: Laurence's African Stories." In Woodcock, *A Place to Stand On*, 113–34.

Nicholson, Colin. "A Woman Speaking." *Canadian Literature* 136 (Spring, 1993): 182–3.

– ed. *Critical Approaches to the Fiction of Margaret Laurence*. London: Macmillan, 1990.

Niven, Alastair. *The Legon Observer* 4, 12 (6–19 June 1969): 15–17.

Nkosi, Lewis. "A Question of Literary Stewardship." *Africa Report* 14, 5–6 (1969): 69–71.

Nwapa, Flora. *Efuru*. African Writers Series 26. London and Ibadan: Heinemann Educational Books, 1966.

Okigbo, Christopher. *Heavensgate*. Ibadan, Nigeria: Mbari, 1962.

Osachoff, Margaret. "Colonialism in the Fiction of Margaret Laurence." *Southern Review* 13, 3 (Nov. 1980): 228–38.

– "Moral Vision in *The Stone Angel*." *Studies in Canadian Literature* 4, 1 (1979): 139–53.

Ostry, Elaine. "In the Flush of Youth: Offerings from the Juvenilia Press." *Canadian Children's Literature* 24, 3/4, no. 91/92 (1998): 158–60.

Packer, Miriam. "The Dance of Life: *The Fire-Dwellers*." *Journal of Canadian Fiction* 27 (1980): 52–3.

Palmer, Robert. *The Rolling Stones*. London: Sphere Books, 1984.

Pell, Barbara. "The African and Canadian Heroines: From Bondage to Grace." In Riegel, *Challenging Territory*, 33–46.

– Review of *Embryo Words: Margaret Laurence's Early Writings*. Edited by Nora Foster Stovel. *English Studies in Canada* 26 (2000): 366–9.

Pett, Alexandra. "Writing a Woman's Life: Celebration, Sorrow, and Pathos in Margaret Laurence's Memoir *Dance on the Earth*." In Coger, *New Perspectives on Margaret Laurence*, 203–15.

Pollack, Claudette. "The Paradox of *The Stone Angel*." *The Humanities Association Review / La Revue de l'Association des Humanités* 27 (1976): 267–75.

Poovey, Mary. *Uneven Developments: The Ideological Work of Gender in Mid-Victorian England*. Chicago: University of Chicago Press, 1988.

Potvin, Elizabeth. "'A Mystery at the Core of Life': Margaret Laurence and Women's Spirituality." *Canadian Literature* 128 (1991): 25–38.

Pound, Ezra. "The Seafarer." *Selected Poems of Ezra Pound*. New York: New Directions, 1957, 18–21.

Povey, John F. "M. Lawrence (*sic*), Long Drums and Cannons: Nigerian Dramatists and Novelists (Book Review)." *Journal of Asian and African Studies*. 8, 1–2 (1973): 109–10.

Powell, Barbara. "The Conflicting Inner Voices of Rachel Cameron." *Studies in Canadian Literature/Études en littérature canadienne* 16 (1991): 22–35.

Powers, Lyall. *Alien Heart: The Life and Work of Margaret Laurence.* Winnipeg: University of Manitoba Press, 2003.

– "Margaret Laurence's Long Journey Home: 'I Love the Damn Country, That's the Trouble.'" *Great Plains Quarterly* 19, 3 (1999): 203–9.

– "Stacey Cameron MacAindra: The Fire This Time." In Coger, *New Perspectives on Margaret Laurence,* 29–39.

Quinby, Lee. "The Subject of Memoirs: The Woman Warrior's Technology of Ideographic Selfhood." In Smith and Watson, *De/Colonizing the Subject,* 297–300.

Ravenscroft, Arthur. "Africa in the Canadian Imagination of Margaret Laurence." In *Re-Visions of Canadian Literature.* Proceedings of Seminar in Canadian Literature, University of Leeds, Leeds, Apr. 1984. Edited by Shirley Chew. Leeds: University of Leeds Press, 1984, 29–40.

Read, S.E. "Margaret Laurence, *The Stone Angel.*" *B.C. Library Quarterly* 28 (July–October 1964): 41–4.

– "The Maze of Life: The Work of Margaret Laurence." *Canadian Literature* 27 (Winter 1966): 5–14.

Renault, Mary. "On Understanding Africa." *Saturday Review* (10 December 1960): 23–4. Reprinted in New, *Margaret Laurence,* 103–4.

Richards, David. "'Leave the Dead some room to dance!': Margaret Laurence and Africa." In Nicholson, *Critical Approaches to the Fiction of Margaret Laurence,* 16–34.

Riegel, Christian, ed. *Challenging Territory: The Writing of Margaret Laurence.* Edmonton: University of Alberta Press, 1997.

– "Hagar's Work of Mourning." *Writing Grief: Margaret Laurence and the Work of Mourning.* Winnipeg: University of Manitoba Press, 2003, 21–43.

– "Introduction: Recognizing the Multiplicity of the Oeuvre." In *Challenging Territory,* xi–xxiii.

– "Preface." In Stovel, *Long Drums and Cannons: Nigerian Novelists and Dramatists, 1952–1966.* Edmonton: University of Alberta Press, 2001, xi–xii.

– "'Rest Beyond the River': Mourning in *A Bird in the House.*" In *Challenging Territory,* 67–80.

– *Writing Grief: Margaret Laurence and the Work of Mourning.* Winnipeg, University of Manitoba Press, 2003.

Rimmer, Mary. "(Mis)Speaking: Laurence Writes Africa." In Riegel, *Challenging Territory,* 1–18.

Rooke, Constance. "Fear of the Open Heart." In Neuman and Kamboureli, eds, *A Mazing Space,* 256–69.

– "A Feminist Reading of 'The Stone Angel.'" *Canadian Literature* 93 (1982): 26–41.

– "Hagar's Old Age: *The Stone Angel* as *Vollendungsroman*." In Gunnars, *Crossing the River*, 25–42.

Roy, Wendy. "Anti-imperialism and Feminism in Margaret Laurence's African Writings." *Canadian Literature* 169 (Summer 1999): 33–57.

– "'I Was Against It': Margaret Laurence and British Imperialism in Somalia." *Maps of Difference: Canada, Women, and Travel*. Montreal & Kingston: McGill-Queen's University Press, 2005, 151–209.

Runte, Roseann. "Reading Stones: Travels to and in Canada." *University of Toronto Quarterly* 45, 3 (1996): 523–33.

Sandburg, Carl. "Chicago." *Chicago Poems*. New York: Holt, 1916, 3–4.

– "Losers." *Smoke and Steel. Complete Poems of Carl Sandburg*. New York: Harcourt Brace, 1920, 87.

Sellin, Eric. "Neo-African and Afro-American Literatures." *Journal of Modern Literature* 1, 2: 249.

Sendak, Maurice. *Where the Wild Things Are*. New York: Harper and Row, 1963.

Seyersted, Per. "The Final Days: Margaret Laurence and Scandinavia." In Gunnars, *Crossing the River*, 207–13.

Shields, Carol. "Leaving the Brick House Behind: Margaret Laurence and the Loop of Memory." *Recherches anglaises et nord americaines* 24 (1995): 75–7.

Smith, Sidonie. *A Poetics of Women's Autobiography: Marginality and the Fictions of Self- Representation*. Bloomington: Indiana University Press, 1987.

– *Subjectivity, Identity, and the Body: Women's Autobiographical Practices in the Twentieth Century*. Bloomington: Indiana University Press, 1993.

– and Julia Watson, eds. *De/Colonizing the Subject: The Politics of Gender in Women's Autobiography*. Minneapolis: University of Minnesota Press, 1992.

Snow, C.P. *The Two Cultures and the Scientific Revolution*. Cambridge: Rede Lecture, 1959.

Socken, Paul, ed. *Intimate Strangers: The Letters of Margaret Laurence and Gabrielle Roy*. Winnipeg: University of Manitoba Press, 2004.

Soyinka, Wole. *The Interpreters*. London: Deutsch, 1965.

Sparrow, Fiona. *Into Africa with Margaret Laurence*. Toronto: ECW Press, 1993.

– "Margaret Laurence of Hargeisa: A Discussion of *A Tree for Poverty*." In Coger, *New Perspectives on Margaret Laurence*, 129–35.

Sproxton, Birk. "The Figure of the Unknown Soldier: Home and War in *The Fire-Dwellers*." In Staines, *Margaret Laurence*, 79–100.

Staines, David, ed. *Margaret Laurence: Critical Reflections*. Ottawa: University of Ottawa Press, 2001.

Stanley, Marni. "Travelers' Tales." In Neuman and Kamboureli, *A Mazing Space*, 51–60.

Steele, Charles. *Taking Stock: The Calgary Conference on the Canadian Novel*. Downsview, ON: ECW Press, 1982.

Steichen, Edward. *The Family of Man*. New York: Simon and Schuster, 1955.

Stovel, Bruce. "Coherence in *A Bird in the House*." In Coger, *New Perspectives on Margaret Laurence*, 81–96.

Stovel, Nora Foster, ed. *Colors of Speech: Margaret Laurence's Early Writings*. Edmonton: Juvenilia Press, 2000.

– ed. *"Embryo Words": Margaret Laurence's Early Writings*. Edmonton: Juvenilia Press, 1997.

– "Female Excalibur as Literary Legacy: Ethel Wilson's *Swamp Angel* and Margaret Laurence's *The Fire-Dwellers*." *The International Fiction Review* 21 (1994): 25–31.

– "Lawrencean Legacy: D.H. Lawrence's *Sons and Lovers* and Margaret Laurence's *Stone Angel*." In *The Cosmic Adventure: Critical Essays on D.H. Lawrence*. Edited by Laurence Gamache and Ian McNiven. Nepean, ON: Borealis Press, 1997, 48–74.

– ed. *Margaret Laurence's Heart of a Stranger*. Edmonton: University of Alberta Press, 2003.

– ed. *Margaret Laurence's Long Drums and Cannons: Nigerian Dramatists and Novelists, 1952–1966*. Edmonton: University of Alberta Press, 2001.

– *Rachel's Children: Margaret Laurence's* A Jest of God. Toronto: ECW Press, 1992.

– *Stacey's Choice: Margaret Laurence's* The Fire-Dwellers. Toronto: ECW Press, 1993.

Styron, William. *Sophie's Choice*. New York: Random House, 1976.

Sullivan, Rosemary. "An Interview with Margaret Laurence." In Woodcock, *A Place to Stand On*, 61–79.

Swayze, Walter E. "Knowing Through Writing: The Pilgrimage of Margaret Laurence." In Gunnars, *Crossing the River*, 147–168.

– "Margaret Laurence: Novelist-as-Poet." In Coger, *New Perspectives on Margaret Laurence*, 3–16.

Tapping, Craig. "Margaret Laurence and Africa." In Gunnars, *Crossing the River*, 65–80.

Tennyson, Alfred. *In Memoriam*. Edited by Michael Davis. London: Macmillan, 1960.

Thomas, Clara. Afterword. *The Prophet's Camel Bell*. Toronto: McClelland and Stewart, 1988, 265–8.

– "Ascent and Agony." *Canadian Literature* 42 (1969): 91–3.

– "Bashing On." *Canadian Literature* 50 (Autumn 1971): 88–90.

– "Celebrations: Frye's *The Double Vision* and Margaret Laurence's *Dance on the Earth."* *English Studies in Canada* 19, 2 (June, 1993): 126. Reprinted in *The Legacy of Northrop Frye*. Edited by Alvin Lee and Robert D. Denham. Toronto: University of Toronto Press, 1994, 164–70.

– "A Conversation about Literature: An Interview with Margaret Laurence and Irving Layton." *Journal of Canadian Fiction* 1 (1972): 65–9.

– *"Dance on the Earth,"* *Canadian Woman Studies* 11, 2 (Fall, 1990): 88.

– *The Manawaka World of Margaret Laurence*. Toronto: McClelland and Stewart, 1976.

– *Margaret Laurence*. Toronto: McClelland and Stewart, 1969.

– "Margaret Laurence." *The Canadian Encyclopedia*, 2nd edition.

– "Margaret Laurence and the Patterns of Pilgrimage." *Canadian Woman Studies / Les cahiers de la femme* 5, 2 (1983): 96–8.

– "'Morning Yet on Creation Day': A Study of *This Side Jordan*." In Woodcock, *A Place to Stand On*, 93–105.

– "'Planted firmly in some soil': Margaret Laurence and the Canadian Tradition in Fiction." In Nicholson, *Critical Approaches to the Fiction of Margaret Laurence*, 1–15.

– "Saving Laughter." *Canadian Woman Studies* 8, 3 (1987): 46–8.

Tillyard, E.M.W. *The Elizabethan World Picture: A Study of Order in the Age of Shakespeare, Donne, and Milton*. New York: Vintage, no date.

Torgovnick, Marianna. *Closure in the Novel*. Princeton: Princeton University Press, 1984.

Toubia, Nahid. *Female Genital Mutilation: A Call for Global Action*. New York: Rainbo, 1995.

Tutuola, Amos. *The Palm-Wine Drinkard*. London: Faber, 1952.

Twigg, Alan. "Margaret Laurence: Canadian Literature." *For Openers: Conversations with Twenty-Four Canadian Writers*. Madeira Park, BC: Harbour, 1981, 161–71.

van Herk, Aritha. "The Eulalias of Spinsters and Undertakers." In Gunnars, *Crossing the River*, 133–46.

– "Margaret Laurence: The Shape of the Writer's Shadow." In Staines, *Margaret Laurence*, 135–44.

Vauthier, Simone. "Images in Stone, Images in Words: Margaret Laurence's *The Stone Angel*." In Nicholson, *Critical Approaches to the Fiction of Margaret Laurence*, 46–70.

Verduyn, Christl. "Cavewomen Div(in)ing for Pearls: Margaret Laurence and Marian Engel." In Staines, *Margaret Laurence*, 23–38.

– "Language, Body and Identity in Margaret Laurence's *The Fire-Dwellers*." In Verduyn, *Margaret Laurence*, 128–40.

– ed. *Margaret Laurence: An Appreciation. Journal of Canadian Studies* 13, 3 (1988).

Wainwright, J.A., ed. *A Very Large Soul: Selected Letters from Margaret Laurence to Canadian Writers.* Dunvegan, ON: Cormorant, 1995.

– "You Have To Go Home Again: Art and Life in *The Diviners.*" *World Literature Written in English* 20 (1981): 292–311.

Walker, Alice and Pratibha, Parmar. *Warrior Marks: Female Genital Mutilation and the Sexual Blinding of Women.* New York: Harcourt Brace & Company, 1993.

Ware, Tracey. "Race and Conflict in Garner's 'One-Two-Three Little Indians' and Laurence's 'The Loons.'" *Studies in Canadian Literature/Études en littérature canadienne* 23, 2 (1998): 71–84.

Warwick, Susan. *River of Now and Then: Margaret Laurence's* The Diviners. Toronto: ECW Press, 1993.

Waterston, Elizabeth. "Double Is Trouble: Twins in *A Jest of God.*" In Nicholson, *Critical Approaches to the Fiction of Margaret Laurence,* 83–92.

Watt, F.W. Review of *The Fire-Dwellers. Canadian Forum* (1969) 87. Reprinted in New, *Margaret Laurence,* 198–9.

Waugh, Evelyn. *Put Out More Flags.* London: Little, Brown and Company, 1942.

"Ways into Africa." *Times Literary Supplement* (2 January 1969) 8.

Wilson, Budge. "Margaret Laurence, Listener." *Canadian Woman Studies-Les cahiers de la femme* 8, 3 (1987): 13.

Wilson, Ethel. *Swamp Angel.* Toronto: McClelland and Stewart, 1954.

Wilson, Lois. "Faith and the Vocation of the Author." In Staines, *Margaret Laurence,* 151–62.

Winslow, Donald J. *Life-Writing: A Glossary of Terms in Biography, Autobiography, and Related Forms.* University Press of Hawaii, 1980.

– "Margaret Laurence's Somali Translations." *Canadian Literature* 135 (1992): 33–48.

Wiseman, Adele. "Somali Literature." Review of *A Tree for Poverty: Somali Poetry and Prose* by Margaret Laurence. *Queen's Quarterly* 62 (1955–56): 610–11.

Woodcock, George. "Afterword." *This Side Jordan.* Toronto: McClelland and Stewart, 1989, 283–8.

– "The Human Elements: Margaret Laurence's Fiction." *The World of Canadian Writing.* Edited by George Woodcock. Vancouver: Douglas and McIntyre, 1980, 40–62.

– *Introducing Margaret Laurence's* The Stone Angel: *Reader's Guide.* Toronto: ECW Press, 1989.

– "Many Solitudes: The Travel Writings of Margaret Laurence." *Journal of Canadian Studies* 13 (Fall 1978): 3–12. Reprinted in Woodcock, *A Place to Stand On,* 135–51.

– "Speaker for the Tribes." *Canadian Woman Studies / Les cahiers de la femme* 8, 3 (Fall 1987): 20–22.
– ed. *A Place to Stand On: Essays by and about Margaret Laurence.* Edmonton: NeWest, 1983.
Woolf, Virginia. "Mr. Bennett and Mrs. Brown." London: Hogarth, 1924.
– *A Room of One's Own.* London: Hogarth, 1929.
– *To the Lighthouse.* New York: Harcourt, Brace, Jovanovich, 1927.

Xiques, Donez. "Introduction." *A Tree for Poverty: Somali Poetry and Prose* by Margaret Laurence. Toronto: ECW Press, 1993, 7–17.
– *Margaret Laurence: The Making of a Writer.* Hamilton, ON: Dundurn Press, 2005.
– "Margaret Laurence's Somali Translations." *Canadian Literature* 135 (1992): 33–48.

Yeats, W.B. "Among School Children." *The Collected Poems of W.B. Yeats.* London: Macmillan, 1961, 242–5.
York, Lorraine. *The Other Side of Dailiness: Photography in the Works of Alice Munro, Timothy Findley, Michael Ondaatje, and Margaret Laurence.* Toronto: ECW Press, 1988.

Zirker, Herbert. "Metaphorical Mapping in Margaret Laurence's Narrative." In Gunnars, *Crossing the River,* 169–82.

Index